TRANSATLANTIC VISTAS

TRANSATLANTIC VISTAS

ON THE LITERATURES OF WALES AND THE UNITED STATES

M. Wynn Thomas

EDITED BY
KIRSTI BOHATA AND
DANIEL G. WILLIAMS

FOREWORD BY
HELEN VENDLER

UNIVERSITY OF WALES PRESS
CARDIFF
2024

www.uwp.co.uk

British Library Cataloguing-in-Publication Data
A catalogue record for this book is available from the British Library.

ISBN 978-1-83772-159-7
eISBN 978-1-83772-160-3

Printed by CPI Antony Rowe, Melksham, United Kingdom
Typeset by Marie Doherty

Literature tills its crops in many fields, and some may flourish, while others lag. What I say in these Vistas has its main bearing on Imaginative Literature, especially Poetry, the stock of all. In the department of Science, and the specialty of Journalism, there appear [...] promises, perhaps fulfilments, of highest earnestness, reality, and life. These, of course, are modern. But in the region of imaginative, spinal and essential attributes, something equivalent to creation is imperatively demanded. For not only is it not enough that the new blood, new frame of Democracy shall be vivified and held together merely by political means, superficial suffrage, legislation, &c., but it is clear to me that, unless it goes deeper, gets at least as firm and as warm a hold in men's hearts, emotions and belief as, in their days, Feudalism or Ecclesiasticism [...] its strength will be defective, its growth doubtful, and its main charm wanting.

—WALT WHITMAN, *Democratic Vistas* (1871)

Contents

Editors' Acknowledgements

The previously uncollected essays, interviews and reviews that appear in this volume reflect some of M. Wynn Thomas's abiding concerns. They have been edited here, with gratitude and admiration, in celebration of his 80th birthday. We are profoundly grateful to Alice von Rothkirch for her visual tribute and to the distinguished critic Helen Vendler for contributing a foreword to the volume. Helen Vendler died on 23 April 2024, making her contribution a particularly moving record of a valued friendship.

Those essays that have already appeared in print are culled from many different sources. We are grateful for the permission to reproduce them here.

'Till I hit upon a name': 'Calamus' and the language of love
An expanded version of an article that first appeared in the *Huntington Library Quarterly*, 73/4 (December 2010), 643–57.

Whitman and the Labouring Classes
Published in Donald D. Kummings (ed.), *A Companion to Walt Whitman* (Malden, Massachusetts: Blackwell Publishing, 2006), pp. 60–75.

States United and United States: Whitman's national vision in 1855
Revised version of a chapter originally published in Susan Belasco, Ed Folsom and Kenneth M. Price (eds), *Leaves of Grass: The Sesquicentennial Essays* (Lincoln: University of Nebraska Press, 2007), pp. 62–83.

Whitman, Tennyson, and the poetry of old age
First published as 'Whitman, Tennyson, and the Poetry of Old Age', in Stephen Burt and Nick Halpern (eds), *Something Understood. Essays and Poetry for Helen Vendler* (Charlottesville: University of Virginia Press, 2009), pp. 161–82. The first section is based on material first published in 'A Study of Whitman's Late Poetry', *Walt Whitman Review*, 27/1 (March 1981), 3–14

The Pioneer: D. H. Lawrence's Whitman
Previously unpublished.

'He was one of ours': American 'bards' and Dylan Thomas
Unpublished in this form. Some of this material appeared in a book chapter co-written with Daniel G. Williams, '"A Sweet Union"?: Dylan Thomas and Post-War American Poetry', in Gilbert Bennett et al. (eds), *I Sang in My Chains: Essays and Poems in Tribute to Dylan Thomas* (Swansea: The Dylan Thomas Society of Great Britain, 2003), pp. 68–79.

'There's words': Dylan Thomas, Swansea and language
The text of a keynote lecture delivered at an International Dylan Thomas Conference held at the University of Bordeaux in Autumn 2014. Published as '"There's words": Dylan Thomas et la langue', Pascale Sardin et Christian Gutleben (eds), *Lire et Relire Dylan Thomas, Cycnos*, 31/2 (2015), 29–56.

The Real Manafon
Previously unpublished.

Bury My Heart: R. S. Thomas and Native America
Previously unpublished.

Interview with Jorie Graham
Swansea Review, 16 (1996), 1–8.

Interview with Rita Dove
Swansea Review, 19 (1995), 158–63.

Interview with Helen Vendler
Swansea Review, 16 (1996), 1–8.

'The heart of the matter', review of Dannie Abse, *New Selected Poems: Anniversary Collection, 1949–2009* (Hutchinson, 2009), *The Guardian*, 30 May 2009.

Charles Bukowski, *The Pleasures of the Damned, Poems 1951–1993*, ed. John Martin (Canongate, 2010); Howard Sounes, *Charles Bukowski: Locked in the Arms of a Crazy Life* (Canongate, 2010), *Acumen* 67 (May 2010), 103–6.

'Full fathom five', review of Jorie Graham, *Sea Change* (Carcanet, 2008), *The Guardian*, 3 May 2008.

'Review: *A Hospital Odyssey* by Gwyneth Lewis', *The Guardian*, 17 April 2010.

'*Oraclau/Oracles* [Clutag Press, 20210] by Geoffrey Hill – a review', *The Guardian*, 16 October 2010.

'Written in water', review of W. S. Merwin, *Selected Poems* (Bloodaxe, 2007), *The Guardian*, 2 June 2007.

'Flesh knew itself, and spoke', review of Sharon Olds, *One Secret Thing* (Cape Poetry, 2009), *The Guardian*, 21 March 2009.

'The best sort of crank', review of Charles Mundye (ed.) *Keidrych Rhys: The Van Pool* (Seren, 2012), *The Welsh Agenda*, 47 (Summer 2012), 82–3.

'Age, the equaliser', review of Anne Stevenson, *Stone Milk* (Bloodaxe, 2007), *The Guardian*, 13 October 2007.

Kirsti Bohata and Daniel G. Williams

Foreword

Helen Vendler

In the early 1980s, a journal asked me to evaluate a piece on Whitman submitted for publication. I was so astonished by its originality that I felt I should transmit my admiration to the author and asked the editor for the author's address. I could scarcely believe his answer. What? Someone in Wales had sent it? Not an American? Bemused and curious, I wrote to the author, explaining that I had myself three times tried and failed to write a book on Whitman – and that he was now brilliantly succeeding in writing the very analysis of the poet's art that I had been unable to formulate. I urged him to complete the book on Whitman that he had it in him to write. (Scholarly books on Whitman at that time tended to be biographical, topical, and cautious; they did not have much to say about Whitman's art – the sources of its vocabulary, its idiosyncratic structures, its relation to earlier poetic tradition.) And I was capable only, as I dejectedly put it to myself, of running after Whitman applauding poem after poem, while the sources of his miraculous living language remained hidden from me. But Wynn Thomas, the young Welsh author of the article, lived inside Whitman's language and imagination as I could not.

Wynn answered my letter, and our correspondence has never ceased. I came to learn, to my amazement, that this young professor had never visited the United States, yet he seemed to know the geography of Whitman's Brooklyn and Manhattan as readily as a native, and to have inhabited the wide political and civil framework of Whitman's century. What distinguished Wynn's perception, above all, was his historical understanding of the verbal world in which Whitman lived – the populist milieu of newspapers, stump speeches, advertisements, party debates, nationalist exhortations, factional sermons, and public affairs. Like other critics, I had been able to appreciate the poet's familiarity with the Bible and English poetry, as well as his ecstatic relation to music, but I discovered, through Wynn's pioneering work, that I had overlooked in Whitman's verse the subterranean populist atmosphere of his day: its vocabulary, its oratorical rhetoric, its flouting of the conventions of socially acceptable speech. Wynn intuited exactly what a populist poem would 'sound like': he knew the common man's tones of speech, what might be his occasions for exhortation, and which of his collective emotional expressions were lying ready for Whitman's pen to plunder and profit from. Wynn could see into Whitman's public passions and popular communication without losing any sense of Whitman's extraordinary intimacy in the more inward or private poems. (A later and fuller rendering of Wynn's pioneering work on Whitman's populist resources, called 'Whitman and the Labouring Classes', is included here.) From the beginning of his life as a critic, Wynn has had that absolute pitch that can identify each melodic intervention in the composition of a poetic whole. (Like many bilingual writers, Wynn, who learned English at five, grew up aware of the distinct melodies of differing languages.)

It had often been claimed, during my postgraduate education, that historical understanding was indispensable to the understanding of poetry, and poetry, studied in chronological order, was classified principally by the characteristics of its 'period' (while the concept of a 'period' was itself of course established by an artificially divided span of time). However, I had never seen the indissolubility of poetry and history conclusively proved on the planes of poetry that chiefly interested me then (and now): its choice of language, its architectural structures, its varying melodic inventiveness, and its emotional volatility. Critics seemed to use history mainly as a topical 'background' for their essays, but to me the analytic dimensions of the two disciplines – the wide graphic arc of history, constantly re-imagined and rephrased, and the vitally unchangeable structures of poetry which if disturbed relinquished the very art they exemplified – seemed too different to mix. To my mind, the analysis of the inimitable idiolect of the individual poet could not be interwoven with the grand discourse of historical analysis.

As I learned from Wynn, it was because I simply did not possess in the necessary detail the nineteenth-century populist and collective American language that I could not perceive how crucial it was, moment to moment, to Whitman's originality. Wynn perceived how Whitman's unlimited sense of popular language as it appeared in prose and in speech brought a new 'unpoetic' vocabulary and a rhetoric of the streets forcefully into the precincts of his aesthetic imagination. As

I finished Wynn's thrilling essay, and understood his revelatory sense of Whitman's conjunction of historical colloquiality and imaginative discourse, a Hopkins passage sprang into my mind:

These things, these things were here and but the beholder
Wanting; which two when they once meet,
The heart rears wings [...]

My heart reared wings, suddenly lifted into understanding Whitman after decades of longing and three failed books. I was now receiving Whitman's poetry from a mind that had mastered it by absorbing, often from working-class prose, multiple sources of both its vocabulary and its speech-acts that I had never thought to explore.

The instruction to my mind from Wynn's pages has continued for the past forty years, down to his newest essay (included here), a surprising and vivid meditation on D. H. Lawrence's struggle with Whitman. Over the years, I realised that Wynn can do anything with literature: translate it, historicise it, narrow it down to a single work, or broaden it out into the rendition of a whole culture. His curiosity has led him down many unusual paths (what were the Mormons doing in Wales? what did Whitman think of Tennyson?), but it has also drawn him into deeper investigations of the two poets he is closest to, the Welsh R. S. Thomas and the American Walt Whitman. His passionate attention to their work does not excuse faults, whether R. S. Thomas's sentimental nostalgia or Whitman's nativist bluster, but Wynn never forgets, even when noting faults, how many experiments must be tried by any artist probing outward possibilities and inner capacities.

I am missing, of course, any acquaintance with the fundamental underlying drive of Wynn's critical and scholarly work because I do not know Welsh and have not his learning in Welsh history and literature from medieval times to the present. Nonetheless, Wynn and I are both 'poetry people', committed in both affection and scholarship to that genre, whose glory lies in its imaginative transformations of language. (I should add that Wynn is also a 'novel person', and a 'history person', such is the reach of his talent as a critic.)

Before reading Wynn, I knew little of Wales. I had indeed visited north Wales in 1955, tracking the footsteps of Hopkins; in the 1980s, I had gone to R. S. Thomas's stern reading at the University of

Cambridge; and ever since I was thirteen I had been reading and thinking about the poetry of Dylan Thomas. I was present in 1953 at the
spellbinding evening at Harvard when Thomas read aloud, with infal-
lible intonation, all the parts of *Under Milk Wood*. But that was the extent
of my brushes with things Welsh. In later years, had I not had Wynn's
illuminating voice from the page – as well as his voice in person when
he was my colleague at Harvard – I would have had no living context
for Welsh writing. I am, then, a figure for all the readers and students
who have been informed and inspired by Wynn's eloquent writing and
teaching over the past decades. His constellations of words shine for me
over the cultural maps of Wales in time and space.

As I was rereading the essays collected here, two seemed especially
characteristic of Wynn's range, and I'll close with a look at each. The
first is Wynn's impressive and dashing piece of American literary history,
as he catches on the wing – from diaries, personal letters, newspaper
articles, reviews, interviews, obituaries and elegies – the responses of
contemporary American poets to Dylan Thomas's poetry and to his four
visits to the United States. The title of the essay begins with a quotation
from the American critic Elizabeth Hardwick, saying (with some surprise)
of Dylan Thomas, 'He was one of ours.' Wynn's subtitle is 'American
"bards" and Dylan Thomas', and its survey is not only entertaining but
also reliable: Wynn is amusing and amused in his choice of quotations,
ranging from the scabrous to the exalted, from both the quarrelsome
American poets and Thomas himself. Along the way, Wynn exposes the
deep fissures among the American poets of the 1950s. He groups them
under the usual rubrics (New Critical, Californian, Black Mountain,
Objectivist, and so on), but ingeniously links them by how often they look
back from Dylan Thomas to Whitman as they 'Americanise' his exotic
Welshness. Unlike the British poets and critics, who tended to connect
Thomas retrospectively with Wordsworth or Blake, American poets,
while sometimes looking back to Whitman, were energetically looking
forward, anticipating the neo-Romantic emergence of the Beat poets
(Rexroth, Ginsberg, Ferlinghetti), as well as the poets of the New York
School (Ashbery and O'Hara). Wynn's narrative brims with a current of
colourful dialogues, memories and vignettes coursing around Thomas's
work and his American readings: Robert Lowell writing to Elizabeth
Bishop, Bishop writing back to Lowell; John Malcolm Brinnin (who
arranged Thomas's visits to America) introducing the poet to a genial

e. e. cummings, who had been so moved by Thomas's earlier reading that afterwards he walked the streets alone for hours; the thronging audiences relishing Thomas's performative brio; John Berryman keeping vigil at Thomas's deathbed; Allen Ginsberg kneeling at Thomas's grave to say Kaddish. Through Wynn's lively sketches of the poets' outspoken warm and cold responses (and his pungent quotations from Thomas on America), I was encountering a striking (and diverting) literary history of my own time, most of which I had never seen before.

The second essay I would cite is a grave one. 'The Real Manafon' is an enlightening study of R. S. Thomas's poems about the parish of Manafon (where he served as an Anglican priest for twelve years, began to learn Welsh and to consolidate his views of the rural region and of his parishioners). Critics who have treated these poems as accurate transcriptions of the parlous conditions of farm life are overlooking, Wynn suggests, both the poet's frequent depressions and the necessary bending of the arc of fact to the aesthetic law of the poem. That law may demand a simplification of landscape, an exaggeration of poverty, a sympathy either intensified or diminished as the poem evolves. To demonstrate the surgery practised by Thomas on rural fact, Wynn invokes a remarkably complex and beautifully expressive book – *Life in a Welsh Countryside*, by the Welsh anthropologist Alwyn D. Rees, published in 1950, but reporting on field work done in 1939–40 (when Thomas lived in Manafon). Rees is far more appreciative of the social dimensions of life on the upland farms than Thomas could bring himself to be. Thomas's Calvinist view of human nature did not concern itself with the family networks and social gatherings of the farms, but saw the rustic farmer as an 'isolato' (as Wynn borrows Melville's drastic epithet for a tragic person). Wynn's penetrating commentary on the Manafon poems is strict and oriented to the aims of poetry, making it a revisionary critical guide to the farm poems as projections of their author's temperament and sensibility. The passage of time allows R. S. Thomas to distinguish his post-Manafon poems from those written while he lived in the parish: as Wynn says, by the time Thomas composes the later poetry he has acknowledged, with anguished bitterness, that his Manafon poems have already become anachronistic and irrelevant. And he also begins to fear that his early poems may have been 'demeaning and self-serving after all' as he himself – transcribing his views from the stance of a privileged spectator – escapes the grim facts of rural life.

Wynn's description of the ideal hope, shared by Thomas and Rees, for an alternative and more merciful postwar existence, government-sponsored, which would preserve the intimate connections between the farmer and his land, makes available to the modern reader the elegiac sentiment mourning, in anthropologist and poet alike, the plight of those who saw a mechanised future supplanting the existence of that communal and familial farm-labour which had conferred a regional solidarity. As I arrived, in my first reading, at the end of 'Manafon', and began to look at the footnotes, I was touched when I came to the one saying simply, 'Alwyn Rees was my uncle.'

No matter Wynn's subject – whether the tragicomic narrative of Thomas's American visits, or the serious plight of Manafon in agricultural decline – he takes his reader into two experiences at once: a direct encounter with a specific life-episode, and a philosophical reflection on the larger question of which his essay gives an instance. Under all of Wynn's writing one feels a warmth of engagement and a solicitude for an adequacy of portrayal: his work embodies an almost familial commitment to be faithful in representation and just in judgement. Even in Wynn's most abstract moments of political or historical scrutiny, one feels the undercurrent of personal expression, because the scholar's voice is always aroused by a human concern and directed to a human ear.

At the time of her passing on April 23rd, Helen Vendler (1933–2024) was A. Kingsley Porter University Professor Emerita at Harvard. Described in The New York Times *as 'the leading critic of poetry in the United States', she had been consultant poetry editor to* The New York Times, *president of the Modern Language Association, and poetry critic for* The New Yorker. *An authority on the poetry of George Herbert, John Keats, W. B. Yeats, Wallace Stevens and Seamus Heaney, she also published classic explications of Shakespeare's sonnets and Emily Dickinson's poems. In 2004, she delivered the Jefferson Lecture (the highest honour awarded in the humanities by the Federal Government), and in 2023 was the recipient of the Gold Medal of the American Academy of Arts and Letters.*

Introduction:
'Where I'm Coming From'

Daniel G. Williams

I begin with a story about the Austrian philosopher Ludwig Wittgenstein. As is well known, Wittgenstein changed the orientation of his philosophy after 1929, urging us to accept that the 'forms of life' that we inhabit form the explanatory bedrock of social and cultural thought. He traced this 'anthropological' shift in his thought to a discussion with the Italian economist Piero Sraffa.[1] In response to Wittgenstein's argument that a proposition and what it describes must have the same 'logical form', Sraffa offered a Neopolitan gesture of contempt by brushing his fingertips outwards from beneath his chin. 'What is the logical form of this?' he enquired.[2] The question led Wittgenstein to consider the damage wreaked by a reductive propositional view of human communication. Returning to his theory of language he was faced with repairing 'a torn spider's web' with his 'fingers'.[3] From then on 'forms of life' – the social contexts of all utterances as manifested in everyday actions, gestures and rituals – became the basis for his understanding of linguistic practice.

In making this case Wittgenstein was rejecting referential theories in which words denote objects or ideas (as in empiricism, and as in his own early writings), and departing from formal systems in which meaning derives from internal relations between signs (as in Saussurean structuralism). He used the term 'language game' to indicate that the 'speaking of language is part of an activity, or a form of life'.[4] Issues of value and rationality therefore arise from within a form of life and within the practices of a certain community. It is only against such a shared background that questions such as 'is this so' or 'is that reasonable' can be asked. We cannot imagine ourselves as independent from our loyalties and convictions because 'living by them is inseparable from understanding ourselves as the particular persons we are'.[5] The earlier Wittgenstein of the *Tractatus Logico-Philosophicus* (1922) comprehended the world as a 'whole', a bounded realm of 'facts': 'The World is all that is the case'.[6] In the *Philosophical Investigations* (1953) the universe is no longer comprehended as 'a whole regulated by the universal conditions of language'. It is, rather, made of 'lateral connections between partial domains'.[7] This shift in perspective also entails a shift in tone. Several critics have noted that whereas Wittgenstein adopted a voice in the *Tractatus* that spoke in direct assertions and logical propositions with no space for dissent, *Philosophical Investigations* contains voices in dialogue and is therefore less assertive and more exploratory in approach. A common interlocutory voice is that of a stranger: 'Suppose you came as an explorer to an unknown country with a language quite unknown to you.'[8] Wittgenstein argues that 'a philosophical problem has the form: "I don't know my way about"'.[9]

One of the sites of Wittgenstein's spatial confusion was Swansea, for between 1942 and 1947 he would visit his Welsh-American friend, acolyte and philosopher at the then University College of Wales, Swansea, Rush Rhees (1905–89). Indeed, Alfred Schmitt suggests that 'a substantial part of the *Philosophical Investigations*, as they were published posthumously by his executors in 1953, was written at Swansea, expanding the work to about twice its original size'.[10] As an undergraduate student at University College, Swansea, M. Wynn Thomas was taught by Rhees. While Wittgenstein is a not a central figure in Thomas's thought, he does make occasional telling appearances in his work, such as the passage in *In the Shadow of the Pulpit* when the 'celebrated aphorism' '[t]he limits of my language are the limits of my world' is used to relate the 'linguistic turn' in criticism to our understanding of religion, or when Emyr Humphreys's exposure to Wittgenstein's claim that '[w]hat we cannot speak about we must pass over in silence' is seen to explain the novelist's 'new spare style of writing' in the early 1960s.[11] In the present volume, the essay on Walt Whitman's 'Calamus' draws suggestively on Wittgenstein's reflections on the language of love. If utterances can only be understood within the broader context of a 'form of life', Wynn Thomas is always aware of the social and biographical contexts of his own thought. Wittgenstein's insistence that there can be no metalanguage – that analysing language by means of language is an impossibility akin to a 'tin opener slic[ing] itself open' – finds its equivalence for a cultural critic in the awareness that there is no dispassionate, objective position from which to speak.[12] An introduction of this kind might be expected to reconstruct the ways in which the formative influences of Thomas's early personal circumstances – from Ferndale to Gorseinon and via a thoroughly Anglophone education at Gowerton Grammar School to an evolution from student to Professor at Swansea University – influenced the core structure of his subsequent thinking and writing. But there is little point in doing that here, for Thomas has already done so himself in the introduction to a prior collection of essays, *All That is Wales* (2017).[13] It is notable that many of Thomas's studies begin with moving, autobiographical accounts of their inspiration and gestation, partly due to the fact that he traces the 'inadequacies' of his work to the 'weakness of my strengths, in the sense that they are the result of "where I am coming from"', in both the Welsh and the American senses of that phrase'. In other words, the self-acknowledged inadequacies 'are the result of my own limited socio-cultural background'.[14] If such declarations of one's own 'positionality' are common in works of cultural criticism, and may be said to have a Wittgensteinian provenance, the reference to the different Welsh and American inflections of the phrase 'Where I'm Coming From' draws our attention to the 'forms of life' that have – as manifested in their literary traditions – preoccupied Thomas throughout his career.

For over half a century M. Wynn Thomas has been one of the foremost literary critics in Wales. His method combines a deep historical knowledge of the Welsh-language and English-language literary traditions, a commitment to pluralism, and an approach to the text that is both sympathetic in its approach and detailed in its analysis. He is a literary and intellectual historian, a critical essayist, a translator, a gifted lecturer and teacher, an institution builder, editor, broadcaster and literary executor. He is among Wales's most distinguished public intellectuals whose 'concern to understand Wales's embeddedness in the wider world' is informed by 'a respect for the complex inner dynamics of myriad other small cultural units world-wide' that are routinely overlooked by majoritarian criticism.[15] With *Transatlantic Vistas* – this latest book in the CREW series on 'Writing Wales in English' that he founded – we celebrate M. Wynn Thomas's eightieth birthday at the end of a remarkable decade of activity in the development of these twin goals. In addition to the collection mentioned above, there was a parallel Welsh-language collection, volumes dedicated to R. S. Thomas and Emyr Humphreys, an excavation of the 'richly diverse potentialities' of Wales as a nation in the fin de siècle, a study of Welsh Europeanism (itself an act of cultural resistance after the Brexit vote of 2016), an analysis of the strikingly sacramental nature of Welsh poetry in the twentieth century, a popular collection of poetry documenting the history of Wales, that was itself followed by an anthology of the ways in which the Welsh have written of love from the medieval period onwards.[16] This volume contains uncollected essays on authors that have been of abiding interest throughout Thomas's career – Walt Whitman, Dylan Thomas and R. S. Thomas – coupled with examples of his work and activities, in the form of interviews and reviews, that have not been collected nor documented in book form.

As the essays, interviews and reviews collated in this volume amply testify, Welsh and American literatures raise questions which – while resembling those asked elsewhere regarding aims, methods, modes of representation – arise in specific contexts and should not be answered simply by translating the terms and answers that have proved useful to others. Wittgenstein insisted that we 'don't think, but look!'[17] He was worried that patterned expectations would be forced on data, crushing the circumstantial use of ordinary language which is what matters for meaning. Marjorie Perloff celebrates the 'anticlosural bent of Wittgenstein's investigative mode', and this resistance to closure is a characteristic of Wynn Thomas's modes of engagement whether as critic, reviewer or interlocutor.[18] Literature is the realm of alternatives and possibilities for a critic impatient with the philosophical and theoretical tendency to fix boundaries and meanings. To allow literature its play of ambiguities and differences is not, however, to ignore its contextual forms of life. It was Thomas's ability to contextualise that first drew the attention of the leading American critic Helen Vendler to his work: 'Thomas had mastered in his research (as I had not) all the underpinnings of Whitman's culture – the newspapers, the stump speeches, the editorials, the war dispatches – and therefore his study moved in historical synchronicity with Whitman's mind'.[19]

Thomas is a critic who resists systematisation, seeking to open democratic vistas as opposed to offering definitive pronouncements. Wittgenstein's worry regarding the imposition of reductive models on complexity and variousness is reflected in Walt Whitman's late fear that his 'philosophy' would be seen to rest 'upon braggadocio, noise, rough assertion, such integers'. Whitman noted his 'assent to this as a part of the truth', but felt that 'I am on the whole to be thought of in other terms'.[20] That Wynn Thomas draws our attention to Whitman's concern in this volume is significant, for recent summaries of his work, and that of those of us working under the umbrella of CREW (The Centre for Research into the English Literature and Language of Wales) at Swansea University, may lead us to wish that we, also, would be assessed by other terms. A celebration of M. Wynn Thomas's eightieth 'year to heaven' seems an appropriate place to attempt an adequate account of the values informing the Centre's myriad activities as we draw on his inspiration for the future.[21]

In his recent autobiography, *Off the Track*, the historian Dai Smith speaks warmly of his time at CREW.[22] Smith joined us in 2006, making a series of key contributions by completing his biography of Raymond Williams in 2008 and arranging that the Williams papers would be deposited in Swansea University's archives.[23] He offers a generous tribute to 'this collective of literary scholars', despite not sharing 'all of the broad agenda at CREW, namely to relate an English-language literature of Wales to a Welsh-language culture in a kind of desirable organic symbiosis'.[24] He is right about the desire to relate particulars within the Welsh experience, but an abiding concern of Thomas's work – and of Kirsti Bohata, Geraint Evans and myself who joined him in what Smith describes as a 'consistency of mission' – was to avoid and indeed to deconstruct all claims to organic wholeness. Wynn Thomas draws on Homi Bhabha's work in *Corresponding Cultures* in order to question 'the essentialist idea of a nation as simply unitary, as wholesomely "organic"', and notes the 'particular significance' of the postcolonial theorist's work 'to those of us who acknowledge the validity of the different kinds of Welshness that are highlighted by (although by no means identical with) the differences between the Welsh-language and the English-language cultures of twentieth-century Wales'.[25] Indeed, it is Smith himself who tends to collapse into forms of organicism such as when he clothes his legitimate case against the marginalisation of the post-industrial valleys in the language of nativism. Part of their claim upon us today, he argued, is that the valleys constitute 'a conurbation in which from eighty to ninety five percent are native born'.[26] These lines are quoted approvingly in Daryl Leeworthy's volume on 'political radicalism and social democracy in South Wales', *Labour Country* (2018), and forms a partial basis for his own 'imagined community'; a South Wales that eschews 'the framework of a nationalist perspective' for one in which Gwaun-cae-gurwen and Garnant are seen to have more in common with Barry than they have with villages to their west, or that Pandy has more in common with Cardiff than with the rural villages of Herefordshire to its east. That's not to say that there are not significant connections of economy and culture between the villages of the western coalfield, or the rural settlements of the border country, and the major coal ports of south Wales. But it is to say that any attempt at framing history, whether temporally, geographically, or culturally, will entail acts of exclusion. When Leeworthy turns his attention to the literary and cultural critics associated with CREW, he sees a collective that shares a 'mutual discomfort with the collective nature and reality of South Walian society after the First World War, its individual and collective traumas, and the political rhythms of that place which were orientated towards (and around) social class, not nation or language'. The tendency of this school of critics, according to Leeworthy, is to focus on 'the negative consequences of "spoiled" Welshness – an identity as much defined by the Edwardian Liberal institutions of chapel, language and nation, as by its modern devolved variant and the darkness of mood which such spoliation occasioned'.[27] Leeworthy takes his notion of 'spoiled Welshness' from Wynn Thomas's chapter on 'spoiled preachers' in *In the Shadow of the Pulpit*.[28] This is not Thomas's coinage. It is taken from a poem by the poet T. Harri Jones who, long domiciled in Australia, described himself as being

> From a hungry parish, a spoiled preacher
> Guiltily taking the surplus of your sunshine,
> And still afraid of hell because I've been there.[29]

The hell, notes Thomas, is both that evoked by the preachers in Jones's 'narrow chapel' at Beulah, and the 'hell that his childhood became because of such preaching'. Nonconformity entered early 'the very marrow of his being', a case of 'childhood development under what might broadly be suggestively termed a hegemonic power'.[30] Thomas argues that Jones was in no way unique in this respect and a series of ground-breaking analyses of south Walian writers – Rhys Davies, Gwyn Thomas and Idris Davies – follow. I have no space to summarise the subtleties of Wynn Thomas's arguments here. A quotation from the conclusion of his moving analysis of poet Idris Davies, long affected by the 'stern and grey' Calvinistic Methodism of his Uncle Edward Williams, must suffice:

> Of his Methodist uncle he registered how he 'was furious against Pharaoh' without ever recognizing his own class enslavement in the enslavement of the Jews. Davies also implicitly acknowledged how his own secular discourse of social revolution – its lexicon, imagery, intellectual structure and tone – was itself a direct translation of the religious language with which he had been surrounded as a boy [...] [H]is was not a case of 'spilt religion', in T. E. Hulme's celebrated phrase, but rather of infusing life and meaning into religious language by re-connecting it with the Reality Principle – with the social, economic and political realities of the proletariat which it had so obstinately, persistently, and culpably avoided facing. 'Once he crawled in the barbarous gloom', he wrote of the south Wales miner, 'As the trembling slave of theology'.[31]

Thomas states explicitly that his exploration of Wales's 'nonconformist heritage' should be 'distinguished from any wish to see the return of the chapels of Wales to their one-time dominance'.[32] To suggest that his nuanced account of the ambivalent literary responses to Nonconformist Protestantism amounts to a defence of Edwardian Liberal Welshness in the face of an allegedly 'discomforting' industrial experience is to misunderstand the analysis in a fundamental manner.

Yet, the distortion is repeated in the work of literary critic John Goodby, who traces the centrality of 'community' in 'WWE [Welsh Writing in English] criticism' not to the cultural materialism of Raymond Williams but to an 'idealistic hankering after the pre-1920 Nonconformist-Liberal hegemony (and its projection into a future of unification and independence) of a certain kind of Nationalism'.[33] In introducing his study of Dylan Thomas, Goodby acknowledges M. Wynn Thomas's innovative use of critical theory, but argues that his 'cymrocentric readings' – rooted in a 'linguistic culturalism' that sees the Welsh language at the core of national distinctiveness – results in a reductive understanding of Homi Bhabha's concept of 'hybridity' that 'avoids its more radical structural implications'.[34] Hybridity, notes Goodby, involves more than 'the inversion of the binary terms of a relationship'. He quotes Homi Bhabha to underline the fact that hybridity represents 'that ambivalent "turn" of the discriminated into the terrifying, exorbitant object of paranoid classification [...], it is not a third term that resolves the tension between two cultures'. M. Wynn Thomas's work, according to Goodby, is unfortunately predicated on the desire to find such 'third terms'.[35]

It is striking that these critiques share a common structure. Dai Smith believes that the members of CREW seek a 'desirable organic symbiosis' of Wales's English and Welsh language traditions. For Leeworthy, Thomas and 'a nationalist school of literary criticism' yearn for a homogeneous society that was 'spoiled' by industrialism.[36] According to Goodby, Thomas seeks a 'third term', a site of resolution. It seems then that what characterises CREW's 'consistency of mission' involves the search for a cultural homogeneity or symbiosis that fails to acknowledge the historical ruptures of the past or the inherent pluralism of the present.

Is this true? There is no doubt that Wynn Thomas has focused on 'the co-existence of two literatures in modern Wales and the many consequences that flow form that single complex fact', that he has argued that 'before Wales can fully know itself for what it is, it must confront acknowledge and carefully consider its bilateral character', and that he has explored key aspects of Welsh religious thought by eschewing what E. P. Thompson described as 'the enormous condescension of posterity'.[37] Furthermore, he has traced the foundations of his bilateralism to his childhood in Ferndale, Rhondda Fach:

> The fact that my first world mainly spoke English meant I grew up never doubting that English was fully a Welsh language and furious whenever it was suggested otherwise. But nor did I suppose that Welsh was somehow an 'illegitimate' language of the Valleys experience that had no right to speak.[38]

There is something profoundly counter intuitive, if not perverse, about a situation where critics who work primarily in one language and focus on English-language sources, criticise a body of work that is bilingual in methodology and expression for its alleged desire for homogeneity and organic symbiosis. Goodby has argued that there is a 'non-correspondence' between the 'linguistic culturalism' that he ascribes to many of us working in the field of Welsh Writing in English and the 'incorrigibly mongrel Anglo-Welsh poetry' produced by a Dylan Thomas whose 'innumerable links to English poetry' are indicative of 'an uneven, transcultural, dynamic productive of hybridity'.[39] It might be pertinent, in the face of such distortion, to make the obvious point that all contemporary Welsh-speakers over the age of around five are at least bi-lingual, whereas the majority of English-speakers in Wales are monolingual.[40] Thus, in a Welsh variation on a pattern witnessed elsewhere, the discourse of multicultural hybridity is deployed by a majoritarian culture against that which is, in fact, the most 'hybrid' element within Welsh society: the Welsh language that is spoken by around 20% of the three million inhabitants of Britain's westernmost peninsulas.[41] Slavoj Žižek has noted the tendency by postmodern cosmopolitans to think of their own culture as hybrid and progressive, while dismissing minority cultures as inherently essentialist and racist. We should be careful when people emphasise their hybrid and universalist credentials, warns Žižek, for the key question is 'do these same people also allow the Other to have the same credentials?'[42] The term 'linguistic culturalism' that Goodby adopts from Dai Smith, is designed to deny that diversity to Welsh language communities.[43] There is, it seems, nothing that may be designated 'linguistic' nor 'cultural' about the English language. The term is based on the delusion that English is the neutral and natural vehicle for a cosmopolitan citizenship that lies beyond the reach of linguistic minorities.

Doris Sommer notes that the acknowledgment of other language games can fail 'because of our underdeveloped skills for hearing differential meanings'.[44] If the misreadings described above suggest that a deficiency in hearing has been a problem for the reception of M. Wynn Thomas's writings, it seems also to have been the case for Ludwig Wittgenstein. It is striking how often Wittgenstein stresses transformation in language. He accepts that concepts can have 'blurred edges', for example, and notes that 'diversity' in language 'is not something fixed, given once for all; but new types of language, new language-games, as we may say, come into existence'.[45] Nevertheless, due to his emphasis on particular language games, Wittgenstein is viewed as a philosopher of limits and of impermeable boundaries. The result is that his philosophy is accused of leaving 'everything as it is', or 'simply … underwrit[ing] the commonplaces of ordinary parlance'.[46] The duty of the philosopher for

Wittgenstein, according to this misleading reading, is 'the stability of the set'.[47] Commentators and critics seem unwilling to allow for a position that argues for the integrity of particularistic language games *and* for the possible impact and influence of one form of life on another. The case for a particularism that is the local manifestation of a cosmopolitan universalism fails, it seems, to convince. To argue for the legitimacy of the particular is seen to entail a desire for homogeneity and stasis.

The problem, perhaps, lies in the question of influence; by what mechanism can one culture or 'form of life' impact another without that entailing some form of assimilation? 'To bring the foundation of a certain linguistic game to the surface' notes Paolo Virno, 'is the only way to move gradually onto a different game, one governed by a different set of rules.'[48] Comparison is presumably one way of bringing one language game into dialogue with another, of exposing the foundational rules of the games being juxtaposed. M. Wynn Thomas's work is consistently comparative, as amply illustrated in this volume. This is nowhere more revealingly the case than in the interview with African American poet Rita Dove. Drawing explicitly on his bicultural formation, Thomas ask Dove about the

> sense of your place, vis-à-vis other American poets, Langston Hughes, for example, Gwendolyn Brooks, Michael Harper, Robert Hayden – or, for that matter, to think differently about you, James Wright, and his poetry relating to Ohio. Is that the way you place yourself?[49]

Like Ralph Ellison before her, Dove is resistant to being read in relation to a single predetermined ancestral canon, though is happy to express her affinity with the African American poets named by Thomas.[50] She notes, nevertheless, that no one had previously suggested an affinity with the Ohioan James Wright, a poet whom she also greatly admires. Thomas suggests that his own biculturalism led him to suggest that an affinity with a white Ohioan writer might co-exist with the commitment to an African American canon.[51] Such multiple affinities, characteristic of minority writers, are only possible if there is some degree of mutual accessibility between cultures. This brings its own dangers. There is, for instance, the trap that Wittgenstein identified in the work of the Victorian ethnologist James Frazer; that we make the practices of others plausible to people who think as we do.[52] In the current volume this is a tendency that Wynn Thomas detects in R. S. Thomas's review of Dee Brown's history of American Indians, *Bury My Heart at Wounded Knee*. Wynn Thomas responds, characteristically, by exploring the particularistic histories of the relevant tribes before analysing the Welsh poet's uses and understanding of that indigenous experience.[53] On the other hand, there's the potential inability to recognise another culture at all. This is a danger in what Wynn Thomas identifies as 'Dylan Thomas's imaging of [...] Nonconformist discourse as authoritarian, univocal to the point of being totalitarian'.[54] If the slit throat of the 'desolate boy ... In the dark coffin' symbolises a cultural rupture in Thomas's 'After the Funeral', he is not wholly alienated from the culture of his forebears.[55] For to express acknowledgment, sympathy, or criticism, entails a mutuality between cultures or selves. Stefan Collini notes that even the most hostile critics require a 'bridgehead' or 'some commonality of values' with the objects of their scorn if their views are 'to gain any purchase at all'.[56] A. C. Grayling makes the same point in a more philosophical vein when he notes that 'if we are to talk of "other forms of life" at all we must be able to recognize them as such; we must be able to recognize the existence of practices which go to make up a form of life'.[57] Moreover, 'if we are to see that another form of life is different from our own we have to be able to recognize the differences; this is only possible if we can interpret enough of the other form of life to make those differences apparent'.[58] This, it seems to me, is precisely what M. Wynn Thomas achieves in his criticism. The turn to Wittgenstein in this introduction has been an attempt at offering an adequate account of Wynn Thomas's achievement, and the cultural vision that has informed the work of CREW and those inspired by Thomas's work in the wider field of Welsh Writing in English. Accusations of organicism and Edwardian nostalgia are so very wide of the mark that they betray a fundamental unwillingness to acknowledge and understand forms of life that are not one's own. The model of language games is much closer to the pluralist vision of Wales espoused in Wynn Thomas's writings. It is this pluralism that forms the basis for his comparative explorations of Welsh literatures in relation to European cultures (as in his recent *Eutopia*) and American literatures (as in the collection *Gweld Sêr*).[59] Thomas's pluralism is rooted in his acknowledgement that the Welsh- and English-language literary traditions of Wales have a validity in their own right. From here he can begin to identify times when 'a shared history may ... have resulted in interesting "congruities" between the two cultures' and also those times when they responded to each other 'in a spirit of mutual suspicion'.[60] Contrary to many, Doris Sommer argues that Wittgenstein is no 'quietist'; he is not one who interprets established practices as being unchangeable. Rather, he is 'a philosopher of human agency who enjoins us to leave prejudice behind and investigate how meanings are made'.[61] If we replace 'philosopher' with 'literary critic', it strikes me that this description is equally applicable to M. Wynn Thomas.

Where Thomas's work usefully supplements Wittgenstein's philosophy of language is in relation to those cases, common in bilingual societies, where individuals and communities may simultaneously occupy more than one language game. Despite the fact that his *Tractatus* was published as a parallel German-English facing text, and despite his own multilingualism (even ending one of his letters from Swansea to his lover Ben Richards with the correctly mutated 'pob llwyddiant yn y flwyddyn newydd as I always say when I'm speaking Welsh') Wittgenstein never explored bilingualism and largely clung to the 'delusion of "normal rule-governed" monolingualism'.[62] The delusion, notes Doris Sommer, 'is a wily player' of language games, getting the better of 'very smart agonists'. Freud, for example, 'translated the Yiddish out of his Jewish jokes in order to make a universal science of humour', while Derrida claimed that his monolingual frustrations were universal, 'as if all of us live, dream, write, speak, in one language that is not our own'.[63] In Wales, as we have seen, some find it easier to associate the Welsh language with an Edwardian past, rather than engage with the bilingual games being played around us in the present. Recognising that the Welsh language can be the vehicle for expressing a plurality of experiences, and that Welsh-language culture is evolving and can be as internally diverse as English language culture is at the root of what Thomas describes, borrowing from the Irish critic Michael Cronin, as his 'micro-cosmopolitanism'.[64] Working for much of his career in institutions where Anglophone monoculturalism continued to be the norm, Wynn Thomas is the prophetic critic of a future genuine pluralism rooted in the nation's bilingualism. He does not underestimate the task ahead. 'A genuinely fruitful "correspondence", in the sense of creative co-operation between the two cultures of Wales seems to me still a very long way away,' he noted in 1999, 'and conditional upon a radical psycho-cultural restructuring of the country that is likely to involve little less that a revolution in consciousness.'[65] What are the prospects of such a revolution today? Influential accounts of our contemporary 'postmodern condition' argue that the teleological grand narratives of modernity have collapsed, whether they be a belief in an evolutionary progress towards the common standards of consent (Friedrich Hayek, Karl Popper), or the view that the persistence of ethno-nationalisms and primitivist rituals indicate that modernity remains an 'unfinished project', yet to fulfil its potential (Jürgen Habermas).[66] In place of participation in the 'grand narratives' of the past, we are trapped, argues Jean-François Lyotard, in a plethora of 'language games'.[67] This analysis of the 1980s seems prophetic as social media intensifies the sense that people are screaming at each other from predetermined subject positions within their isolated silos, as opposed to working towards consensus through dialogue. Expressed in more positive and affirmative terms, we might argue that the coerced sameness fostered by narratives of assimilationist universalism in the past have now given way to a pluralised world in which linguistic and cultural particularity and diversity can be articulated and developed. What is required, perhaps more than ever, is a medium in which alternative positions can be voiced, and a critical approach open enough to test each language game by the criteria of its others within the context of 'a deeply felt and enacted human solidarity'.[68]

This leads me to close with a defence of the discipline in which Wynn Thomas and the editors of this volume work. For it is in the field of literature that we discover forms that are subtle enough to account for the presence and traces of distinct languages and particularistic voices. Literature has, perhaps uniquely, the ability to bring these languages and voices together and to set them in both antagonistic and sympathetic dialogues. Literary criticism explores, through a variety of approaches, the formal and contextual 'rough ground[s]' of their annunciation, and measures the similarities and incongruities between forms of life as expressed and mediated through language.[69] A fully bilingual culture in Wales may not yet sound realisable in a post-Brexit Britain where regurgitated neo-imperial dreams of cultural coherence continue to blunt the senses. Wittgenstein's therapy for the damage caused by the rigidity of rules and restrictions was to acknowledge the intricate spontaneity and creativity of everyday languages. The work of CREW in the next decade will be pursued in this spirit and informed by a truth taught us by M. Wynn Thomas; that monocultural dreams are a greater threat to our common humanity than are bilingual disturbances.

Notes

1. Ludwig Wittgenstein, *Philosophical Investigations*, trans. G. E. M. Anscombe, P. M. S. Hacker and Joachim Schulte (1953. Oxford: Wiley-Blackwell, 2009), p. 4e. Henceforth PI followed by section number.
2. For Wittgenstein's argument regarding logical form see *Tractatus Logico-Philosophicus* (1922. New York: Routledge, 2001), pp. 12–22. On Saffra see Amartya Sen, 'Saffra, Wittgenstein and Gramsci', *Journal of Economic Literature*, 4/4 (December 2003), 1249–55.
3. PI §106.
4. PI §23.
5. Michael Sandel, *Liberalism and the Limits of Justice* (Cambridge: Cambridge University Press, 1982), p. 179. Sandel is quoted by Kwame Anthony Appiah, *The Ethics of Identity* (New Jersey: Princeton University Press, 2005), p. 46.
6. Wittgenstein, *Tractatus*, p. 5.
7. Slavoj Žižek, *Less than Nothing: Hegel and the Shadow of Dialectical Materialism* (London: Verso, 2012), p. 756.
8. PI §206.
9. PI §123.
10. Alfred Schmidt, '"It's good to be away from Cambridge and to be here, and among friendly people": Wittgenstein's Letters to Ben Richards and his Philosophical Work in Swansea', in Alan Sandry (ed.), *Wittgenstein in Swansea* (Cardiff: University of Wales Press, forthcoming).
11. M. Wynn Thomas, *In the Shadow of the Pulpit* (Cardiff: University of Wales Press, 2010), p. 124. M. Wynn Thomas, *All That Is Wales: The Collected Essays of M. Wynn Thomas* (Cardiff: University of Wales Press, 2017), p. 151. M. Wynn Thomas will also contribute a chapter to the forthcoming volume edited by Alan Sandry, *Wittgenstein in Swansea*.
12. PI §120–4. See Marjorie Perloff, *Wittgenstein's Ladder: Poetic Language and the Strangeness of the Ordinary* (Chicago: University of Chicago Press, 1996), pp. 71–2. The 'tin-opener' analogy is from Terry Eagleton, 'My Wittgenstein', in Terry Eagleton, *The Eagleton Reader*, ed. Stephen Regan (Oxford: Blackwell, 1998), p. 336.
13. Thomas, *All That Is Wales*, pp. 1–29.
14. M. Wynn Thomas, *Internal Difference: Twentieth-century writing in Wales* (Cardiff: University of Wales Press, 1992), p. xiv.
15. Thomas, *All That Is Wales*, p. 3.

Introduction

16. M. Wynn Thomas, all University of Wales Press. In the order in which they are described: *Cyfandir Cymru: Ysgrifau ar Gyfannu Dwy Lenyddiaeth Cymru* (2017); *R. S. Thomas: Serial Obsessive* (2013); *Emyr Humphreys: Writers of Wales* (2018); *The Nations of Wales, 1890–1914* (2016); *Eutopia: Studies in Cultural Euro-Welshness, 1850–1980* (2021); *R. S. Thomas to Rowan Williams: The Spiritual Imagination in Modern Welsh Poetry* (2022); *The History of Wales in Twelve Poems* (2022); *A Map of Love: Twelve Welsh poems of romance, desire and devotion* (2023).

17. PI §66. See also PI §340.

18. Perloff, *Wittgenstein's Ladder*, p. 14.

19. Helen Vendler, '*Under Milk Wood*: Lists, Made and Undone', in Alyce von Rothkirch and Daniel Williams (eds), *Beyond the Difference: Welsh Literature in Comparative Contexts* (Cardiff: University of Wales Press, 2004), p. 100.

20. Thomas, 'Whitman, Tennyson, and the poetry of old age'. In this volume, p. 106.

21. The phrase is from Dylan Thomas, 'Poem in October', in *The Collected Poems of Dylan Thomas: The New Centenary Edition*, ed. John Goodby (London: Weidenfeld and Nicolson, 2014), pp. 160–2.

22. Dai Smith, *Off the Track: Traces of Memory* (Cardigan: Parthian, 2023), p. 370.

23. Dai Smith, *Raymond Williams: A Warrior's Tale* (Cardigan: Parthian, 2008).

24. Smith, *Off the Track*, p. 370.

25. M. Wynn Thomas, *Corresponding Cultures: the two literatures of Wales* (Cardiff: University of Wales Press, 1999), p. 45.

26. From a lecture delivered by Dai Smith at Chapter Arts Centre in November 2014. Quoted in Daryl Leeworthy, *Labour Country: Political Radicalism and Social Democracy in South Wales 1831–1985* (Cardigan: Parthian, 2018), p. 16.

27. Daryl Leeworthy, *Fury of Past Time: A Life of Gwyn Thomas* (Cardigan: Parthian, 2022), pp. 6–7.

28. M. Wynn Thomas, *In the Shadow of the Pulpit: Literature and Nonconformist Wales* (Cardiff: University of Wales Press, 2010), pp. 153–81.

29. Quoted by Thomas, *In the Shadow*, p. 154.

30. Quoted by Thomas, *In the Shadow*, p. 154.

31. Thomas, *In the Shadow*, p. 179.

32. Thomas, *In the Shadow*, p. 337.

33. John Goodby, *The Poetry of Dylan Thomas: Under the Spelling Wall* (Liverpool: Liverpool University Press, 2014), p. 24.

34. Goodby, *The Poetry of Dylan Thomas*, pp. 28, 29.

35. Goodby, *The Poetry of Dylan Thomas*, pp. 28–9.

36. Leeworthy, *Fury*, p. 6.

37. Thomas, *Internal Difference*, p. xiv. *Corresponding Cultures*, p. 6. E. P. Thompson, *The Making of the English Working Class* (1963. London: Penguin Classics, 2013), p. 12.

38. Thomas, *All that is Wales*, p. 6.

39. John Goodby, *The Poetry of Dylan Thomas*, p.31.

15

40. *https://statswales.gov.wales/Catalogue/Welsh-Language* (accessed 1 July 2023).

41. See, for example, Senka Božić-Vrbančić's work on multiculturalism within Maori culture in New Zealand: Senka Božić-Vrbančić, *Tarara: Croats and Maori in New Zealand: Memory, Belonging, Identity* (Dunedin: Otaga University Press, 2008). I am grateful to Simon Brooks for drawing my attention to this work.

42. Slavoj Žižek and Glyn Daly, *Conversations with Žižek* (Cambridge: Polity, 2004), p. 157.

43. John Goodby, *The Poetry of Dylan Thomas*, pp. 25, 28.

44. Doris Sommer, *Proceed with Caution, when engaged by minority writing in the Americas* (Cambridge MA: Harvard University Press, 1999), p. 7.

45. PI §71, PI §23

46. 'It [philosophy] leaves everything as it is' is Wittgenstein's own phrase. PI §124. Perry Anderson, *English Questions* (London: Verso, 1992), p. 66.

47. Perry Anderson, *English Questions*, p. 67.

48. Paolo Virno, *Multitude: Between Innovation and Negation*, trans. Isabella Bertoletti, James Cascaito and Andrea Casson (Los Angeles: Semitexte, 2008), p. 129.

49. Thomas, Interview with Rita Dove. In this volume, p. 293.

50. Ralph Ellison, 'The World and the Jug' in *Shadow and Act* (1964. New York: Quality Paperback Book Club, 1994), pp. 107–43.

51. Thomas, Interview with Rita Dove. In this volume, pp. 293–4.

52. Ludwig Wittgenstein, 'Remarks on Frazer's *Golden Bough*', in *Philosophical Occasions, 1912–1951*, ed. James C. Klagge and Alfred Nordmann (Indianapolis: Hackett, 1993), p. 119.

53. Thomas, 'Bury My Heart: R. S Thomas and Native America'. In this volume, pp. 243–90.

54. Thomas, '"There's Words": Dylan Thomas, Swansea and language'. In this volume, p. 185.

55. Dylan Thomas, 'After the Funeral', *The Collected Poems of Dylan Thomas*, pp. 101–2.

56. Stefan Collini, *Speaking of Universities* (London: Verso, 2017), p. 223.

57. A. C. Grayling, *Wittgenstein: A Very Short Introduction* (1998. Oxford: Oxford University Press, 2001), p. 121.

58. Grayling, *Wittgenstein*, p. 121.

59. Thomas, *Eutopia: Studies in Cultural Euro-Welshness*. Thomas (ed.), *Gweld Sêr: Cymru a Chanrif America* (Caerdydd; Gwasg Prifysgol Cymru, 2001).

60. Thomas, *Corresponding Cultures*, p. 1.

61. Doris Sommer, *Bilingual Aesthetics: A New Sentimental Education* (Durham NC: Duke University Press, 2004), p. 162.

62. Quoted by Alfred Schmitt in a paper at the Wittgenstein in Swansea Conference, 16 June 2022. The Welsh means 'I wish you every success in the New Year'. On translation and the *Tractatus*, see Michael North, *Reading 1922: A Return to the Scene of the Modern* (Oxford: Oxford University Press, 1999), pp. 31–52.

63. Sommer, *Bilingual Aesthetics*, p. 167. Sommer is summarising the arguments found in: Sigmund Freud, *Jokes and Their Relation to the Unconscious*, ed. and trans. James Strachey (1905. New York: W. W. Norton, 1960); Jacques Derrida, *Monlingualism of the Other or The Prosthesis of Origin*, trans. Patrick Menash (1996. Stanford: Stanford University Press, 1998).

64. Thomas, *All that is Wales*, pp. 1–4. See Michael Cronin, 'Global Questions and Local Visions: A Microcosmopolitan Perspective', in Rothkirch and Williams (eds), *Beyond the Difference*, pp. 186–202.

65. Thomas, *Corresponding Cultures*, p. 5.

66. Friedrich A. Hayek, *The Road to Serfdom* (London: Routledge, 1944). Karl Popper, *The Open Society and its Enemies* (London: Routledge, 1945). Jürgen Habermas, *Strukturwandel der Öffentlichkeit* (Darmstadt: Mermann Luchterhand, 1962). Translated as *The Structural Transformation of the Public Sphere: An Inquiry Into a Category of Bourgeois Society* (Cambridge: Polity Press, 1989).

67. Jean-François Lyotard, *The Postmodern Condition*, trans. Geoff Bennington (Manchester: Manchester University Press, 1984), p. 4.

68. The phrase is from Daniel Boyarin, *A Radical Jew: Paul and the Politics of Identity* (Berkeley: University of California Press, 1994), p. 257.

69. PI §107.

I.
ON WALT WHITMAN

'Till I hit upon a name':
'Calamus' and the language of love

One feature of the 1860 edition of *Leaves of Grass* interests me particularly. Simply put, the great poems in the previous editions of 1855 and 1856 tended to deal with the complexities of life by separating out the different strands of human experience and dealing with them sequentially. This simple procedure is integral to the otherwise elaborate structure of 'Song of Myself,' as the poem alternates rhythmically between responding to a sequence of different internal impulses of instinct, feeling, thought, and responding to external stimuli. But with 'A Word Out of the Sea' and 'Calamus', Whitman seems no longer insouciantly content to contradict himself, but instead seeks to capture the inherent contradictoriness, the ingrained ambivalence, of all the deepest human experiences. No longer are we invited to swing between great opposites – life and death, joy and sorrow, love and loss. We're now confronted with a new understanding of these contraries as implicated in each other, so that love is understood as predicated upon loss and vice versa. Interestingly enough, Ellen M. Calder – who, as the then wife of William D. O'Connor, was probably as close as anyone to Whitman during his Civil War years in Washington (1862–5) – could still vividly remember, decades later, the popular verse of the period he was so fond of reciting:

> A mighty *pain* to love it is,
> And yet a pain that love to miss;
> But of all pain, the greatest pain
> It is to love, but love in vain![1]

This is a trite formulation of the electric new recognition that powers some of the greatest poems of the 1860 edition. Whitman's sensibility seems to have been deepened and enriched by a much subtler, impacted, and in some ways newly tragic, sense of the complexities of human experience.

An alteration of consciousness has occurred that makes possible the emergence of a new Whitmanian poetry – an authentic poetry of love. Because it is only when the inherent, disturbing ambivalence of love and passion are fully registered that a great romantic love poetry becomes possible. Both 'A Word out of the Sea' and 'Calamus' testify most compellingly to the birth in Whitman of this new understanding by conveying to us the 'demonic' side of love. So new, and so dangerous, a vision is this for Whitman that he is understandably frightened by it. As early as the opening, signature and programmatic poem of 1860, 'Proto-Leaf,' he lets slip what seems to be a real anxiety in this connection: 'Proceed, comrade,/ It is a painful thing to love a man or woman to excess – yet it satisfies – it is great'.[2] But this is still carefully generalised sentiment, the insight defused and rendered safe. Not so, however, in 'A Word Out of the Sea':

'O throes!
O you demon, singing by yourself – projecting me,
O solitary me, listening – never more shall I cease imitating,
    perpetuating you,
Never more shall I escape,
Never more shall the reverberations,
Never more the cries of unsatisfied love be absent from me,
Never again leave me to be the peaceful child I was before
    what there, in the night,
By the sea, under the yellow and sagging moon,
The dusky demon aroused – the fire, the sweet hell within,
The unknown want, the destiny of me.' (276)

The culminating phrases in this deliberately reverberative passage echo the age-old tropes in traditional poetry lamenting the anguish and the torments of heterosexual love – the very tropes, we might note, that are to be found reduced to the banal in that little verse Whitman so loved to recite during his Washington years. And in such phrasing, or so it seems to me, lies a premonition of the 'Calamus' poems to come.

'A Word Out of the Sea' also awakens uncontrollable echoes from other classic texts on love. (Not the least powerful feature of the poem is the way it thus carries within the very body of its language the terrible knowledge that in the very moment of his initiation into love the child is caught up by forces over which he no longer has any

21

control. He is reconstituted out of the impersonal, unpredictable and irresistible 'voices' of passion.) Take the tipping point in the poem's psycho-narrative: 'For I that was a child, my tongue's use sleeping,/ Now that I have heard you,/ Now in a moment I know what I am for – I awake' (275–6). These lines bear the unmistakeable, and indelible, mark of the memorable passage from the thirteenth chapter of Paul's majestic First Epistle to the Corinthians: 'When I was a child, I spake as a child, I understood as a child, I thought as a child; but when I became a man, I put away childish things.' The context is, of course, the celebration of love, called 'charity' in the King James version of the English Bible.

By echoing Paul, Whitman is underlining the fateful, sacred character of the human awakening to love; he's emphasising that in such an awakening can be felt the stirring within us of strange gods, strange powers that will never be fully under our control. And he's explicitly stating that it's the stirring of those powers that can be heard in the adult tongue, most potently and unpredictably of all when it gives reverberative voice to poetry. The whole passage is an astonishing one. It's a confession to having awakened simultaneously to adulthood and to poetry by finding his voice; that is, to having been involuntarily blessed – and cursed – with the language of love, through a kind of Pentecostal descent of some dubious spirit: 'demon or bird,' as he put it in his later, revised version of the poem.

In seeking for an adequate 'language of love' he instinctively turns to one of his greatest passions: opera. With its remarkable collection of arias, 'A Word out of the Sea' is evidently a composition modelled on such music, as scholars have already amply noted. Indeed, it might prove fruitful to set alongside the distracted 'song' of the thrush the great 'mad' scene from Donizetti's *Lucia di Lammermoor*, one of Whitman's favourite operas,[3] and one he alludes to in his ecstatic salute to the music of the world, 'Proud Music of the Storm': 'Across the stage with pallor on her face, yet lurid passion,/Stalks Norma brandishing the dagger in her hand.// I see poor crazed Lucia's eyes' unnatural gleam,/ Her hair down her back falls loose and dishevel'd' (406). Comparison with the *bel canto* masterpieces of Donizetti and Bellini not only highlights but clarifies the deliberately 'stylized' expression of the madness of love in Whitman's poem (a feature, too, of some of the greatest 'Calamus' poems) – although equally illuminating would be a recollection of the powerful scenes of distraction from, say, Shakespeare's love tragedies, with which Whitman was so passionately 'inward.'

Some of the greatest poetry of the 1860 edition is in the form of this authentic language of love, new in Whitman's poetry. And it is no doubt legitimate for scholars to speculate that it derived from some great psychic upheaval within Whitman, as he found the poetic strategies he'd so brilliantly devised and deployed in 1855–6 were no longer adequate for dealing with the desperate political (and perhaps personal) circumstances in 1860. But in some important ways, whether or not there had been an actual biographical or political crisis is immaterial. All that matters is the appearance of this new kind of writing, inscribed in which is a new awareness of how life's opposites are compressed, crushed together into every iota of intense human experience.

Nowhere is this more evident than in the 'Calamus' cluster. And there it results in writing that is sometimes astonishing. Take 'Calamus 15' (later 'Trickle Drops'), which captures, with an honesty so naked that it is almost embarrassing, the grotesqueness that can attend passion. It's a poem that conveys what it's like to be *in extremis*, to be beside oneself, as we say. It's about self-wounding, self-crucifixion, self-mutilation, self-abuse. And it's a lyric of self-abasement that confesses to its own shame – 'Saturate them,' (the pages of the poem) 'with yourself all ashamed and wet,' Whitman beseeches his blood, 'Glow upon all I have written or shall write, bleeding drops,/ Let it all be seen in your light, blushing drops.' (361) The erotic charge in the writing – the implicit association of blood with semen, and the suggestion that this is a kind of seduction poem to the reader – is extraordinary.

As to the sense conveyed that confession is somehow emotionally and sexually arousing and gratifying, a form of masochism, well that's an insight we associate more with Dostoevsky than with Whitman. This is the kind of thing I mean when I say that 'A Word Out of the Sea' and the poems in 'Calamus' are great love poetry – for poetry of like density of character, insight and expression one would probably have to turn back to the Elizabeth and Jacobean age, the golden age of English love poetry. As Ian Robinson trenchantly noted four decades ago, 'Love poetry is the creation of sexual passion in language. Poetry is some demon or other uttering himself in common speech; in love poetry the demon belongs to the not wholly respectable family of Venus and Cupid.'[4] In Whitman's case, the accents of that demon can clearly, and uniquely, be heard in the great love poems in the 1860 edition. Because it is there alone he writes as one haunted by passion, although, as we'll see below, this impression is created by means as studied and 'theatrical' as those in *Anthony and Cleopatra* or Donizetti's operas.

A Language Experiment

The foregoing observations may be usefully connected to a remark Whitman makes in the glorious scatter of notes published posthumously as *An American Primer*. While celebrating the American lexicon, incomparably 'rich and juicy' thanks to its hybrid character, he adds the following:

> Words of approval, admiration, friendship. This is to be said among the young men of These States, that with a wonderful tenacity of friendship, and passionate fondness for their friends, they yet have remarkably few words of names for the friendly sentiments – They seem to be words that do not thrive here among the muscular classes, where the real quality of friendship is always freely to be found. – Also, they are words which the muscular classes, the young men of these states, rarely use, and have an aversion for; – they never give words to their most ardent friendships.[5]

Mark Bauerlein and others have demonstrated that Whitman's concept of language primarily centred on a 'representational' model, which assumed the pre-existence of phenomena and experiences for which a 'corresponding' vocabulary then had to be found. Implicit in his actual practice – as, perhaps, in the practice of every poet – is a different intuition: that to some extent, experience is not fully evolved and present in us until we already have a language for it.[6] Hence his conviction that his poetry was not a mere accompaniment to democracy – a recording of an already safely established social reality – but rather a vital means of establishing a genuine democracy in America. The implications of this notion for our present concerns are made clear in Ian Robinson's *The Survival of English* (1973), a study that draws fruitfully on those models of language outlined so scrupulously yet cryptically in the later work of Wittgenstein:

Is 'love' just a label like (in some cases) 'moon', for something we can't help seeing in the world and which is there whether we name it or not? It is tempting to say so, and I don't want to argue that 'love' would make any sense unless there were something answering to it really present in the world. It is also true that love is far from being kept in bounds by language or anything else, in some cases. I shall argue all the same that there *is* an interaction between the thing and the word which makes the word more than a label, that the use of the word affects the sense of the thing, and that since the sense [...] is the real existence of the thing, even here words affect things and love as we really know it in life varies with the way we use 'love'.[7]

The 'love' in question here is specifically of the 'romantic' kind that has been a dominant mode of experience in Western societies, according to many scholars, at least since the period of the troubadours and their language of courtly love. And particularly relevant in the present context is the further scholarly suggestion that courtly love developed partly as an attempt to evoke a heterosexual love relationship to counterbalance the predominantly masculine and overbearingly paternalistic character of medieval society. Whitman may be regarded in 'Calamus' as conversely attempting to establish a male-male socio-erotic axis to offset the heavily heterosexual American society of his own time. And in so doing, there is even a sense in which he is reversing the process that actually produced the *Amour Courtois* phenomenon; as scholars have again pointed out, courtly love may be regarded as the defiant 'translation' into heterosexual terms of the kind of social and sexual relationships that had, in antiquity, been regarded as the exclusive feature of the intimate bonds between males.[8] Thus, citing a celebrated passage on homosocial and homoerotic love from Plato's *Phaedrus*, Maurice Valency has noted that the 'whole mechanism of romantic love is inherent in this passage pretty much as the Renaissance lyricists conceived it – it is quite the same, all but the gender of the pronouns.'[9]

Viewing 'Calamus' in this context allows us to read it as a 'language experiment', to apply one of Whitman's most celebrated descriptions of *Leaves of Grass* as a whole. By 'experiment' is not meant, though, that it was an exercise coolly, objectively, dispassionately undertaken. The very opposite is in fact true. This was a search he had been both enabled and compelled to make for an 'answerable' language: a language for recognising, comprehending and sharing the deepest, the richest, and in some ways too the darkest, ranges of same-sex relationship. It was a search for a language of same-sex love as subtly inflected and comprehensive as the language of heterosexual love.

And this experiment probably meant an enormous amount to him – it was probably connected at that juncture with his most intimate, troubled personal experiences. But we go then astray, it seems to me, if we proceed to puzzle over whether or not Whitman was homosexually active, in the sense of enjoying sex with other men. That is, in a way, irrelevant. What the most intimate passionate poems in 'Calamus' are about is not having sex but about making love – which is very different. Whitman was anxious to develop a language that would allow same-sex relations to include the same kind and quality of human relationship that characterised heterosexual relationships. In short, he wanted to create a new language of love – or rather, perhaps, to extend the existing language of love to make possible the full recognition of the whole continuum of male-male relationships from transient friendship through episodic, and even furtive, homosocial and homoerotic encounters to 'grand passions' and what we would nowadays term a full, multi-faceted, sexually active, same-sex relationship.

This is not to deny Mark Doty's assertion that there was already a language for homosexual encounters available to Whitman in 1860.[10] It is rather to doubt whether Whitman – for all his love of the fluid, floating character of such casual sexual transactions – was fully satisfied with the limited discourse of a sub-culture and the correspondingly limited modes of relating inscribed within it. He anticipated modern philosophers like Wittgenstein, as well as modern sociolinguists and discourse theorists, in realising that before an experience can assume substantial, developed and thoroughly integrated form it needs first a language that, by articulating it, can call it into fullness of socialised being. That is why, for instance, Shakespeare's great comedies feature lessons in the language of love – think of Rosalind, dressed as a boy, teaching Orlando radically to review the idealising, limiting language of romantic love with which he has become infatuated.[11] Taking advantage of the 'liberties' allowed her by her cross-dressing, (s)he demonstrates for him that the risqué language of bawdy is not only compatible with but vital for a fulfilling heterosexual love relationship.

Erotic Tropographies

So, then, 'Calamus' may fruitfully be approached as a language experiment in the above senses; an attempt to give voice to a power of 'romantic love' that was both 'demon and bird'. And Whitman's ambition to develop a language capable of acknowledging the full range of male-male relations is explicitly announced in 'Calamus 4' (later 'These I Singing in Spring'):

> These I, singing in spring, collect for lovers,
> (For who but I should understand lovers and all their sorrow
>   and joy?
> And who but I should be the poet of comrades?) (370)

It is usual to assume unthinkingly that 'lovers' and 'comrades' are synonyms here; that they're interchangeable because they're just two variant words for the same thing. But it might be read otherwise. If we understand 'lovers' to signify a relationship instinct with sex and 'comrades' to signify a relationship instinct with affection, then we see that in these lines Whitman is in fact spanning the whole spectrum of the same-sex relationships he's trying to find a language for in 'Calamus'. That would seem to bring us to the collection's raison d'être, and to be its great achievement.

Before pursuing this theme further, it is important to recall how slowly, and painstakingly, composed the 1860 text of 'Calamus' was. As Fredson Bowers brilliantly demonstrated over a half-century ago, 'Calamus' was some five years in the growing, with the pungent, potent organising symbol Whitman eventually settled on for title occurring only towards the very end of the protracted process.[12] Some of the poems were already complete by 1857, although at that stage he had no idea what to do with them. Then came the twelve poems grouped deliberately together under the working title of 'Live Oak with Moss', before the rival possibilities of the 'Calamus' plant as a central and informing feature began to emerge during the summer of 1859. Finally, yet more poems were added as the whole began to consolidate into a clear cluster. Hence, as I pointed out in an essay published forty years ago, we should be wary of mining 'Calamus' for direct, straightforward, 'confessional' evidence. Indeed, even some of those passages that seem to be most immediate and intimate turn out, upon examination of the manuscript evidence, to have been significantly revised and altered. 'The climate of feeling of the "Calamus" group,' I suggested, 'is one that Whitman not only recognized but deliberately fostered.' Whitman, I concluded, was constructing 'from his own experiences, a sort of model of the passional life as he knew it. [The poems] are more of a poet's self-possessed investigation of the parameters of passion, than the direct testimony of man by passion possessed.'[13]

One recent commentator to take the implication of these revisions and developments intelligently on board is Allen Helms, and his interpretation may be regarded as broadly representative of recent approaches, in gay criticism, to Whitman's achievements in 'Calamus'. Tending to prefer the 'Live Oak with Moss' group of poems to the more evolved and multifaceted (and in his opinion more diffuse and verbose) 'Calamus' collection, he points out all the disfiguring linguistic tics in the latter that, as they accumulate, increasingly betray Whitman's acute discomfort at writing about 'manly love' for mainstream public consumption. 'Insofar as "Calamus" is more ambitious than "Live Oak" and published besides,' Helms argues, 'the tension between the need to speak and the prohibition against doing so becomes excruciating.'[14] Similarly, Mark Doty contends that Whitman encased the powerful 'Live Oak' sequence within the more anodyne 'Calamus' sequence because he lost his nerve: 'Even Walt got the willies!'[15] Such readings are very much in line with current orthodoxy on 'Calamus' in seeing many of the distinctive lexical choices and rhetorical strategies of the collection as expressive of Whitman's distressing psycho-social situation. According to this line of argument, Whitman has constantly to take evasive action because of the internal inhibitions and the external obstacles and prohibitions that in his time bedevilled any attempt at speaking of same-sex relations.

That this is a powerful and compelling aspect of 'Calamus' seems to be beyond dispute. But to limit oneself to this perception may be to risk skewing reading of the collection. Approached in this spirit, tropes, for example, can suddenly appear to be not unique modes of experiential apprehension and articulation but rather pathetic substitutes for plain, direct statement. Reading can then rapidly deteriorate into exercises in 'decoding' the 'surface' text. It can also quickly become suspicious of the whole decorum of the writing – its deliberately formal and stylized qualities. Helms, for example, accurately notes how conventional

Whitman's writing has now in some respects become, but sees this only as symptomatic of the fatal decline of his early radicalism.[16] In what follows I should like to suggest that not only may the dignity and decorum of the 'high style' that Whitman adopts in 'Calamus' be viewed as directly pertinent to his liberationist aims in that collection but that the tropes, too, should be valued for their unique heuristic properties.

Given the prevailing climate of our anti-poetic culture we should always beware of reinforcing, however unintentionally, already powerful literal-minded opinion that metaphors and similes are modes merely of decoration or of concealment. It is the contrary, surely, that is true? Poetic tropes are actually unique modes of disclosure. When Donne, excitedly viewing his mistress undress, breaks out into 'O my America, my new founde land', it isn't because he's too shy and tongue-tied to name the relevant delectable body parts that are heaving so enticingly into view. No, he is registering the way in which another's body may, to an excited lover, seem like a mysterious, virginal continent of treasures. And Donne underlines the drift of his trope in the pun in a succeeding line: 'How blest am I in this discovering thee'.[17] To uncover is to discover: this affirmation is the natural outcome of a trope that has enabled us, as readers, to share with the lover the sacred thrill of the very moment of that discovery. There is no shortage in 'Calamus' of similar rhetorical feats. Indeed, one of the most powerful achievements of the volume is Whitman's creation of what might be termed erotic tropographies – tropes (figures of speech) that intimately map a whole topography of private erotic experience. So, in 'These I, Singing in Spring', he wanders beyond bounds:

> but soon I pass the gates,
> Now by the post-and-rail fences, where the old stones thrown
> there, picked from the fields, have accumulated,
> Wild-flowers and vines and weeds come up through the stones,
> and partly cover them – Beyond these I pass,
> Far, far in the forest, before I think where I get,
> Solitary, smelling the earthy smell, stopping now and then in
> the silence (347).

Landscape and body here become versions of each other.[18] There are hints of erotic biomorphic features everywhere (passing the gates;

post-and-rail fences; earthy smell), although nowhere are these crudely allegorised. As with Donne, what Whitman is after is not the biological 'facts' of transgressive relationships but the delicate, suggestive registering of the strange, elusive, wondrous world of experience to which they uniquely admit entry. And, as with so much romantic love poetry, the ecstatic enlargement of consciousness his tropes faithfully register results from transport beyond the ordinary bounds of selfhood. It comes from wandering 'far, far in the forest, before I think where I get' (370). It is also figured as the experience of being carried beyond the bounds of familiar language, even perhaps beyond the bounds of language itself. Thus, 'These I, Singing in Spring' not only shows us Whitman's new language of love actually coming into being, it conveys to us something of the very pressure of the conditions that call it so inexorably into existence.

The heroic 'originality' of this writing is beyond question, as are the oppressive contemporary circumstances militating against it. But in dwelling exclusively on it we run the risk of ignoring its studied conventionality. We may miss, for example, its continuity with the great love poems of Donne and his contemporaries, although to note that does not mean to suggest Whitman was familiar with them. He was no disciplined, scholarly reader, but he was a voracious scanner and cannibaliser of all sorts of unlikely texts. Alan Helms is one of several critics to notice resemblances between 'Calamus' and Shakespeare's sonnets, but my understanding of the implications of such resemblances is rather different from his consensus view. Not too far beneath the surface of the text of 'These I, Singing Spring' lurks a figure traditional to love poetry – the moping, distracted lover, perhaps carving names on trees, perhaps dreaming of passionate romantic trysts, perhaps reflecting on the indifference of the hard-headed world to his plight. To this figure Whitman, the socio-sexual outcast, gives a poignant twist, as he does to a whole range of other conventional features of romantic love poetry. Indeed, if one reads the 'Calamus' sequence with eyes informed by the great tropes, motifs and rhetorical figures that have traditionally constituted Western (heterosexual) love poetry, one can discern the lineaments of these everywhere. And in the process, one begins to intuit how Whitman is, probably intuitively, aligning his poetry, and his experiences, radically 'original' and 'transgressive' though they may both have been, with long established, respected, socially sanctioned modes of feeling and expression.

In other words, he is in part unconsciously attempting to bestow upon the passionate and affectionate relationships between members of his beloved working class the respect and human dignity that heterosexual relationships have long commanded in his society. In order to do that, he has to integrate his own language of 'new' love into the 'language of love' that already exists, without jeopardising in the process full acknowledgement of the necessary differences between homo- and hetero-sexual experience; and without underplaying the painfully crippling contemporary constraints on same-sex relations. Moreover, as his collection demonstrates, the traditional discourse of romantic love is itself bound to be substantially modified as it admits full recognition of this 'other,' 'alternative,' and previously 'alien' dimension of experience.

An Inventory of Devices

To reinforce these points it is worth drawing up (by way of example and with no implication of 'influence') a brief, crude inventory of some of those features in 'Calamus' that approximate to the staple devices of romantic love poetry, even as of course they deviate from them. There are, for instance, hints of the dangerous, demanding, wayward, alternative religion of love in 'Whoever you are holding me now in hand':

> The way is suspicious – the result, slow, uncertain,
>   may-be destructive;
> You would have to give up all else – I alone would expect to be
>   your God, sole and exclusive,
> Your novitiate would even then be long and exhausting,
> The whole past theory of your life, and all conformity to the
>   lives around you, would have to be abandoned. (345)

The repeated Gospel echoes here have been widely noticed, and Whitman's equivocal invitation to us to be his disciples is obviously very much in the spirit of a traditional worshipper of Eros. Such a subversive use of the sacred discourse of religion, has of course, been a staple device of love poetry for millennia. Notable examples include Donne's 'The Relique' ('he, that digges us up, will bring/ Us, to the

Bishop and the King') and 'The Canonisation' ('As well a well wrought urne becomes/ The greatest ashes, as half-acre tombs').[19]

Admission to a secret fellowship of lovers is the great theme of several of the 'Calamus' poems, and in several cases it is closely connected with mention of the secret language of passionate relationship. 'For who but I should understand lovers, and all their sorrow and joy?' is the question in 'These I, Singing in Spring', while a powerful feature of other poems is their development of a complex erotic vocabulary of plants and flowers. A prominent example is 'Calamus 13' (eventually 'Roots and Leaves Themselves Alone are These'). Roots, leaves, scents from the wild woods and pond-side, 'breast-sorrel and pinks of love', 'Frost-mellowed berries, and Third Month twigs' – all these, and more, it is alluringly promised, will reveal their secret meaning to those who recognise them as 'love-buds' and provide them with the 'aliment and wet' that promote their growth to fullness of sensual expression.[20] The whole suggestive poem daringly naturalises the processes of sexual arousal, yet it is based on the familiar conceit of the language privately shared by lovers. A related example is provided in that marvellously haunting and haunted poem 'These I Singing in Spring'. In its most heart-rending moments, it brings to mind the mad Ophelia distributing her sad tokens of remembrance to all and sundry:

> Plucking something for tokens – something for these, till I hit
>   upon a name – tossing toward whatever is near me,
> Here! lilac with a branch of pine
> Here, out of my pocket, some moss which I pulled off a
>   live-oak in Florida, as it hung trailing down,
> Here, some pinks and laurel leaves, and a handful of sage (348).

There are parallels in the poem even to Ophelia's wistful trust that her flowers and herbs will nurture in her recipients the fidelities of attachment so tragically absent from her own experience of love and its treacheries: 'And this, O this shall henceforth be the token of comrades – this calamus root shall,/ Interchange it, youths, with each other! Let none render it back!' (348). And in the case of both Ophelia and Whitman these tokens give expression to feelings for which there is no adequate existent language – 'Plucking something for tokens – something for these, till I hit upon a name', as Whitman trenchantly puts it.

Thus does his poetry enact that very search for a 'language of love' that lies at its troubled heart.

This constant effort to 'hit upon a name' is Whitman's permanent – and permanently thwarted – undertaking throughout 'Calamus'. And again, whenever he specifically addresses this problem, he is likely to end up reworking a familiar rhetorical figure from romantic love poetry. Take the following celebrated instance from "Calamus 2' (subsequently 'Scented Herbage of My Breast'):

> Come, I am determined to unbare this broad breast of mine –
>   I have long enough stifled and choked;
> Emblematic and capricious blades, I leave you – now you serve
>   me not,
> Away! I will say what I have to say, by itself,
> I will escape from the sham that was proposed to me [...]
>   (366–7).

Such frustrated outbursts against the fancy language of simile, metaphor and the whole obstructive paraphernalia of poetry are a commonplace of romantic (as of religious) verse – a recognised move, so to speak, in the elaborate rhetorical game of love; staged evidence of sincerity and authenticity. A fine example of this is provided in the opening Sonnet of Sidney's great sequence *Astrophil and Stella*, a definitive pattern-book of rhetorical devices appropriate to the exploration of love. Having strained throughout the octave to seek 'fit word to paint the blackest face of woe;/ Studying inventions fine, her wits to entertain', Sidney ends his sestet with an impatient rebuke to his besotted, ingenious self:

> Thus, great with child to speak, and helpless in my throes,
> Biting my truand pen, beating myself for spite,
> 'Fool,' said my Muse to me, 'look in thy heart and write.'[21]

Likewise, Whitman's dismissal of 'the sham that was proposed to me' parallels Sidney's gesture in another sonnet from the same sequence. Mocking those who 'do dictionary's method bring/ Into your rimes', he accuses them of taking 'wrong ways; those far-fet [i.e. far-fetched] helps be such/ As do bewray [betray] a want of inward touch,/ And sure, at length, stol'n goods do come to light' (178).

As for the torments of love, this is perhaps the most familiar staple of all in love poetry. 'To rage, to lust, to write to, to commend,/ All is the purlewe [preserve] of the God of Love', wrote Donne: 'Oh were wee wak'ned by this Tyrannie/ To'ungod this child againe' (78). One of Whitman's most abandoned expressions of these peremptory passions is 'Calamus 6' (later 'Not heaving from my ribbed breast only'), simple in structure because it consists only of a list of the extreme physical symptoms of love's suffering before it concludes with the deliberately flat assertion that his passion need no more reveal itself in these tortures than in his songs – the implication being that relief, of sorts, can come only through the public expression that may bring the salve of shared recognition of his anguish. Compare this, again, with lines such as the following from *Astrophil and Stella*:

> Grief, find the words, for thou hast made my brain
> So dark with misty vapours which arise
> From out thy heavy mould that inbent eyes
> Can scarce discern the shape of mine own pain,
> Do thou then – for thou canst – do thou complain
> For my poor soul, which now that sickness tries
> Which even to sense, sense of itself denies. (208)

There are other motifs from traditional love poetry in abundance scattered throughout 'Calamus'. 'Calamus 8', for example, rewords the claim so familiar from Elizabethan love poetry that the poet, waylaid by love, will now renounce his public duties (in Whitman's case, that of the national bard), nay, that he will even abandon his calling to poetry altogether, in order to 'go with him I love,/ It is to be enough that we are together – We never separate again' (379). 'Calamus 10' is an elaboration on this in the form of another familiar conceit. This time the poet addresses 'bards of ages hence', charging them not to pay tribute to his poetry but rather simply to 'Publish my name and hang up my picture as that of the tenderest lover,/ The friend, the lover's portrait, of whom his friend, his lover, was fondest,/ Who was not proud of his songs, but of the measureless ocean of love within him, and freely poured it forth' (380).

One comes in 'Calamus 17' across further familiar evidence of a lover's distempered mind in the form of a sinister fantasy of loss: 'Of him I love day and night, I dreamed I heard he was dead,/ And I dreamed I went where they had buried him I love – but he was not in that place' (387). What have we here but a reworking of the theme previously explored in 'Strange Fits of Passion', one of the most celebrated of Wordsworth's 'Lucy' poems? There, too, we first encounter the reluctance, so frequently mentioned again in 'Calamus', to share a lover's confidences with anyone save another lover: 'I will dare to tell,/ But in the Lover's ear alone,/ What once to me befell'. To any sane person Wordsworth's subsequent disclosure would, he implies, seem nothing but plain incontrovertible proof of insanity:

> My horse moved on; hoof after hoof
> He raised, and never stopped;
> When down behind the cottage roof,
> At once, the bright moon dropped.
>
> What fond and wayward thoughts will slide
> Into a Lover's head!
> 'O mercy!' to myself I cried,
> 'If Lucy should be dead!'[22]

There, the deliberate banality of the horse's regular animal movements ('hoof after hoof/ He raised, and never stopped') serves only to highlight the wild uncontrollable unpredictability of the human mind whenever it falls victim to passion. But whereas Wordsworth offers this little anecdote simply as a kind of instructive psychological curiosity, Whitman instead insists that through the wayward ministrations of passion he has, in fact, been vouchsafed a glimpse of universal truths about the human condition that previously had been closed to him:

> I found that every place was a burial-place,...
> – And what I dreamed I will henceforth tell to every person
>   and age,
> And I stand henceforth bound to what I dreamed [...] (362).

Liebestod

Whitman's preoccupation with death, of course, remains one of the strangest and most disturbing features of the 'Calamus' sequence. Of late, it has been customary to interpret this, again, as a displaced form of expression; a means of indirectly voicing the experience of repression, of the psychic death that was Whitman's fate as he so damagingly internalised his age's prohibition against same-sex relations. But while such explanations may indeed carry almost as much weight as they do current conviction, I find it nevertheless impossible to make satisfactory sense of all Whitman's mentions of death in these terms. There is for example the unsettling and irreducible strangeness – not to mention the distastefulness – of 'Calamus 2' (later 'Scented Herbage of My Breast'), which opens by conflating the printed leaves of the poem with the hair on his chest, insistently representing both as 'tomb-leaves, body-leaves, growing up above me, above death' (342). But he does not mean that these luxuriant growths are a kind of triumph over death, a transmutation of death into glorious life, as becomes apparent as his poem proceeds. Instead, its mood becomes ever more death-fixated, not out of frustration, anxiety or fear, but rather out of a positive infatuation with whatever death seems to signify in this context (although not until the very end is this explicitly specified):

> Yet, you are very beautiful to me, you faint-tinged roots – you
>   make me think of Death,
> Death is beautiful from you – (O what indeed is beautiful,
>   except Death and Love?)
> O I think it is not for life I am chanting here my chant of
>   lovers – I think it must be for Death (343).

Nor is this by any means merely a staging post in the development of Whitman's feelings in this particular poem. In fact, he goes on to insist that Death is no less than the true Muse of his whole collection: 'Indeed, O Death, I think now these leaves mean precisely the same as you mean' (343).

'Calamus 2' culminates in a great ecstatic and erotic love-song to the deathly object of his passion, which needs to be quoted at length for its strangeness to register:

> Through me shall the words be said to make
>   death exhilarating,
> Give me your tone therefore, O Death, that I may accord
>   with it,

> Give me yourself – for I see that you belong to me now
>   above all, and are folded together above all – you Love and
>   Death are,
> Nor will I allow you to balk me any more with what I was
>   calling life,
> For now it is conveyed to me that you are the
>   purports essential,
> That you hide in these shifting forms of life, for reasons – and
>   that they are mainly for you,
> That you, beyond them, come forth, to remain, the real reality,
> That behind the mask of materials you patiently wait, no
>   matter how long,
> That you will one day, perhaps, take control of all,
> That you will perhaps dissipate this entire show of appearance,
> That may be you are what it is all for – but it does not last so
>   very long,
> But you will last long (344).

With his customary cruel accuracy, D. H. Lawrence pointed to a passage such as this as Whitman's 'postmortem effects'. And in a further comment agitated by his own fearful homophobia he scathingly identified a dominant strain both in *Enfans d'Adam* and in 'Calamus':

> Merging! And Death! Which is the final merge.
> The great merge into the womb. Woman.
> And after that, the merge of comrades: man-for-man love.
> And almost immediately with this, death, the final merge
>   of death.[23]

For me, the path towards an understanding of Whitman's thanatopsis leads first back to 'A Word Out of the Sea'. At the poem's celebrated climax, the waves lisp to Whitman 'the low and delicious word DEATH,/ And again Death – ever Death, Death, Death' (350) as it creeps ever insinuatingly nearer, seductively hypnotising the listener with its sensual intimations and ecstatic promises. As has already been noted, Whitman's models for writing this poem are known to have been Donizetti and Bellini. Yet it is not they who spontaneously come to mind when reading 'A Word Out of the Sea'. No, when it reaches its most intense pitch the poem seems eerily reminiscent of Wagner, most specifically those surges of sound at the orgasmic conclusion of *Tristan and Isolde*. And intriguingly, there is possible evidence to suggest Whitman himself came approvingly to notice the resemblance between his poetry and Wagner's music. The following passage occurs in a review of *Leaves of Grass* printed in *The Critic* in 1881:

> [Whitman's] rhythm, so much burlesqued, is all of a part with the man and his ideas. It is apparently confused: really most carefully schemed; certainly to a high degree original. It has what to the present writer is the finest thing in the music of Wagner – a great booming movement or undertone, like the noise of heaving surf.[24]

The review is anonymous, but Furness has demonstrated there are sound grounds for supposing the author was actually Whitman himself. And, of course, the mention of 'the noise of heaving surf' immediately brings to mind the opening section of 'A Word Out of the Sea'.

The word 'Liebestod' was coined to describe the peculiar fusion of love and death in *Tristan und Isolde*, composed in 1854 and first performed at the very time when Whitman – who could therefore not have heard it – was constructing his 'Calamus' sequence. Wagner was directly indebted to the writings of his hero, Schopenhauer, for the distinctive view of love and death taken at his great opera's finale. But he added his own twist to the philosopher's vision. The most transporting heterosexual passion, Wagner was convinced, could find ecstatic fulfilment only in death, because it was rooted in an instinctive recognition that the kind of perfect union which it craved could never be achieved in the illusory world of fleshly experience. It therefore strained beyond the 'phenomenal' towards the 'noumenal' world of supernal spiritual existence. Hence the suicide pact not uncommon between besotted lovers.[25]

These sentiments at the very core of the *Liebestod* experience seem present not only in 'A Word Out of the Sea', with its carol of inconsolable loss, but also in 'Calamus 2'. And it threatens to recur in 'Calamus 7', where Whitman initially dwells on 'the terrible question of appearances,/ … the doubts, the uncertainties…/ That may-be identity beyond the grave is a beautiful fable only' (353). This corrosive doubt is consistent with Schopenhauer's account of the phenomenal world. But in this particular case, the Wagnerian solution is specifically reversed. The next world seems to offer no more final satisfaction than this. Therefore instead of passion leading irrevocably to consummation through death, it is here depicted as alone capable of supplying on earth a measure of the reassurance and fulfilment that both flesh and spirit crave: 'I am satisfied,/ He ahold of my hand has completely satisfied me' (353). The whole poem could be read not only as an unintentional answer to Wagner but also as countering the *Liebestod* theme so seductively sounded elsewhere in 'Calamus'.

A Democracy of Comrades

Whitman's reworking of the *Liebestod* theme may be regarded as yet another powerful example of the way formations seminal to the artistic treatment of heterosexual romantic love reappear in mutated form in 'Calamus'. But in refusing the option of limiting his sub-section to the 'Live Oak with Moss' sequence, he chose not to focus only on homoerotic passion. His claims for the love he celebrated were altogether more ambitious than that. 'Over and over he says the same thing,' noted Lawrence: 'the new world will be built on the love of comrades, the new great dynamic of life will be manly love. Out of this manly love will come the inspiration for the future ... This is to be the new Democracy of Comrades. This is the new cohering principle in the world.'[26]

In this important connection, again, Whitman may be seen as adapting an established heterosexual model of love's powers for his own, different, purposes. Some forty years before the writing of 'Calamus', a youthful, enthusiastic Shelley had announced the socially liberating and redemptive powers of heterosexual love in his poetry. 'Those who now live have survived an age of despair', he announced in his Preface to 'The Revolt of Islam',[27] written after the reactionary powers that had triumphed over Napoleon had effectively re-established the ancien regime and successfully turned the clock of European politics back to pre-Revolutionary days. His remedy? A vision of love as the true, indestructible revolutionary principle, possessed of a power to '[re]animate the social institutions of mankind'. In Shelley's poem, 'Love is celebrated everywhere as the sole law which should govern the moral world' (148). So revolutionary, indeed, was his conception of that power that it was originally embodied in an incestuous relationship between brother and sister. In the Preface he unrepentantly accounted for this by asserting that he had 'appealed ... to the most universal of feelings, and [had] endeavoured to strengthen the moral sense, by forbidding it to waste its energies in seeking to avoid actions which [were] only crimes of convention' (149). Whitman never remotely ventures to be as transgressive as this.

'Can man be free if woman be a slave?' asks Shelley in 'The Revolt of Islam', a poem that deserves to be recognised as an important contribution to women's struggle for equal rights (182). His vision of heterosexual love includes the concept of a partnership of equals that can then form the nucleus of a genuinely democratic society. Only in such relationships may 'hearts beat as mine now beats, with such intent/ As renovates the world' (182). The final martyrdom of his lovers, Laon and Cythna, releases a spirit of forgiveness and reconciliation out of which what Hart Crane would term a new 'visionary company of love' may one day be born. A similar hope permeates the conclusion of 'Lines Written Among the Euganean Hills', where Shelley imagines that he and his beloved may be able to retreat to some island refuge where an alternative society may spontaneously form around them:

> We may live so happy there,
> That the spirits of the air,
> Envying us, may even entice
> To our healing paradise
> The polluting multitude;
> But their rage would be subdued
> By that clime, divine and calm,...
> And the love which heals all strife
> Circling, like the breath of life,
> All things in that sweet abode
> With its own mild brotherhood:
> They, not it would change; and soon
> Every sprite beneath the moon
> Would repent its envy vain,
> And the earth grown young again. (350–1)

In attempting to establish the 'institution of dear love of comrades' in the form of a 'brotherhood of lovers', Whitman is, then, treading in the footsteps of Shelley and others whose ideal societies were to be founded on romantic love. And, as has already been noted, Whitman opens 'Calamus' with a series of poems in which, like Shelley, he stages a strategic retreat from the polluted world as prelude to his formation of an alternative community. Also, and again like Shelley, he bases his hopes on the belief that a passionate desire for this new liberating order for which he yearns is already latent in every man. 'These', he says, referring to his 'leaves', 'depict you as myself – the germs are in all men';

> I believe the main purport of These States is to be found a
>   superb friendship, exalté, previously unknown,
> Because I perceive it waits, and has been always waiting, latent
>   in all men. (374)

The spying out of what lies hidden; the calling forth of what is secluded; the formal realisation of what is inchoate: these are tropes and rhetorical figures fundamental to 'Calamus'. Hence Whitman's comment, following an ecstatic account of the effect music (and particularly the human voice in song) has on him, that 'I am moved by the exquisite meanings ... I do not think the performers know themselves – But now I think I begin to know them' (366). His own 'songs' (and the word is insistently ubiquitous in 'Calamus') are therefore instances of performances that, in 'knowing' themselves, bring others, too, to the fullness and finality of self-knowledge for the first time. And when his 'brothers' do achieve a mutuality of relationship with a kindred soul and body, Whitman registers this through the joyous gerunds of release found in 'Calamus 26':

> We two boys together clinging,
> One the other never leaving,
> Up and down the roads going...
> With birds singing – With fishes swimming – With trees
>   branching and leafing,
> Cities wrenching, ease scorning, statutes mocking,
>   feebleness chasing,
> Fulfilling our foray. (369)

'Cities wrenching': the phrase is resonant with Whitman's hope that there is seismic power enough in the love he's intent on releasing to shake existing society to its very foundations.

All this brings us back to our initial concern with Whitman's interest in creating a language of love, because it is by providing others with the words that give shape to their frustrated, fumbling need for full self-realisation that his poetry enables them at last to become truly themselves. He likened this to an intimate process of uncovering, as in 'Calamus 25':

> The prairie-grass dividing – its own odor breathing,
> I demand of it the spiritual corresponding,
> Demand the most copious and close companionship of men,
> Demand the blades to rise of words, acts, beings. (368)

When he later revised the opening phrase to read 'the prairie-grass accepting', he muffled that search for the latent that is the clear impulse behind the phrase in its original form. And the delicately discriminating intimacy of that initial gesture of dividing opens the lines that follow up to polymorphous suggestions of the odorous secret bodyscape of sensual experience. What is significant in the present context, though, is that, when Whitman comes to look for the shoots of this new life to appear, it is to 'words' he turns first, treating them implicitly as necessary facilitators of 'acts' and 'beings'.

As for the lines that follow, these remind us, if such a reminder be needed, of the perilous political circumstances under which the 'Calamus' sequence was being constructed. There is praise for

> Those that go their own gait, erect, stepping with freedom and
>   command – leading, not following,
> Those with a never-quell'd audacity –those with sweet and
>   lusty flesh, clear of taint, choice and chary of its love-power,
> Those that look carelessly in the faces of Presidents and
>   Governors, as to say *Who are you?*
> Those of earth-born passion, simple, never constrained,
>   never obedient,
> Those of inland America. (368)

This conveys Whitman's hope that the western territories would produce a new kind of American, a 'mechanic' capable of rescuing the imperilled nation from the immanent disaster he blamed on eastern seaboard politicians, in league with undemocratic business interests. This is the vision memorably advanced in a contemporary passage from *The Eighteenth Presidency!*, that scurrilous unpublished squib attacking the 'deformed, mediocre, snivelling, unreliable, false-hearted men' who were governing the country (1310). These, Whitman argued, in his most fiery free-soil vein, were allies of the 'Southern disunionists' (1316), joined with them in the advancing of a sinister secret agenda, 'the entrance and establishment of slave labor through the continent' (1316). To counter these dangers, Whitman summons up in 'Calamus' his fantasy figure:

> I would be much pleased to see some heroic, shrewd, fully-informed, healthy-bodied, middle-aged, beard-faced American blacksmith or boatman come down from the West across the Alleghanies, and walk into the Presidency, dressed in a clear suit of working attire, and with the tan all over his face, breast, and arms (1308).

Once noticed, it becomes impossible to ignore the ubiquitous presence in 'Calamus' of the political crisis of the period. When, in 'Calamus 5', Whitman enquires rhetorically 'States!/ Were you looking to be held together by the lawyers/ By an agreement on a paper? Or by arms?' (348), we now become aware of the way in which rival interpretations of the American constitution lay at the very, troubled, heart of the North-South dispute over slavery. And when Whitman replaces that revered but equivocal constitution with the much more binding brotherhood of lovers, we note the significance of the promise that 'One from Maine or Vermont' shall be friends with 'a Carolinian and an Oregonese' (350). His attack on 'institutions' takes on a new complexion in the light of political circumstances, as does his determination to replace them with 'the institution of the dear love of comrades' (368). His dismissal of 'the President in his Presidency' in favour of 'the brotherhood of lovers' (370) becomes poignantly redolent of his hopes and fears. Even the physical orientation of his songs betrays the politics of his geography: 'I and robust love belong among you, inland,

and along the Western Sea,/ For These States tend inland, and toward the Western Sea – and I will also' (371). His address 'To the Kanadian of the north – to the Southerner I love' (374) now evidently possesses an urgent contemporary dimension. Given his fear that the cities – and most particularly his own beloved 'Manahatta' – were given over to the 'doughfaces' and 'copperheads' who were the northern advocates of slavery, the references in 'Calamus' to glimpses within the urban scene of a secret redemptive brotherhood that can form the nucleus of a new 'City of Friends' (373) are piercingly pointed. No longer can even the mention of the two boys 'North and South excursions making' (369) seem so innocent and carefree; nor does it seem incidental that it is down south in Louisiana that he sees the impressive Live-Oak growing.

Conclusion

Every bit as much as Shelley's, then, Whitman's vision of a community of love was deeply rooted in despair at the existent society of his time and place. In developing its language of love, 'Calamus' makes consistent reference not only to the plight of 'gays' in Whitman's world but also to the plight of the United States themselves. And just as he seems to have found in the established 'mainstream' tradition of western heterosexual romantic love poetry an inspiration for his solitary, brave attempt at creating a subtly modulated and richly inclusive discourse of same-sex love, so he seems to have found in that same source authority for envisaging a visionary community of lovers that could offer him and his country not only a refuge from the present political crisis but the promise of a different world, and an infinitely better one. The 'language of love' he creates in 'Calamus' therefore contains within it the germ of an alternative political, as well as personal, dispensation.

Notes

This is an expanded version of an article that first appeared in the
Huntington Library Quarterly, 73/4 (December 2010), 643–57.

1. Ellen M. Calder, 'Personal Recollections of Walt Whitman', in Joel Myerson (ed.), *Whitman in His Own Time* (Detroit: Michigan University Press, 1991), p. 199.

2. *The Collected Writings of Walt Whitman: Leaves of Grass: A Textual Variorum of the Printed Poems*, ed. Scully Bradley et al., vol. 2, *Poems, 1860–1867* (New York: New York University Press, 1980), p. 280. Subsequent references to Whitman's poetry are to this volume, except where otherwise indicated.

3. Walt Whitman, *Complete Prose Works* (Philadelphia: David McKay, 1892), p. 20.

4. Ian Robinson, *The Survival of English: Essays in Criticism of Language* (Cambridge: Cambridge University Press, 1973), p. 191.

5. William White (ed.), *The Collected Writings of Walt Whitman: Daybooks and Notebooks:* vol. 3, *Diary in Canada, Notebooks, Index* (New York: New York University Press), pp. 740–1.

6. Mark Bauerlain, *Whitman and the American Idiom* (Baton Rouge: University of Louisiana Press, 1991).

7. Robinson, *Survival*, p. 19.

8. Maurice Valency, *In Praise of Love: An Introduction to the Love-Poetry of the Renaissance* (New York: New York University Press, 1961). It is interesting to note that while Eleanor of Aquitaine presided over a Court of Love in her native region, her favourite son, Richard Coeur de Lion, was gay.

9. Valency, *In Praise of Love*, p. 33.

10. Mark Doty, 'Form, Eros, and the Unspeakable: Whitman's Stanzas', *Virginia Quarterly Review* 8/2 (2005), 66–78 (74).

11. Shakespeare, *As You Like It*. First published in 1623.

12. C. J. Furness (ed.), *Walt Whitman's Workshop* (New York: New York University Press, 1964).

13. M. Wynn Thomas, 'Whitman's Achievements in the Personal Style in "Calamus"', *Walt Whitman Quarterly Review* (1983), 36–46 (39 and 42).

14. Alan Helms, 'Whitman's "Live Oak with Moss"', in Robert K. Martin (ed.), *Continuing Presence: The Life after the Life* (Iowa City: University of Iowa Press, 1992), pp. 185–205.

15. Doty, 'Form, Eros', p. 89.

16. Helms, 'Whitman's Achievements'.

17. John Donne, *The Complete English Poems*, ed. A. J. Smith (Harmondsworth: Penguin, 1971), p. 30.

18. The obvious comparison would be with Shakespeare's 'Venus and Adonis'. Relationships between 'Calamus' and Shakespeare's Sonnets are usefully explored in Nils Clausson, '"Hours Continuing Long" as Whitman's rewriting of Shakespeare's Sonnet 29', *Walt Whitman Quarterly Review* 26 (2009), 131–42.

19. Donne, *Complete English Poems*, pp. 76 and 48.

20. Cf. Donne's 'Love's Growth', *Complete English Poems*, p. 69.

21. Sir Philip Sidney, 'Astrophil and Stella: 1', in Gerald Bullet (ed.), *Silver Poets of the Sixteenth Century* (London: Everyman, 1972), p. 173. Subsequent references to Sidney's poems are to this volume and given in the text.

22. William Wordsworth, *Poetical Works*, ed. Thomas Hutchinson (London: Oxford University Press, 1969), p. 86.

23. D. H. Lawrence, *Studies in Classic American Literature* (1923), ed., Ezra Greenspan, Lindeth Vasey and John Worthen (Cambridge: Cambridge University Press, 2002), p. 399.

24. *The Critic*, 22/5 (1881), in Graham Clarke (ed.), *Walt Whitman: Critical Assessments* (Mountfield: Helm Information Ltd, nd), vol. 2, 149–53 (51).

25. Bryan Magee, *The Philosophy of Schopenhauer* (Oxford: Oxford University Press, 1997), p. 388.

26. Lawrence, *Studies*, p. 398.

27. Percy Bysshe Shelley, *Selected Poetry, Prose, Letters*, ed. A. S. B. Glover (London: Nonesuch, 1951), p. 142. Subsequent references to Shelley's poems are to this volume and are given in the text.

Whitman and the Labouring Classes

As youthful contributor to *The New-York Democrat*, Walt Whitman gave expression to what was to become his life-long creed: 'labor creates real wealth. It is to labor that man owes every thing possessed of changeable value. Labor is the talisman that has raised him from the condition of the savage.'[1] It followed that, as he put it two years later in a piece for *The Brooklyn Eagle*, 'There is hardly anything on earth, of its sort, that arouses our sympathies more readily than the cause of a laborer, or a band of laborers, struggling for a competence' (*J*, 303). He was writing from personal experience. Throughout much of Whitman's childhood and youth his father had worked in the building trade, as later did his brother Andrew, and so the family had suffered (and no doubt also benefited) at first hand from the dramatic changes in the life of the working population that had been effected by the United States' transition to a new phase of capitalist activity. But in using the word 'competence', the young Whitman was using the vocabulary of a past period and betraying his origins in a time when workers could still expect to control their own livelihood.

Nor was it only the urban workforce with which Whitman felt a strong sense of solidarity. In *Specimen Days*, his friend John Burroughs, writing to Whitman's dictation, observed of the poet's farming ancestors on Long Island that 'both sexes labor'd with their open hands – the men on the farm – the women in the house and around it'.[2] And those sections of *Specimen Days* in which Whitman recalls his earliest years on the island he affectionately called 'Paumanok' is full of fond, detailed references to the ordinary workers, farmers and fishermen. Moreover, the passion of Whitman's identification with the workers never really waned – neither when he himself became a successful middle-class journalist; nor when he became an explosively controversial poet; nor in his old age, when an instinctive faithfulness to his earliest experiences prevented him from ever appreciating the real character of working life in the America of the Gilded Age, polarised between corporate power and an increasingly unionised labour movement.

So ingrained was Whitman's sense that his own creativity, even as writer, was continuous with the 'creativity' of labour ('a framer framing a house is more than the equal of all the old-world gods' [*WCP*, 74]) that he instinctively turned to his family's trade (his father was primarily a carpenter) for images of creative self-construction: 'Sure as the most certain sure … plumb in the uprights, well entreatied, braced in the beams … I and this mystery here we stand' (*WCP*, 28); 'my foothold is tenoned and mortised in granite' (*WCP*, 46). But equally significantly, and no doubt equally unconsciously, he also conceived of himself (and of every person) as not to be limited by the constraints of any such traditional trade identity. By declaring 'Unscrew the locks from the doors!/ Unscrew the doors themselves from their jambs!' (*WCP*, 50) he was in effect declaring for a new liberty of personal development, as unimaginable as it was unavailable to an earlier society in which personal fulfilment was achievable only through the performance of an ascribed social role. As such, Whitman was the typical product of the new society of individual, and individualising, opportunity being produced by the new economic order that had replaced the working world of his own childhood and youth. Yet he simultaneously continued to prize the values of that largely disappeared artisanal order, for the continuation of which his father and his generation of workers had fought so bitterly during the 1820s and 1830s – indeed Whitman's very insistence on the labour theory of wealth was a conscious reaffirmation of that older politics in the face of the new world's demonstration of the primary wealth-creating powers of money, in the form of capital and its powers to profit quite unscrupulously from any 'band of laborers, struggling for a competence'.

Prefabricated buildings – a typical product of the post-artisanal period – helped put Whitman's father out of work. And when he asks 'Who learns my lesson complete?' and answers 'Boss and journeyman and apprentice' (*WCP*, 341) he is compressing into a single phrase the incompatible features of the artisanal and post-artisanal orders. 'Boss' was a term that entered New York English (from the Dutch *baas*) in the 1820s to describe a new kind of social and economic phenomenon which involved not the old master-apprentice relationship of the craft world but a new relationship of employers to labour. So when Whitman elsewhere, speaking ecstatically of his rapport with the dreams of sleepers, exclaims 'I am their boss' (*WCP*, 108), he is doing what he repeatedly did in the early editions of *Leaves of Grass*. He is trying to reform the new emergent socio-economic order by refashioning the key terms of its vocabulary and hence redefining its governing concepts. Time and time again, from the 1855 Preface onwards, the terms of profit, loss, speculation, gain, spending, and the like are employed by him in senses designedly contrary to their current usage in his time: 'What is commonest and cheapest and nearest and easiest is Me,/ Me going in for my chances, spending for vast returns' (*WCP*, 38). And even his stance as a loafer, fundamental to the working of 'Song of Myself', was in part an act of dissent, a conscious opting out of a world in which, increasingly, time meant money. Thus did Whitman conduct, on the field of language, a guerilla action against the new capitalism. But if he mounted a counter-attack, he never intended a counter-revolution. Whitman was never disaffected with capitalism *per se*, as were the socialists of his day. On the contrary, he thrived on the vitality, the energy, the variety, the inventiveness, of the very new world of labour and capital whose values he in other ways so deeply distrusted.

And radically divided as he thus was in his sympathies – between the new individualistic, laissez-faire libertarianism and an older collectivist, collaborative ethos – he found in poetry a unique medium that offered him the indispensable means of reconciling these two otherwise incompatible systems of value. So, in claiming that 'neither a servant nor a master am I', he seeks to place, and thus define, himself as existing outside the social categories produced by, and in turn producing, the emergent economic order. Similarly, when he states that 'I take no sooner a large price than a small price' he is substituting the notion of a 'fair' price for that of 'market value', in a gesture that is implicitly a criticism of the whole system of values promoted by a new capitalism.

It was in the guise – or, in one important sense, in the disguise – of an ordinary worker that Whitman first studiedly introduced himself as a poet. Whereas earlier visual images represent him as a fashionable successful urbanite, in the famous frontispiece engraving which served in lieu of an author's name in the first (1855) edition of *Leaves of Grass* he chose to appear in the jauntily angled hat and unfashionably informal (un)dress of an ordinary worker. And while the self-portrait was in part a literary allusion – a kind of paradoxically fashionable act of homage to the cult of the carpenter created by George Sand – there was behind this affectation a sincere sense of his role as the voice of the largely silenced class that had produced him. This was, in turn, his authority to release 'many long dumb voices,/ Voices of the interminable generations of slaves,/ Voices of prostitutes and deformed persons,/ Voices of the diseased and despairing, and of thieves and dwarfs' (*WCP*, 50). It was indeed his authentic right, his birthright as child of the working class, to act as spokesperson for the suppressed and the dispossessed; and for examples both of prostitution (the modern term 'hooker' actually derives from Whitman's New York, from the blue-light district of the Hook, on the East River, frequented by sailors, stevedores and workmen) and of psychological deformity he needed to look no further than his immediate family, still largely working-class in its struggling character, with whom Whitman chose to continue living for most of his years as working journalist and emergent poet.

'The floormen are laying the floor – the tinners are tinning the roof – the masons are calling for mortar,/ In single file each shouldering his hod pass onward the laborers' (*WCP*, 41): when Whitman records the world of work he does so with all the respectful inwardness of understanding, all the loving care and wondering attention, that characterise the jewelled miniatures of contemporary life captured by monkish scribes in the lunettes of medieval manuscripts. They are his hymns to creation – the creation of more than wealth, the creation of a plenitude of artefacts, through the scrupulous, satisfying exercise of trade skills and craft skills. But as such they are also his unacknowledged elegy for a lost world; the artisanal world of small masters, craftsmen, skilled workers and apprentices. It was an arrangement he retrospectively idealised; 'masters' could be as tyrannical as bosses, and there was no great satisfaction to be gained from being subject, as farmer's son or daughter, to omnipotent patriarchal power.

So when he builds his great celebratory structures of praise of the working world he seems to model his rhetoric on the visual rhetoric of the pageants organised by the self-promoting artisans in their erstwhile pomp, when they marched behind the proud emblems of their respective trades – the chairman's chair, the schooner of the shipwrights, the arm-and-hammer of the General Society:

> Manufactures .. commerce .. engineering .. the building of
>   cities, and every trade carried on there .. and the implement
>   of every trade,

> The anvil and tongs and hammer .. the axe and wedge .. the
>   square and mitre and jointer and smoothingplane;
> The plumbob and trowel and level .. the wall-scaffold, and the
>   work of walls and ceilings .. or any mason work (*WCP*, 95)

In passages such as this he implicitly affirms the labour theory of value, in the face of the reality of contemporary capitalism, representing products as the end-product of the creative process of skilful work. He also succeeds, by a sleight of rhetoric, in making a world which is co-operative merely in the sense of temporally co-active seem co-operative in the ethical sense. He thus substitutes collaboration for competition as the motor of the new economy and the new society:

> Where the triphammers crash ... where the press is whirling
>   its cylinders;
> Wherever the human heart beats with terrible throes out of
>   its ribs;
> Where the pear-shaped balloon is floating aloft ... floating in it
>   myself and looking composedly down;
> Where the life-car is drawn on the slipnoose ... where the heat
>   hatches pale-green eggs in the dented sand. (*WCP*, 60)

Through parataxis, work activities are cunningly humanised by being linked metaphorically to human metabolism (the rhythmic repetitive crash of triphammers is associated with the beatings of the heart), and they are also naturalised as creative acts by being treated as part of the cosmic process of procreation ('where the heat hatches pale-green eggs in the dented sand'). The same rhetorical device of juxtaposition is used elsewhere to suggest that in the world of labour Whitman actually heard America singing: 'The pure contralto sings in the organloft,/ The carpenter dresses his plank ... the tongue of his foreplane whistles its wild ascending lisp' (*WCP*, 39). The Whitman who yearned for an indigenous form of American musical theatre found it in precisely such moments. It is no accident that Whitman's exclamation 'I hear the chorus ... it is a grand-opera ... this indeed is music!' occurs in 'Song of Myself' at exactly the point of transition between his relish of 'The heav'e'yo of stevedores unlading ships by the wharves ... the refrain of the anchor-lifters' and a tenor's aria, 'The orbic flex of his mouth is pouring and filling me full' (*WCP*, 54). It is therefore appropriate that the poem 'I hear America singing' turns out to be entirely about working America:

> The mason singing his [carol] as he makes ready for work, or
>   leaves off work,
> The boatman singing what belongs to him in his boat, the
>   deckhand singing on the steamboat deck,
> The shoemaker singing as he sits on his bench, the hatter
>   singing as he stands. (*WCP*, 174)

No hint there of the discords caused by New York's headlong laissez-faire capitalism.

Those artisanal pageants were, however, in some ways at their most impressive during the very period – the period of Whitman's childhood and youth – when the artisanal order was making its last stand, desperate to demonstrate how central it still was to the maintenance of republican values. Whitman's writing remained steeped in these values, even as he welcomed not only the new freedoms of the post-artisanal society but also the plethora of new products made available by the bounty of commercial capitalism – in his early journalism he typically waxes lyrical over 'rare specimens of art' in the form of the false teeth crafted by Dr Jonathan W. Dodge, 'such as would almost tempt a man to knock out his own and have some from Dr D instead' (*J*, 225). But while he delighted in celebrating in his poetry the newest devices for revolutionising the world of work (the Singer sewing machine is featured as soon as it appears on the market), he can also declare 'No labor-saving machine … have I made … But a few carols vibrating through the air I leave,/ For comrades and lovers' (*WCP*, 182).

Whitman was certainly imaginatively excited by the new capitalism's exuberant inventiveness. In particular, he revelled in its incomparable powers to accomplish transformations, miraculous acts of metamorphosis. 'Materials here under your eyes shall change their shape as if by magic,' he declared (*WCP*, 345), and, as 'Song of the Broad Axe' shows, he saw human progress in American capacity, if not to beat swords into ploughshares, then at least to change the barbarous weapons of Europe's feudal past into the all-conquering ax that enabled the American frontiersman and settler to hew fertile ground out of wilderness. It was through work – emblematised by the axe – that the

United States would build a new, democratic society, the eventual site of which would be not the established cities of the east but the as-yet 'virgin lands' of the west (once the aboriginal inhabitants had finally died out, as Lamarckian evolution decreed that they must).

Meanwhile, Whitman celebrates the labour, country-wide, that is setting this final work in progress, sensuously envisaging 'The flexible rise and fall of backs, the continual click of the trowels striking the bricks' and 'The brisk short crackle of the steel driven slantingly into the pine,/ The butter-color'd chips flying off in great flakes and slivers,/ The limber motion of brawny young arms and hips in easy costumes' (*WCP*, 326). Such a passage is a revelation not least of how sensuous, not to say sexual, was Whitman's homoerotic response to the world of masculine work, and how correspondingly sensitive he was to the way in which the new socio-economic order, which crammed men in their young physical prime together into boarding-houses, had created what historians have called an intensely 'homosocial city,' ripe with opportunities for sexual intimacy.[3] Same-sex relations – 'homosexual' did not yet exist either as a term or a concept – were usually viewed with relative indulgence by the civic authorities. Most of Whitman's own friendships were with young working-class men like Thomas Sawyer and Pete Doyle, friendships that were undoubtedly passionately intimate and that may have found sexual expression. In this sense, Whitman's *Calamus* poems, with their celebration of 'the need for comrades', their commendation of the 'salute' of manly kissing, and their memories of a youth glimpsed 'among a crowd of workmen and drivers in a bar-room around the stove late of a winter night' (*WCP*, 283), capture – albeit with a singular anguished intensity and complexity of ambivalent feeling – a defining feature both of his own experience and of the New York labour scene: 'I am enamoured of …/ Men that live among cattle or taste of the ocean or woods,/ Of the builders and steerers of ships, of the wielders of axes and mauls, of the drivers of horses' (*WCP*, 38). Yet Whitman openly professed himself dismayed at the limited vocabulary of feeling among the 'muscular classes', at their aversion to thus admitting their 'passionate fondness for their friends'. *Calamus* may therefore be read as a deliberate attempt to extend that vocabulary, to develop a proper language of love, to demonstrate to them a language for 'their most ardent friendships', and thus to enrich the consciousness of the working class that it was 'where the real quality of friendship is always freely to be found'.[4]

Whitman was very conscious that his poetry was as much of a product of this new society of labour as was 'the ring on your finger ... the lady's wristlet' (*WCP*, 96) and other manufactured artefacts which he also viewed as the product of creative acts. In those passages of his late prose work *Specimen Days* in which he offers his own account of 'the growth of a poet's mind' – so different from boyhood in the Lake District, the locale in which Wordsworth experienced the fair seed-time of his soul – he recalls roaring out lines from Shakespeare above the din of city streets while riding the top deck of one of the horse-drawn 'stages' whose drivers became his close friends; and he lists the names of the most colourful of those drivers, now long dead, as if they were Homeric heroes: 'George Storms, Old Elephant, his brother Young Elephant (who came afterward), Tippy, Pop Rice, Big Frank, Yellow Joe' (*WCP*, 703). Whitman relished the tang of their names every bit as much as he loved the ripeness of their 'largely animal' characters.

One of the greatest gifts of the labouring world to Whitman was that of language – including slang, the sign of the imaginative vitality of working life; the inventive new language of the teeming streets, bred of the mingling of peoples and races in a city. Slang was 'lawless', Whitman declared exultantly, and he revelled in the 'powerfulness' of its transgressive expressions. His ear was attuned to 'the recitative of fish-pedlars and fruit-pedlars ... the loud laugh of workpeople at their meals' (*WCP*, 54) – the inflections of speech every bit as much as its grammar and vocabulary ('pronunciation is the stamina of language', as Whitman vividly noted). Working America was a language experiment, just like *Leaves of Grass* itself, and in places slang seems to erupt spontaneously out of Whitman's mouth – 'I do not snivel .../ That life is a suck and a sell' (*WCP*, 45); 'The blab of the pave ... the tires of carts and sluff of bootsoles' (*WCP*, 33); 'Washes and razors for foofoos ... for me freckles and a bristling beard' (*WCP*, 48); 'The spotted hawk swoops by and accuses me ... he complains of my gab and my loitering./ I too am not a bit tamed ... I too am untranslatable,/ I sound my barbaric yawp over the roofs of the world' (*WCP*, 87).

But it was not just in slang that Whitman the poet delighted, welcome evidence though it was, like leaves of grass, of the heedlessly rank abundance of life, and of the procreant urge of the world. The American world of labour was a verbal cornucopia of new possibilities which were also new necessities – words born of the need to articulate new experiences, new processes, new products, new businesses, new developments, new inventions: 'shipping, steam, the mint, the electric telegraph, railroads ... Mines – iron works – the sugar plantations of Louisiana ... all these sprout in hundreds and hundreds of words, all tangible and clean-lived, all having texture and beauty' (*AP*, 3). If words were always for Whitman 'magic' they were also 'acts' and 'things', and he was confident that the United States would prove equal to the challenge of producing a 'renovated English speech', adequate to the articulation of a vast new world of work experience – 'Words of Modern Inventions, Discoveries, engrossing Themes, Pursuits, ... Words of all kinds of Building and Constructing' – because its English was 'enriched with contributions from all languages, old and new' (*AP*, 27).

It was the same process of mixing, of hybridisation, that character-ised the new forms of popular entertainment that thrived in the famous working-class district of the Bowery where 'a full-blown working-class entertainment strip' had developed (Burrows and Wallace, 486). In some ways, nothing more clearly demonstrates how Whitman, whose family had in any case always tended towards the 'respectable' end of the working-class spectrum, had become middle-class in outlook than the reservations he expressed at such raucous popular forms of entertainment as the circus. And nowhere does he mention the rat fights of the Bowery. Moreover, while he can include the 'brothels, porter-houses, oyster houses, dance halls, and gambling dens' of the district in his poetic panoramas, it was to the Bowery Theatre that Whitman was in fact primarily drawn, as much as to the colourful street theatre that was the district's everyday 'performance'. And while he idolised the great contrasting tragedians Booth and Forrest, he also mentioned seeing popular entertainers such as 'Daddy Rice'. It is an interesting reference, because it was Thomas Dartmouth 'Daddy' Rice who brought burlesques, in the form of 'Negro' (blackface) songs and dances, to the Bowery stage in the late 1820s. 'Guised in blackface, the artist could safely mock elites, snobs and condescending moralists', and Whitman evidently warmed to such broad, subversive humour.[5] Out of such materials Rice was to fashion the 'minstrel' shows. In one respect an appalling travesty of black experience and of indigenous black entertainment, minstrelsy was also 'an exercise in creative cultural amalgamation, something for which New York would become famous. It blended black lore with white humour, black banjo with Irish fiddle,

African-based dance with British reels.'⁶ As such, it anticipated, and perhaps encouraged, Whitman's own turn to 'hybridity' in 'Song of Myself', a poem that bewilderingly mixes genres and changes registers, and whose vocabulary switches constantly from racy street-talk to Biblical sonority to dignified discourse.

And when a contemporary reviewer described the Whitman of the first edition of *Leaves of Grass* as 'a compound of the New England transcendentalist and New York rowdy', the latter epithet again perceptively placed the poet in the context of the working-class culture of the Bowery, one of whose most dominant and colourful specimens of character was the 'Bowery B'hoy'. In social reality, the 'B'hoy' was a product of the gangland culture of working-class New York, a swanking thug but also a cultural conglomerate: 'a multiethnic construction, part native American rowdy, part Irish "jackeen", part German "younker"'.⁷ By the time that Whitman came to model his persona in the original 'Song of Myself' on 'one of the roughs' of this kind, something interesting had happened to the B'hoy. He had come to be represented by popular, best-selling middle-class writers like George Foster as the quintessential American; a free spirit, impulsive, warm-hearted, brave, strong, and high-spirited; the urban equivalent of the trapper of the Rockies. And the B'hoy hated financiers, bosses, businessmen, and all the types that the new capitalist culture had spawned. The B'hoy and his G'hal belonged to 'the great middle class of free life under a republic of which they are the types and representatives.'⁸ Whitman found this kind of idealising aggrandisement of the New York labourer irresistible, and in many ways his persona in 'Song of Myself' – 'one of the roughs, large, proud, affectionate, eating, drinking, and breeding' (*WCP*, 50) – is modelled on such middle-class romances of the working class as this. Moreover, Foster sentimentally claims that when the B'hoy and his G'hal ostentatiously drive along fashionable Broadway (the Bowery's near neighbour but class opposite), differences of class are 'Macadamized' (i.e. levelled and smoothed) like the avenue itself. 'Song of Myself' is a similar dream of social integration, Whitman's attempt to reconcile the two halves of a world in which, in actual fact, the labouring class, from which he had himself in a sense derived, was tensely opposed to the middle class of owners, businessmen – and journalists (albeit their in some ways ambivalent social position) such as Whitman himself.

In some ways, it was a relish for language, as typical of a street-wise journalist as it was of a poet, that led him to haunt the Bowery B'hoy's working class culture. Not for nothing had coarse invective traditionally been dubbed 'billingsgate', after the London fish-market; the working-world had always been renowned for its ability to spawn 'vulgar' expletives. It is therefore appropriate that a Whitman who relished 'coarseness, directness, live epithets, expletives, words of opprobrium, resistance', and who took 'pleasure in the use, on fit occasions, of traitor, coward, liar, shyster, skulk, doughface, trickster, mean, curse, backslider, thief, impotent, lickspittle' (*AP*, 16), most vigorously exercised his talents for words aggressively 'whirled like chain-shot rocks' (*AP*, 14) in his unpublished 1856 pamphlet, 'The Eighteenth Presidency!' Addressed to the workingmen and workingwomen of the United States, this squib, intended to influence the outcome of the presidential elections of that year, gave final, and fullest, expression to the radical politics of labour that Whitman had originally derived from his father, Walter Whitman, Senior. During the 1820s and 1830s the crisis in the craft system had steadily deepened, as the old master-journeyman-apprentice system changed into a new socio-economic system central to which was the relationship between entrepreneurial employers and unskilled wage earners, a relationship governed strictly by market forces. New political alignments appeared in response to this stratification and degradation of labour, a process accelerated by the surge in the power of New York capital in the wake of a boom in building railways and the opening up of western markets. Walter Whitman was interested in the radical solutions offered by figures such as Fanny Wright, Robert Dale Owen and William Leggett, all of whom advocated economic and political programs specifically designed to promote social egalitarianism and based on respect for the primary wealth-creating power of labour. The Democratic Party itself developed a radical 'Locofoco' wing, in an attempt to contain labour agitation within the established mainstream of contemporary politics. One lasting outcome of these labour movements was the democratisation of the press through the publication of new cheap 'penny' papers aimed at a mass market. Walt Whitman was to spend many years editing such newspapers, as he was also to account himself a 'Locofoco' for the whole of his writing life. He shared the movement's hatred of business monopolies, paper money, banks, the exploitation of female labour, and all the other social ills it attributed to a political system in which government (deeply mistrusted by the Locofocos) had been usurped by an un-American monied class.

In many ways, 'The Eighteenth Presidency!' is a Locofoco tract updated to take account of the 1856 political situation. An unremittingly scurrilous attack on the corrupt contemporary political system ('dough-faces, office-vermin, kept-editors' [*WCP*, 1309]), alienated as it had become from the interests of the masses, it calls upon the authentic representatives of democracy, the working people, to assert their power and so to bring a truly egalitarian, authentically American, society into being. The workers particularly favoured by Whitman are those of the new western territories, since it is from there that he expects a new political force, 'a new race', to appear. This will embody 'the young genius' of America and will revolutionise the old, Europeanised, and thus corrupted, societies of the seaboard states. It is also from there that he imagines a Redeemer President will emerge, a figure strikingly prefigurative of Abraham Lincoln as Whitman was later to view him: 'some heroic, shrewd, fully-informed, healthy-bodied, middle-aged, beard-faced American blacksmith or boatman [will] come down from the West across the Alleghanies, and walk into the Presidency, dressed in a clean suit of working attire' (*WCP*, 1308).

The future of the West is, in fact, the focal concern of 'The Eighteenth Presidency!' Whitman was a convinced Free Soiler, believing that the states being formed out of the western territories should be kept free of slaves so as to be reserved exclusively for white labour. Indeed, such was the passion of his belief that a truly democratic America could be developed only in and through the new western societies, that upon the outcome of the Free Soil issue hung, for him, the very future of democracy in the United States – and hence the very future of that vanguard of democracy, the labouring classes. But in allowing a newly formed state to decide for itself whether it should be 'slave' or 'free', the 1854 Kansas-Nebraska Bill had turned the mid west into the bloody cockpit of political struggle for the future of America. The Bill led to the shattering of the established system of political parties, out of which was formed the Republican Party which Whitman implicitly supports in 'The Eighteenth Presidency!' and which was for him to continue to be the truest party of labour throughout the turbulent years ahead.

What the pamphlet clearly shows is how Whitman's devotion to the working class limited his human and social sympathies quite as much as it served to promote them. On the one hand, his repeated insistence on explicitly including 'workingwomen' amongst his target audience as well as 'workingmen' is a reminder of his substantially enlightened attitudes on gender issues – although nowhere visible in his work are black washerwomen. He was particularly fond of Mattie, the wife of his favourite brother, Jeff. She made shirt-fronts for a local manufacturer, and thus helped Whitman gain personal insight into the working conditions of the army of seamstresses, milliners, dress-makers and other female outworkers, mill-workers and piece-workers in mid-century New York who are given 'bit parts' in his poetic panoramas ('The spinning girl retreats and advances to the hum of the big wheel' [*WCP*, 39]). Their working-conditions were frequently dismal, 'too confining for health and comfort' as Whitman somewhat euphemistically put it in *Democratic Vistas*. As for their pay, it was often short of bare subsistence and could leave them at starvation level. Some – including his brother Andrew's wife, Nancy – turned to prostitution to augment their income, and Whitman's sympathy with 'hookers' may well be partly rooted in his awareness of their social situation. 'Not till the waters refuse to glisten for you and the leaves to rustle for you, do my words to glisten and rustle for you,' he writes in a poem which is deliberately structured on a customer's making of an 'appointment' to meet 'A Common Prostitute' (*WCP*, 512).

When it came to recognising and honouring black American labour, however, Whitman was altogether less defiantly outspoken. Even as, in the 1855 'Song of Myself', he was becoming 'the hounded slave ... I wince at the bite of the dogs' (*WCP*, 65), he was insisting in 'The Eighteenth Presidency!' that fugitive slaves should be returned to their southern masters, and throughout that pamphlet slavery is consistently represented, not as an inherent evil, but purely as a threat to the interests of white labour. Whereas securing the future of white 'democracy' in America demanded urgent immediate action, the abolition of slavery was deferred by Whitman to some future period and was left to the cold care of 'progress'. Nor did he spare very much space in his poetry for free black labour, although in saluting both the 'drudge of cottonfields and emptier of privies', he did implicitly recognise that the plight of New York's blacks (to whom were largely entrusted only menial jobs, like the nightly emptying of privies) might be little better than that of southern plantation workers. Because they were menials, they had to compete with the newly arrived immigrants to scrape a living in such

trades as drayage, construction and domestic service. When Whitman
eulogises the physical beauty of the black carter – 'I behold the picturesque giant and love him' (*WCP*, 37) – he does not recognise the fact that
in New York blacks were debarred from all the better work for cartmen
that required a municipal licence. And little would one realise from his
poetry that the 'free' blacks of his city were a ghettoised underclass, that
there was constant tension between them and white workers, and that
they went in fear of 'blackbirders' who snatched free blacks in New York
for bounty offered by Southern slave-owners.

But then, it would be unwise ever to trust to Whitman's poetry
for an accurate representation of working life in his America. As Alan
Trachtenberg has wisely observed, 'Whitman's laborer tends to be a
person in the condition of potentiality: not so much a social figure
but, like America and democracy, a literary figure, a trope of possibility'.[9] One needs to turn to his journalism for a more faithful mapping
of the contemporary world of the working classes – the concept of a
single unified white 'labour' force, opposed to the interests of capital
appeared in fledgling form in the 1830s but was consolidated only during the class-torn and correspondingly class-conscious post-war period.
His newspaper articles and editorials do exist on the same plane as such
social realities as the Five Point slums, the opium dens, the race riots,
and all the other disturbing and disfiguring features of mid-century New
York. When these occur in the poetry, as they do in parts of 'Song of
Myself' and 'The Sleepers', they are offered more as distressing aspects
of the dynamics of urban experience than as sites and occasions for
remedial action. But in his editorials Whitman campaigned for reforms.
He deplored the hold of liquor over working people's lives, argued
for reduction in transport costs (particularly ferry charges), demanded
that clean drinking water be supplied, and pleaded for the provision of
decent housing.

One other salient fact is also registered much more bluntly in the
journalism – that the majority of the New York workforce was in fact
not American but immigrant. In his editorials, Whitman was more than
capable of railing against some of the socio-political consequences of
this – the campaigns of Bishop John Hughes in the early 1840s for separate Catholic schools provoked the poet to verbal attacks on the Irish as
a threat to American values, attacks so vehement that he found himself
publicly defending his writing against the charge that it was Nativist and

xenophobic. For a variety of reasons – partly a wish to avoid ethnic tensions in the face of the political power of Nativism in 1855, and partly because, for all the sincerity of his repeated affirmations of welcome, he could himself be disconcerted by the obstinacy with which foreigners remained perplexingly attached to their foreignness – Whitman downplayed in his poetry the fact that the New York workplace was overwhelmingly immigrant in character. Instead, he devised a grammar of integration, writing, for instance, of 'Mechanics, Southerners, new arrivals'. Indeed, with regard to the world of labour, Whitman's purpose in his poetry was almost always to mediate it through a rhetoric of integration, thus occluding the extent to which, in historical reality, it was a social space riven by class and ethnic divisions – by 1855 the massive ethnic enclave of Kleindeutschland alone, with its tens of thousands of non-English-speaking foreigners, was the largest German city in the world apart from Berlin and Vienna.

Whitman's real constituency was white America, and his favourite constituents by far were the working-class 'boys' and 'comrades' who, for him, constituted the best hope of a future American democracy. Tragically, however, the fullest confirmation of his grounds for trust in them was to come not in peace but in war and in the form of his experiences nursing the desperately wounded in the great hospitals of Civil War Washington. Whitman saw that war not as one to liberate the slaves, and not even as one between North and South, but as a 'class war' of sorts. He believed it was fought between the Northern rural and urban working class, that for him represented true American democracy, and the class of owners (in which Southern slave-owners were allied with Northern businessmen) who oppressed not only the blacks but also the white working population of both the Northern and the Southern states. 600,000 lives were lost as the United States tried to solve its labour problems. It was in these terms that the Civil War was, for him, a war for 'democracy'; for social, political and economic egalitarianism. And it was the workingmen who won that struggle, as much through their powers of suffering and endurance as through their military prowess.

From beginning to end, Whitman's Civil War collection, *Drum-Taps*, is his highly idealistic memorial tribute to the ordinary soldiers. It is they who, when war is declared, spring voluntarily and enthusiastically to arms, leaving 'the houses ... and the workshops, ... / The mechanics arming, (the trowel, the jack-plane, the blacksmith's hammer, tost aside

with precipitation, .../ The driver deserting his wagon in the street)'
(*WCP*, 416–17). And it is they who, at war's end, return peacefully to
their task of building a better society. In the heat of battle, it is the 'tan-
faced prairie boy' and his urban counterpart who distinguish themselves
through their bravery, not least when they are brought to hospital. The
greatest heroes, wrote Whitman, were 'working on farms or at some
trade before the war – unaware of their own nature' (*WCP*, 739). In
their transformation he found final evidence of the heroic potential
of American democracy. When he saw them en masse 'it fell upon me
like a great awe'. When he encountered them as the young inarticulate
illiterates he nursed in hospital wards he devoted himself to their service,
not least by writing simply worded letters on their behalf. And Lincoln
he regarded as an embodiment of their stalwart working-class qualities, as those had been further Americanised, and thus more perfectly
democratised, in the west, the real, capitalist nature of which Whitman
never confronted. In his great elegy for Lincoln, 'When Lilacs Last in
the Door-yard Bloomed', it is to the world of work that he turns to find
the dead president's lasting memorial – to 'pictures of growing spring
and farms and homes', and 'the city at hand with dwellings so dense,
and stacks of chimneys,/ And all the scenes of life and the workshops,
and the workmen homeward returning' (*WCP*, 462).

How cruelly, however, was Whitman to be disappointed in that
vision of a post-war America in which labour, and with it democracy,
came into its own. In the event, the war ironically made possible,
through the huge boost it had given industrialisation, the ways in which
it had fostered a centralisation of economic and political power, and
its creation of a disciplined class of aggressive leaders, a society deeply
divided along class lines, and a business culture in which financially
bloated industrial tycoons and predatory corporations thrived. In
response, an alienated labour force turned in self-defence to weapons,
such as unionism and strikes, which Whitman regarded as un-American
and of which he deeply disapproved. For him, prose was better suited
than poetry to wrestle with such conditions, and in works like *Democratic
Vistas* he struggled to keep faith with his vision, focusing on the belief
that the social jungle of the Gilded Age would evolve into a society in
which all workers would be property-owners. But even his most affirmative writing seems now shadowed by darkness. Unable to confront
his anxieties directly – to have admitted the depth of his uncertainty

about the future of working class America would have been to begin to doubt the purpose of that hideously destructive war in which he had watched so many young working men die – he found alternative means of expression. In his late, obsessive, passion for Jean François Millet's heroic picture of labour, 'The Sower', may be detected both a nostalgia for a lost world of work and perhaps an unspeakable sympathy with the social radicals of the French Revolution. He was particularly shaken by what he called 'the tramp and strike question', those worrying symptoms of serious social disorder. Meeting a homeless family on the road, he fails to make out the woman's features under her large bonnet, almost as if he were unwilling to look such suffering in the face. Analogously, he finds it increasingly difficult in his post-war poetry actually to home in on those telling details of working-life that, in his pre-war poetry, had been incandescent with his belief in the immanent potential of the American labouring classes. Then he had been writing 'the evangel-poem of comradeship and love'.

He did, however, continue to write a poetry of work, one that tended to be as vague in its rhetoric as it was strident in its optimistic affirmations. Also, by attaching the annexes *Passage to India* and *After All, Not to Create Only* to the post-war (1871) edition of *Leaves of Grass* he continued to try to find means of integrating the best qualities of the old artisanal order with the inventiveness of the new ruthlessly productive economy. Perhaps his most ambitious attempt to spiritualise the post-war nation's frenetic materialism was his commissioned piece for the 1871 National Industrial Exposition, where the Muse is addressed, with somewhat cumbersome irony, as if she were an illustrious immigrant. She is reduced to a gawking visitor awed by the assembled evidence of the New World's superiority to the Old and discerning in it the westward march of civilisation. Among the amazements on offer are 'the Hoe press whirling its cylinders, shedding the printed leaves steady and fast,/ The photograph, model, watch, pin, nail, shall be created before you' (*WCP*, 345). But for all its ostensible celebration of modern mass-production, the text occasionally betrays its origins in Whitman's artisanal sympathies, as when he claims the function of the Exposition is 'to teach the average man the glory of his daily walk and trade ...' (*WCP*, 347). And in a reversal of the Cinderella story of old Europe, Whitman amusingly declares that the Muse 'is here, installed amid the kitchen ware!' (*WCP*, 343).

Behind all this boosterism, however, lie darker imperatives, evident when Whitman uses the Exposition to banish the nightmare of the recent carnage ('Hence from my shuddering sight to never more return that show of blacken'd, mutilitated corpses' [*WCP*, 346]). It becomes clear that, in the Exposition, Whitman finds comforting evidence of the triumph of the democratic United States, a workers' collective, as emblematised by the Union flag ('But I have seen thee bunting, to tatters torn upon the splinter'd staff' [*WCP*, 350]). And the poem further confesses its origins in anxiety when Whitman hopefully represents the Exposition as a site for reconciliation between polarised classes: 'The male and female many laboring not/ Shall ever here confront the laboring many/ With precious benefit to both, glory to all,/ To thee America, and the eternal Muse' (*WCP*, 346).

Another interesting, if neglected, instance of Whitman's post-war poetry of labour is 'Outlines for a Tomb', which may be briefly described as a recycling of his great elegy to Lincoln in the form of an elegy addressed to that unlikely subject, for Whitman, a businessman. One sign of Whitman's post-war disorientation was his (reciprocated) admiration, in old age, for that hammerer of labour, Andrew Carnegie. But it is to the memory of a businessman of a quite different character, the millionaire philanthropist George Peabody who founded museums at Yale and Harvard, that the poem is dedicated. In a rhetorical turn that repeats the way in which Whitman had imagined decorating the walls of Lincoln's tomb, he here imagines scenes for Peabody's mausoleum. And, as in the case of Lincoln, what he comes up with are scenes from working life – 'among the city streets a laborer's home appear'd,/ After his day's work done, cleanly, sweet-air'd, the gaslight burning,/ The carpet swept and a fire in the cheerful stove' (*WCP*, 506). 'All, all the shows of laboring life' are conjured up as tribute to the millionaire who had so kindly supplied all the wants of labour, with a magnanimity equal to that of nature itself: 'From thee such scenes, thou stintless, lavish giver,/ Tallying the gifts of earth, large as the earth,/ Thy name an earth, with mountains, fields and tides' (*WCP*, 507).

It is a remarkable poem, embarrassing in its effusions if placed next to the great, 'Locofoco' poetry of the earlier Whitman. But what it represents is an ageing man's attempts to believe, in the face of such dire evidence to the contrary as the great railroad strike of 1877 and the Chicago Haymarket riots of 1886, that a humane alliance between

business and labour was still possible and that in it lay the hope for progress towards a truly democratic American society. Yet as ever Whitman's
prose starkly and faithfully registered an altogether different reality, and
warned 'of the unjust division of wealth-products, and the hoggish
monopoly of a few, rolling in superfluity, against the vast bulk of the working people, living in squalor'. Moreover, in 1871, Whitman had included
a new section entitled 'Songs of Insurrection' in his new edition of *Leaves
of Grass* as a protest against 'the more and more insidious grip of capital'.

There was also another disappointment evident towards the end.
Whitman had not only wished to write *of* American labour, he had
wished to write *for* American labour. But American labour had plainly
showed that it was not listening. While Whitman was heartened by the
evidence of appreciation that came from such British lower middle-
class supporters of his work as the members of the Bolton Group (who
succeeded in creating a public labour day in honour of Whitman that
continued to be observed for much of the twentieth century), he was
not to live to see how much his poetry would come to matter to Eugene
Debs and other leaders of labour in the United States. Nor was he ever
to know how important he was to become for several figures influential
within the Socialist movement in the British Isles.[10]

Yet, for all his disappointment and bewilderment, Whitman's concern not just for the condition but for the cause of labour and the
labouring classes never really slackened, alienated though he had
become, by the end of his life, from the (to him un-American) forms
that the politics of labour had taken, and baffled though he was, at the
end, by the class polarities within his society. The writer who, in the 1855
Preface to *Leaves of Grass*, had praised 'the noble character of the young
mechanics and of all free American workmen and workwomen ... the
general ardor and friendliness and enterprise – the perfect equality of
the female with the male ... the large amativeness' (*WCP*, 8) was still
reaffirming that vision, that faith, in the very last years of his life:

> Without yielding an inch the working-man and working-woman
> were to be in my pages from first to last. The ranges of heroism
> and loftiness with which Greek and feudal poets endow'd their
> god-like or lordly born characters – indeed prouder and better
> based and with fuller ranges than those – I was to endow the
> democratic averages of America. I was to show that we, here and

today, are eligible to the grandest and the best – more eligible now than any times of old were. (*WCP*, 668)

And if that had been his intention, then such, too, had been his achievement. For all his shortcomings and blindnesses Whitman remains the great Homeric poet of American labour. It is certainly too much to claim, adapting a phrase from that early statement of his in *The New-York Democrat*, that 'it is to labor that [he] owe[ed] everything'. But there is surely some truth in the assertion that but for 'the democratic averages' he might well not have been a poet at all.

Notes

Previously published in Donald D. Kummings (ed.),
A Companion to Walt Whitman (Malden, Massachusetts:
Blackwell Publishing, 2006), pp. 60–75.

1. Walt Whitman, *Journalism 1834–1846: Volume 1*, ed. Herbert Bergman et al.; part of *The Collected Writing of Walt Whitman*, ed. Gay Wilson Allen and Sculley Bradley (New York: Peter Lang Publishing, 1998), p. 197. All subsequent quotations from this edition will appear following a *J* in the text.
2. Walt Whitman, *Walt Whitman: Complete Poetry and Collected Prose*, ed. Justin Kaplan (New York: The Library of America, 1982), p. 694. Subsequent references to this volume, abbreviated as *WCP*, are given in the text.
3. Edwin G. Burrows and Mike Wallace, *Gotham: A History of New York City to 1898*. (Oxford: Oxford University Press, 2000).
4. Horace Traubel (ed.), *An American Primer by Walt Whitman* (1904. Wisconsin: Holy Cow! Press, 1987), p. 15. Subsequent references to this volume, abbreviated as *AP*, are given in the text.
5. Burrows and Wallace, *Gotham*, p. 489.
6. Burrows and Wallace, *Gotham*, p. 490.
7. Burrows and Wallace, *Gotham*, p. 753.
8. George G. Foster, *New York by Gas-Light: With Here and There a Streak of Sunshine* (New York: np, 1850), p. 109.
9. Alan Trachtenberg, 'The Politics of Labor and the Poet's Work: A Reading of "A Song for Occupations"', in Ed Folsom (ed.), *Walt Whitman: the Centennial Essays* (Iowa City: University of Iowa Press, 1994), pp. 120–32 (123).
10. See M. Wynn Thomas, *Transatlantic Connections: Whitman US/Whitman UK* (Iowa City: University of Iowa Press, 2005).

States United and United States: Whitman's national vision in 1855

I

Allen Grossman opens his important essay comparing Whitman and Lincoln with a summary of the first principles of his study:

> To begin with, I shall suppose that both policy and art are addressed to the solution of problems vital to the continuing social order, and therefore, to the human world. In the period of America's Civil War (the 'renaissance' moment both of America's literary and its constitutional authenticity) there arose two great and anomalous masters, the one of policy and the other of poetry: Abraham Lincoln and Walt Whitman.[1]

This present study proceeds from a similar working assumption about the congruence of politics and literature in mid-nineteenth-century America, while substituting for Lincoln another political giant of the period – John C. Calhoun – whose relationship to Whitman has hitherto received very little attention.

There is abundant evidence of Whitman's fascination with the whole wide field of language. *An American Primer* makes manifest a gargantuan appetite in this respect that leads directly to the growth of the poetry; showing how Whitman is excited by a range of different discourses, including the languages of contemporary politics. Indeed, although it is undoubtedly the vehicle of conviction politics, his unpublished 1856 pamphlet, 'The Eighteenth Presidency!', can also be read as a conscious exercise in one of those languages. It is also proof – if proof were needed, given Whitman's record as sometime campaigning Democrat, passionate Free Soiler and highly politicised journalist – of his alertness not only to the political issues, personalities and arguments of his day but also to the terms of thinking and utterance that held sway in the fast-moving world of contemporary political affairs. But while

Betsy Erkkila has authoritatively mapped Whitman's poetry onto the shifting political concerns of the period, work remains to be done to explore the ways in which his poetry was, to some extent, composed out of elements of the political discourses that were circulating at the time he was writing.[2] And this work may proceed from a greater awareness of the political figures with whom Whitman is known to have been particularly fascinated. As Grossman's nevertheless singular essay reminds us, Whitman's wartime and postwar infatuation with Lincoln has, of course, been extensively investigated. But far less attention has been paid to those figures of the pre-war period to which he makes pointed or impassioned reference. Indeed, several of them remain entirely overlooked by Whitman scholarship, and the subject of this discussion is one of these, a towering antebellum politician whose 'alternative' rhetoric of unionism was arguably as powerfully influential, even on Whitman himself, as was that of his polar opposite Lincoln.

Calhoun was known, even to many of his exasperated friends, as 'John Crisis Calhoun' because, every time he opened his mouth, he seemed to be prophesying disaster for the South and catastrophe for the Union of States. A more unlikely figure to attract Whitman's admiration than this austere, forbidding, formidable ideologue of Southern separatism could, on the face of it, scarcely be found. That perhaps is partly why the archetypal New Yorker's obsession with this grand apologist for the Southern cause has hitherto passed unnoticed. Yet, there is substantial evidence to indicate the depth of Whitman's ambivalent regard for an ideological adversary who seems, in some ways, to have provided his pre-war self with the kind of whetstone for his democratic unionism the post-war Whitman found in Thomas Carlyle. It may, indeed, not to be too much to assert that Whitman's antebellum poetic discourse and ideology of unionism may in part have developed in complicated concert with his developing fascination with Calhoun's grand, seminal statements on this subject.

II

Evidence for Whitman's interest in Calhoun may be found in three different periods of his writing life. The bulk of it occurs in the form of striking and sometimes extended passages from the journalism and notebooks of the early and mid forties. There is a further reference in the mid-fifties, of particular significance because it coincides with the appearance of the first editions of *Leaves of Grass*. And finally there is a remarkable, and indeed haunting, post-war passage in *Specimen Days*. What this material appears to indicate is that Whitman was aware not only of the general terms of Calhoun's defiant thinking but also of the specific language in which he advanced his powerful model of unionism. It seems clear that Whitman had access (probably by the usual journalistic means of the day) to transcripts of some of Calhoun's key speeches, and that he was very powerfully affected by the great Southern statesman's eloquent prosecution of his case.

The first of Whitman's references to Calhoun appeared in the *New York Aurora* (11 March 1842) and it immediately shows how conflicted his views of him were: 'John C. Calhoun ... is a statesman, and, we have no doubt, a patriot. But that nullification business – ah, that's the rub!'[3] By 'that nullification business' Whitman means, of course, Calhoun's notorious assertion in 1832, when he was Jackson's Vice President, that any federal law passed by Congress might be rendered null in any state whose legislature voted against it, and that if two thirds of the states so voted, then it could no longer stand as federal law. It was on these 'nullification' grounds, deriving in part from statements Jefferson had earlier made, that, the same year, Calhoun's own state of Southern Carolina promptly rejected the law recently passed by Congress imposing a tariff on goods of foreign manufacture. A dramatic instance of Calhoun's extreme and impassioned belief in states rights, the nullification declaration precipitated a political crisis that jeopardised the Union, and only a compromise measure proposed by Henry Clay saved the day.

Whitman's deep mistrust of Calhoun as what he later repeatedly and obsessively termed 'a disunionist' was, therefore, to be expected, but it was to some degree most unexpectedly offset by his admiration – an admiration he was repeatedly to voice, with escalating passion – for Calhoun's 'patriotism.' From the very beginning, Whitman recognised in Calhoun an identification with 'his country' the equal, in its belligerent ferocity, of his own, and sadly unequalled, or so Whitman came increasingly to feel, by any contemporary Northern politician. The key to Whitman's fascination with Calhoun is almost certainly to be found here: the Southerner exemplified the kind of unqualified, unwavering, uncompromising and fearless commitment to the cause of the South that Whitman yearned to find matched in Northerners' attachment to the democratic Union. One obvious complication was the fact that the primary loyalty of 'this pride of Southern chivalry' was deeply sectional in character but, as Whitman explained in another newspaper article later in 1842, 'we admire his very faults – his devotion to his native south, and his ardent advocacy of her interests beyond all else'. Whitman must, nevertheless, sorrowfully deplore Calhoun's adherence to the doctrine of nullification, because 'we can never admire anything which puts in jeopardy the well being of our beloved Union' (*J*, 52).

But then, in 1846, Calhoun seemed briefly to masquerade as a convinced Unionist. The position he took that year on the question of whether or not the United States should prepare for war against Great Britain to resolve the future of Oregon attracted Whitman's enthusiastic approval, because it seemed to indicate that the Southerner was capable of a unionist sentiment that, in its intensity, uncannily resembled Whitman's own. He was therefore moved to repeated encomiums of the following unbridled kind:

> Until we read Mr. Calhoun's speech, we never saw so fully realized the towering grandeur and strength of this republic! We never saw so clearly its far stretch of future greatness, width, and the compulsive happiness it will be able one day to bestow on its citizens, as far as government can bestow happiness. (*J*, 296)

Moreover, Whitman placed Calhoun in the very midst of his personal pantheon of exalted American heroes:

> Mr Calhoun deserves well of the American people – and they will not forget it – for this effort in behalf of their highest, truest interests. As it was the lofty agency of Washington's to hew out with the unsheath'd sword what nothing but the sword could have achieved – as it was Jefferson's to put down the great landmarks, by which shape the province of government, and to know the rights of the people – as it was our beloved Jackson who both in battle and the cabinet exemplified the excellence of both these prototypes – is it too much to add that *Calhoun* follows in the same category – a warrior whose ponderous hand lifts up the clearest, most useful principles of political truth, and rallies in their behalf

a support of intellect and hear-eloquence surpassed by hardly any man living. (*J*, 297)

No greater endorsement by Whitman could possibly be imagined than this. So what had Calhoun said that was worthy of such a paean? The following passage from his senate address on the Oregon crisis may help account for Whitman's rapturous acclamation of his 'sense and patriotism':

> Providence has given us the inheritance stretching across the entire continent, from East to West, from ocean to ocean, and from North to South, covering by far the greater and better part of its temperate zone. It comprises a region not only of vast extent, but abundant in all resources, excellent in climate, fertile and exuberant in soil, capable of sustaining, in the plentiful enjoyment of all the necessaries of life, a population of ten times our present number. Our great number, as a people, is to occupy this vast domain, to replenish it with an intelligent, virtuous, and industrious population, to convert the forests into cultivated fields, to drain the swamps and morasses, and cover them with rich harvests, to build up cities, towns and villages in every direction, and to unite the whole by the most rapid intercourse between all parts.[4]

This could easily be mistaken for a passage by Whitman, an impression confirmed when one reads other sections of the same speech: 'Magic wires are already stretching themselves in all directions over the earth, and when their mystic meshes shall have been united and perfected, our globe itself will become endowed with sensitiveness, – so that whatever touches on any one point, will be instantly felt on every other' (*Speeches*, 283–4).

During the course of repeated excited commentaries on Calhoun's 1846 speech – and he was so enthralled by it that he returned to it on four occasions – Whitman clearly revealed how his enthusiasm for the Southerner was rooted in his dismay at the lack of an equivalent patriotic spirit amongst the unionist politicians of the North:

> We like a bold honest *morally* heroic man! We therefore like John C. Calhoun ... We admire it the more that it is so rare in these degenerate days. We believe that a higher souled patriot never

trod on American soil, than is John C. Calhoun. He reminds
us of some of those old Roman heroes who in great crises sat
calm as the rocks of Heaven, while every thing else was turmoil
and disquietude – the hero-senators that stood disdainfully in
the capitol with their robes about them, when the approach of
a conquering invader scattered all the rest of Rome. (*J*, 363–4)

Although these responses mark the zenith of Whitman's admiration for
Calhoun, it is evident not only that the Southerner had left a deep and
indelible mark on his consciousness but that Whitman continued to pay
rapt attention to all the South Carolinian's subsequent senatorial utterances, and that even after his death he recognised that his remained an
immensely powerful influence on the political scene right down to the
Civil War. In many ways, Calhoun was, for Whitman, the very spirit
of the South, and the epitome of everything he both intensely hated
and devoutly admired about that region. That this Southerner was very
much in his mind when addressing the crisis of the Union in the first
edition of *Leaves of Grass* may reasonably be inferred from the way in
which, a mere few months later, he treated Calhoun in 'The Eighteenth
Presidency!' as the architect of the anti-egalitarian philosophy which not
only underpinned the institution of slavery but also potentially threatened the freedoms even of white northern workers:

> Calhoun, disunionist senator, denounces and denies, in the pres-
> ence of the world, the main article of the organic compact of
> These States, that all men are born free and equal, and bequeaths
> to his followers, at present leaders of the three hundred and fifty
> thousand masters, guides of the so-called democracy, counsellors
> of Presidents, and getters-up of the nominations of Buchanan
> and Fillmore, his deliberate charge, to be carried out against the
> main article, that it is the most false and dangerous of all polit-
> ical errors; such being the words of that charge, spoken in the
> summer of the 73d year of These States, and, indeed, carried out
> since in the spirit of congressional legislation, executive action,
> and the candidates offered by the political parties to the people.[5]

This makes it clear that Whitman felt that the 'words' Calhoun had
notoriously spoken in 1848, during a second debate on the Oregon

question (to which we shall return), had in effect functioned down to 1856 as the pernicious 'law' secretly governing all government policy and action. Those 'words' had, indeed, been permanently recorded for posterity in the great edition of Calhoun's works that appeared a year after his death in 1850. Nor did Whitman only hold Calhoun primarily responsible for the calamitous state of political affairs during the fifties. He also later regarded him as the villain of the Civil War, in contrast to its hero, Abraham Lincoln. When Whitman came to write the epitaph of the old South in *Specimen Days* he chillingly entitled the passage 'Calhoun's Real Monument', and composed it in the form of words he claimed to have heard spoken by a Union veteran:

> I have seen [Calhoun's monument]. It is the desolated, ruined south: nearly the whole generation of young men between seventeen and thirty thousand destroyed or maim'd; all the old families used up – the rich impoverish'd, the plantations cover'd with weeds, the slaves unloos'd and become the masters, and the name of southerner blacken'd with every shame – all that is Calhoun's real monument. (*WCP*, 773)

It was Calhoun's sombre monument, surely, that was at the back of Whitman's mind when, in 'When Lilacs Last in the Dooryard Bloom'd', he went searching for a mausoleum fitting for Lincoln, and found it, not in a desolated, ruined land, but in 'The varied and ample land, the South and the North in the light, Ohio's shores and flashing Missouri/ And ever the far-spreading prairies cover'd with grass and corn' (*WCP*, 463). For Whitman, the victory of North over South in the name of the democratic Union was most naturally and dramatically figured as the final victory of Lincoln over Calhoun, and 'When Lilacs' may, therefore, be read as an elegy as much for Calhoun as for Lincoln.

III

If, in 'The Eighteenth Presidency!' Whitman felt that Calhoun's reactionary 'words' had replaced the Constitution itself as the malign guiding spirit of American government, then those same words may also be said to be invisibly influencing much of Whitman's own writing in the

1855 edition of *Leaves of Grass*. Take, for instance, the very first word in the volume, the word 'America' with which the Preface opens. 'America' was a word as necessarily absent from Calhoun's discourse as it was necessarily omnipresent in Whitman's. It was a seminal term in both of their political lexicons. Calhoun abhorred the word because it implied that the United States was a single, unitary, socio-political entity; that it was, in short, a 'nation' – another term that was complete anathema to Calhoun, whereas it was fundamental and indispensable to Whitman's philosophy: 'it is attempted to subvert the federal Government, plainly established by [the Constitution], and rear in its place a great national consolidated government – to expunge the word "Union" and insert in its place that of "Nation"' (*Speeches*, 357). 'The Americans of all nations at any time upon the earth have probably the fullest poetical nature', the second paragraph of the Preface audaciously replies: 'The United States themselves are essentially the greatest poem' (*WCP*, 5). The parallel syntax here insists on 'America' and 'The United States' as being synonyms – which for Calhoun they could not be – just as it takes it for granted that 'The United States' are inhabited by a single people ('Americans') – again an assumption that Calhoun would certainly have challenged, insisting as he did that the United States was a confederation of different peoples, not a single people. Calhoun even baulked at the term 'United States', finding its apparent neutrality suspicious. To it he preferred the term 'the States United', because that made clear that the States had priority over the Union.

That Whitman may even sometimes have had Calhoun consciously in mind when employing what, for the Southerner, were such highly loaded political terms in such an apparently innocent and matter-of-fact manner is suggested by another phrase he uses a little later in this same paragraph. 'Here', writes Whitman of his 'America', 'is not merely a nation but a teeming nation of nations' (*WCP*, 5). This may be a deliberately distorting echo of Calhoun's assertion in 1842: 'Instead of a nation, we are in reality an assemblage of nations, or peoples (if the plural noun may be used where the language affords none), united in their sovereign character immediately and directly by their own act, but without losing their separate and independent existence' (*Speeches*, 81). It is interesting to see that Calhoun is here constrained by his ideology – as Whitman was constrained by his – to coin neologisms ('peoples'). But whereas Calhoun uses the phrase 'an assembly of nations' to distinguish between the different 'peoples' of the different States, Whitman uses 'a teeming nation of nations' to differentiate between the native inhabitants of the States and immigrant newcomers from so many of the countries of old Europe.

To realise that, during this period of deep political instability, when the future of the democratic Union seemed desperately uncertain, Whitman's political imagination was however reluctantly in thrall to Calhoun's is to discover that the apparently innocent language he uses in the first edition of *Leaves of Grass*, both in the Preface and the poetry, trails, in fact, a dark shadow of political controversy. And nowhere is one more aware of Calhoun's thinking as the 'dark matter' of Whitman's mental universe – an invisible presence secretly shaping that which is visible – than in the case of the geopolitical vision which is a cornerstone of Whitman's nationalist unionism. In replying to remarks made by Senator Simmons of Rhode Island in 1847, Calhoun made the following significant statement:

> [The Senator] dwelt for some time on the interpretation which I gave to the term United States ... I said it meant the "States United", my object was to get clear of the geographical idea which, in common parlance, is attached to the United States. As commonly used, it is intended to designate that portion of this continent which Providence has allotted to us, and has come to receive this meaning, because there is no specific name to express it. But that is not its meaning in the constitution. As used in that instrument, it is intended to designate all the States that are members of this union. (*Speeches*, 357)

Calhoun is here deliberately renouncing the holistic geopolitical idea of the United States as a providentially ordained continental 'nation' in favour of the constitution's model of the United States as a confederation of separate, intrinsically independent but voluntarily interdependent political units. The thrust of Whitman's writing in 1855 was, of course, exactly opposite to this, his mistrust of the constitutional model being equal to Calhoun's absolute trust in it, and his exploitation of the political implications of a continental model of the US being exactly what Calhoun most feared: '[T]he character of the Government has been changed', Calhoun charged in 1850, 'from a federal republic, as it originally came from the hands of its framers, into a great national consolidated democracy ... What was once a constitutional federal republic, is now converted, in reality, into one as absolute as that of the Autocrat of Russia, and as despotic in its tendency as any absolute government that ever existed' (*Speeches*, 551).

'The largeness of nature or the nation were monstrous without a corresponding largeness and generosity of the spirit of the citizen', wrote Whitman in his 1855 Preface, eliding nature and nation so that the latter seems the 'natural' counterpart of the former. As self-appointed national bard Whitman proceeds to characterise the responsibilities of an authentically American poet: 'His spirit responds to his country's spirit ... he incarnates its geography and natural life and rivers and lakes' (*WCP*, 7). It is the beginning of one of those great, sweeping, trans-continental, visionary panoramas that stud both the prose and the poetry of the first edition of *Leaves of Grass*. In 'Song of Myself', they famously take the form of a kind of national audit, an epic listing of the nation's geographical assets. Never again was Whitman to 'ground' his vision of nation so eloquently, and therefore so convincingly, in his land, from Great Lakes to Gulf and from coast to coast. This was the very bedrock of Whitman's nationalism, but, as Donald Pease has reminded us, such 'visionary compacts' also served to conceal from himself what in worrying political reality he knew, and what Calhoun had starkly emphasised: viewed in the august light of the Constitution, this vision of organic nationhood was based on very shaky ground indeed.[6] A metaphor was being used to usurp the authority of the founding statutes of the United States.

Not that Calhoun was above using that same geographical model himself to advance his own, very different, political purposes, when it suited him. As not only the number of free states but also the size of their populations began rapidly to outstrip those of the slave states so Calhoun's opposition to a concept of democracy based on the idea of rule by the numerical majority understandably intensified: 'As the Government approaches nearer and nearer to the one absolute and single power, – the will of the greatest number – its action will become more and more disturbed and irregular' (*Speeches*, 92). Whitman responds to this looming problem in his own characteristic way: 'The American bard shall delineate no class of persons ... and not be for the eastern states more than the western or the northern states more than the southern' (*WCP*, 15). As for Calhoun, he responded by proposing an alternative model of democracy, based on the recognition of a balance of justice between the frequently conflicting interests of different regions of an internally highly diverse country. (His was a plea for pluralism against majoritarianism, to use today's political jargon.) In a speech on the veto power in February, 1842, he warned against giving 'the dominant interest, or combination of interest, an unlimited and despotic control over all others', asking 'what, in a country of such vast extent and diversity of condition, institutions, industry, and productions, would this be, but to subject the rest to the most grinding despotism and oppression?' (*Speeches*, 82). For the model of democracy as governed by the will of the people he therefore substituted one that respected the will of the peoples. And he found the 'full, perfect, just and supreme voice of the people [as redefined by Calhoun], embodied in the constitution' (*Speeches*, 93).

Contrast Calhoun's use of this argument from geo-political diversity with that of the 1855 *Leaves of Grass*. Whenever he advances his national vision in trans-continental terms, Whitman does so either by emphasising the 'natural' complementarity and harmonious interdependence of richly diverse 'regions' he is careful to characterise in non-political terms, or by a deliberately promiscuous listing that completely scrambles all those categories of difference upon which Calhoun's political philosophy depended:

> I see not merely that you are polite or whitefaced ... married
> or single ... citizens of old states or citizens of new states ...
> eminent in some profession ... a lady or gentleman in a
> parlor ... or dressed in the jail uniform ... or pulpit uniform,
> Not only the free Utahan, Kansian, or Arkansian ... not only
> the free Cuban ... not merely the slave ... not Mexican
> native, or Flatfoot, or Negro from Africa. (*WCP*, 90)

Specifically using Calhoun's notion of America as 'an assemblage of nations', and this time in the same sectionalist sense in which the Southerner had intended it, Whitman proclaims in 'Song of Myself' that he is 'One of the great nation, the nation of many nations – the smallest the same and the largest the same,/ A southerner soon as a northerner, a planter nonchalant and hospitable,/ A Yankee bound my own way ... ready for trade ... my joints the limberest joints on earth and the sternest joints on earth./ A Kentuckian walking the vale of the Elkhorn in my deerskin leggings' (*WCP*, 42). What he does to defuse the fraught situation created by Calhoun's sectionalist politics, is to represent American diversity not in terms of an awkward patchwork of different, fiercely independent, states but in terms of a parti-colored weave of individual activities: 'The cleanhaired Yankee girl works with her sewing-machine or in the factory or mill,/ ... The Missourian crosses the plains toting his wares and his cattle,/ ... The coon-seekers go through the regions of the Red river, or through those drained by the Tennessee, or through those of the Arkansas' (*WCP*, 40–1). This by-passing of the state is consistent with the radical view of the American constitution Whitman advances in 'The Eighteenth Presidency!', when he states that 'the whole American government is itself' not an agreement between independent states but rather 'simply a compact with each individual of the thirty millions of persons now inhabitants of These States' (*WCP*, 1319).

Such strategies as these were necessary not least because Whitman had, in fact, considerable sympathy for Calhoun's states rights stance, an indelible respect for the political integrity of the states that led him frequently to contradict himself in his writings. Thus the Whitman who, in 'Song of Myself', is friend to the escaped slave is also the Whitman who, in 'The Eighteenth Presidency!', declares that, under the terms of the Constitution, 'runaway slaves must be delivered back' (*WCP*, 1320). So how, then, to account for 'Boston Ballad', that savage attack on Boston in the 1855 *Leaves of Grass* for implementing the Fugitive Slave Law – as Calhoun had repeatedly demanded the North should, and as had been agreed it would under the terms of the reinforced Law? Whitman's answer is to evoke the doctrine of states rights in order to distinguish between the Law (to which he objected) and the Constitutional injunction: the former could be defied with impunity because it was a Federal imposition that interfered with the freedom of states.

Nor is 'Boston Ballad' the only poem in the 1855 *Leaves of Grass* to address issues specifically highlighted by Calhoun. There are many others. Take, for instance, 'A Song for Occupations'. In a senate speech of February 1847, Calhoun had declared that 'where wages command labor, as in the non-slaveholding States, there necessarily takes place between labor and capital a conflict, which leads, in process of time, to disorder and revolution, if not counteracted by some applica-tion and strong constitutional provision' (*Speeches*, 360). Here, again, Calhoun was touching on a raw nerve. Whitman was acutely anxious about labour conditions and labour relations in pre-war, post-artisanal American society. It was, of course, easy enough to counter Calhoun's arguments at the level of political reasoning. So, for instance, Whitman could (and did, in 'The Eighteenth Presidency!') deliberately misrepre-sent Calhoun's remarks as indicating his willingness to 'enslave' white northern labour were he given the chance. Alternatively, and more fairly, Calhoun could be used to bolster Whitman's main argument – that there was a malign anti-labour alliance between Southern planters and Northern businessmen. After all, Calhoun had in effect indicated as much by stating that 'in all conflicts which may occur in the other portion of the Union between labor and capital, the South will ever be found to take the conservative [i.e. "preservative"] side' (*Speeches*, 360–1).

But to allay Whitman's deepest misgivings, a more compelling rhet-oric of national solidarity transcending class conflict had to be found and, as always, he could supply this only by turning to poetry. The result was 'A Song for Occupations', and Whitman's manufacturing of a persona professedly independent of class positioning: 'Neither a servant nor a master am I/ I take no sooner a large price than a small price' (*WCP*, 89). Calhoun might well have snorted at the preposterousness of such a naive claim, such a social impossibility. But Whitman manages to maintain his improbable stance within the special rhetorical world of the text by insistently instancing a distinction between a socially ascribed role (as of workman or owner) and the 'real' individual. And then, when eventually he reassembles his individuals into a socially recognisable whole, he does so on terms carefully calculated to exclude any possible grounds for social conflict. The distance between workers and owners is dissolved as Whitman treats them all without distinction as makers and producers, and thus sees them as expressing through their production and their products the creative imagination that is the defining char-acteristic of human kind: 'Goods of gutta-percha or papier-mache … colors and brushes … glaziers' implements,/ The veneers and glue-pot … the confectioner's ornaments … the decanter and glasses … the shears and flatiron;/ The awl and kneestrap … the pint measure and quart measure … the counter and stool … the writingpen of quill or metal' (*WCP*, 97). Insofar as this is a profoundly equalising vision, rooted in a passionate belief in the uncontainable freedom of human creative self-expression, it constitutes, of course, an implicit advocacy of a democratic politics diametrically opposite to that of Calhoun's.

Thus, then, did Whitman attempt to counter Calhoun's claim that, were it deprived of the stabilising social presence of the slave-owning South, the North would be helpless to prevent the Union from descending into social chaos: 'The North ... would have no central point of union, to bind its various and conflicting interest together; and would, with the increase of its population and wealth, be subject to all the agitation and conflicts growing out of the divisions of wealth and poverty, and their concomitants, capital and labor, of which already there are so many and so serious' (*Speeches*, 533). The spectre of that possibility also haunted Whitman's imagination in 1855 and in 'Song for Occupations' he sought to exorcise it by demonstrating that northern society was held together not by a 'central point of union' but by the mutuality of its inhabitants' common commitment to freedom of self-realisation. In Calhoun's eyes, this kind of belief was dangerously 'revolutionary' and could lead only to the bloody social conflicts that typified so many of the states of contemporary Europe. The value of the Southern states was therefore that they represented the 'conservative portion of the country', the only portion capable of conserving the Union. The doctrine of equality preached in the North 'is the leading cause among those which have placed Europe in its present anarchical condition, and which mainly stands in the way of reconstructing a good government in the place of those which have been overthrown, – threatening thereby the quarter of the globe most advanced in progress and civilization with hopeless anarchy, – to be followed by military despotism' (*Speeches*, 511–12). It is partly in the light of such assertions that one should read that relatively neglected poem in the 1855 *Leaves of Grass*, 'Europe the 72d and 73d Years of These States', an elegy for the revolutionary democrats who were the victims of the 1848 upheavals: 'Not a grave of the murdered for freedom but grows seed for freedom ... in its turn to bear seed,/ Which the winds carry afar and re-sow, and the rains and the snows nourish' (*WCP*, 134).

Calhoun made those inflammatory remarks about Europe during the course of his famous last great speech to Senate 'On the Slavery Question', 4 March 1850. A dying man, he was too ill to deliver his speech in person and had to sit and listen to a companion read it for him. A speech that seared itself on Whitman's memory, it included a memorable declaration, addressed to the non-slave-owning majority:

> It is time, Senators, there should be an open and manly avowal on all sides, as to what is intended to be done. If the question is not now settled, it is uncertain whether it ever can hereafter be, and we, as the representatives of the States of the Union, regarded as governments, should come to a distinct understanding as to our respective views, in order to ascertain whether the great questions at issue can be settled or not. If you, who represent the stronger portion, cannot agree to settle them on the broad principle of justice and duty, say so: and let the States we both represent agree to separate and part in peace. (*Speeches*, 572–3)

It was these words that moved an incensed Whitman to brand Calhoun the 'disunionist senator'. But inflamed though he was by these remarks, Whitman was even more enraged by other arguments Calhoun had advanced, with his characteristic meticulous rationality, during the course of his second Oregon speech two years earlier. There the Southerner had set about exposing the fallacy of Rousseau's famous proposition that 'all men are born free and equal' (*Speeches*, 505). This was nonsense, Calhoun argued, since babies are wholly dependent on others for their very survival. And even as children, they remain 'subject to their parents'. Only as they mature through a process of socialisation do 'they grow to all the freedom of which the condition in which they were born permits, by growing to be men'. Calhoun then turned to the famous formulation in that sacred founding text, the American Declaration of Independence, with its assertion 'that "all men are created equal"'. This, too, was nonsense, not only for the reasons already advanced against Rousseau but also because, according to the Bible, only two human beings were ever created, 'and of these one was pronounced subordinate to the other' (*Speeches*, 507–8). Calhoun therefore argues that a person's 'freedom' is a function of their existence as both a social and a political being (the social order being dependent on political organisation for its very survival). It therefore follows that 'individual liberty, or freedom, must be subordinate to whatever power may be necessary to protect society against anarchy within or destruction without' (*Speeches*, 510).

But why devote so much time to tracing Calhoun's line of thought on this issue? Well, to be aware of it, and to be aware of Whitman's scandalised response to it – he was, as we have seen, still making extended and heated reference to it in 'The Eighteenth Presidency!' – is to become aware, in turn, of the political dimensions of a poem from the 1855 edition of *Leaves of Grass*, which would otherwise seem wholly apolitical in character. 'There was a child went forth' has been repeatedly read as a poem of human growth, possibly based on Whitman's own experience of development as person and as poet. Scarcely ever has it been understood as possessing a political dimension and as constituting a clear political statement. But to read it alongside Calhoun's account of a child's gradual, carefully managed and supervised growth into the freedom possible only for a maturely social being is surely to realise how different from Calhoun's – and how expressive of Whitman's democratic vision – is the model of childhood and its development that the poem offers. Even the pseudo-biblical rhythms and vocabulary Whitman employs seem to be in conscious defiance of Calhoun's use of Genesis to sneer at the notion of every individual human being as 'created' free and equal to every other. By contrast, Whitman not only endows his infant with freedom, he pointedly treats that gift with religious reverence. He also makes the child entirely its own teacher, showing how it learns only through its own free and spontaneous actions, and its own wholly unplanned and unsupervised encounters. Indeed, when Calhoun's socialising agents appear – notably in the form of parents – the child is shown as learning quite as much by rejecting their example as by following it. And, given the Southerner's racist convictions, it may not be entirely coincidental that Whitman includes 'the barefoot Negro boy and girl' right next to 'the tidy and freshcheeked [white] girls' in his list of encounters from which the child profits (*WCP*, 138).

IV

To the victors the spoils. When, long after the Civil War, Whitman set out to trace the 'Origins of Attempted Secession', he began by asserting, with all the unchallengeable authority of the victor, a view of the conflict directly opposite to that which Calhoun, spokesman now for the defeated, would have taken:

I consider the war of attempted secession, 1860–65, not as a struggle of two distinct and separate peoples, but a conflict (often happening, and very fierce) between the passions and paradoxes of one and the same identity – perhaps the only terms on which that identity could really become fused, homogeneous and lasting. (*WCP*, 994)

One nation under God – that was the established character of the post-war United States: it was now indubitably not a 'nation of nations' in Calhoun's pre-war sense of that phrase. And as if to emphasise how total had been the defeat of Calhoun's cause, Whitman proceeded to associate him, later in his discussion, with the southern extremists who together, as Whitman scrupulously noted, with their numerous fellow-travellers in the north, had been the cause of the war:

Behind all, the idea that it was from a resolute and arrogant determination on the part of the extreme slaveholders, the Calhounites, to carry the states' rights portion of the constitutional compact to its farthest verge, and nationalize slavery, or else disrupt the Union, and found a new empire, with slavery for its corner-stone, was and is undoubtedly the true theory. (*WCP*, 997–8)

Thus did the post-war Whitman propose to dispose of Calhoun. But for the antebellum Whitman dispatch of his great Southern antagonist would not have been so simple, not only because of Calhoun's undoubted influence over contemporary thinking both south and north at that time, but because Whitman's relationship to him was itself complex; Calhoun was, in some ways, simultaneously an enemy thinker, an *alter ego*, and a necessary adversary.

As historians have pointed out, the pre-war decades saw the emergence of sectionalist ideology in both the South and the North – although the latter's claim to be not sectionalist but national in outlook was, in the event, to be 'confirmed' in and by its eventual military victory. The truth however was, as again history has established, that the 'national outlook' of the north was itself narrowly sectional to the extent that it conceived of 'the nation' exclusively on its own ideological terms – terms that specifically excluded the existing society of the South.

Furthermore, by the late 1840s a new generation of southern politicians was beginning to claim that the south was home to a 'nation' different from that of the north – in other words, the south began to develop a rhetoric of nationalism equal and answering to that of the north. What historians have further pointed out is that during this period the sectionalist/national ideologies of the south and the north respectively were developed with reference to, and by definition against, each other. Moreover, it has been claimed that, after the Compromise of 1850, the 'nationalist' thrust of southern political thinking was blunted for a while, and that, denied a political voice, it found expression instead in the field of southern literature.

To place Whitman's 1855 *Leaves of Grass*, with its implied conversation with Calhoun, in this historical context is to become newly aware of it as very much a textual product of its political times. As in the south so in the north, the nationalist feelings of the early fifties found expression not directly by political means but indirectly through literature – such literature as *Leaves of Grass*, an idiosyncratic but still classic instance of northern nationalism. As is well know, the volume was in part the result of Whitman's own disappointed turn away from the political life in which he had been so deeply immersed in 1848 – a turn occasioned by his total disillusionment with existing political parties, which he saw as being pro-southern in sympathy and thus dangerous to his own northern nationalist vision of a radically egalitarian democratic society. And in fashioning his vision through, and as, a radically new poetry he also, or so this essay has attempted to suggest, developed his nationalist ideology with intimate, formative reference to the antithetical nationalist ideology of the South.

And even after the Civil War, Whitman remained capable of a response to Calhoun's pre-war south very different from that he voiced at the beginning of 'Origins of Attempted Secession' – a response that corresponded more subtly, and thus more completely, to the feelings of his pre-war self. In his essay on 'Poetry To-day in America – Shakspere – The Future', Whitman included one of his finest statements of his generous vision of American society, a statement the authority of whose challenge remains undimmed to this day:

> For the meanings and maturer purposes of these States are not
> the constructing of a new world of politics merely, and physical

comforts for the million, but even more determinedly, in range with science and the modern, of a new world of democratic sociology and imaginative literature. If the latter were not establish'd for the States, to form their only permanent tie and hold, the first-named would be of little avail. (*WCP*, 1014)

It is a sobering statement of an intoxicating vision – the finest kind of nationalist ideology and the vindication of Whitman's pre-war adherence to the 'northern cause'. But a few paragraphs later there is another passage which stands in interesting relationship to the first:

> It almost seems as if only that feudalism in Europe, like slavery in our own South, could outcrop types of tallest, noblest personal character yet – strength and devotion and love better than elsewhere – invincible courage, generosity, aspiration, the spines of all. Here is where Shakespeare and the others I have named perform a service incalculably precious to our America. Politics, literature, and everything else, centers at last in perfect *personnel*, (as democracy is to find the same as the rest;) and here feudalism is unrival'd – here the rich and highest-rising lessons it bequeaths us – a mass of foreign nutriment, which we are to work over, and popularize and enlarge, and present again in our own growths. (*WCP*, 1015)

There is a tragic paradox here – that the 'feudal' society of the antebellum south, a society founded on a great human evil, had nevertheless been able to produce individuals of a quality that Whitman, mired in the moral quagmire of the Gilded Age, can only wistfully dream that American democracy might one day be capable of producing. This is the insight that Whitman had had as early as 1842, when he had first praised John C. Calhoun as a peerless patriot. It is therefore surely not too fanciful to imagine that when here, in his later age, Whitman brings to mind the great human products of feudalism and mentions that they were to be found not only in Europe but also 'in our own South', the grand ghost of John Caldwell Calhoun was stalking his imagination for one last time.

Notes

Revised version of a chapter originally published in Susan Belasco,
Ed Folsom and Kenneth M. Price (eds), *Leaves of Grass: The Sesquicentennial
Essays* (Lincoln: University of Nebraska Press, 2007), pp. 62–83.

1. Allen Grossman, 'The Poetics of Union in Whitman and Lincoln: An Inquiry toward the Relationship of Art and Policy', in Walter Benn Michaels and Donald E. Pease (eds), *The American Renaissance Reconsidered* (Baltimore: Johns Hopkins University Press, 1985), p. 183.
2. Betsy Erkkila, *Whitman the Political Poet* (New York: Oxford University Press, 1989).
3. Walt Whitman, *Journalism 1834–1846: Volume 1*, ed. Herbert Bergman et al.; part of *The Collected Writing of Walt Whitman*, ed. Gay Wilson Allen and Sculley Bradley (New York: Peter Lang Publishing, 1998), p. 50. All subsequent quotations from this edition will appear following a *J* in the text.
4. John C. Calhoun, *Speeches of John C. Calhoun*, vol. IV, ed. Richard K. Crallé (New York: Russell and Russell, 1998), p. 285. Subsequent references to Calhoun's speeches are to this volume and are given in the text.
5. *Walt Whitman: Complete Poetry and Collected Prose*, ed. Justin Kaplan (New York: The Library of America, 1982), pp. 1316–17. Subsequent references to this volume, abbreviated as *WCP* and are given in the text.
6. Donald E. Pease, *Visionary Compacts: American Renaissance Writings in Cultural Context* (Madison: University of Wisconsin Press, 1987).

Whitman, Tennyson, and the poetry of old age

'Why should the agèd eagle stretch its wings?'[1] It was a question that troubled Whitman increasingly as he approached seventy. Why, when half-paralysed, confined to a cramped room in a tiny Camden cottage, and no more capable of soaring than the cheeping pet canary on whose caged company he so doted, should he continue to scribble? Why, above all, should he continue to publish? The question, voiced and unvoiced, haunts the two annexes he attached to the final edition (1892) of *Leaves of Grass* – 'Sands at Seventy' and 'Good-Bye My Fancy'. And answers are multiplied, both in the numerous prose *apologia* in which Whitman explained his intentions and in the annexes themselves. There is, for instance, an arresting grimness, a taciturnity, about the end of 'L. of G.'s Purport':

> I sing of life, yet mind me well of death:
> To-day shadowy Death dogs my steps, my seated shape, and
>   has for years –
> Draws sometimes close to me, as face to face.[2]

There is no ringing conclusion. The poem does not even end. It simply stops: the rest is silence. The impression is of a man disconcerted by death, even perhaps a little unnerved by it. And this is confirmed in the splendid 'After the Supper and Talk' (636). An old man's progress towards death is likened to a guest after supper, reluctant to leave the company for the dark:

> Shunning, postponing severance – seeking to ward off the last
>   word ever so little,
> E'en at the exit-door turning – charges superfluous calling
>   back – e'en as he descends the steps...

Soon to be lost for aye in the darkness – loth, O so loth to depart!
Garrulous to the very last. (636)

A new, sobering use is here found for the participial form so favoured by Whitman in his prime for exultantly conveying the restless, ceaseless procreant urge of the world. In this instance it functions as a psychological ploy to evade the finality of 'closure'. In extreme old age (for so seventy was for him) Whitman discovers a motive for continuing to write which is different from those offered previously in his poems and prefaces. He writes, it now poignantly emerges, because he is afraid of the final, dead silence after his last full stop, and because his poems are the means of clinging to the company (and the 'communion' as the poem expressively puts it) of the living. It is an account by Whitman of his relationship to his poetry, and through it with his reader, which is all the more marked by pathos for its contrast with the confident claiming of relationship that fills the clamorous poetry of his prime.

But counterpointing and counterbalancing these motives for old-age poetry there are others prominently advertised in the two Annexes. These texts elsewhere repeatedly insist that they were published primarily as proof of 'undiminished faith' (614), and intended as a 'résumé', a 'repetition' (614). Sparse leaves they might be, but 'confirming all the rest' (633) of *Leaves of Grass*. Puzzling over the reasons why 'folks dwell so fondly on the last words, advice, appearance, of the departing', pointing out that 'those last words are not samples of the best, which involve vitality at its full, and balance, and perfect control and scope', Whitman finally concluded that dying words 'are valuable beyond measure to confirm and endorse the varied train, facts, theories and faith of the whole preceding life' (639).[3] Published as a footnote to the poetic text, this statement forms part of that running argument with himself which Whitman conducted throughout his last years, over whether he should continue to write and publish or not. Characteristically he managed to make fine public and literary capital out of these doubts themselves, exploiting their dramatic potential in both his poetry and his prefaces. One of the bright cluster of qualities that had belonged to Whitman as a poet in his prime remained with him in his declining years: the gift for fashioning in poetry and out of his life a compelling dramatic personality. The result is not only a scatter of fine individual poems but a masterly, or old-masterly performance; the gradual construction of a character of himself in old age.

Whitman's ways of describing or addressing himself to his broken body greatly contribute to this achievement and are particularly worth remarking. There is his impatience at his own querulousness, and fear that his life may be dishonoured by weakness at the last:

> As I sit writing here, sick and grown old,
> Not my least burden is that dulness of the years, querilities,
> Ungracious glooms, aches, lethargy, constipation,
>   whispering *ennui*,
> May filter in my daily songs (614)

As he wonders what his 70th year will bring he displays a pitilessly bleak self-knowledge:

>   Wilt stir the waters yet?
> Or haply cut me short for good? Or leave me here as now,
> Dull, parrot-like and old, with crack'd voice harping,
>   screeching? (615)

And there is his shockingly brutal recognition of the isolating nature of physical decline:

>   a torpid pulse, a brain unnerv'd,
> Old age land-lock'd within its winter bay – (cold, cold, O cold!)
> These snowy hairs, my feeble arms, my frozen feet. (623)

The cool detachment of such self-appraisal, the fastidious distaste he shows for his own grotesqueness, is reminiscent of the tone of Ben Jonson's 'My Picture Left in Scotland':

> Oh, but my conscious feares,
>   That flie my thoughts betweene,
>   Tell me that she hath seene
>   My hundreds of gray haires,
>   Told seven and fortie yeares.
> Read so much weast, as she cannot imbrace
> My mountaine belly, and my rockie face,
> And all these through her eyes, have stopt her eares.[4]

Recognising in Jonson's poem a rare and wry honesty of self-recognition, W. B. Yeats tried to emulate it in his late poetry. And Whitman, too, strove to attain a similarly naked, unaccommodated vision of his drastically reduced physical condition in some of the poems in his two late Annexes.

A little masterpiece of this kind is 'The Dismantled Ship':

In some unused lagoon, some nameless bay,
On sluggish, lonesome waters, anchor'd near the shore,
An old, dismasted, gray and batter'd ship, disabled, done,
After free voyages to all the seas of earth, haul'd up at last and
    hawser'd tight,
Lies rusting, mouldering (634)

Its effectiveness, like that of the later Imagist poetry to which it bears a passing resemblance, lies in its apparent innocence of its own power of suggestion. That is what saves it from sentimentality, as Whitman resists the impulse to license certain feelings in himself about his condition. In his description of the ship, he concentrates, and is thus able to shed, all his feelings of physical helplessness, uselessness, worthlessness and loneliness. At the same time he refuses to identify with those feelings outright by representing himself as a dismantled ship. Whitman resists the lure of such self-indulgent despair: 'I know, divine deceitful ones, your glamour's seeming', as he puts it in 'Fancies at Navesink' (619).

The continuing alertness of mind in Whitman to which 'The Dismantled Ship' implicitly testifies is an indispensable source of the dramatic life and moral honesty of the best of the late poems. As an old man, he continues, as far as his flagging mental energy will permit, to be an explorer of his many-charactered old age. He can use a poem not only to confirm another but also to qualify, or even contradict, the impressions already made. 'You Lingering Sparse Leaves of Me' (633) sensitively works out a comparison between his late poems and the 'lingering sparse leaves … on winter-nearing boughs'. 'The faithfulest – hardiest – last': the pun there at the end contributes its quiet, unassertive strength to the conclusion. But the next poem deliberately, startlingly, works the same simile out to a very different purpose, partly in the spirit of a kind of rebuke to, or at least reaction against, his previous accept-ance (half-melancholy, half-defiant) of his diminished self. The very first line of this poem (532) contains unemphasised within it the dynamics of vision of the whole poem: 'Not meager, latent boughs alone, O songs! (scaly and bare, like eagles' talons)'.

That simile within a simile is very interesting: the songs may be like winter boughs bare as eagles' talons – but then eagles' talons are themselves instinct with power. In other words, the second simile, while apparently obediently echoing and buttressing the first, has without registering the fact effected a radical shift of emphasis which completely subverts, and even inverts, the original meaning. It is a beautiful example of how a poem can remain secretly faithful and obedient to the deepest inclination of the poet's meaning rather than serve his conscious will. It is a kind of Freudian slip through which the inner self betrays its secret stubborn obsession with joy and proves itself to be incorrigibly defiant and irredeemably hopeful. And the rest of the poem proceeds, all unconscious of having been anticipated, to produce hope in its own more sober way out of the original image. Life is represented as latent in these meagre poems, ready to blossom at the first touch of spring. It is one of Whitman's last and most touching images for the meeting between his poems and some future reader. It is now enough for him to believe that his 'leaves' may become 'verdant' again and rejuvenated – 'the stalwart limbs of trees emerging': implicit in the whole description, and adding a generosity of tone to it, is Whitman's recognition that such spring and summer can never return for him.

There is, then, genuine affirmation to be found in some of these poems which bring George Herbert to mind:

> Go birds of spring: let winter have his fee;
> Let a bleak paleness chalk the doore,
> So all within be livelier then before.[5]

Feelings about old age similar to these marvellous and ringing lines of Herbert's give rise to two particularly fine poems in these collections. One is 'Sounds of Winter' (646), where the senses quietly harvest the richly distinctive sounds and sights of winter and leave the mind to glean a meaning of its own at the end. 'Where are the songs of Spring? ... Think not of them, thou hast thy music too':[6] Keats's famous encouragement to another season is very much in the spirit of Whitman's tribute to winter, and both poets affectionately emphasise the kindliest aspects of their respective seasons.

But there is one remarkable poem in which Whitman, accepting all that the natural and human season can bring, uncompromisingly celebrates the very wintriness of winter. 'Of that Blithe Throat of Thine' (623) is perhaps the old Whitman's greatest vindication of the philosophy of life which he had propounded so confidently in his youth: the wholehearted commitment of oneself to physical existence in all its aspects and implications because it is God-given. The poem is a quiet triumph, all the more impressive for Whitman's refusal to celebrate it. Nothing better distinguishes him from other life-worshippers such as Hemingway than his tough-spirited insistence on persisting in joy:

> Not summer's zones alone – not chants of youth, or south's
> warm tides alone,
> But held by sluggish floes, pack'd in the northern ice, the
> cumulus of years,
> These with gay heart I also sing. (623)

In this one poem, at least, Whitman acquires what Wallace Stevens called 'a mind of winter'.[7]

These last poems are offered by Whitman, in impressive part, as final incontrovertible testimony that his seasoned central vision is apt for all seasons. They may therefore seem entirely dependent on *Leaves of Grass* for their meaning. But that is not the case. The two annexes may be regarded as the flying buttresses of the massive edifice of *Leaves of Grass*, humbly designed to take the potentially oppressive weight of the earthward thrusts of its soaring central affirmations. Many different elements have contributed towards the fashioning of these buttresses, and one of them, it seems to me, is the relationship between Whitman's democratic ideology of ageing and the old age writings of a giant rival figure who continued to trouble his dreams.

II

Five days before he died, Whitman startled his young friend and amanuensis Horace Traubel. Racked by pain, his voice often choked and reduced to a whisper, he was lying helpless on his bed, when

Suddenly, his voice rose, quite firm and easy again for a minute at the start, then lapsing into the disastrous struggle now becoming his norm. 'Horace,' he said – and his voice stirred me by a something mandatory in his tone, 'Horace, if I wrote anything more, I would compare Tennyson, Whittier and me, dwelling quite a bit on the three ways we each have treated the death subject: Tennyson in 'Crossing the Bar', Whittier in 'Driftwood' – both ecclesiastical and theoretical – and my 'Good-Bye, My Fancy' – based, absorbed in, the natural. That that I've just said is quite a significant' – here he broke off from vain effort to say more.[8]

Obsessed with his great English contemporary to the very last, Whitman continued, in the unabated anxiety of his long jealous rivalry with Tennyson, to travesty the relation between them as poets. As Christopher Ricks has noted, far from being conventionally 'ecclesiastical', the Laureate's religious faith in old age 'remained humane and disconcertingly unorthodox'. The old man was said to have remarked, 'There's a something that watches over us; and our individuality; and our individuality endures; that's my faith, and that's all my faith.'[9] Thus phrased, it seems a faith as vague, as hetorodox, and as un-'theoretical' as Whitman's own.

But Whitman's very faith in himself as poet had long been predicated on an initially violent, but later much more conciliatory, repudiation of everything Tennyson represented. The compelling complex narrative of this unreciprocated obsession has been succinctly summarised by the editors of Whitman's *Notebooks and Unpublished Prose Manuscripts* in the form of a note on several scraps of prose about Tennyson from the 1860s and 1870s.[10] These fragments are themselves eloquent testimony to the stammering intensity of Whitman's Tennysonian obsession, since they are the debris of his repeated attempts to piece together a statement about the English poet sufficiently powerful to exorcise his ghost.[11]

Even more than Emerson, to whom he felt an uneasy filial tie, and Carlyle, who was a worthy but not dangerous opponent, Tennyson was the contemporary who troubled WW. At the beginning of his career he announced anonymously...that he was about to replace the kind of poetry Tennyson represented and kept saying the same thing for the next twenty years. By 1870,

he seems not to have been so sure. Possibly his growing awareness that his country was not accepting him led to a number of
mildly foolish efforts to promote himself ... For all these reasons
he felt a deep need for Tennyson's approbation and in 1871 sent
him books through a mutual acquaintance ... Tennyson was
courageous and understood the *Leaves* well enough to pronounce
that they had 'go' ... WW was immensely and pathetically proud
of this approbation from the Highest Source. (*NUPM* 5, 1760)

Indeed, to track Whitman's relations with Tennyson during the last
two decades of his life through the Correspondence and the Traubel
volumes is not infrequently to be embarrassed by the painful evidence of
the American's repeated, and sometimes desperate, attempts to assure
others, but primarily himself, of the high regard in which he was held
by the Englishman.

It was, of course, Whitman himself who had made the first direct
overtures by sending Tennyson a sample of his work in late 1870, and
when he received a polite acknowledgement, he could not stop boasting
to his friends that the Laureate had even gone so far as to invite him to
visit. For the next five years, he took immense pride in the fact that he
received regular, politely cordial letters from the Englishman; but then
he did not hear for two and fretted so terribly that he sent Tennyson a
pitiful, half-beseeching rebuke.[12] Having tried unsuccessfully in 1885 to
persuade William Sloane Kennedy to write a 'criticism on Tennyson
and Walt Whitman' he produced one himself less than two years later
(*C3*, 391). Anxious as ever to make Tennyson immediately aware of
what he'd written, he sent him a copy, exulting when he received a
courteous acknowledgement: 'Is not this the only instance known',
he eagerly enquired, 'of the English Laureate formally "noticing a
notice"?'[13] And when his determined disciple, R. M. Bucke, proposed
paying a visit to the by then extremely frail, mentally confused and
mostly bedridden Tennyson, Whitman furnished him with a personal
introduction. Learning from Bucke that the poet's family was under
doctors' orders to exclude all visitors, Whitman held his breath to see
whether his own name and recommendation would be sufficient to
work a rare open sesame. Always harbouring deep – and very well-
founded – misgivings about whether or not Tennyson really did regard
him as his poetic equal, Whitman clearly felt that this was the moment

of conclusive proof. So when Bucke proudly reported that not only had he been granted the rare privilege of a brief audience but the poet's son, Hallam, had uttered bland commendations of Whitman, he was delighted. Yet he remained 'cute' enough not to be wholly convinced. Bucke himself had conceded in his report that 'none of the Tennysons I imagine ... have read you as really to understand you or what you are after – but have read you enough to know in a more or less vague way that you are a great force in this modern world'.[14]

Bucke's words were confirmation of a suspicion long held by Whitman and clearly voiced on 15 April 1888, 'I don't think [Tennyson] ever quite makes me out.' 'But,' he had then hopefully added, 'he thinks I belong: perhaps that is enough – all I ought to expect.'[15] It was much more, alas, than was actually the case. It is just as well that he was never made privy to the kind of blunt remark Tennyson had made only three years previously in private conversation with George Walter Prothero: 'Walt Whitman [is] no real poet.'[16] Contrast such sentiments with Traubel's touching report that 'I remember a letter from Tennyson, surrounded by its ribs of black, redolent with savor of wind and water, a strain of poetry in itself, which Whitman for a long time carried in his vest pocket' (*C8*, 583). In the days after receiving Bucke's report, Whitman continued to worry about where he stood with Tennyson. A letter was forwarded to him, via Bucke, from someone trying to recall the exact words Tennyson had used many years before when talking about Whitman. 'It certainly seems to me,' said the correspondent, 'that his expression was "one of the greatest poets" or "he surely is a great poet" or words to that effect. But I could not be sure of the words or the form of the statement' (*C8*, 441–2). Clutching at the straw offered by Traubel – that the very vagueness of the report was proof of its honesty – Whitman asked for the letter to be left near him overnight, so that he could give it his concentrated attention in an effort to determine exactly what Tennyson had said. 'Oh! yes,' he concluded pitifully, 'I guess there need be no doubt but Tennyson is very friendly towards me – has a genuine admiration, of a sort' (*C8*, 442).

These incidents are worth noting, because they indicate the depth and extent of Whitman's concern with Tennyson during his final years. Whitman scholarship has hitherto concentrated almost exclusively on Tennyson's influence on the early Whitman that even took the form, on occasion, of poetic response. A great admirer of 'Ulysses', Whitman seems in part to have modelled 'Prayer of Columbus' on it, and to have taken from it the trochaic measure for 'Pioneers'; and Ken Price has further suggested that 'Pictures' may have been a kind of reply to 'The Palace of Art'.[17] All such responses are governed, of course, by the model Whitman had early established and thereafter assiduously cultivated, of himself as the ideological opposite of Tennyson, playing democrat to his 'aristocrat' and relegating him to the 'feudal' European past. But then, Whitman knew full well that 'nations or individuals, we surely learn deepest from our unlikeness, from a sincere opponent, from the light thrown even scornfully on dangerous spots and liabilities' (898).

It has already been well understood by scholars that Whitman in his prime drew considerable creative energy from his 'unlikeness' to the likes of Carlyle and of Tennyson. But no attention has been paid to the possibility (to put it no more strongly) that Whitman continued to do so during his final years, when his always uncertain confidence in his poetry began to be seriously sapped by his deteriorating physical condition, the attendant mental stress, and the doubts expressed even by some of those to whom he was closest about his occasional effortful excursions into shockingly short-breathed poetry. '[William] O'Connor kicks against [Sands at Seventy],' he noted in 1888, he 'is unfavorable – seems to regard the new poems as in some sense a contradiction of the old – alien to the earlier poems – as if I had gone back on myself in old age.' That, Whitman insisted, was not the case,

Am I, as some think, losing grip? – taking in my horns? No – no – no: I am sure that could not be. I still wish to be, am, the radical of my stronger days – to be the same uncompromising oracle of democracy – to maintain undimmed the lights of my deepest faith. I am sure I have not gone back on that – sure, sure. The Sands have to be taken as the utterances of an old man – a very old man. I desire that they may be interpreted as confirmations, not denials, of the work that has preceded ... I recognize, have always recognized, the importance of the lusty, strong-limbed, big-bodied American of the Leaves. I do not abate one atom of that belief now, today. But I hold to something more than that, too, and claim a full, not a partial, judgment upon my work.[18]

His old age was to be represented as the old age of an indomitably convinced democrat. And who better than Tennyson, the contemporary author of celebrated old-age poems, to sharpen awareness of what it meant to be, in one's declining years, 'an uncompromising oracle of democracy'?

III

'Dear old man', Tennyson teasingly opened a letter to Whitman in January 1887, before gracefully proceeding to describe it as sent from an 'elder old man' (*C*4, 63). The Laureate was ten years older than his correspondent, and had, in 1885, published a notable collection of 'old age poems'. These attracted the immediate attention of a Whitman who always kept anxiously abreast of Tennyson's poetry, and his response came in the form of the essay 'A Word about Tennyson'. First published in *The Critic* (January 1887), it was incorporated in 1888 into *November Boughs*, where it kept company with 'Sands at Seventy', as if inviting a comparison between 'the old man at Farringford' (1164) and the old man at Camden.

In the consistency of point of view between 'Locksley Hall' and the recently published 'Locksley Hall Sixty Years After' Whitman found confirmation of his own consistent characterisation of Tennyson as the splendidly eloquent, elegiac voice of a dying society. Both poems are 'essentially morbid, heart-broken, finding fault with everything, especially the fact of money's being made (as it ever must be, and perhaps should be) the paramount matter in worldly affairs' (1161). The insouciance of such a statement was somewhat disingenuous, given the ageing Whitman's own rageing's against his dollar-driven America, but then Tennyson acted as a lightning-rod for many of the unacknowledged anxieties and misgivings Whitman had about his country – hence the intensity and complexity of his concern with the 'royal English laureate'. Professing here to believe that 'the course of progressive politics (democracy) is so certain and resistless ... that we can well afford the warning calls, threats, checks, neutralizings, in imaginative literature' (1163), Whitman is able to pronounce that Tennyson, like Carlyle, is a valuable adversary: 'As to his non-democracy, it fits him well, and I like him the better for it. I guess we all like to have (I am sure I do) some one who presents those sides of a thought, or possibility, different from our own' (1163). He then revealingly adds, 'different and yet with a sort of home-likeness'. This is a moment of honest self-knowledge on Whitman's part, before he concludes his essay by condescending to Tennyson, damning him with the faint praise that American readers 'owe to him some of their most agreeable and harmless and healthy hours' (1165). That Whitman should have then sent a copy of this essay post-haste to Tennyson is surely indicative of how blind the anxiety of his obsession had made him to the impression that such a piece – ingratiatingly patronising when it wasn't grandly dismissive – was very likely to make on its unfailingly polite recipient.

In 'Locksley Hall Sixty Years After', the aged Tennyson's blistering commentary on what he regarded as his own bellicose, exploitative, materialistic and degenerate age, the convulsive energy of dark nihilism ('Chaos, Cosmos! Cosmos, Chaos! once again the sickening game' [1364]) moderates into the outrage of social denunciation: 'Is it well that while we range with Science, glorying in the Time,/ City children soak and blacken soul and sense in city slime?/ … There the smouldering fire of fever creeps across the rotted floor,/ And the crowded couch of incest in the warrens of the poor' (1367–8). Through the poem there echoes a 'Poor old voice of eighty crying after voices that have fled!/ All I loved are vanish'd voices, all my steps are on the dead' (1368). The bitter despair in the poetry provoked at least one British reviewer to protest against this 'rhymed recapitulation of the bad-blooded objurgations of gout-stricken Toryism'.[19] And the poem's prediction that 'Demos [would] end in working its own doom' (1363) must certainly have provoked Whitman. Moreover, it is likely that he would have read the poem in the context of a collection in which gloom bleaks through much of the poetry. So in some ways it does through Whitman's, but his manner of expressing it, and of coping with it, are very different – 'democratic' in character (in his terms) as opposed to what he regarded as Tennyson's aristocratic response. For instance, he firmly links his 'ungracious glooms' to his decrepit physical condition with its 'aches, lethargy, constipation, whimpering *ennui*'. Thus, instead of donning the singular mantle of the doomed prophet he appears as everyman, sometimes grumpy victim of those great levellers, the mundane infirmities of body and of mind. Just as, for old age's angry yearnings for lost youth – Tiresias's 'I wish I were as in the years of old' – he substitutes the equanimity of a fondness for 'the meditation of old times resumed – their loves, joys, persons, voyages', thus substituting a model of life as continuity for the model of life as violent rupture. For Whitman, the 'word of the modern, the word En-Masse' meant a faith that 'Nothing is ever really lost, or can be lost' (620). And his fussing over the exact form of the title of the Second Annex (*Good-Bye My Fancy* should not, he insisted, terminate with an exclamation mark, although the poem of the same title did), may be attributed to his wanting to emphasise the matter-of-factness of the salutation. This was because, as he pointedly noted, 'Behind a Good-bye there lurks much of the salutation of another beginning – to me, Development, Continuity, Immortality, Transformation, are the chiefest life-meanings of Nature and Humanity' (639).

However, before further considering such contrasts, perhaps deliberately measured by Whitman, it is worth noticing points of unexpected convergence between his outlook and Tennyson's. The latter's poem 'The Wreck' is a Victorian melodrama about a forced and loveless marriage, resulting in a tragically unloved baby, a passionate adultery and, finally, overpowering guilt. It includes a significant characterisation of the cold husband as follows: 'He would open the books that I prized, and toss them away with a yawn,/ Repelled by the magnet of Art to the which my nature was drawn/ The word of the Poet by whom the deeps of the world are stirr'd./ The music that robes it in language beneath and beyond the word!/ My Shelley would fall from my hands when he cast a contemptuous glance/ Even where he was poring over his Tables of Trade and Finance' (1336). Here, as elsewhere in this late collection, Tennyson the darling of his country despairs at the impotence of his fame, frankly recognising what the older Whitman, too, knew, that poetry changed absolutely nothing in society.

This is a feeling most compellingly worked out by Tennyson in the 'Tiresias' sequence of poems.[20] It begins with a genial Horatian epistle of friendship addressed to his old friend Edward Fitzgerald, famous author of *Omar Khayam*, quietly rejoicing that 'we old friends are still alive,/ And I am nearing seventy-four,/ While you have touched at seventy-five' (1318). The main body of the sequence then follows in the form of the poem 'Tiresias', a product of Tennyson's youth he here resurrects and offers as a gift to Fitzgerald. The theme of this poem is the ancient Tiresias's desperate attempt to convince Menoeceus to sacrifice his own life in order to save Thebes from the dreadful fate that,

the prophet foresees, will otherwise certainly befall it. Tiresias's desperation derives, of course, from the fact that Pallas Athene had inflicted on
him a terrible punishment when he was young for having accidentally
glimpsed her radiant nakedness: 'Henceforth be blind, for thou hast
seen too much,/ And speak the truth that no man may believe' (570).
Such had been his terrible fate ever since – the accursed gift of barren
prophecy, from which he could not escape even when now dwelling in
'oldest age in shadow from the night'. All his long life he had therefore
been condemned to experience 'the faces of the Gods – the wise man's
word,/ Here trampled by the populace underfoot' (574). Repeating in
his old age this story that he had first rehearsed in his youth must,
for Tennyson, have powerfully reinforced his identification with the
ancient, disregarded Tiresias. And this is an experience underlined by
the epilogue to the poem. There Tennyson reveals that Fitzgerald, the
intended recipient of the poem, had died before ever it could be completed and sent. What more poignantly conclusive evidence could be
adduced for the poem's core truth? – that the words of a prophet or a
poet are powerless in the face of life.[21]

Reflections such as these also haunted Whitman in his old age,
evidence again that though his vision may have differed centrally from
that of Tennyson, there were also many 'sort[s] of home-likeness' that
complicated and enriched the picture. Reluctant to express in poems the
racking self-doubts he confessed to Traubel, since (as Tennyson's lines
indicated) that would mean indicting his beloved democratic masses,
he resorted to such indirect expression as 'To Those Who've Failed',
with its revealing mention of 'many a lofty song and picture without
recognition' (613), and 'The Bravest Soldiers' who 'press'd to the front
and fell, unnamed, unknown' (638). Insisting that 'this late-years palsied
old shorn and shell-fish condition of me [was] the indubitable outcome
and growth' of 'those hot, sad, wrenching times' of his war-service
in the Washington hospitals (638), he found repeated expression for
his chronic fear that he (and his democratic vision) had been wholly
ignored by his society in his old-age poems about unwelcome veterans
of past wars who 'amid the current songs of beauty, peace, decorum'
interject the unwelcome false note of 'a reminiscence – (likely 'twill
offend you)' (631).[22]

Primarily, though, Whitman seems to me to have used Tennyson's
old age poems as a foil for his own. Take, for instance, the Englishman's

fondness for seeing in the ocean an image of what he feared most (and therefore denounced most loudly), a vision of the brutal senseless power of a Godless material universe. So, in 'Despair', a married couple seek to drown in the sea their despair at a universe in which they see 'No soul in the heaven above, no soul on the earth below,/ A fiery scroll written over with lamentation and woe' (1300). To such would-be suicides, the Whitman of 'Fancies at Navesink' gives short shrift: 'Some suicide's despairing cry, *Away to the boundless waste, and never again return.*// On to oblivion then!/ On, on, and do your part, ye burying, ebbing tide!/ On for your time, ye furious debouché' (619).

For a Tennyson whose spirit had always been darkly shadowed by the dread that 'Doubt is the lord of this dunghill and crows to the sun and the moon', stability could be kept only by clinging to the belief in a remedying afterlife. Mortal existence, he repeatedly affirms, can only be justified (and then only doubtfully) by the promise of a world to come.[23] And it is here, perhaps, that Whitman was most fruitfully able to oppose his own vision in old age to that of his great rival, by expressing his unqualified commitment (however effortful at times) not to an afterlife but to ongoing life. This, too, he believed to be an expression of a devout democratic relish for every one of life's minute particulars. This might be supposed to have come naturally to the poet who, in his prime, had so unforgettably celebrated 'fog in the air and beetles rolling balls of dung' (51). But there is a different, darker, richer timbre to his old-age affirmations; they radiate a humility in the face of the lustre of 'the commonplace'. To ward off the prostration that threatened him after the death of his beloved mother, following as it did hard on the heels of his first paralytic stroke, Whitman had assiduously trained himself to live in the moment, to magnify its gifts. 'The trick is, I find, to tone your wants and tastes low down enough, and to make much of negatives, and of mere daylight and the skies' (780). Accompanying the course of physical rehabilitation he underwent at Timber Creek was a therapeutic course of mental and spiritual re-education, a gradual teaching of each of his senses to appreciate how their powers of apprehending the world could be paradoxically enlarged by the reduction of physical mobility and the straitening of circumstance. He concentrated intensely on 'distilling the present hour' (809). The result was a new kind of writing, which should be recognised as being as much of an achievement as, say, the new poetic style William Carlos Williams so arduously and remarkably produced in the aftermath of his own stroke. The bent form of Wordsworth's Old Cumberland Beggar, proceeding at snail's pace, sees not 'hill and dale,/ and the blue sky' but 'some straw/ Some scattered leaf, or marks which, in one track,/ The nails of cart or chariot-wheel have left/ Impressed on the white road'.[24] Unconsidered trifles came to bulk similarly large in the stricken Whitman's experience, and they are registered, in *Specimen Days*, in the luminous spareness of a prose that is the real poetry of his post-war period:

> autumn leaves, the cool dry air, the faint aroma, – crows cawing in the distance – two great buzzards wheeling gracefully and slowly far up there – the occasional murmur of the wind, some-times quite gently, then threatening through the trees – a gang of farm-laborers loading corn-stalks in a field in sight, and the patient horses waiting (794).

Not, however, until his late annexes, and little pieces of Adamic purity of wonder like 'Out of May's Shows Selected', does he himself seem to have realised that such writing constituted the different poetry of his old age.[25]

> Apple orchards, the trees all cover'd with blossoms:
> Wheat fields carpeted far and near in vital emerald green:
> The eternal, exhaustless freshness of each early morning;
> The yellow, golden, transparent haze of the warm
>   afternoon sun;
> The aspiring lilac bushes with profuse purple or white
>   flowers (617).

The self-contained, end-stopped lines – syntactically and experientially the very opposite of the early writing, with its hectic forward momen-tum – indicate the self-sufficiency, and sufficiency for the self, of each discrete sensation. 'The simple shows, the delicate miracles of earth', says Whitman again in 'Soon Shall the Winter's Foil Be Here', are returned so that 'Thine eyes, ears – all thy best attributes – all that takes cognizance of natural beauty,/ Shall wake and fill' (630). In old age, his senses are still the means, as they were in 'Song of Myself', to fulfil-ment; the realising of self through a coming alive to the sensory world.

No wonder, then, that in wishing his poems on 'the death subject' to be contrasted with those of Tennyson, the dying Whitman stressed that his be recognised as 'based, absorbed in, the natural'. He had, no doubt, forgotten that he had himself already written the very essay he was urging Traubel to write. His 'A Death-Bouquet' (1266–8) was a brief comparison of the ways death had been treated by several poets, including Whittier and Tennyson (he singled out the very recently published 'Crossing the Bar'). Noting that they, and poets as ancient as Phrynichus of 'old Athens', had become absorbed in contemplating the movement of tides and of ships as the most richly suggestive tropes for dying, he wryly asked 'Am I starting the sail-craft of poets in line?' (1267). Indeed he was, and very much, it seems, with a view to adding his own vessels to this stately textual procession. The piece concludes with his little poem 'Now, land and life, finalé, and farewell!' (1268). And in the light of the train of thought followed in this brief essay, it seems reasonable to suggest that at least two of the poems in *Good-Bye My Fancy*, 'Sail Out for Good, Eidólon Yacht!' and 'Old Age's Ship & Crafty Death's', are exercises in extending this tradition he had so sympathetically identified. Moreover, published as they were in 1891, they seem specifically to involve conversations with 'Crossing the Bar' (1888). For the fade-out of the poem in which Tennyson gently acquiesces in dying, Whitman, ever the ebullient indomitable democratic individualist, pointedly substituted a robust yo-ho! of 'challenge and defiance – flags and flaunting pennants added,/ As we take to the open – take to the deepest, freest waters' (642).

In a piece published in *Lippincott's Magazine* to coincide with the appearance of *Good-Bye my Fancy* he had boasted that 'every page of my poetic or attempt at poetic utterance therefore smacks of the living physical identity' (1345). While this 'new last cluster' is 'a lot of tremolos about old age', and 'the physical just lingers but almost vanishes', the book 'is garrulous, irascible (like old Lear)'. He was right so to characterise it, as he was also right to insist that, to the very last, his poems were deliberately composed 'in style often offensive to the conventions' (1345). And as his late writing and recorded oral comments indicate, he associated the conventional approach to old age and dying with Tennyson. Indeed, one of the essays he included in *Good-Bye my Fancy* itself notes that Tennyson, 'over eighty years old', had 'sent out long since a fresh volume, which the English-speaking Old and New Worlds are yet reading'. He then reiterated his view of the Laureate's poetry, that it was 'flowery' and the author 'the poetic cream-skimmer of our age's melody, *ennui* and polish' (1255). In going on to associate Tennyson with Shakespeare he was paying him a back-handed compliment, at once advertising his greatness and drawing attention to his superannuation. The same strategy is followed even in the poems of *Sands at Seventy*, when, in 'To Get the Final Lilt of Songs', he speaks of the kind of wisdom granted old age – 'to know the mighty ones/ Job, Homer, Eschylus, Dante, Shakespeare, Tennyson, Emerson' (624). Tennyson is pointedly included there among the dead, as he was in 'Song of the Exposition': 'Pass'd! pass'd! for me, forever pass'd, that once so mighty world, now void, inanimate, phantom world, .../ Blazon'd with Shakespeare's purples page,/ And dirged by Tennyson's sweet sad rhyme' (343).

IV

Whitman was a consummate salesman and inveterate self-publicist to the last. In a late reprise of the kind of feyness he had most famously exhibited in 'Calamus', he enticingly offered *Good-Bye my Fancy* to his readers as a mystery wrapped up in a riddle: 'It will have to be ciphered and ciphered out long – and is probably in some respects the most curious part of its author's baffling works' (1345). Perhaps. What this essay has, at least suggested, is that it might be worth considering the possibility that concealed in the two late annexes was Whitman's obsessive conversation with Tennyson, 'the boss of us all' and the one great contemporary figure who contested with him the privilege of being the supreme poet of old age. And there is one possible final twist to their poetic relationship. The very last poem Whitman completed was 'A Thought of Columbus', the piece he handed to Traubel just ten days before his death in which, aware of himself as 'A flutter at the darkness' edge as if old Time's and Space's secret near revealing', Whitman reverses his life-long practice of addressing the future and addresses instead this phantom from the past in a final paradoxically prophetic act of homage and of (self-) acclamation.

What is interesting for present purposes is that Whitman had long associated Columbus with Tennyson. As has been noted, his own 'Prayer of Columbus' had been modelled on Tennyson's 'Ulysses'. A few years later Tennyson had himself, as Whitman could surely not have failed to notice, published his own 'Columbus'. And then, on 4 April 1891, Traubel records Whitman's warm approval of the following notice that had appeared in the *Illustrated American*:

OUR POET LAUREATE – That was a very foolish thought of the managers of the World's Fair – to ask a poem from Lord Tennyson in honor of the occasion.

Tennyson is a great man. But his day is over. His recent work – especially the last song. 'To Sleep!' – has detracted from rather than added to his reputation. Better, far better, he should relapse into silence. Moreover, he is a foreigner – a member, too, of the nation which scorned Columbus and refused his proffer of a new world. A Spaniard, even an Italian, would be better. Among the exponents of the latter-day renaissance of song in either country, it might be possible to find one who could do justice to Columbus, to Chicago, to America.

But best of all would be an American poet. The children of the New World, which Columbus revealed to the Old, are best fitted to celebrate the glories of the new dispensation.

Walt Whitman would be the ideal choice. He is an American, a democrat in the largest and best sense of the word, a son of the soil. He could give us a splendid chant, full of virility and breadth and wisdom. But we have not yet reached the ideal stage where we can appreciate him or his true worth. Lowell is a choice that would better please the more finical and dainty and scholarly mind. (C 8, 126)

The editors of the Comprehensive Reader's edition of *Leaves of Grass* note that the Columbus poem Whitman handed to Traubel at the very end of his life consisted of several fragments, some of which dated back to 1891 – the date of this notice.[26] One wonders, therefore, whether that last poem might not after all be Whitman's final act of engagement with – and triumph over – his great rival, Tennyson. Because in this poem, Whitman pointedly lays claim to the privilege, as American poet, of being Columbus's heir. In his long (one-sided) argument with Tennyson, Whitman may thus have ensured he had the very last word. And if his last spoken words are reputed to have been a request to be turned on his waterbed – the simple, pitiful, 'Shift, Warry' – then the last words he authorised for publication were words of tribute to the great 'Discoverer' who had unknowingly called a new, modern, democratic world into being:

> (An added word yet to my song, far Discoverer, as ne'er before
>   sent back to son of earth –
> If still thou hearest, hear me,
> Voicing as now – lands, races, arts, bravas to thee,
> O'er the long backward path to thee – one vast consensus,
>   north, south, east, west,
> Soul plaudits! acclamation! reverent echoes!
> One manifold, huge memory to thee! oceans and lands!
> The modern world to thee and thought of thee!) (*LGRE*, 582)

As the heir of Columbus, Whitman laid claim himself to being a 'Discoverer', as Tennyson was not. 'For all these new and evolutionary facts,' he wrote, surveying the dying nineteenth century in his late essay *A Backward Glance O'er Travel'd Roads*, and for all the new 'meanings, purposes, new poetic messages, new forms, expressions are inevitable' (659). In his prime, Whitman had altered expression repeatedly, as epic, elegy, war poetry, love poetry all assumed new, democratic forms in his work. And now, at life's end, he succeeded in working one final miracle of transformation, producing a democratic poetry of old age. It did not, however, take the form he had longed for. To him was denied that mellow serenity and wisdom in age that, he had so long dreamt, would be the finest expression of the democratic spirit. Lacking that, he instead turned his very condition – paralysed, exhausted but indomitable – into the physical sign of the as yet unfulfilled promise of American democratic society. His old age poetry faithfully recorded this truth and, greatly reduced in power and scope though he full well knew it to be, it retained a shy hold on his affections. As he wistfully remarked to Traubel, 'Howells, James and some others appear to think I rest my philosophy, my democracy, upon braggadocio, noise, rough assertion, such integers'. It is a tendency that, despite the best efforts of Randall Jarrell and many others, has persisted to the present day. But, he then added, 'while I would not be afraid to assent to this as a part of the truth I still insist that I am on the whole to be thought of in other terms' (*C1*, 272). It is a telling remark, all the more compelling because it is uttered so quietly and modestly. No wonder that he therefore warmed to Traubel's speaking of the 'dignity' of *Sands at Seventy*. And, in the light of such comments, it is perhaps time that we, however belatedly, take the advice Traubel gave in an Appendix he published after Whitman's death, to read the old age poems 'as indicating how this giant man, sitting here in the freedom which no physical disorder can destroy, is establishing a very heaven of purposeful stars' (*C8*, 586).

Notes

First published as 'Whitman, Tennyson, and the Poetry of Old Age', in Stephen Burt and Nick Halpern (eds), *Something Understood. Essays and Poetry for Helen Vendler* (Charlottesville: University of Virginia Press, 2009), pp. 161–82. I am grateful to Larry Buell, Alan Trachtenberg and Gerhard Joseph for their advice on an earlier version of this essay. The first section is based on material first published in 'A Study of Whitman's Late Poetry', *Walt Whitman Review*, 27/1 (March 1981), 3–14.

1. 'Ash Wednesday', in *T. S. Eliot: Collected Poems, 1909–1962* (London: Faber and Faber, 1963), p. 95.

2. All quotations from Whitman's poetry and prose, unless otherwise stated, are taken from Justin Kaplan (ed.), *Walt Whitman's Complete Poetry and Collected Prose* (New York: The Library of America, 1982). Subsequent page numbers will appear in the text; here, p. 653.

3. Whitman's responses to dying and to death are subtly considered by Harold Aspiz in *So Long! Walt Whitman's Poetry of Death* (Tuscaloosa: University of Alabama Press, 2004).

4. George Burke Johnston (ed.), *Poems of Ben Jonson* (London: Routledge and Kegan Paul, The Muses Library, 1962), p. 128.

5. 'The Forerunners', in F. E. Hutchinson (ed.), *The Works of George Herbert* (London: Oxford University Press, 1971), p. 177.

6. 'To Autumn', in H. W. Garrod (ed.), *The Poems of John Keats* (London: Oxford University Press, 1966), p. 219.

7. 'The Snow Man', *Collected Poems of Wallace Stevens* (London: Faber, 1969), p. 9.

8. Horace Traubel, *With Walt Whitman in Camden* 9 (1 October 1891–3 April 1892), ed. Jeanne Chapman and Robert MacIsaac (Oregon House, CA: W. L. Bentley Books, 1996), p. 576.

9. Christopher Ricks, *Tennyson* (London: Macmillan, 1972), p. 296.

10. Edward F. Grier (ed.), *Walt Whitman: Notebooks and Unpublished Prose Manuscripts* 5 (New York: New York University Press, 1984), pp. 1757–68 [hereafter, NUPM]. For the mixed reception the US afforded to Tennyson's earlier poetry, see John

Olin Eidson, *Tennyson in America: his reputation and influence from 1827 to 1858* (Athens: University of Georgia Press, 1943). The relationship between Tennyson and Whitman is usefully outlined by Harold Blodgett in *Walt Whitman in England* (Ithaca, NY: Cornell University Press, 1934), pp. 122–35. And while theirs was in many respects a complex rivalry, the earlier Whitman was nevertheless indebted to the Englishman, not least for a poetry that had revealed to him the potentialities of soundscapes and of metric. See Laurence Buell's important essay 'Walt Whitman as an Eminent Victorian', in Susan Belasco, Ed Folsom and Kenneth M. Price (eds), *Leaves of Grass: The Sesquicentennial Essays* (Lincoln: University of Nebraska Press, 2007), pp. 282–98.

11. It is interesting to note Christopher Ricks's opinion that 'The best criticism of Tennyson is by Walt Whitman', *Tennyson*, p. 312.

12. Edwin Haviland Miller (ed.), *Walt Whitman: The Correspondence* 3 (1876–85) (New York: New York University Press, 1964), pp. 52, 133 [hereafter page numbers will appear in the text prefaced by *C3*]. Edwin Haviland Miller (ed.), *Walt Whitman: The Correspondence* 2 (1868–75) (New York: New York University Press, 1961), p. 125. Whitman first heard from Tennyson in July 1871.

13. Edwin Haviland Miller (ed.), *Walt Whitman: The Correspondence* 4 (1886–9) (New York: New York University Press, 1969), p. 76.

14. Horace Traubel, *With Walt Whitman in Camden* 8 (11 February 1891–30 September 1891), ed. Jeanne Chapman and Robert MacIsaac (Oregon House, CA: Bentley Books, 1996), p. 431 [hereafter page numbers will appear in the text prefaced by *C8*].

15. Horace Traubel, *With Walt Whitman in Camden* 1 (New York: Rowman and Littlefield, 1961), p. 36.

16. Cecil Y. Lang and Edgar F. Shannon, Jr. (eds), *The Letters of Alfred Lord Tennyson* 3 (Oxford: Clarendon Press, 1990), p. 332.

17. For Tennyson's influence on Whitman see Floyd Stovall, *The Foreground of Leaves of Grass* (Charlottesville: University of Virginia, 1974). Kenneth M. Price, *Walt Whitman and Tradition: the poet in his century* (New Haven, CN: Yale University Press, 1990). See also the relevant entry in J. R. LeMaster and Donald D. Kummings, *Walt Whitman: An Encyclopedia* (New York and London: Garland Publishing, 1998).

18. Horace Traubel, *With Walt Whitman in Camden* 2 (16 July 1888–31 October 1888) (New York: Rowman and Littlefield, 1961), p. 9.

19. J. M. Robertson, 'The Art of Tennyson' (1889), in John D. Jump (ed.), *Tennyson: the Critical Heritage* (London: Routledge and Kegan Paul, 1967), p. 412.

20. It is noteworthy that Whitman scribbled some notes for Bucke on the verso of pages from the 1885 *Tiresia* (*NUPM*, 1536). It therefore seems reasonably safe to assume his familiarity with this text.

21. Another poem relevant to this theme is 'The Dead Prophet', an astonishing attack on Froude for publishing a biography that revealed the clay feet of one of

Tennyson's idols, Carlyle: 'Dumb on the winter heath he lay,/ His friends had stript him bare,/ And rolled his nakedness everyway/ That all the crowd might stare.' Quotations from Tennyson's poems are from *Alfred Lord Tennyson, The Poems of Tennyson*, ed. Christopher Ricks (Harlow: Longmans, 1969); here, p. 1324.

22. Whitman also had another motive for thus accounting for his physical condition in old age: '"That which you told me the other day – that some, even of our fellows, question whether this paralysis came of the war, was not the result of the youthful" – he hesitated and laughed – "indiscretions, so to say – that was news to me. Yet it is not the worst that has done duty against me"' (*C8*, 79).

23. Tennyson's struggle with himself, even in old age, to overcome the temptations of a nihilistic atheism is powerfully expressed in 'The Ancient Sage' (1349). As for his imaging of old age, in personal correspondence the Tennyson scholar Professor Gerhard Joseph shrewdly noted for me that Tennyson 'adopted "the mask of great age" (as W. D. Paden first called it in *Tennyson in Egypt: a Study of the imagery in hie earlier works*) as a juvenilian melancholic pose that he carried into his mature poetry, so that there's always something more or less theatrical to Tennyson's old age poems from, say, "Ulysses" on down[.] Quite different from Whitman?'

24. William Wordsworth, *Wordsworth: Poetical Works*, ed. Thomas Hutchinson, revd Ernest de Selincourt (Oxford: Oxford University Press, 1969), p. 443.

25. The equivalently affirmative old-age piece by Tennyson is 'Early Spring', a lovely lyric relishing the way 'the Heavenly Power/ Makes all things new,/ And domes the red-plumed hills/ With living blue' (1314). But this is a reworking of an early (1834) poem.

26. Harold W. Blodgett and Sculley Bradley (eds), *Leaves of Grass: Reader's Edition* (New York: New York University Press, 1965), 581 [henceforth *LGRE*].

The Pioneer:
D. H. Lawrence's Whitman

'Whitman, the great poet, has meant so much to me. Whitman, the one man breaking a way ahead. Whitman the one pioneer. And only Whitman. No English pioneers, no French.'[1] I opened my extensive discussion of the complex relationship between Lawrence and Whitman in *Transatlantic Connections* with that familiar assertion from the final version of *Studies in Classic American Literature* published in 1923.[2] And in the chapter that followed, I particularly emphasised how the image of Whitman with which Lawrence obsessively and viscerally engaged over a crucial decade in his own development as a writer was in significant part the selective and distorted image of him mediated by his many contemporary admirers on the Left in England. 'The English Whitman that most concerned Lawrence', I suggested, could be said to include the Democratic Whitman (beloved alike of Reform Liberals and Socialists), Comrade Whitman (the darling of Socialists and gays), the loving Whitman (attractive to more conventional, mainstream progressives such as Amy Locke), Whitman the Nature Poet (also sentimentally admired by mainstream readers), the Prophetic Whitman (acclaimed by any number of progressive movements), and the Cosmic Whitman of some of his more ecstatic adherents. Furthermore, I suggested, Lawrence's engagement with these, and through them with Whitman, took an oppositional and dialectical form much influenced by his contemporary reading of Nietzsche, Heraclitus – and of course *The Marriage of Heaven and Hell* with its famous maxim: 'Without contraries is no progression.' Lawrence's seemingly uncanny affinity with Whitman, I finally concluded, owed much to the symmetries not only between the deep structure of their respective natures but also between their respective socio-cultural situations. Their relationship could therefore be characterised as that of 'secret sharers', in Joseph Conrad's suggestive phrase.

But while in that chapter I endeavoured to address a very wide range of affinities between Whitman and Lawrence, I also had to admit that the approach I had chosen to adopt had one very obvious and very serious limitation. It failed to take into account the extraordinary creative issue of Lawrence's involvement with Whitman, particularly as expressed in and through the Englishman's poetry. In short, Lawrence is surely the only English writer of genius to have turned his obsession with the American into a poetry distinguished not by its derivativeness but by its astonishing originality – an originality in part mysteriously, and as we shall see paradoxically, enabled, rather than disabled as was the case with lesser writers, by his great predecessor. It may very well be a classic instance of Bloom's celebrated theory of the Anxiety of Influence, but I shall deliberately avoid any neat application of Bloom's model in what follows.[3]

Recent Lawrence scholarship has thrown enticing new light on two interestingly connected Lawrence texts, *Look! We Have Come Through!* and *Studies in Classic American Literature*. As Mark Kinkead-Weekes has shown, *Look! We Have Come Through!* may contain a substantial number of poems written from 1912–13 onwards, but it nevertheless remains in essential respects a work of 1917, since Lawrence revised all the existing texts in that year during the course of adding new material.[4] And while the poems undoubtedly originated in intimate marital experiences, the revisions of 1917 serve to emphasise the fictional, dramatic character of the collection in its published form and the representative nature of its testimony.

The volume may now clearly be seen as reflecting Lawrence's ideas of male-female and of male-male relationship in the specific form in which those restlessly evolving ideas existed in 1917, at a turbulent time in his life when he was desperately adjusting his understanding of love in the light of his tumultuous marriage to Frieda, while also struggling to come to terms with his own bisexuality and with the continuing magnetic pull of his relationship to his dead mother. And, as Mark Kinkead-Weekes has indicated, *Look! We Have Come Through!* bears the marks of the reading Lawrence had recently done, most notably the American texts and authors he had been exploring for the project that eventually became *Studies in Classic American Literature*. Of those authors, the one who most strongly and permanently fascinated Lawrence was, of course, Walt Whitman.

By 1917, this fascination had a 'long foreground', to quote the celebrated phrase Emerson applied in 1855 to a *Leaves of Grass* whose complex genesis he was acute enough to recognise. Although Lawrence first quotes from Whitman in *The White Peacock* (1911), correspondence with Jessie Chambers allows us to trace his familiarity with the poet back at least as far as 1908, and, as I have attempted to demonstrate in *Transatlantic Connections*, the terms on which he engaged with Whitman may, at least in part, have been heavily influenced by the discussions of the American's writings and philosophy that were widespread in radical Liberal and Socialist circles during the first decade of the twentieth century. In particular, Lawrence may have been reacting, however unconsciously, against the images of Whitman that had been circulating in the pages of *The New Age*, the influential intellectual journal that Lawrence is known to have favoured at this time. Until recently, the earliest draft known to be extant of Lawrence's historic Whitman essay for *Studies in Classic American Literature* was that written in 1921. But Lawrence scholarship has now unearthed an earlier version of 1919, available in the new Cambridge edition of *Studies*, which leaves only the version known to have been completed in 1918 still unaccounted for. Taken in conjunction with Lawrence's important comments on Whitman to Henry Savage in December 1913, the 1919 essay allows us to map *Look! We Have Come Through!* more clearly than before onto Lawrence's five-year obsession with the American's writing.

Valuable work on Whitman as 'a major force behind the poetry' in this volume has, of course, already been done. For instance, Roberts W. French has well noted the importance to Lawrence of Whitman as an extender of limits, as a pioneering spirit 'adventurous, unashamed, tenacious, relentless in its pursuits, firm in its convictions', and as a prophet with 'a commanding sense of human possibility'.[5] As *Look! We Have Come Through!* makes clear, Lawrence shared Whitman's belief that 'the greatest poet is necessarily a teacher'. And since the lesson both poets sought to teach was the value of the passing moment, the incomparable immediacy of lived experience, they scorned the laboured artifice of traditional art, and embraced an aesthetics of directness, incompleteness and spontaneity of utterance. As French further explains, it was, indeed, Whitman who had primarily educated the Lawrence of *Look! We Have Come Through!*, with its 'quick nervous rhythms' (111), in the rhetoric of spontaneity, which Lawrence recognised was a technique necessary for exploring the charged erotic aspects of male-female and male-male relationship. But at the same time, there was a fundamental difference between the poets' respective concepts of spontaneity: 'Whitman ... was much more open and receptive, much more willing to give of himself, in his relationships than Lawrence, who seemed always to be trying to determine how he could form deep attachments and at the same time retain his fierce independence' (109).

Confirmation that Whitman's aesthetics of spontaneity had excited Lawrence into new creative expression may readily be found in the 1919 version of the Whitman essay. It concludes with a memorable passage of lyrical tribute to Whitman's verse: 'There is the sheer creative gesture, moving the world in wonderful whirls. The whole soul follows its own free, spontaneous, inexplicable course, its contractions and pulsations dictated from nowhere save from the creative quick itself. And each separate line a pulsation and contraction' (*Studies*, 369). As is suggested by the mingling here of the terminology of spirit ('soul') with the metabolism of the body to characterise what is essentially an expressive act of creative consciousness, Lawrence is approvingly registering Whitman's integrated approach to human being. A few lines earlier Lawrence had specifically commended the psychosomatic vision that had allowed Whitman to ensure that 'the whole soul speaks at once: sensual impulse instant with spiritual impulse, and the mind serving, giving pure attention' (*Studies*, 368).

But although he here seems wholly to be endorsing the concept of spontaneity inscribed in Whitman's poetic practice, elsewhere in the 1919 essay he makes it clear that for him Whitman ultimately mistakes what he is about, as he 'mix[es] all up with emotion and merging, that merging which is the breaking-down of being. He believed in fusion – which is pure loss' (*Studies*, 366). Taking our clue from comments such as this, and from Roberts W. French's implied perception of their relevance to *Look! We Have Come Through!*, it may prove fruitful to return to that volume, and to consider in particular the ways in which it is informed by a dialogue with Whitman, a dialogue which centrally involves a critique of the American's understanding of spontaneity. Attention to these matters may help illuminate some of the paradoxes of Lawrence's volume, such as that whereas Lawrence himself at the time of its writing was (largely thanks to Whitman) becoming deeply interested in the kind of free verse that seemed best suited to the articulation, and indeed the vital enactment, of spontaneity, and whereas he even went so far as to claim that his volume consisted of 'unrhyming poems', almost all the poems in *Look! We Have Come Through!* are in fact notably faithful to traditional rhyme and metre.

The best place to begin, however, is not with Lawrence but with Whitman. 'Spontaneous Me', from the 'Children of Adam' section of *Leaves of Grass*, is that rarity; a poem by Whitman that actually features the word 'spontaneous' – and even then the word had been absent from the text in its original 1856 form, when it was entitled 'Bunch Poem'. Its virtual absence from Whitman's lexicon may itself be instructive. Whereas spontaneity was for him undoubtedly an article of personal and poetic faith, and while there is scarcely a line of his poetry in which it is not inscribed, it nevertheless did not involve the self-tormenting psychosomatic conundrum that in many ways it did for Lawrence, for whom it was inseparable from the whole vexed issue of selfhood's unavoidable implication in interpersonal relationships.[6] And to read 'Spontaneous Me', whose crucial first line was added only in the 1860 edition of *Leaves of Grass*, by the jagged lightning flashes of Lawrence's stormy obsessions is to begin to understand the difference he was doomed to have with Whitman on this subject, a difference that is reflected quite as much in the poetic forms of *Look! We Have Come Through!* as in its content.

'Spontaneous me, Nature': the calculatingly unguarded opening line, genially granting, through an unproblematic use of the term 'nature', complete authority to free self-expression, immediately warns us that we are here entering a very un-Lawrentian world of experience. This is confirmed by everything that follows, including the poem's central concern with auto-eroticism (and with the resultant practice of masturbation, which Lawrence could conceive of only negatively, as a symptom of deathly narcissism); its celebration of what (in 'Song of Myself') Whitman so memorably termed 'the procreant urge of the world'; and its casual trust in the free association of ideas. This last signature aspect of the poem is embedded deeply in its very rhetorical structure, which prominently features listing, repetition of grammatical patterns, and the regular use of present participles. These are the kinds of features of Whitman's writing that Lawrence explicitly addresses and criticises in the Whitman essay of 1919, and they are also implicitly critiqued in *Look! We Have Come Through!*

While Whitman actually only uses the term 'spontaneous' in three of his poems (*E*, 683) the concept is integral to all his writing, including his prose. The absence of spontaneity was, for him, a clear and worrying symptom of the poor social and political health of mid-century America, as is made clear in an important passage commenting on the way the Fourth of July was celebrated by New York city in 1856. Whitman deplored the regimentation evidenced by the way the different professions, trades and services were neatly dragooned into order to march in public procession on this festive occasion. He saw it as a perfect image of the new urban politics that had been ushered in by the mayor Fernando Wood, whom historians have come to label, with a mixture of admiration and regret, as the first example of the modern figure of the 'city boss', who has ever since played such a key role in the political life of the United States. In an excoriating article for *Life Illustrated* he fulminated at length against this new social and political order, and contrasted it with the kind of celebrations he believed appropriate to a truly democratic nation. Such, he proclaimed, should be days of authentic 'national thanksgiving and pride, with rustic festivals and friendly hospitality, with public triumphs, *if spontaneous* [Whitman's emphasis], but not by chilly management of squabbling civic authorities ... in short with spontaneous and affectional displays of joy, in civil and decorous forms'.[7]

Whitman equated spontaneity with the personal freedom he believed to be the preserve of truly democratic societies. For him, it flowed from an innate trust in the potentialities not only of human life, as expressed alike in the physical and spiritual existence of liberated individuals but also in the progress both of history and of the vast cosmos itself. And this trust was rooted in a teleological outlook, an ideology common to virtually all Americans, of course, in the hopeful age of 'Manifest Destiny'. As for Whitman, he was originally clearly influenced by Lamarck's pre-Darwinian model of 'purposeful evolution', a model he adapted late in life to accommodate a highly selective reading of Hegel's philosophy. Needless to say, Lawrence was never tempted to entertain such optimistic outlooks, and thus was far less inclined to the kind of universal trustfulness that underwrote Whitman's enthusiastic commitment to spontaneity.

'Beautiful dripping fragments, the negligent list of one after another as I happen to call them to me or think of them', writes Whitman evocatively in 'Spontaneous Me', identifying the generative principle of his poetics.[8] 'List after list of additions to himself he gives us' (*Studies*,

360), Lawrence complains in his 1919 Whitman essay. His objection to this practice is based primarily on the belief that Whitman treats all the phenomena in the world as fuel for his own ineffable selfhood, failing to take into account their inalienable difference, and therefore insuperable distance, from himself. Lawrence reduces all the rhetorical forms of Whitman's poetry ('catalogues, lists, enumerations' etc. [359]) to 'one cry: I am everything and everything is me. I accept everything – nothing is rejected' (*Studies*, 359). And, although he does not mention it, Whitman's notorious fondness for participial forms may well not have escaped Lawrence's censorious attention, judging by the seemingly pointed difference in the use he himself makes of them in *Look! We Have Come Through!*

Whether Whitman is speaking of 'The boy's longing, its glow and pressure as he confides in me what he was dreaming', or of 'The dead leaf whirling its spiral whirl and falling still and content to the ground', or of 'The pulse pounding through palms and trembling encircling fingers', he uses the continuous present to propose what might be called a 'steady state' theory of the cosmos's generative sexual dynamic. The present participle is used as a device for assimilating the experience of the moment to a universal norm, but without thereby diminishing its pressing immediacy. Contrast this with Lawrence's use of the same verbal form in *Look! We Have Come Through!* Take 'River Roses',[9] for example, in which participial forms are given such prominence, through their hypnotically repeated use as end-rhymes, that they could reasonably be said to constitute an intimate part of the poem's meaning. They function as a means of suggesting a moment strangely suspended out of ordinary time, and filled with brooding presentiment. They therefore serve to magnify the utter singularity of that moment, and that is the main characteristic of Lawrence's use of participles, as can again be seen in the beautiful 'Fireflies in the Corn', with its delicate evocation of 'dear fireflies wafting in between/ And over the swaying corn-stalks' (*CP*, 221). It is the same need to isolate the moment, and to assign to it its own unique 'truth', that prompts Lawrence to identify the precise location in which each of the poems in *Look! We Have Come Through!* is set and/or was written. The tendency of critics to take this simply as Lawrence's way of anchoring the poems in, and thus somehow 'verifying' them by, autobiographical experience is, as Kinkead-Weekes and others have shown, fundamentally mistaken.

In the different use of participial forms can, then, be descried a fundamental difference in ideology, and in related notions of spontaneity, between Lawrence and Whitman. But in order to see this properly, one needs to cultivate a genuinely evenhanded approach; a scrupulously bifocal vision – one as capable of attending sympathetically to Whitman's central concerns as to those of Lawrence. 'Spontaneous Me' is a magnificent poem, demonstrating as it does Whitman's powers of body imaging. For him the human body is 'the poem of the mind', most compellingly so in its sensual presence and most particularly so in the form of its most secret genital parts. Late in life he explicitly outlined his convictions in this regard:

> Perhaps the inner never lost rapport we hold with earth, light, air, trees etc., is not to be realized through eyes and mind only, but through the whole corporeal body, which I will not have blinded or bandaged any more than the eyes (807).

Consistent with this approach is not only his impassioned interest in auto-eroticism and self-arousal, but his daring conception of masturbation as a 'natural' act revealing how human sexuality is rooted in the imagination. But then, the human imagination is, for Whitman, also rooted, in its turn, in sexuality, and so (given the patriarchal character of his thinking in this particular connection) he is supplied with a number of key equivalences – phallic potency, masturbation and artistic creation can all be treated as versions of one another. With the addition of one other factor, it is this nexus of equivalences that constitutes the verbal and experiential armature of 'Spontaneous Me'. That additional factor is the cosmos, the sexualised body of the natural world. This body, too, is informed by 'imagination' insofar as it takes the dynamic, restlessly metamorphosing shape of eternal, insatiable desire. So, if Whitman seems briefly to imagine cosmic desire as assuageable ('The hairy wildbee that murmurs and hankers up and down, that gripes the full-grown lady-flower, curves upon her with amorous firm legs, takes his will of her, and holds himself tremulous and tight till he is satisfied'), then the very next moment he is reaffirming the cosmos's sexually aroused, expectant state ('The wet of woods through the early hours'). The tumescent natural world is thus added to Whitman's list of cognates for human sexuality and forms an integral part of his poetic grammar of sexuality.

'Spontaneous me, Nature': the finely judged ambivalence of this opening line may now be appreciated. Its grammatical form allows it to be understood as indicating either that the two terms 'nature' and 'spontaneous me' are synonyms, or that 'nature' is different from and therefore additional to the self but the closest of kin to it, since both are the offspring of spontaneity. Either way, the effect of this annunciatory exclamation is to initiate us into Whitman's distinctive world, in which the psycho-somatic human self is constantly discovering itself in, through and as the cosmos, and the cosmos is constantly realising itself in, through and as the psychosomatic self: and spontaneity is the *primum mobile* that generates and regulates this whole process. This is the vision that is woven into Whitman's poetry at every level, from the macro-form of structural dialectics to the micro-form of specific passages and lines. 'Song of Myself' is an astonishing example of spontaneity writ large, as the whole poem is developed structurally in terms of the rhythmic alternation between excursion (the self discovering itself in the cosmos) and incursion (the cosmos entering constitutively into the self), an alternation that Whitman specifically images in the most basic and life-sustaining of physiological terms ('My respiration and inspiration, the beating of my heart, the passing of blood and air through my lungs' [29]). And within the 'body' of the poem as a whole occur wonderful passages in which it is virtually impossible to tell whether Whitman is imaging the human body as landscape or the natural landscape as a human body. The greatest of these, perhaps, are those incomparable paragraphs in Section 24 that include the famous credo ('I believe in the flesh and the appetites') and proceed to demonstrate how 'If I worship one thing more than another it shall be the spread of my own body, or any part of it' (53).

These were the impulses of spontaneity that at once most excited Lawrence in Whitman's poetry and most disturbed him. Accordingly, they elicited from him not only an impassioned critique (in the 1919 essay) but also a powerful poetic response. The finest examples of body-language in *Look! We Have Come Through!* are those where the body is dramatically lit by the emotional equivalent of chiaroscuro, and where, at the very moment of supreme affirmation, it seems to stand out in fragile relief against a background of wary mistrust. 'Frohnleichnam', for instance, concludes as follows:

> Only to dance together in triumph of being together
> Two white ones, sharp, vindicated,
> Shining and touching,
> Is heaven of our own, sheer with repudiation. (*CP*, 210)

But the following poem, 'In the Dark', is the woman's complaint that 'You cast/ A shadow over my breasts that will kill me at last' (*CP*, 212). And the same dialectic between light and shadow, emotional trust and mistrust, spontaneous giving and equally spontaneous withholding, is apparent in that most lovely of poems 'Gloire De Dijon'. There the bathing woman's body is caught by sunlight so that 'down her sides the mellow/ Golden shadow glows'. Lawrence will not, however, rest content with that vision. Instead, he characteristically notes the way that, as she drips herself with water, 'her shoulders/ Glisten as silver, they crumple up/ Like wet and falling roses/ and I listen/ For the sluicing of their rain-dishevelled petals'. It is out of this glimpse of ruin that he salvages his recuperative final vision of the sunlight concentrating 'her golden shadow/ Fold on fold, until it glows as/ Mellow as the glory roses' (*CP*, 217).

In such poems is registered the dialectic of spontaneity, as Lawrence, unlike Whitman, conceives of it. And at the root of that perception, of course, lies Lawrence's obsessively insistent belief that all human relationships are an alloy of love and hate, of identity and difference. Authentic 'spontaneity' offers no escape from this. Rather, it gives the most perfect existential expression to the inherently ambivalent, iridescent, mercurial character of the feelings that are constitutive of human selfhood and out of which human relationships are hesitantly and warily, if wondrously, fashioned. 'Yet all the while you are you, you are not me./ And I am I, I am never you./ How awfully distinct and far off from each other's being we are!': the full stops at the end of the first two lines signify human life as punctuated, and thus constrained, by fate – the singleness and finality of each of the two symmetrical utterances is underlined, even as the sentences are recognised as co-operating to define the fateful double-bind of human existence: 'To be faithless and faithful together/ As we have to be', as Lawrence strikingly writes elsewhere (199).

Read in the light of the foregoing, a poem such as 'She Said As Well To Me' seems to be an implied rebuke to Whitman's most joyful poetry of self-exposure. The male protagonist bridles at the loving intimacy of his partner's teasing celebration of his body. Her exclamation 'I admire you so, you are beautiful: this clean sweep of your sides, this firmness, this hard mould!' (*SP*, 255) brings to mind Whitman's 'If I worship one thing more than another it shall be the spread of my own body, or any part of it,/ Translucent mould of me it shall be you!/ Shaded ledges and rests it shall be you!' (53). In Lawrence's poem, the man's response to the woman's erotic compliments is fiercely self-protective: 'You would think twice before you touched a weasel on a fence/ as it lifts its straight white throat' (*CP*, 255). That spontaneous impulse of recoil takes us, of course, to the very quick of Lawrence's writing about human relationships, particularly when they are sexually charged.

The lack of such an impulse is, for him, a symptom of psychic ill-health, as certainly as the lack of any reflex action of the bent, suspended leg when the knee is struck is an indication of neurological damage. Hence Lawrence's diagnosis of Whitman in the 1919 essay. And hence, too, his corrective dramatisation in *Look! We Have Come Through!* of the conflicting impulses at work not only in the man-woman relationship but also in the human relationship to what Whitman styled the 'cosmos'. In 'A Doe at Evening' what is registered is the startled alertness of the creature even after her instant flight from the human intruder: 'On the sky-line/ she moved round to watch,/ she pricked a fine black blotch/ on the sky' (*CP*, 222). This is a world away from Whitman's cosmos. Even when he is recording 'Where the panther walks to and fro on a limb overhead, where the buck turns furiously at the hunter' (62), he insinuates himself comfortably into such scenes in a way that suggests his own easy intercourse with all living forms. Whitman's vision is single whereas Lawrence's is always double, and double-edged in a way that makes for an excited, and exciting, edginess in his writing.

Nowhere is Lawrence's fearful hostility towards Whitman's nevertheless fascinating concept and practice of spontaneity more furiously evident, though, than in his treatment of sexual relations. It is as if his experience with Frieda since their marriage had made Lawrence anxiously sensitive to the issue of 'free love' – how, after all (particularly given her history of previous infidelities), was the 'spontaneity' with which she had left her husband and children to be distinguished from the spontaneity of promiscuity? And he seems also to have come to equate free love with Whitmanian free verse. So, he uses the conventional, distancing, generic form of the ballad in 'Ballad of a Wilful Woman' (Lawrence's shockingly heretical version of the story of Joseph and the Virgin Mary), the poem in which he most openly wrestles with the issue. The poem is a frank exposure of the endless 'cruel journey' which the woman takes with her last partner 'through harsh, hard places/ Where strange winds blow' (202). But it is also an uncompromising assertion that it is the very hardship of this life that can alone guarantee its unique quality, making it infinitely more fulfilling than all she has known before: 'And she woke to distil the berries/ The beggar had gathered at night,/ Whence he drew the curious liquors/ He held in delight' (*CP*, 202).

In this, her final and supreme act of spontaneity, the woman has left behind not only her husband but her children too. In this way, Lawrence touches on one of the most charged aspects of his relationship with Frieda, and the one that recurs most harrowingly in *Look! We Have Come Through!* Not only does the sequence repeatedly give us a woman haunted by memories of her abandoned children, it also gives us a woman who continues – to her partner's frustration – to believe that children are not just the incidental product but the very *raison d'être* of a fulfilling emotional and sexual relationship. In other words, the sequence gives us a woman for whom maternity is of the very essence of identity, and whose maternal 'instincts' 'spontaneously' seek expression. In 'She looks back', resulting male jealousy is given full, unbridled expression, as the male protagonist rails against the 'mother-love [that] like a demon drew you from me/ Towards England' (*CP*, 206). Embittered, he feels the 'burning of powerful salt, burning, eating through my defenceless nakedness'. Likening himself to 'Lot's wife', he cries out that he has been 'thrust into white, sharp crystals,/ Writhing, twisting, superannuated'. Add to this the tormented relationship with his own mother to which Lawrence continues to bear disturbing compulsive witness in this volume, and it is not surprising that in the 1919 essay he savages Whitman's preoccupation with the maternal figure: 'He has no idea that each woman is, in truth, a *being*, a single, instant human being, not in any way to be generalized. To Whitman each woman is a Female, a Womb, the Magna Mater' (*Studies*, 363).

Later in his Whitman essay, Lawrence insists that 'sexual love of a man for a woman' is 'deeper' than 'the great passional emotions of family love', such as when 'a woman feels her "bowels drawn" in a child'. This is because 'the sexual consummation between man and woman is the fiery, electric establishing of the perfect life-current, the vital circuit between the two' (*Studies*, 365). He is here continuing that ceaseless, tormenting argument between himself and Frieda that is given generalised, stylised expression in *Look! We Have Come Through!* In 'Rose of all the World', he constructs a debate between two voices within the male speaker, two voices that interpret the image of a rose-bush in contrasting ways. One suggests that a heterosexual relationship finds fulfilment only in issue, and so argues 'The seed is purpose, blossom accident,/ The seed is all in all, the blossom lent/ To crown the triumph of this new descent' (*CP*, 218). While the other asks 'How will you have it? – ... The sharp begetting, or the child begot?/ Our consummation matters, or does it not?' (*CP*, 219). And by the end of the poem, it is this second voice with which the male speaker unequivocally and emphatically identifies. He does so partly in the name of the 'liberation' of women from their enslavement to motherhood. That women like Frieda seemed not to view maternity in such a light is the unstated point of another of his comments in his Whitman essay: 'It is no wonder men complain of the humbug [of Whitman's treatment of the female in his poetry]. It is a wonder more women do not complain. For surely it is humbug to translate the individual into a function – an integral woman into a Female, a Womb' (*Studies*, 364).

It is in the light of this tortuous, conflicted understanding of the nature of the primary human instincts that Lawrence's concept of spontaneity needs to be examined, and his use of poetic forms studied. For him, spontaneity took the form of an involuntary upsurge of a whole complex of interconnected emotions. It was an intricate structure of feeling, and so poetry needed to be answerably subtle, sufficiently nuanced to catch the instress of spontaneity and to trace its inscape. Free verse as actually practised by Whitman, exhilarated though Lawrence was by its potential, could not provide him with the means of such expression, because it was moulded to Whitman's (mis)conception of spontaneity. This, I would suggest, is why the bulk of the poems in *Look! We Have Come Through!* function through traditional poetic rhymes, rhythms and metres. An examination of the way these devices work *in situ* repeatedly confirms that they serve to convey the dynamics of a given relationship. In 'Sunday Afternoon in Italy', for example, full rhymes are used to convey the fearful symmetries of contrasted male and female feelings: 'Nourish her, train her, harden her/ Women all!/ Fold him, be good to him, cherish him/ Men, ere he fall' (*CP*, 228). The constantly shifting patterns of rhyme in 'A Bad Beginning' mirror the shifting moods of the emotional exchange between man and woman, and so constitute a kind of sexual counterpoint. 'Paradise Re-entered' (*CP*, 241–3) affords particularly intricate examples of the grammar of rhyme. As the lovers become enfolded in a paradisal state, mono-rhymes come to dominate every stanza, and to these are added mono-rhymes repeated across stanzas, linking the final line of each to its successor and forming a close weave of sounds.

Rhymes assume a similarly emblematic role in the paired poems 'Giorno Dei Morto' and 'All Souls' (*CP*, 232–3). In the former a limited number of full rhymes is used to create a claustrophobic sense of villagers rapt in their conventional deathly ritual of commemorating the departed, whereas in the latter, unrhymed verse is used to convey the speaker's triumphant conversion of a tribute to his dead mother into an energised reaffirmation of his own life force: 'I am busy only at my life./ But my feet are on your grave, planted./ And when I lift my face, it is a flame that goes up/ To the other world, where you are now' (*CP*, 233). As for 'Both Sides of the Medal', it seems to constitute a kind of implicit meditation on the merits of rhymed verse. Rhyme is used to show lovers coming to terms with the fact that their relationship is constrained by the dialectic of love and hate. They learn 'to submit/ each of us to the balanced, eternal orbit/ wherein we circle on our fate/ in strange conjunction' (*CP*, 235). And it is implied that circling in 'strange conjunctions' (of rhyme as well as of relationship) is preferable to the alternative, which is not 'freedom' but 'chaos': 'A disarray of falling stars coming to nought' (*CP*, 237).

Although poems in relatively free form do occasionally occur throughout *Look! We Have Come Through!*, it is only in the last few pages that free verse fully comes into its own, as if Lawrence had 'come through' not only to a new vision but also into a new style and poetic. That, in its movements, this free verse is both reminiscent of Whitman's and yet unmistakably distinct from it is, of course, part of the point. For the thrusting propulsive energy of Whitman's rhetoric Lawrence substitutes an altogether different rhythm – that of 'fine consciences', to adapt Henry James's phrase – intended to track the finessing of feeling and the deepening and refining of sensuous reflection. Nowhere is the difference between the two writers more evident than in their respective use of repetitions, parallelism and related doublings. Whereas Whitman often uses these for cumulative effect, and for building momentum, Lawrence uses them for subtilising and intensifying experience:

> I, in the sour black tomb, trodden to absolute death
> I put out my hand in the night, one night, and my hand
> touched that which was verily not me,
> verily it was not me.
> Where I had been was a sudden blaze,
> a sudden flaring blaze!
> So I put my hand out further, a little further
> and I felt that which was not I,
> it verily was not I,
> it was the unknown. (*CP*, 259)

Having clearly marked the difference between Whitman's sense of spontaneity and his own, Lawrence can now safely experiment with the free verse form that Whitman had pioneered.

Confirmation of this new assuredness can also be found in the form of Lawrence's Introduction to *New Poems* (1920). Surely one of the most exhilarating defences of poetry written in the twentieth century, it is from beginning to end a paean of unqualified praise to Whitman as the pioneer of a free verse that captures 'the insurgent naked throb of the instant moment'.[10] 'All this should have come as a preface to *Look! We Have Come Through!*', Lawrence writes of his essay in its concluding paragraph. But, as has been suggested here, it may very well be that Lawrence had not actually been in a psychological state to write such an essay in 1917. Although he may have resolved the issue of spontaneity by writing *Look! We Have Come Through!*, it could be that only after he had been able to consolidate his new understanding in the 1918 essay on Whitman that has survived in its 1919 form did he become capable of unguarded, wholehearted tribute to the great American. So, by 1920, he could note that '[t]he quick of the universe is the *pulsating, carnal self*, mysterious and palpable … Because Whitman put this into his poetry, we fear him and respect him so profoundly' (*SLC*, 87). 'It is because his heart beats with the urgent, insurgent Now, which is even upon us all', Lawrence adds, 'that we dread him' (*SLC*, 87). Interestingly enough, it is again in terms of 'fear' that he pays further, related, tribute to Whitman three years later. Singling out the line 'When lilacs last in the dooryard bloomed', he comments: 'It is a string of words, but it makes me prick my innermost ear … There is an element of danger in all new utterance. We prick our ears like an animal in a wood at a strange sound' (*SLC*, 94). 'Fear' seems, then, to have continued to be an integral, complex element in Lawrence's 'spontaneous' admiration for Whitman, and, as this discussion has sought to demonstrate, it is in this vivifying 'fear' – and trembling – that he seems to have written *Look! We Have Come Through!*

The opening line from 'When Lilacs' is quoted again in the 1919 Whitman essay, a study the history of the composition of which reveals how Lawrence's work on it substantially overlapped with his completion of *Look! We Have Come Through!* Scholarship has established how Lawrence first embarked on a systematic rereading of Whitman sometime after requesting, in January 1917, that a copy of *Leaves of Grass* be sent to him. By August of that year, he was fully committed to a sustained study of that text along with the group of other texts that were to form the basis of what eventually became *Studies in American Literature.* He was, therefore, deeply engaged with Whitman's work several months before the publication of *Look! We Have Come Through!* on 26 November 1917. By June 1918, he was completing an essay on Whitman that was, however, omitted from the set of essays on American authors he published in *English Review* between November 1918 and June 1919. On the face of it, this omission was surprising because, as was recently noted in the Cambridge Edition of Lawrence, the essay 'presumably served as the *Consummatum est*' of his work, 'for in all versions of *Studies* known to arrive at a culminating essay on Whitman, the latter was to be the figure with whom Lawrence wrestled, to use the figure dear to both men to describe the engagement of the artist with the self and the universe' (*Studies*, xxxv). Lawrence seems to have kept this 1918 essay very much to himself – the text has not survived – probably because it contained materials that would have scandalised the censors. The 1919 version of the essay, which has survived and is therefore the first extant version of Lawrence's treatment of Whitman in what became *Studies in American Literature,* still contains such materials, but in what is presumably a form sufficiently modified as not to have risked legal prosecution. For instance, the sections recommending male anal intercourse are couched in the most arcane of terms, concocted out of a pseudo-neurology heavily indebted, via contemporary fashionable theosophy, to Eastern notions of the several distinctive centres of consciousness located in different parts of the human body.

In his 1919 essay, Lawrence therefore deals with the nexus of ideas that he associated with spontaneity in a fashion that is as eccentric and bizarre as, or so it has been argued, it is richly suggestive. Easier access to the conclusions Lawrence had reached on the subject is afforded by 'Democracy', another essay of 1919, commissioned by the Dutch periodical *The Word*, and one that is openly keyed throughout to Whitman's work.[11] John Turner has usefully recorded the extent of Lawrence's concern with spontaneity throughout this period, starting with *Women in Love*:

> The word is used 17 times here; it is used 43 times in the 1918–19 *Studies in Classic American Literature*, 24 times in the 20 pages of the 1919 essay 'Democracy'; 41 times in the 12 chapters of the essay 'Education of the People', first written in 1918 and extended in 1920, 26 times in the 50 pages of *Psychoanalysis and the Unconscious* (1920) and 45 times in *Fantasia of the Unconscious* (1921).[12]

As I have attempted to show elsewhere, Lawrence was at this time probably very aware of the fierce debate about the nature of true democracy that had raged in the pages of *The New Age* and other radical intellectual publications of the era. Whitman's name was frequently invoked in such a context, and so it is natural that he should figure so prominently in 'Democracy', divided as it is into three sections addressing the two terms that seemed to Lawrence central to Whitman's democratic philosophy: '(1) the Law of the Average and (2) the Principle of Individualism, or Personalism, or Identity.'

Developed in Lawrence's typical style – staccato, brusque, assertive, sweeping – the argument is that, properly understood, the first of these 'principles' relates only to man's material needs: translated into social operation, respect for the average takes the form of ensuring that every person has access to the bare necessities of life. So, in the first section of the essay, he establishes that the democratic State should 'make proper facilities for every man's clothing, feeding, housing himself, working, sleeping, mating, playing, according to necessity as a common unit' (66). Here, as the editors of the definitive Cambridge edition have noted, may be discerned the remnants of Lawrence's own Socialist beliefs in the abolition of private ownership of property, including land and industry. The trouble with Whitman, though, was that his vision of the Average was far more ambitious than this and extended to matters of spirit and consciousness. It was, argues Lawrence, predicated on the false supposition that 'we are all one, and therefore every bit partakes of all the rest. That is, the Whole is inherent in every fragment. That is, every human consciousness has the same intrinsic value as every other human consciousness, because each is an essential part of the Great Consciousness' (71).

He turns on this concept with all the manic ferocity of disavowal that he was again, of course, to voice in the final, familiar study of Whitman as published in *Studies in Classic American Literature*. And it is when, in the second section of 'Democracy', he begins to fashion his own, alternative, sense of identity that he begins obsessively – one might almost say hysterically – to multiply the use of the term 'spontaneity'. To be exposed to such obsessive repetition (which is to undergo a kind of verbal assault and battery) is to feel the justice of John Turner's insight that this term, and quality, was for Lawrence one that was psychically charged to the most intense degree: that it was, indeed, crucial to his own psychic survival, his own (frail) identity. Emotionally formed, as he had been, through his unusually intimate relationship with his depressive mother, he had early instinctively felt that to be noticed, to be loved, and thus psychically to exist, he needed incessantly to bring that relationship to life through what could therefore only have been a heightened, exaggerated, desperately willed and acted vitality. The result was the oxymoronic sense of willed spontaneity that, disguise it as he might with talk of each and every individual life bubbling spontaneously from the 'fountainhead, 'the unfathomable well-head' of being (73), is to be felt in his bullying (because self-bullying) verbal insistence.

In the third and fourth sections of his essay, Lawrence sets about correcting Whitman, substituting his own concept of 'identity' for the specious one he has attributed to the American and proposing 'the first great purpose of Democracy: that each man shall be spontaneously himself – each man himself, each woman herself, without any question of equality or inequality entering in at all' (80). The trouble is that 'in his present state of mechanical degeneration, man is unable to distinguish his own spontaneous integrity from his mechanical lusts and aspirations' (81). The comment is an important one, because it illuminates a crucial feature of Lawrence's sense of spontaneity, and a crucial weakness he therefore supposed to exist in Whitman's; namely, that spontaneity is always in danger of mutating into some malignant form of itself. His relationship to the spontaneous was therefore as agonistic as his attitude to its presence in Whitman could be antagonistic. Hence the guardedness we have noticed as being inscribed, even at the level of rhythm, rhyme and syntax in *Look! We Have Come Through!*. And hence, too, his at times angry contempt – a contempt surely rooted in fear – for what he thought was the unguardedness, the promiscuous hospitality, of Whitman's openness to all kinds of inner and outer promptings.

As for Whitman, it is surely true that for him the problem lay not in any such complex, conflicted and ambivalent sense of what constituted authentic spontaneity as obsessed Lawrence but rather in all those psycho-social barriers he saw as inhibiting its active operation in his own society. In order to allow the expression of 'nature without check with original energy', it was essential to hold 'creeds and schools in abeyance' (*Reader's Edition*, 29). Therein, for him, lay the challenge, and he intended his poetry to be instrumental in releasing such repressed spontaneity. And while 'nature' was his preferred term for indicating its source, implicit in his celebration of nature's irrepressible energies was the belief that they ultimately derived from the very source of being itself. He thus conceived of himself as a prophet, in the specific sense in which he used that word in his late posthumous tribute to his own hero and antagonist Thomas Carlyle. Properly understood, he there stated, the word prophecy meant much more than predictive powers: 'it means one whose mind bubbles up and pours forth as a fountain, from inner, divine spontaneities revealing God' (887). This, he added, 'is briefly the doctrine of the Friends or Quakers', and he is obviously recalling the teachings of Elias Hicks, that unorthodox Quaker whose teaching had at one time so appealed both to his mother and to his youthful self.[13] With an unorthodoxy more than the equal of that of Hicks, he had subsequently evolved partly out of the Quaker's teachings his own theology of spontaneity, whose prophet he, as poet, had duly become.

That Lawrence was, indeed, right to identify 'spontaneity' as a term of seminal importance to any understanding of Whitman's writing, the latter seemed to confirm at the very end of his life. Probably the last poem he completed was 'A Thought of Columbus' – by Traubel's account, it was handed to him by the poet just ten days before he died, although it seems likely that Whitman had been working on it since November, 1891.[14] Its opening is a final demonstration of how important a term 'spontaneity' was in Whitman's lexicon of freedom:

> The mystery of mysteries, the crude and hurried ceaseless
>   flame, spontaneous, bearing on itself,
> The bubble and the huge, round, concrete orb!
> A breath of Deity, as thence the bulging universe unfolding!
> The many issuing cycles from their precedent minute!
> The eras of the soul incepting in an hour,
> Haply the widest, farthest evolutions of the world and
>   man (580).

That first line is one Lawrence himself could almost have written, expressive of a vision to which he surely would have enthusiastically subscribed. But the rest of the stanza is pure Whitman. Spontaneous, as well as garrulous, to the very last, Whitman shared Lawrence's chronic addiction to vitality even while he evaded the tortured complexion the psychically wounded Englishman never ceased to put on it. Whitman used it, as ever, on his own teleological terms.

Notes

1. D. H. Lawrence, *Studies in Classic American Literature*, ed. Edward Greenspan (Cambridge: Cambridge University Press, 2003), p. 155. All subsequent references are to this edition, unless otherwise specified. For a detailed analysis of the complex composition history of this text, see M. Wynn Thomas and John Turner, '"Whitman, the great poet, has meant so much to me": Lawrence's *Studies in Classic American Literature*, 1919–1923', *Walt Whitman Quarterly Review*, 21/2 (Fall, 2003), 41–64.

2. Chapter Eight, 'The English Whitman', in M. Wynn Thomas, *Transatlantic Connections: Whitman US/Whitman UK* (Iowa: Iowa University Press, 2005).

3. Harold Bloom, *The Anxiety of Influence* (Oxford: Oxford University Press, 1973).

4. Mark Kinkead-Weekes, 'The Shaping of *Look! We Have Come Through!*', in Howard Erskine-Hill and Richard A. McCabe (eds), *Presenting Poetry: Composition, Publication, Reception* (Cambridge: Cambridge University Press, 1995), pp. 214–34.

5. Roberts W. French, 'Whitman and the Poetics of Lawrence', in Jeffrey Meyers (ed.), *Lawrence and Tradition* (Amherst: University of Massachusetts, 1985), pp. 91–114.

6. For a useful summary of Whitman's interest in spontaneity, see the entry on the subject by Edward W. Huffstetler, in Donald D. Kummings and J. R. LeMaster (eds), *Walt Whitman: An Encyclopedia* (New York and London: Garland Publishing, 1998), pp. 683–4. Hereafter *E*.

7. In addition to the following analysis, see *Transatlantic Connections*, p. 39.

8. Harold W. Blodgett and Sculley Bradley (eds), *Walt Whitman: Leaves of Grass, Reader's Edition* (London: University of London Press, 1965), p. 103. All references are to this edition.

9. D. H. Lawrence, 'River Roses', in *Complete Poems* (New York: Penguin, 1993), p. 216. Hereafter *CP*.

10. Anthony Beale, *D. H. Lawrence: Selected Literary Criticism* (London: Heinemann, 1964), 88. Hereafter *SLC*.

11. 'Democracy', in Michael Herbert (ed.), *D. H. Lawrence: Reflections on the Death of a Porcupine* (Cambridge: Cambridge University Press, 1988), pp. 63–83.

12. I quote from J. F. Turner, 'In Search of Spontaneity: The Madeleine Davies Memorial lecture', p. 7. I am very grateful to my friend Dr Turner for sharing this unpublished text with me.

13. See the entry on Hicks in *E*, pp. 276–7.

14. See the footnote to the poem in *Leaves of Grass: Reader's Edition*, p. 581.

II.
ON DYLAN THOMAS

'He was one of ours':
American 'bards' and Dylan Thomas

I

It is 'Late April 1952', and Allen Ginsberg is 'in San Remo'[1] sitting
relaxed 'toward closing time' when 'Dylan Thomas and someone else
with a big bruise on right forehead' walk in. Ginsberg – yet to become
the leading poet of the Beat Generation with the publication of *Howl
and Other Poems* in 1956 – is asked whether he knows 'who this is' by
Thomas's companion. 'Of course man it is obvious', answers the young
poet. Thomas, who boasts that 'I have the shortest legs in the world,
my belly hangs down to my groin', is looking for an obliging girl. But
Ginsberg persuades him to end his evening's drinking in his attic. At
this point, Thomas's companion reminds him that 'Caitlin is waiting',
and Ginsberg recalls in his journals that

> … Thomas decided to go, and I closed a cab door on them,
> ran to other side & stuck my tongue in window at him which I
> immediately regretted tho I meant it as a friendly gesture. He
> stared out at me drunkenly without response …
>
> Ah, Dylan Thomas, I would have liked to know you that
> night, wish I could have communicated who I was, my true feel-
> ing, and its importance to you. For I too am a lover of the soul.
>
> How disappointing to come away empty-handed with no
> recognition from this Chance meeting – I feel sick and unhappy
> because I could not make a great sweet union of the moment
> of life – now this is 45 minutes after, it will pass but it is sad
> and true.[2]

Ginsberg's failure to effect that 'sweet union' found an echo in an event
almost fifty years later. One evening in early summer, 1995, my wife and
I were sitting, along with a number of others, in the Windsor Lodge
Hotel, Swansea. We had been invited to dine with Allen Ginsberg,

who was in town to read his poetry: it was the year Swansea had been designated the UK millennial City of Literature. Seven o'clock came and went, and so did eight o'clock and then nine o'clock. It was obvious by then that Ginsberg was not going to show up. Only later did the full story emerge. Met off a plane from Ireland, where he had been royally and riotously entertained, a grumpy Ginsberg had informed his 'minders' somewhere on the M4 between Heathrow and the Severn Bridge that he wanted to meet two Welsh poets. The first was John Ceiriog Hughes. The second Dic Jones. Once it was explained to him that meeting Ceiriog might prove a trifle difficult, given his demise a century earlier, Ginsberg homed in on Dic Jones.

He stuck obstinately to that particular gun, and the very morning of our expected meeting with him, he had been taken – by a Dafydd Rowlands made nervous by Ginsberg's reputation as a predator – to Aberystwyth, where Dic was reading at a 'Barddas' convention.[3] Arrived there, Ginsberg had attended a session of 'Talwrn y Beirdd', an oral poetry competition, had applauded the unintelligible performers wildly for five minutes and had then fallen asleep. Waking at the end, he'd indulged in another bout of frenzied applause before announcing that he now wanted to pay his respects to Dylan Thomas at Laugharne. That rather lengthy detour reluctantly accomplished by the compliant Rowlands, Ginsberg headed for the graveyard, where he sank to his knees before Dylan Thomas's grave and began very publicly to chant a kaddish, a Jewish lament for the dead.

At once comic and moving, the episode can be seen as American poetry's fitting tribute to one who, to adapt the remark Philip Larkin made on hearing of Thomas's death, had helped alter the face of poetry not only in the United Kingdom but also in the United States.[4] Writing in the late 1970s, Eric Homberger noted that 'no British poet since Dylan Thomas has made a significant impact on American taste'.[5] The ways in which Dylan Thomas's work intersected with the postwar poetic American culture has been explored in recent years, and this chapter is a contribution to that area of study.[6]

As Kenneth Rexroth remarked in 1961, 'Postwar years are characteristically periods of wholesale literary revaluation. Everybody knows that is what happened after the First World War. It is only now becoming apparent that the same thing occurred after the Second World War.'[7] Even as that war was drawing to its close, American poetry began the

process of transforming itself in the image of changed social, political, economic and cultural circumstances. The young Robert Lowell's
Lord Weary's Castle (1945) already provided some advance notice of the
radical changes that lay a decade ahead, anticipating Lowell's transformation into one of the greatest of post-war poets with the publication
of a new kind of poetry, formally relaxed and seemingly so intimately
and frankly personal in character that it came to be designated 'confessional'. Dylan Thomas had something to do with that change.

But back in 1945, Randall Jarrell, addressing a letter to the young
Lowell, had praised *Lord Weary's Castle* in fervent terms that, suggests
Lowell's biographer Ian Hamilton, 'can be readily forgiven. If the two
choices for a modern poet seemed to be, on the one hand, the learned,
metrical, ironic style of Eliot and Auden and, on the other, the fiery,
bardic line of Dylan Thomas (with the William Carlos Williams free-
verse "Americanist" model as a permanent "other" possibility), then
Lowell's new poems undoubtedly would have seemed to be getting the
best of every possible world.'[8] As if in anticipation of the ambivalence
with which Thomas's impact on American culture was eventually to be
viewed, Jarrell elsewhere less favourably commented that if 'poetry were
nothing but texture, Thomas would be as good as any poet alive. The
what of his poems is hardly essential to their success, and the best and
most brilliantly written pieces usually say less than the worst.'[9]

Lowell's first volume is transitional. It emerges from a New Critical
kind of writing in which he had himself been trained and which had
become enormously powerful on American campuses. But it foreshadows the new, formally relaxed and free-flowing Whitmanesque style of
writing to be variously exemplified in the fifties by Lowell's own 'confessional' poetry, the work of the Beats, the Black Mountain open field
revolution and the New York school's experiments with the demotic.
And Dylan Thomas's work can be illuminatingly seen as implicated in
this process. He was fully aware of the New Critics and was indeed an
admirer of Ransom's poetry, but as Brinnin reported, he was antipa-
thetic to the hardening of such a poetic and practice into dogma: 'he
knew just enough about the perspectives and the jargon of the new critics of poetry to use them in discussion and, as a rule, tended to disparage
the more rigid applications of the approach they represent' (*DTA*, 58).
Interestingly, however, Brinnin also recalls how, at an awkward party
held in Thomas's honour at Yale, when 'all the professors sat around in

a brooding druidic circle apparently awaiting an oracle', 'the exception was Cleanth Brooks [one of the greatest of the New Critics of course] who conveyed by his presence more than by anything he said a sympathetic recognition of Dylan's dilemma' (*DTA*, 30).

It has always astonished me that so few American commentators have realised that, both in its poetic and in its practice, the 'New Criticism' movement was a defensive 'cultural formation', to adopt Raymond Williams's suggestive classification.[10] It was the belated product of the defeated élite culture of the post-bellum White South. It valorised qualities, both social and literary – such as irony, urbanity, emotional reticence, elaborate courtesy, discursive complexity, and obliqueness – that were supposedly the preserve of the 'South', and that pointedly contrasted with the coarse, vulgar, thrusting culture of the 'carpetbagging' North, dominated as it was by a philistine capitalism and industrialism. The poets of post-war America, hailing as several of note did from the Mid-West, the West coast or electric New York City, could scarcely have been expected to tamely submit for long to being cabbin'd, cribb'd and confin'd by such a regressive ideology and its precious aesthetic forms. Having been newly exposed to wide international experiences by the Second World War, they were eager to develop brand new, mould-breaking cultural formations of their own. And that was a process in which some of them instinctively felt the example of Thomas could prove helpful.

Thomas's impact on the early Lowell long antedated Thomas's visits to the States. The American had first registered his work in the late 1930s, because it was intricately wrought, forbiddingly dense, and formally demanding. It was therefore exactly the kind of verse towards which Lowell himself, still heavily influenced by his studies under Ransom (the poet-guru of the New Critical movement) at Kenyon College, had at that time inclined. 'I was also reading Hart Crane and Thomas and Tate and Empson's *7 Types of Ambiguity*,' he later wrote, 'and each poem was more difficult than the one before, and had more ambiguities.'[11]

In the Summer 1947 issue of *The Sewanee Review*, the Bostonian published a long review of works by Thomas, Bishop and Williams.[12] 'He is,' Lowell commented, 'a dazzling obscure writer who can be enjoyed without understanding,' and he unexpectedly compared Thomas with Pound. Both, he suggested, 'tend to be fragmentary, over-ingenious, and to have difficulty in finding a subject. Several of Thomas's best poems have the child-like directness and magic of "Cathay"' (493). Lowell did, however, concede that Thomas most closely resembled Hart Crane, even though he 'comes from another world' from that of the American. Of living poets, he added, 'Wallace Stevens is the only [one] who can hold a candle to him'. Annoyed, however, by the slavish admiration for Thomas expressed by the likes of Sitwell and Read, Lowell made a point of underlining his limitations and weaknesses. He listed these as 'Repetition and Redundancy' and 'Overloading'. His carefully considered conclusion was that 'Thomas is a very good poet', some of whose poems would certainly last. The best of all, he felt, was 'Fern Hill', a Wordsworthian 'pastoral of childhood' (496).

As for Lowell's master, John Crowe Ransom, writing in 1951 he disarmingly admitted that he could not decide whether Thomas was a major or a minor poet; and such uncertainty may in part have derived from the ambiguous relation between Thomas's work and the tightly woven, densely packed and multi-faceted poetry that theorists of the New Criticism such as Ransom had long practised.[13] Lowell could write about Thomas with some annoyance and asperity. In a 1948 letter to R. W. Flint, he passingly observes that 'it seems to me that maturity of experience makes Williams so wonderful – by comparison a gorgeous poet like Thomas seems wordy, green, living in an imaginative darkness'.[14] There seems to be a hint of envy here as well as of disapproval. Two years later he reported to Peter Taylor on Thomas's stay in the Lowell household that 'somehow he was kept on beer most of the time, but he'd begin at 7 in the morning and end at 12 – no meals except breakfast'. He then proceeds to sketch a rapid, vivid caricature of his guest:

> About the best and dirtiest stories I've ever heard – dumpy, absurd body, hair combed by a salad spoon, brown-button Welsh eyes always moving suspiciously, a fixing on the most modest person in the room.

And he signed off with a phrase that might well serve as epitaph for the American Thomas: 'a great explosion of life, and hell to handle' (*LRL*, 155).

The gossipy letter Lowell wrote to Elizabeth Bishop on 19 November 1953 following Thomas's death shows the American in a different and rather unfavourable light. 'The details', he informed her cattily, 'are rather gorgeously grim'. And he went on to recount with tasteless relish the melodrama attendant upon the event: 'He was two days incommunicado with some girl on Brinnin's staff in some New York hotel. Then his wife came, first calling "eternal hate", and tried quite literally to kill and sleep with everyone in sight. Or so the rumours go in Chicago and Iowa City.' He then readjusted his tone to conclude that '[i]t's a story that Thomas himself would have told better than anyone else; I suppose his life was short and shining as he wanted it – life, alas, is no joke' (*LRL*, 202).

Bishop's reply was much more sympathetic, as she recalled that 'I liked [Dylan Thomas] so much. Well, "like" isn't quite the word, but I felt such a sympathy for him in Washington, and immediately after one lunch with him, you knew perfectly well he was only good for two or three years more.' Why was he taken so young, she ended up wondering, 'when people can live to be malicious old men like Frost, or maniacal old men like Pound, or –'.[15] But in the end, her response to Thomas's poetry was, like that of Lowell, predictably guarded and ambivalent even while frankly admiring. 'I agreed with your review of Dylan Thomas completely,' she wrote to him on 14 August 1947, 'his poems are almost always spoiled for me by two or three lines that sound like padding or remain completely unintelligible. I think that last stanza of "Fern Hill",' she generously added, 'is wonderful – although I don't know what he means by "the shadow of his hand" – I haven't got the poem or the review to go by.'[16] As for Lowell, by 11 October 1957, he was writing to Randall Jarrell that '[t]here's a new English poet called Larkin that I like better than anyone since Thomas. I've been reading him since the Spring and really like him better than Thomas' (*H*, 234). By then, the brief feverish era of Thomas-mania triggered by his three eventful and melodramatic visits to the States had come to an end.

II

Thomas flew to New York for his first visit to America on 20 February 1950. Five days later he wrote to Caitlin admitting how overwhelming was the experience of finding himself in the 'very loud, mad middle of the last mad Empire on earth … the last monument there is to the insane desire for power that shoots its buildings up to the stars & roars its engines louder and faster than they have ever been roared before and makes everything cost the earth & where the imminence of death is reflected in every last power-stroke and grab of the great money bosses, the big shots, the multis, one never sees'.[17] Before leaving Wales, he had expressed the hope that he might be allowed to read the work of some American poets he admired, mentioning John Crowe Ransom as one of those (*CL*, 730). He mentioned 'Blackberry Winter'. Thomas had been including a poem by Ransom in his public readings from 1937 onwards. As for other American poets with whom he was familiar, they included Richard Eberhart, but he admitted that he had only recently glanced at Lowell's 'Where the Rainbow Ends', and 'The Raid' by William Everson (*CL*, 738).

A few months after returning from his first visit to the States – it is still staggering to learn that he had read at more than forty universities – he wrote his patron, Margaret Taylor, a long, carefully detailed letter. Opening with a set piece description of his adventures – 'I was floored by my florid and stertorous spouting of verses to thousands of young pieces whose minds, at least, were virgin territory' – he then proceeded to anatomise the poetry scene in America for a correspondent who was at that juncture interested in organising events there. From the beginning, he emphasised that 'the majority, the big majority, of poets in America *are* attached to universities' (*CL*, 762). There were only two he knew of, he added, who were not, namely Wallace Stevens and e. e. cummings. There was also the 'G.O.M. of American poetry', Robert Frost, although he earned a tidy income through guest appearances on various campuses.

Interestingly enough, Thomas made no reference to William Carlos Williams, even though he had mentioned his name as far back as 1934, when he was barely out of his teens, in a letter to Geoffrey Grigson expressing pleasure that *New Verse* had 'given [him] one in the eye', in a review of his *Collected Poems, 1921–1931* (*CL*, 120). As for Williams, a comment he made in a letter of 24 May 1950 shows that he was well aware of Thomas before he even visited the States. He remarked that

American poems are of an entirely different sort from [Dylan] Thomas's Welsh-English poems. They use a different language and operate under a different compulsion. They are more authoritarian, more Druidic, more romantic – and they are, truly, more colourful.[18]

As we shall see, several in the United States were to follow Williams in romantically supposing that there were 'Druidic' characteristics (whatever they were fancifully deemed to be) both to Thomas's poems and to their performance. And Williams's tribute to Thomas after his death was notable for its generosity, particularly considering the radical difference between his poetic and that of the Welshman:

> Thomas was a lyric poet and, I think, a great one. Such memorable poems as 'Over Sir John's Hill' and, even more to be emphasized, 'On His Birthday', are far and away beyond the reach of any contemporary English or American poet … You may not like such poems but prefer a more reasoned mode but this is impassioned poetry, you might call it drunken poetry, it smacks of the divine – as Dylan Thomas does also … He had passion and a heart which carried him where he wanted to go, but it cannot be said that he did not choose what he wanted. (*RC*, 324)

Not all poets whose practice was, like that of Williams, fundamentally different from that of Thomas, were inclined to be so generous. The sniffy attitude of the Black Mountain brigade, for example – always excepting their ally Denise Levertov, proud of her own Welsh descent – is effectively voiced by Cid Corman in a lengthy essay dissecting Thomas's career. The dominant note of the discussion is struck in the opening sentence: 'That Thomas is a very limited poet, despite his birth-(love)-death ambit, is almost a constant self-testimony in his work' (*T*, 223). Corman closes in on 'Over Sir John's Hill', pointing out that 'Thomas speaks for the poet as the cantor, the incantatory scribe', and dismissing his spontaneity as nothing but 'a studied grace. Rhetoric is his controlling artifice'. 'Thomas savours his tongue', is Corman's comment on the public readings. 'It is a prime organ with him. Anyone who has heard him read (and who hasn't? and who hasn't, should), remembers the strong syllabic drunkenness (something of an orgy), the craze of sound sometimes running against the flow and the clear sense' (*T*, 225). Conceding that there are beauties in the poetry and instancing some of them, Corman nonetheless insists that Thomas is essentially nothing but a shallow rhetorician given to a sentimentality that vitiates his claims to sincerity.

The most arresting, fascinating and consequential assessment of Thomas from a Black Mountain perspective, however, was that of Charles Olson. It came in the form of private correspondence with Frances Boldereff, and has been expertly analysed by Ralph Maud, a distinguished scholar both of Thomas and of Olson.[19] Olson had gone to hear Thomas read at Washington DC, and been surprised to discover that, far from being a Byronic figure, he was 'a rather wretched rabbit, fat and seedy on the outside', and frightened on the inside. This impression set the tone for Olson's further comments, that have a Freudian tinge in keeping with the Age of Psychoanalysis that was then dawning in the States. Olson pronounces Thomas to be a case of arrested development at around the age of four-and-a-half or five, 'when the world was fresh and round as his mother (precise, in this case); and with language still all apple and honey, and the only articulation known to him terror and incest, so that his verse is full of burning, of green fire, and of curds and cream'. Olson concedes, however, that, for all his lamentable lack of true manliness, there is something of the endearing child-genius about Thomas. In a strange digression, he then confesses to a primitive urge to take this 'child-poet' in his arms, as if Thomas somehow represents a [necessarily] repressed part of his own identity.

All this is prelude to Olson articulating his own view of the needs of a truly 'adult' and 'manly' poetry at that time. In his view, the case of Thomas serves him as an example of how not do it. As he confesses, having deplored Thomas's self-absorbed 'wordiness': 'I am hammering here at the same idea the piece on Projective Verse was after: to stay in the struggle for open verse as against closed, in order to arrive at forms which come not from the outside, inherited ... but from the inside, from the working along the self and the stuff in the open, until some form comes out of it is fresh and implicit to the thing-needed-done itself.' Maud has shrewdly recognised that these sentiments closely parallel those expressed by Olson in passages such as the following in his classic essay on 'Projective Verse':

> Objectivism is the getting rid of the lyrical interference of the individual as ego, of the 'subject' and his soul, that particular presumption by which western man has interposed himself between

what he is as a creature of nature ... and those other creations of nature which we may, with no derogation, call objects. For a man is himself an object ...[20]

And Olson ends his discussion of Thomas by contrasting the Welshman's self-centred and self-confining poetic, as a 'sprawler' poet able to 'sing [only] of himself', and his own ideal of a poet who 'stays inside himself', so that 'contained within his nature' he is 'participant in the larger force', and so 'will be able to listen and his hearing through himself will give him secrets objects to share'.

III

Cid Corman had ended his essay on Thomas by deploring the evidence of his pernicious influence to be found in much of the poetry appearing in American periodicals. In this respect, such periodicals were repaying the interest Thomas had long paid them. He had made sure to familiarise himself with the contemporary poetry scene in America well before his first visit to the United States, prompted in part by the steadily increasing interest shown there in his poems. A particularly important conduit for information was the avid anthologist Oscar Williams (Thomas's 'Little Treasure' and 'label-less hot red potato' [*CL*, 840]), who from the early 1930s onwards had often included a poem by Thomas in his compilations. Surprisingly, the first piece by Thomas to appear in a North American outlet was a short story – 'The Visitor' – that appeared in 1935.

Two years later 'We lying by seasand' was included in a special 'English number' of *Poetry Chicago*. 1939 saw the first publication in America of his collection, *This World I Breathe*. From the beginning, Thomas's interest in the American scene proved to be hospitably eclectic. In a late letter in 8 October 1952, he told Oscar Williams about his reading on the BBC 3rd Programme of poems by Roethke and Lowell, and went on to mention 'a half hour of Spoon River' as well as a series of readings of 'Masters, Lindsay, Robinson & Sandburg, a fine old four for a programme and a booze-up' (*CL*, 841). This is an interesting nod to the Whitmanian tradition of the inter-war years, when the emphasis was primarily on his social radicalism. In some ways, Thomas later came to provide a kind of hinge between that pre-war version of Whitman and the new version that could be said to have begun with the 'Whitmanian turn' in the immediate post-war period in which he himself was unconsciously implicated.[21]

In his letter to Margaret Taylor he had shrewdly surmised that 'the poets [in the States] you are most interested in would be, I imagine, far younger men' than established names like Stevens and Cummings (*CL*, 763). And it was on this emergent generation, and that following, that his influence would prove to be greatest. While he had originally become known to them through his densely worked and sometimes laboriously obscure early poems – grist to the mill for all those currently fascinated by the New Criticism and its poets – his public readings across the US galvanised them by its electric difference from the printed texts. In the (increasingly coarse) flesh, and in full voice, he transformed arid intellectual text into emotionally compelling oral utterance, thereby helping to reawaken Americans' excited interest in their own bardic tradition, stemming from Emerson and Whitman (who had, in turn, been a considerable influence on the young Thomas himself) and paving the way for the American performance poetry of coming decades. As Karl Shapiro put it in his obituary essay: 'it is one thing to analyse and interpret poetry and keep it all in a book: it is another to watch that poetry enter an audience and melt it to a single mind' (*T*, 270). And if Thomas 'was the master of a public which he himself had brought out of nothingness' (thus anticipating the Beats), he was also, Shapiro noted in 1954, 'the first whose journeys and itineraries became part of his own mythology, the first who offered himself up as a public sacrifice', thus anticipating the self-lacerating life studies of the confessionals.[22]

Donald Hall shrewdly surmised 'that his gregariousness was another refuge from pain, the anaesthesia of promiscuous acquaintance', and Brinnin seems to have broadly concurred. Late in life Hall could still recall the thrilling impact of Thomas's readings forty years after hearing him at Harvard in February 1950. He remembered that he'd already listened to him on a Caedmon LP. Yet even that didn't prepare him for the astonishing effect of the live performance. 'Out of this silly body', Hall wrote,

[r]olled a voice like Jehovah's, or the Ocean's, or Firmament's. 'R's' rolled, vowels rose and fell … consonants thudded and

crashed and leapt to their feet again … I hovered five inches above my uncomfortable chair in New Lecture Hall, stunned by the beauty of poem and reading. Although I was later to meet him under different guises, I remember the first DT I saw: a small and disheveled figure bodying forth great poetry in great performance, an act of homage to poetry, an act of love for magnificent words … [T]he voice was partly Thomas's perform-ance and partly the poetry's structure of rhythms and assonance, which inhere and will endure.[23]

Some of the most particular friends Thomas made among the poets on his visits to the States had themselves been harbingers of these changes. Even before the war, Kenneth Patchen had been producing leftist poetry along unacademic, unorthodox lines.[24] The Theodore Roethke whom Thomas came to know intimately and whose biomor-phic vision of the evolution of the human self so uncannily resembled his own, had by 1950 already moved away from his formalist beginnings and begun to anticipate confessional practice, announcing 'himself as the material of his art' and producing a poetry that searched 'for some dynamic correspondence between the human and vegetable worlds'.[25] No wonder Thomas could write to Roethke about the latter's new col-lection, 'I'd like to hear you read them, and to go through them very carefully with you. Perhaps we can learn a little from each other, and anyway it will be enjoyable if we learn and know nothing and only blunder loud about' (*CL*, 895). Brinnin recalls that, on his very first encounter with Thomas, when he had just landed in New York for his inaugural tour, 'the first American writer he asked about was Theodore Roethke' (*DTA*, 5).

It was at Thomas's own request that Roethke reviewed *In Country Sleep and Other Poems* for *Poetry* in December 1952.[26] As the flamboy-ant title 'One Ring-tailed Roarer to Another' would lead us to expect, not only is it an extravagant verbal bagatelle, it is an ingenious act of acculturation, of American appropriation of Thomas. This is signalled in the title itself, which is a slang American expression, deriving from Southern folk humour, for a larger-than-life character; a loud, swag-gering braggart: a ready roisterer and brawler.[27] And in keeping with this, the whole piece is a colourful exercise in verbal brawling, designed to image Thomas as an untamed character after Roethke's own heart.

Has the ring-tailed roarer begun to snore? The limp spirit of a
Peruvian prince taken over his wild psyche? Has he shoved down
the throttle only to find a ramshackle model of patch-work fancies fluttering to a short cough? What time's the train of his spirit
due? To what wonders are we now exposed? (*T*, 211)

At once approximating to Southern tall-tale convention and roughly
imitating Thomas's writings at their most wildly surreal, Roethke seems
out to demonstrate that he and the Welshman are kindred spirits, free
rebel spirits both, walking on the wild side of language and convention,
crazy boyos ready for a verbal punch-up. Roethke devotes a whole paragraph to the ancient art of 'flyting', excoriating 'those loathly wearers
of other men's clothing ... hyenas of sensibility; ... anglo-saxon apostles
of refinement' (*T*, 211).

Roethke was always sympathetic to Thomas's situation as an
undomesticated Welsh outsider out to shock middle-class English establishment culture: 'a home-made halo he has in a sour country where at
least they love a bard. *And* sing' (*T*, 212). Roethke also seems aware that
the Welsh name 'Dylan' comes from the Mabinogion character known
as 'Dylan eil-don', Dylan spume of the sea, because he invokes him as
a 'rare heedless fornicator of language' who 'speaks with the voice of
angels and ravens, casting us back where the sea leaps and the strud-
ding witch walks by a deep well' (*T*, 213). The whole review is clearly
calculated to please Thomas himself. It is a kind of tribute from one
poet to another, whom he regards as his spiritual and poetic twin. And
it is a brilliantly inventive attempt to 'Americanise' Thomas that is, in
part, predicated on his welcome 'un-Englishness'. Many other American
poets were to adopt this approach when dealing with the Welshman.

In the process they often relied on that bogus, but highly influential,
account of 'Celtic magic' that had been peddled by Matthew Arnold in
his (in)famous 1867 lecture *On the Study of Celtic Literature* – a subject on
which he authoritatively pontificated even though he could not read a
word of the literatures involved in their original tongues.[28] In the 'Saxon'
Arnold's condescendingly sexist and racist rendering, the 'Celtic nature'
was characterised by a particular sensibility, 'a nervous exaltation', that
had 'something feminine' about it. 'The Celt', he grandly pronounced,
was 'indisciplined, anarchical, and turbulent by nature', which was the
opposite of 'the Anglo-Saxon temperament, disciplinable and steadily

obedient within certain limits'.[29] The latter was destined to rule, the former to prove an amenable subject.

These politically advantageous English ideas became fused with the fanciful notions of the late eighteenth-century antiquarians about the 'Druids'.[30] And it is to the eighteenth century we also need to look to discover the origin of the idea of the 'Welsh bard' that kept cropping up in American responses to Thomas. It derived from Thomas Gray's famous poem 'The Bard', which was built on the entirely false supposition that Edward I, during his thirteenth-century campaigns to subdue the troublesome Welsh, had ordered his troops to slay all the bards. But behind this legend there did in fact lie a truth: namely that the traditional role of the 'bard' – or 'bardd' in Welsh, which simply means 'a poet' – was to be the remembrancer of his people and the custodian of their traditions. It was this tribal role of the bard, along with the honourable place accordingly assigned to him at all feasts, that Thomas had in mind when he claimed – or perhaps 'usurped' – that role for himself in his poem 'After the Funeral' when describing himself as 'Ann's bard on a raised hearth'.[31]

Roethke's tribute essay after Thomas's 'stunning' death strikes a much more sober note than his rumbunctious review. Regretting that he had had such a short time to get to know him – they had met only some three times – Roethke spoke feelingfully of him 'as a younger brother', while shrewdly noting that 'he was so rich in what he was that each friend or acquaintance seemed to carry a particular image of him' (*T*, 51). Perhaps thinking back to that earlier review, he mentioned that Thomas 'had been built up to me as a great swill-down drinker, a prodigious roaring boy out of the Welsh caves', before adding with wistful honesty, '[b]ut I never knew such a one' (*T*, 50). Thomas had disarmingly preferred to talk instead, Roethke had discovered, 'about Welsh picnics'. And he concluded his short piece by asserting that '[h]e was one of the great ones, there can be no doubt of that. And he drank his own blood, ate of his own marrow, to get at some of the material' (*T*, 52).

More complicated was Thomas's relationship with the poet and critic Karl Shapiro, who was a year older than himself, but his response too included an attempt to 'Americanise' Thomas, albeit in terms different from those of Roethke. Thomas had first come to Shapiro's attention in late 1944, as Thomas singled out for praise a poem of his that had appeared in Oscar Williams's most recent anthology (*CL*, 536). At that point, Shapiro was serving in the Pacific Theatre, but by the time Thomas came to visit the US, he had become an influential figure, winner of a Pulitzer Prize in 1945, Poetry Consultant to the Library of Congress (1946–7) and recently appointed editor of *Poetry* (Chicago). A year after Thomas's death, Shapiro wrote a long, rather convoluted obituary for him that seemed to reflect his own conflicted feelings about both the man and the poetry.[32]

'The death of Dylan Thomas a year and a half ago,' it opened, 'was the cause of the most singular demonstration of suffering in recent literary history' (*T*, 269). He had been the first poet to have been 'both popular and obscure'. But all the wrong things had come to be written about him, as writers seemed mesmerised by an image of him as a kind of overgrown baby. Instead, Shapiro insisted, he was the poet of suffering and he meant to draw attention to 'the live thing, the thing that touched the raw nerve of the world and that keeps us singing in pain' (*T*, 270). 'I doubt,' Shapiro percipiently added, 'that Thomas himself knew how personal poetry might become after him' (*T*, 271). And he took pains to differentiate his Thomas from that of the heirs of the Bohemians and the Symbolists, even as he emphasised that 'Thomas resisted the literary traditionalism of the Eliot school'. Likewise he had distanced himself from Auden and his followers, because he belonged to a generation with no romantic political illusions. After all, he had begun to write in the Depression, 'which was worse in Wales than in America' (*T*, 272). And Thomas had also written in the aftermath of 'the horror of the second war [that] surpassed the historical imagination' and when 'the prescience of the third war paralyzed thought' (*T*, 272). At this point, we begin to see that Shapiro views Thomas very much in the light of his own experiences in the post-war period. He presents Thomas as a spokesman in poetry for Shapiro's own, second 'lost generation' of American veterans.

Shapiro is also shrewd in surmising that Thomas 'was anti-tradition by nature, by place, by inclination', and that his 'love for America can ... be seen in this light; America is the untraditional place, the Romantic country *par excellence*' (*T*, 273). As for Roethke, therefore, Thomas's 'un-Englishness', rooted in a Welshness of which Shapiro has but a vague and Romantic conception, becomes a salient and attractive feature of his writing. There was in the poetry nothing that was original, claims

Shapiro, yet everything that was distinctive. But at this point, he seems to veer off-course as he begins to insist that Thomas 'is quite derivative, unoriginal, unintellectual', and that 'the entire force of [his] personality and vitality is jammed into his few difficult half-intelligible poems' (*T*, 274).

Having thus done a pretty good job of damning him, though, Shapiro suddenly announces that of the ninety or so poems published by Thomas, 'more than thirty ... I think stand with the best poems of our time' (*T*, 274). But as for the more pretentious poems, such as 'Altarwise by Owl-Light', these are merely conventional statements dressed up in fancy language. He is prone to leave us with 'heaps of grotesque images that add up to nothing'. And while 'sex is the chief process in Thomas's view of the world' – and here, Shapiro acidly remarks, he betrays himself to be a contemporary of Henry Miller and Freud – he should nevertheless be accounted an authentically religious poet. In fact, 'there are two minds working in Thomas, the joyous naturally religious mind, and the disturbed, almost pathological mind of the cultural fugitive or clown' (*T*, 278). And Shapiro the war veteran seems to be more attracted to the latter, when 'through the obscurity of the poetry everyone could feel the scream of desperation' (*T*, 279).

IV

As can be seen, any serious attempt to examine the impact of Thomas on the poetic culture of the States must involve a study of what I term the phenomenon of 'cultural translation'. In other words, the various means, or strategies, employed to 'acculturate' his work; to transpose it, so to speak, into the different key of American culture. Today, this process would tend to be labelled 'the construction of the American Thomas'. Yet most discussions of 'Thomas in America' have been limited to attempts – necessarily elusive, if not futile – to establish the precise extent and import of his 'influence' on American poets. (Seemingly so hospitably simple, that word 'influence' in reality conceals a multitude of difficulties.) 'Cultural translation' is a process that is common enough, but it is also invariably complex and elaborate. But in his classic study, Brinnin opens a fascinating window on the process as it relates to Dylan Thomas.

Following Thomas's return to Wales after his first American tour, Brinnin had journeyed there himself, and shortly after his initial arrival in Cardiff had been introduced to Thomas's very important early mentor, Aneirin Talfan Davies. By then, Davies was head of BBC Radio in Wales, and he invited Brinnin to deliver a talk on Dylan Thomas in America. The talk that resulted was both brilliant and brilliantly revealing, because during the course of it Brinnin ventured to propose two reasons – contrasting yet complementary – as to why Thomas had been such a hit in the United States. The first was an exotic 'foreignness' that took the form of his evident Welshness. For Brinnin, Thomas's person and writing exuded a sense of being wrinkled deep in time. It gave the impression of being fraught with an ancient history. Thomas seemed to be working in an old tradition that he was modifying in his poetry: 'he has made of the history in his bones a speech that we come upon with instantaneous enlightenment … As a Welshman rooted deeply in his people and his land, Dylan Thomas speaks to us from sources we have lost, and we are drawn by his native accents with nostalgia and the excitement of vicarious participation' (*DTA*, 97). One of the most common ways in which Americans registered this sense of Thomas was, as Brinnin astutely realised, by characterising the Welshman as 'primitive'.

But the second reason for Thomas's appeal was that Americans could instinctively realise that he was also working in an *American* tradition: the tradition of Walt Whitman. It was a thought that had perhaps struck Brinnin when, in the process of 'borrowing' the garage near the boat house that Thomas had converted into his writing studio in order to draft the text of his radio broadcast, Brinnin's eye had immediately been taken by the fact that 'over the small wooden table that served Dylan for a desk was a handsome portrait of Walt Whitman' (*DTA*, 93).

Brinnin was writing before the important 'Whitmanian turn' in post-war American culture was effectively begun by Gay Wilson Allen's classic 1955 biography, a turn that duly saw Whitman reinstated as the major poet of America as well as a 'prophet'. In writing of the Whitmanian aspects of Thomas, therefore, Brinnin made it clear that he had in mind 'the vigor and breadth of Walt Whitman'. 'We [Americans] read Whitman when we are young,' Brinnin wrote, 'and he implants in us a lively vision of democracy that persists as part of our belief' (*DTA*, 98). 'But as we grow older, we find less and less satisfaction in his qualities as an artist, and finally tend to remember him as a prophet rather than as a poet.' Elsewhere in his study of Thomas, Brinnin emphasised that for him the Welshman's most prominent feature was his radical egalitarianism. Thomas's 'Whitmanianism' was fascinating to Americans, Brinnin concluded, because he somehow managed to combine 'democratic expression and aristocratic artistry which satisfied a dual need which we may not have consciously recognized' (*DTA*, 98).

Shapiro's treatment of Whitman in his essay clearly bears out Brinnin's conclusion, and thus offers yet another angle on the act of 'cultural translation' central to the process of 'Americanising' Thomas. For Shapiro, he has to be cleansed of those several distinctively English designations with which he had arrived encumbered – Bohemian Marxist; Symbolist; one of the Apocalyptic poets. Then he has to be isolated from the disparate foreign traditions to which he had been connected – the English Metaphysical poets, the Welsh-language *cynghanedd* tradition most famously represented by Dafydd ap Gwilym. Nevertheless, his Welshness is not to be denied and discarded utterly, as it is, in fact, his cultural passport to America and the grounds for awarding him honorary American citizenship. It is by virtue of his Welshness that he is a puritan and a provincial, both terms that resonated with American readers, as did the image of the 'primitive' with which Shapiro also very strongly associated him: 'he was another *naïf*, like Rimbaud, a countryman, who, having left the country wanders over the face of the earth seeking a vision'. 'And there are suggestions of Druidism … and primitive fertility rites, apparently still extant in Wales, all mixed up with Henry Miller, Freud and American street slang' (*T*, 277). The absurdities of such claims are, of course, evident. Thomas was no countryman: he was a thoroughgoing 'townie', brought up in the industrial town of Swansea, globally famous as 'Copperopolis' in the nineteenth century and a centre of the worldwide burgeoning metallurgical industries by the beginning of the twentieth century. It was also one of the exporting ports for the great south Wales coalfield. Even more absurd was the notion of 'Druidism' and of 'primitive fertility rites' – notions born of eighteenth-century English fantasies of the supposedly remote and backward 'Celtic fringe'. Although in fairness, Thomas himself loved, particularly in the stories of the 1930s, to play with such romantic materials. For Shapiro, 'he is a self-limited poet; and an exasperating one'; and that exasperation is patently clear in Shapiro's essay. Thomas constantly seeks refuge in childhood, like

D. H. Lawrence, and Shapiro ends his essay by quoting lines from 'I advance for as long as forever is', because to him they sound 'so much like a line of Whitman's that I have searched through Whitman's poems to find it' – but in vain (*T*, 283).

The Americanisation of Thomas by equating him with Whitman came to a head in 1960 when, along with James E. Miller Jr and Bernice Slote, Shapiro brought out the critical volume *Start with the Sun*. First, then, there was Ginsberg's avid reading of Gay Wilson Allen's biography; now this volume put together by a team that, in Shapiro, included a poet. These mark the high point of the coincidence of the post-war poetic and academic interest in Whitman, and Dylan Thomas was implicated in both cases. From then on, the paths of their respective development began to diverge. *Start With the Sun: Studies in Cosmic Poetry* was dedicated to the enthusiastic study of what the authors termed the 'Whitman tradition', a tradition they also termed 'the New Paganism', which they contrasted with the 'Eliot tradition', which they styled 'The New Puritanism'. The former was life-affirming and celebratory, in its delight in all the forces implicated in what Whitman had famously called 'the procreant urge of the world', while the latter was lamentably negative and sterile. The key figures in the Whitman tradition, they asserted, were Whitman, Lawrence, Hart Crane and Dylan Thomas, all of whom resembled Whitman in some way or other in their poetics. But they emphasised that theirs was a study concerned not with 'influences' but with 'relationships, affinities, definitions'. And they observed that 'Crane, Thomas, Lorca and Ginsberg all participate in the creation of a twentieth-century Walt Whitman who was relatively unknown in the nineteenth' – as, one might add, he was to remain largely unknown in twentieth-century America (with the exception of a few admirers such as Crane) until after the Second World War.[33]

In his essay 'James Dickey as a Southern Visionary', the distinguished Southern critic Monroe K. Spears described Dickey in terms that dovetail neatly with the discussion of twentieth-century heirs of 'the Whitman tradition' in *Start with the Sun*.[34] Recalling Dickey's statement that his religious vision 'involves myself and the universe and it does not admit of any kind of intermediary, such as Jesus and the Bible', Spears concludes that 'Dickey belongs to the line of visionaries running from Blake through Rimbaud and Whitman to such modern exemplars as Hart Crane, George Barker, Dylan Thomas and Theodore Roethke'.

As a young man Dickey, a committed Southerner, was prone to mock and dismiss Whitman as a 'bard of the North'. But when addressing a Whitman conference at Camden New Jersey in 1972, he completely changed his tune.[35] He had first read Whitman, he claimed, in the gloom of the cockpit of a trainer fighter during the war, and had suddenly realised that here was a poet he could relate to. Whitman had revealed to him, he added, that he needn't despair of being able to write like Tennyson; that he could draw upon his own experiences and rely on his own style to write a poem. 'I have been doin' so ever since,' Dickey concluded, 'I think he's my great father as a writer.' Dickey's account of encountering Whitman may well have been a stretcher – he was an adept practitioner of the tall tale tradition of the South – but there may have been at least a grain of truth that he had found his way to writing partly through Whitman. Joyce Carol Oates once arrestingly described Dickey as a 'our dark poet', because he embraced the buoyant energies of American individualism, but in forms contaminated by the violence of the twentieth century.[36]

Spears linked Dickey as a visionary not only with Whitman but with Roethke and Thomas, and evidence for his deep admiration for both seems to me to be unequivocal. He remarked that he had been profoundly influenced by Roethke's *The Lost Son* and thereafter had aimed for his 'haunted perceptual clarity'. And during the course of informal discussions held with students at the University of South Carolina (where he taught) Dickey took off for ten enraptured minutes describing his envy for Thomas's effortless and authentic originality of mind and expression. He marvelled at lines in which there seemed a blend of surrealism and Freudianism, and both were combined with a song-like, rhythmic utterance consistent with Thomas's south Wales accent. Such originality he added was inimitable, and so he'd been careful never to be influenced by Thomas. But he had learned from him. And Dickey ended with the typically hyperbolic claim that Thomas 'was the most original poet in English'. The only two who could claim to be his equals, he stated, were Donne and Hopkins, but in the end Thomas was the most original of the three.[37]

Dickey, then, provides another example of how a familiarity with Whitman could facilitate admiration for Thomas in the States. Another who illuminated the process of cultural translation instanced by Thomas's 'Americanisation', but from an intriguingly different angle, was Elizabeth Hardwick. Her essay entitled 'America and Dylan Thomas' (the reversal of the order in the title of Brinnin's book is of course pointed) opens by arrestingly stating that '[h]e died, like Valentino, with mysterious, weeping women at his bedside'.[38] 'Could it have happened quite this way in England?' she quizzically wonders. 'Were his last years there quite as frenzied and unhealthy as his journeys to America? He was one of ours, in a way, and he came back here to die with a terrible and fabulous rightness. (Not ours, of course, in his talents, his work, his joys, but ours in his sufferings, his longings, his demands.)' (*EH*, 153). That 'he was first-rate' she has no doubt, but she is most interested in examining the reasons why he was 'literally *adored* in America'. She concludes that 'he was both a success and a failure in a way we find particularly appealing ... a wild genius who needed caring for ... he was a pattern we can recognize all too easily – the charming young man of great gifts, wilfully going down to ruin. He was Hart Crane, Poe, F. Scott Fizgerald ... and also, unexpectedly, something of a great actor ... in a time when the literary style runs to the scholarly and the clerical' (*EH*, 155). Hardwick also recognises the important contribution made by Brinnin's notorious, 'outlandishly successful' book to the posthumous clinching of this American image of Thomas. (She shrewdly noticed that Brinnin's controversial reportage was a cathartic work, and a work of grieving: it had sprung from the sympathy, sorrow and respect he still felt for his friend.) And she ends her brief study with the remark that Thomas's meteoric American passage had brilliantly illuminated and briefly relieved 'the sober and dreary fact of the decline of our literary life, its thinness and fatigue. From this Thomas was, to many, a brief reprieve' (*EH*, 159).

<h1 style="text-align:center">V</h1>

Thomas had arrived in America at the beginning of what Hardwick's husband (from 1949 to 1972), Robert Lowell, was to term 'the tran-quilized fifties'; the Eisenhower era of what economist John Kenneth Galbraith, in his critique of the period's emergent 'affluent society', described as 'the bland leading the bland'.[39] Out of the traumas first of the Depression thirties and then of involvement in a world war, Americans had emerged into a period of supreme military dominance, political quietism and consumer craving. It was perhaps the golden age of bourgeois America, although shadowed by the spectre of Communism and the threat of the Bomb. That Thomas's visits to the States occurred not only during the Cold War but during the period of Senator McCarthy's witch-hunts is chillingly brought home by an incident reported by Brinnin. 'When he had applied in London for an American visa,' Brinnin recalled, 'he had been subject to questions which made him angry, but also apprehensive.' Thomas had been asked, for instance, whether he would attend a song-recital of Paul Robeson's.[40] He had answered in the affirmative. His interrogator had also quizzed him about his visit to Prague, and Thomas had had to 'admit that his expenses were paid by his hosts behind the Iron Curtain' (*DTA*, 25). Thomas underwent a similar interrogation when he subsequently applied for a visa before his second American visit.

This was the cultural context that produced a backlash in the form of James Dean, Marlon Brando and Elvis Presley, the dissenting culture of the Beats, the lacerating self-exposures of the Confessionals and the ominous psychic landscapes of the Deep Image school. Although Thomas did not survive to see the emergence of this anti-bourgeois counter-culture, he actually lived through its beginnings and helped develop the conditions necessary for its full development. And he was able inadvertently to do so because he already naturally spoke the language of this new generation – a vulgarised Freudian discourse, the anarchist vocabulary of the soft Left, the vatic utterance of a visionary sexual politics. Brinnin is shrewd on Thomas's relationship to the politics of the Left in this period:

> Dylan's political naïveté, it seemed to me, was a consequence of his promiscuous affection for humanity and of his need for emotional identification with the lowest stratum of society. His socialism was basically Tolstoyan, the attempt of the spiritual aristocrat to hold in one embrace the good heart of mankind, a gesture and a purpose uncontaminated by the *realpolitik* of the twentieth century. While he expressed himself strongly on political matters and tended indiscriminately to support the far left, his attitude was a kind of stance unsupported by knowledge, almost in defiance of knowledge. As long as, anywhere in the world, there existed groups of men pilloried by the forces of

propertied power, Dylan wanted to be counted among their sym-
pathizers. (*DTA*, 26)

It is a passage worth dwelling on, because for 'Tolstoyan' Brinnin might
as appropriately have written 'Whitmanian', and the whole thrust of his
comments helps us to understand how and why Thomas came to appeal
to the Beats and even to prepare the way, so to speak, that eventually
was to lead to Woodstock.[41]

If Ginsberg's gesture at Laugharne is one powerful image of
Thomas's influence on postwar American poetry, then it finds its equally
powerful counterpart in the presence of John Berryman at Thomas's
bedside in St Vincent's Hospital, New York, when he passed away on
9 November 1953. Berryman was at that time on the very threshold of
the critical recognition that would begin to come his way with the publication of *Homage to Mistress Bradstreet* in 1956. He had first met Thomas
when he was a student at Clare College, Cambridge in the mid thirties
and had reviewed him for the *Kenyon Review* in 1940. But like Lowell
and so many others, Berryman had come a long way from the formalist
poetry of his early period, and it was a different Berryman who, particularly with the publication of *77 Dream Songs* (1964), was to perfect a new
genre of Freudian lyric, who kept vigil by the dying Thomas's bedside.
It is an appropriate emblem of Thomas's notable importance for a new,
emerging generation of post-war American poets.

Forty years after Thomas's death, researchers found an unpublished
memoir of Berryman's friendship with Thomas that was written in
1959.[42] This includes the usual colourful stories, such as the anecdote
about the occasion Thomas got Berryman drunk in an attempt – vain,
as it turned out – to prevent him making a rendezvous with his hero,
the great W. B. Yeats. Even then, 'I was perfectly clear already that he
was the most important of my generation to come into view on either
side of the Atlantic'. It is, however, by characterising the impression
Thomas made on him as a remarkable reader of poetry that Berryman
most clearly indicates Thomas's contribution to his own development.
'At this time Dylan Thomas was very thin and small,' writes Berryman.
'His face gave the impression of being covered with knobs; he looked
rather like a bug-eyed pixie; he was one of the most delicious clowns
I have ever come on.' Thomas the clown – Roethke likewise recalls
his devotion to the films of Chaplin and of the Marx Brothers – was

well calculated to appeal to the future poet of *Dream Songs*. That is the first of Berryman's significant comments. The second quickly follows: 'His reading then was less mannered, less virtuoso-like, and adapted itself better to whatever the poem was … Later, wonderful as his voice remained, he often used it as a machine into which he fed poems of every sort that came out then all much alike.'

Two points, then: Thomas's gifts as a clown, and his gifts as a reader not of poetry but of poetries: the young Thomas seemed not so much to have a single, sonorous, organ Voice, but a dramatic range of different voices at his disposal. Those are the points to bear in mind when one turns to Berryman's acknowledged masterpiece, and one of the greatest achievements in postwar American poetry – namely the astonishing sequence of poems on which he embarked in the late 1950s and which remained uncompleted at his suicide in 1972. The bulk of these poems are collected under the title *Dream Songs* and constitute a vaudeville theatre of Berryman's psyche. The starring role, so to speak, is given to Henry, an imaginary character representing the unruly impulses of the id – since the anonymous scriptwriter of this vaudeville is in effect Freud, and the whole endless programme of chaotic, tumultuous 'acts' is based on Berryman's experiences. Take the following dialogue between Henry and his side-kick, here functioning as the lugubrious, world-weary voice of common-sense, and speaking with a grotesque Black Minstrel accent, who cuts him down to size by reducing 'Sir Bones' to 'Mr Bones'. It is lustful Henry who speaks first:

> Filling her compact & delicious body
> with chicken paprika, she glanced at me
> twice.
> Fainting with interest, I hungered back
> and only the fact of her husband & four other people
> kept me from springing on her
>
> or falling at her little feet and crying
> 'You are the hottest one for years of night
> Henry's dazed eyes
> have enjoyed, Brilliance.' I advanced upon
> (despairing) my spumoni. – Sir Bones: is stuffed,
> de world, wif feeding girls

Black hair, complexion Latin, jeweled eyes
downcast…The slob beside her feasts…What wonders is
she sitting on, over there?
The restaurant buzzes. She might as well be on Mars.
Where did it all go wrong? There ought to be a law
   against Henry
Mr Bones: there is.[43]

As Kurt Heinzelman has shrewdly remarked, 'rather than saying that Thomas influenced Berryman directly, as he did Les Murray, I would say that Berryman absorbed Thomas; that Thomas's ongoing, though intermittent, presence for him manifested itself in a voice and a manner that Berryman would be projecting in his new *Dream Songs*, begun in the mid-1950s but not published as a volume until 1964'.[44] And Heinzelman also draws attention to the Thomasian resonances of 'In Memoriam', the elegy that Berryman wrote when he was 'in his mid-fifties and hospitalized at least once a year from drink and depression' and starting 'to understand that he may be veering towards the same sad end as Thomas.'[45]

Berryman ruefully remarked that, on meeting Thomas, he immediately noticed that 'his talent for ordinary life was even less than mine'. And he was never so besotted that he failed to protect himself from Thomas's dangerously radioactive presence. He made it clear that the more practiced the Welshman became at public readings, the more inauthentic they became, as 'the voice' took over. He also distinguished between the early Thomas, whose 'work was accomplished, even prodigious, but … overdone and a little inhuman', and the post-war work. And he particularly admired 'Fern Hill' and 'A Refusal to Mourn' – which was one of the poems that made a most profound impression on a substantial number of American poets. Touchingly, he recalled how he and Thomas had enthused together about the unfulfilled promise of the young Welsh poet Alun Lewis, who had tragically died in wartime Burma by his own hand.[46]

Berryman's response to Thomas was in some ways representative of several emergent poets of his generation. One such was Robert Bly, who achieved celebrity in 1990s thanks to publishing a book, *Iron John*, that became the sacred text, the veritable testament, of the men's movement.[47] It was the counter-weight to the new wave of feminism that had emerged during the early 1970s. Parallel with this, Bly embarked on a poetic search for his own 'chosen fathers', or poetic teachers, and one of those was Dylan Thomas, revered by Bly along with Walt Whitman. Once again, then, we find that the 'Americanisation' of Thomas involves providing a fast track back to Whitman. Why so? Because the music of Thomas's poetry, like that of Whitman's, reveals language to be at root not the obedient tool of the rational, functional intelligence but the secret agent of our primal, pre-conscious, sensuous being: it beats to the pulse of our body and moves to the tidal rhythms of our blood, the 'systole and diastole' of the heart hymned by Whitman, and it also reproduces, as does his poetry, 'the procreant urge of the world'. Bly expresses this in his poem 'The Gaiety of Form', addressed to his chosen father, Dylan Thomas:

> How sweet to weight the line with all these vowels!
> Body, Thomas, the codfish's psalm. The gaiety
> Of form lies in the labor of its playfulness.
> The chosen vowel reappears like the evening star
> There, in the solemn return the astronomers love.
> When 'ahm' returns three times, then it becomes
> A noise; then the whole stanza turns to music.
> It comforts us, says: 'I am here, be calm.'[48]

By considering the response of Berryman, Shapiro, Hall and Bly to Thomas, I have highlighted the Welshman's impact in the early fifties on the rising generation of postwar American poets. But as noted earlier, there is also another aspect to his case, namely the way in which Thomas gave new prominence, and decisive new impetus, to existing elements within the American poetry of the time. This is best illustrated by considering the development of Kenneth Rexroth. Some ten years older than Dylan Thomas, Rexroth was already well-known as a poet in America long before Thomas arrived on the scene. He had had a colourful early career, that included backpacking across the country several times, and spending two months in a Hudson Valley monastery. During the 1930s, he became a leading figure of the Left, participating in the Communist party's John Reed Clubs, organisations supporting working-class writers and artists. One area that is just beginning to be investigated is the way in which Dylan Thomas, one of whose closest

friends was the Communist Bert Trick and who himself always professed an attachment to the Left, was regarded by radical writers during
his visits to the States.[49] Certainly, Rexroth is likely to loom large in any
such investigation.

After Thomas's death, Rexroth wrote 'Thou Shalt not Kill', a
memorial that became one of the American's best known performance
pieces. A long work, it treats Thomas's death as emblematising the death
of all artists martyred at the hands of a murderous Capitalist order that
had demonstrated its true, ruthless nature by exploding the hydrogen
bomb over Hiroshima. It accuses Capitalism of 'vaticide' – that is of
slaying the vates, the bardic seer and sayer – and it ends apocalyptically:

> The underground men are not singing
> On their way to work.
> There is a smell of blood
> In the smell of turf smoke.
> They have struck him down,
> The son of David ap Gwilym.
> They have murdered him,
> The Baby of Taliesin.
> There he lies dead,
> By the Iceberg of the United Nations.
> There he lies sandbagged
> At the foot of the Statue of Liberty.
> The Gulf Stream smells of blood
> As it breaks on the sand of Iona
> And the blue rocks of Carnavon.
> And all the birds of the deep sea rise up
> Over the luxury liners and scream,
> 'You killed him! You killed him,
> In your God damned Brooks Brothers suit,
> You son of a bitch.'[50]

Rexroth viewed Thomas, partly courtesy of his Welshness, as an outsider to the Anglo-American Establishment like himself. This becomes
clear, if one recalls his verse report on his fleeting experience of the
London poetry scene in the early 1950s, 'The Dragon and the Unicorn'.
It includes the following passage:

> Intellectual parties,
> Orgies of foolish snobbery,
> Bad manners, and illiteracy.
> The Irish are not considered
> Human, the Scotch and Welsh subject
> To worse chauvinism than
> Can be found in the Deep South.
> Everywhere, here, covetousness
> And envy of money-grubbing
> Americans.[51]

From his early days in Chicago, Rexroth had revelled in the company of odd-balls and crazy marginals: 'Anarchists-Single Taxers, British Israelites, self-anointed archbishops of the American Catholic Church, Druids, Anthroposophists ... Socialists, communists ... Schopenhauerians, Nietzscheans'.[52] He also loved to go to jazz clubs to listen to Louis Armstrong and Bix Beiderbecke. When he settled on the West Coast, in the Bay Area of San Francisco, he revelled in the freedom of mountains and ocean. Also he established groups to discuss politics and read poetry. By the 1950s, these informal gatherings had spawned a new kind of performance poetry, and it was at one such event that Allen Ginsberg heard Rexroth read poems to musical accompaniment, poems that included the elegy to Dylan Thomas.[53]

During the later 1950s, Rexroth therefore became a kind of guru of a new cult movement that came to be labelled Beat. He was revered by figures such as Robert Duncan, Lawrence Ferlinghetti, Gary Snyder and, of course, Allen Ginsberg. Consequently, he was informally dubbed 'the Father of the Beats', although he came to resent such a dubious accolade.[54] He, in turn, regarded Whitman as the great muse and patron of his own visionary imagination, and regarded Dylan Thomas as a kind of reincarnation of Whitman's spirit. Rexroth therefore affords a striking and important example of the way in which Dylan Thomas simultaneously benefited from and dramatically contributed to the development of a new kind of post-war American poetry. With its roots way back in Whitman, and already beginning to burgeon in the early pre-war poetry of Rexroth, this poetry (often emphasising its oral and performative aspects) was enabled – partly through the dramatic intervention of Dylan Thomas – to explode into spectacular growth with the

Beats and then to proliferate into what in the 1960s came to be known as an 'alternative culture' of violent critique of American capitalism and protest against its prosecution of the Vietnam war.

Like Rexroth, Richard Eberhart had also begun to establish a reputation in the States as a poet, albeit a minor one, before Thomas made his appearance there. And Eberhart, who was to reach the pinnacle of success in the 1960s and 1970s, when he won the Pulitzer Prize in 1966 and in 1974 a National Book Award, was another of the American poets that the Welshman mentioned he'd read before any of his trans-Atlantic trips. By December 1949, his attention had been drawn to *War and the Poet*, an anthology co-edited by Eberhart and Seldon Rodman that exemplified man's response to war from ancient to modern times, which received a lukewarm review from John Ciardi in *The Atlantic*.[55] Thomas's interest was very understandable, given his own stance on the Second World War, his horror at Hiroshima and Nagasaki and their implications, and such poems of his as 'A Refusal to Mourn'. As for Eberhart's co-editor, Rodman, he began a review of poetry collections by Macleish and Eberhart in the *New York Times* in November 1953, with the query: 'Now that Dylan Thomas is gone, how many natural poets have we among us? Poets whose habit fits them so well that when they use prose it sounds as though they were writing in a foreign language?' Rodman suggested that the two poets under review had produced poems worthy of Thomas's example.[56]

The two actually got to know each other when Eberhart found himself, with Richard Wilbur among others, trying to 'manage' Thomas when he visited Harvard to read at the Brattle Theatre on his first visit to the United States, and again on his second. After Thomas's death, Eberhart recalled the occasion with a mixture of affection, exasperation and sadness, including the time when he had had to 'get him up in the morning by plugging his mouth with a bottle of beer, this wonderful baby' (*T*, 56). Eberhart settled on the term 'impish' to account for all the 'startling' things Thomas got up to while he was at Harvard, and the impression made on him by his readings stayed permanently with him and affected his own approach to poetry. 'I loved the man', he disarmingly admitted, adding that it was his belief 'that he could no more escape his death than he could his genius; and that he lived and died to exalt mankind and to express something recurrent and ineffable in the spirit of man, the strength of the imagination, the exaltation of the soul'. Immediately following Thomas's death, Eberhart joined with Archibald MacLeish and Richard Wilbur in an evening of readings at the Poetry Theatre in Harvard chaired by I. A. Richards (who was, Helen Vendler assures me, proud of his own Welsh connections), to raise money for Thomas's impecunious widow and her children.[57]

VI

As David Boucher has noted, 'The Beat Generation was nascent at the time of Thomas's death.'[58] The response of the Beats to Thomas (which in many cases was ambivalent) has been covered extensively and excellently elsewhere, as has the fascinating record of his attractiveness for Black American poets, such as Al Young and Bob Kaufman. Amiri Baraka, as Daniel Williams has noted, is a dissenting case.[59] Baraka began, when still LeRoi Jones, by viewing Thomas as a liberating Bohemian presence on the American scene, writing a letter in 1958 to the editor of *Partisan Review* regretting that 'Poor Dylan Thomas carried the ball all by himself in England, and we know what happened when eventually he did get to America.'[60] But once he became Amiri Baraka, he could see Thomas only as a representative of white 'European' cultural ascendancy. For Rexroth and other (mainly white) Beats, Thomas was a kind of poetic equivalent of the African American saxophonist Charlie ('Bird') Parker, part of a wider affinity that the Beats alleged existed between Dylan Thomas and modern jazz.[61]

Of the Beats, it was Ferlinghetti who was most alive to Thomas's influence on the milieu out of which he and his fellows had emerged, and most appreciative of his achievements. During a visit to San Francisco Thomas had given readings to packed houses in the Bay area as well as on the influential KPFA radio station, and those readings made an indelible mark on Ferlinghetti's consciousness: 'His voice,' he recalled years later, 'had a singular beauty and richness, in the great Welsh oral tradition; and the excitement he generated was an early inspiration for a tradition of oral poetry here, the subsequent San Francisco poetry movement being consistently centred on the performance of poetry in public.'[62] By 1957, Ferlinghetti and Rexroth were to begin performing poetry to jazz accompaniment at 'The Cellar', 576 Green Street, and these events were a focus of attention for the Beats as much as the City Lights Bookstore (which had opened in 1953).

In due course, following a visit to Wales, Ferlinghetti wrote his 'Belated Palinode for Dylan Thomas', which opens by setting the scene before continuing in a loose style that allows him to incorporate familiar phrases and references from Thomas's poetry into his own verse:

> In Wales at Laugharne at last I stand beside
> his cliff-perched writing shed
> above the coursing waters
> where the hawk hangs still
> above the cockle-strewn shingle

Ferlinghetti looks out across 'a bold green headland lost in the sun', beyond which lie

> (across an ocean and a continent)
> San Francisco's white wood houses
> and a poet's sun-bleached cottage
> on Bolinas' far lagoon
> with its wind-torn Little Mesa
> (so very like St Johns Hill).[63]

It is a moment of moving self-identification with Thomas and acknowledgement of his contribution to the culture of the Beats.

Other of the Beat poets were more cagey and ambivalent in their responses to Thomas. Corso – who routinely referenced Whitman in his poetry, as did his idol Ginsberg – was taken aback when, during the course of a conversation, the latter responded to Corso's reading of his poem 'Hair' by remarking that 'it's more like Dylan Thomas than you would think ... think of all the mad images in that, that's like Dylan Thomas: "I see the angels washing their oceans of hair" is something that Thomas would have smiled at.' Corso was forced wryly to agree.[64]

By 1967, Charles Bukowski could comment caustically that 'anybody can go the way of Dylan Thomas, Ginsberg, Corso, Behan, Leary, Creeley, sliding down that river of shit. The idea is Creation, not Adulation; the idea is a man in a room alone hacking at the stone and not sucking at the tits of the crowd.'[65] Ironically, it is an observation to which we can imagine Thomas assenting. Bukowski expressed the same sentiments in savagely crude, impassioned poetry:

> and D. Thomas – THEY KILLED HIM, of course.
> Thomas didn't want all those free drinks
> all that free pussy –
> they … FORCED IT ON HIM
> when they should have left him alone so he could
> write write WRITE.[66]

Like Bukowski, Rexroth ended up aghast at Dylan Thomas's prodigal gift for self-destruction, and was accordingly wary of his example. The last time he had seen him, Thomas's condition 'had assumed the terrifying inertia of inanimate matter. Being with him was like being swept away by a torrent of falling stones.'[67]

That a poet of Rexroth's ilk should so admire Thomas's life and work is hardly surprising. Much more so – and therefore in a way evidence even more compelling for his extraordinary saturation effect on American poetic culture, for however brief a period in the early 1950s – is the admiration expressed by poets whose connection with him no one really would have suspected. One such is John Ashbery, who, in a private communication of 12 November 2003, very kindly confirmed to me that half a century earlier he had indeed been interested in Thomas. 'I remember meeting him once at a bar in the Village ("Louis", on Sheridan Square; the building no longer exists), but have no recollection of any conversation we might have had. He was, of course, one of my favorite poets when I was just discovering modern poetry. Frank O'Hara also loved his work, in particular, the poem "Paper and Sticks".' Who would have thought? That elegant formalist Richard Wilbur was an unlikely contact of Thomas's back in the early 1950s.[68] He amusingly recalled the drunken Welshman calling on him at Harvard, 'spinning again and again like a teetotum, before sitting on the couch and declaring himself a "used-up bottle-shaped fraud"'. And he admitted that Thomas's gift for reading his poetry had influenced his own performance style. Galway Kinnell was another who confessed to an early interest in Thomas in a *New Yorker* interview. Recalling his awakening to poetry as a young man, he explained that 'I read a lot of poems. I really set out to read all poetry, from the beginning to now, and some of it I loved and some of it I disliked, and some of it sort of stirred me to write something myself ... I would say Dylan Thomas was one of those.'[69]

As for Kinnell's friend, Philip Levine, he is best known for his gritty poems about the industrial society of Detroit and his powerful poetic protests against the Vietnam war. Yet, in a twenty-minute radio interview with BBC Wales's Carolyn Hitt, Levine spoke at length about his love for Thomas's poetry, which he had first encountered in an Oscar Williams anthology when a Freshman at what became Wayne State University. He had found it refreshing for its exuberant vitality, after slogging in class through the 'gloom and doom' of Eliot's poetry. A few years later he heard him read and was startled both by how different he had then become from his youthful self – in the flesh he proved to be 'Rumpled, stubby, red-faced' – and by his electrifying performance. Thomas had, he still remembered, read not only his own poetry but Crowe Ransom's 'Captain Carpenter', and pieces by Wilfred Owen, Hart Crane and Theodore Roethke, whom he had strongly recommended. Levine, and a group of other excited students, had then met Thomas at the front door of the member of staff who was entertaining him, and still vividly recalled how delighted they all had been when Thomas boomingly announced that 'he had come to meet the students'. Adding 'Fuck the Faculty'.[70]

Levine stressed what a rock star of poetry Thomas had been – the only previous example of anyone vaguely similar had been Edna St Vincent Millay, striking in appearance but a bad poet and terrible reader. What a contrast, Levine archly added, Thomas was to the 'dowager' Marianne Moore and to William Carlos Williams, who always seemed to be humbly embarrassed at being there. Levine had, he explained, later come to see Thomas as belonging to the vatic tradition of Blake and had also come to believe that as a reader he had been somewhat of a ham. But he still loved some of the poems, and still remembered how different his subjects (meadows, birds and pastoral landscapes) had been from those of the survivors of the 1930s, who were still addressing the social and political issues of the Depression years in their poetry. Of his poems, he particularly liked 'In Memory of Ann Jones', 'The Hunchback in the Park', 'Poem in October' and – above all others – 'A Refusal to Mourn', which was the greatest of war poems.

For Levine, Thomas remained a remarkable one-off, and one whose poetry always seemed to sing.[71]

Another unlikely enthusiast for Thomas was the Jamaican-born Louis Simpson, who paid extensive attention to Thomas, alongside Ginsberg, Plath and Lowell, in a book-length study. Although he had moved to the States when he was only seventeen, and had served with distinction in the Pacific Theatre during the Second World War, the Jamaican Simpson remained in many important respects a lifelong outsider to the culture of his adopted country. His most famous poem – and also perhaps his finest – is 'Walt Whitman at Bear Mountain', which includes memorable lines of sad commentary on the state of the USA:

> Where are you, Walt?
> The Open Road goes to the used-car lot.
>
> Where is the nation you promised?
> These houses built of wood sustain
> Colossal snows,
> And the light above the street is sick to death.
>
> As for the people – see how they neglect you!
> Only a poet pauses to read the inscription.[72]

It is not surprising, therefore, that Simpson immediately recognized a fellow outsider in Dylan Thomas, and expressed it through contrasting him with Auden.

Auden's dislike of Thomas had complex roots. Auden was an Englishman of the professional middle class. Anglican in religion, educated at public schools and Oxford or Cambridge. Thomas's people were Welsh dissenters, and anyone who does not know the suspicion with which most Englishmen regard the Welsh, the Scots,[73] and the Irish, knows little of England. Celts are dreamers – they even believe in magic. They are music-hall turns, entertaining there perhaps, but nowhere else. Moreover, not only was Thomas a Welshman, he came of a lower class – his father had raised himself by his own bootstraps. Finally, he was in bad taste; he cadged money, he drank too much, his behaviour was a disgrace.[74]

Auden's style of writing was likewise the very opposite of that of Thomas. He was rational, while the Welshman was 'demonic'. Auden aimed at disenchantment, Thomas at enchantment.

One of the poets Thomas wished to meet during his first visit to New York was e.e. cummings, and Brinnin duly arranged it. 'Dylan and Cummings seemed,' he later recalled, 'happily at ease and inti- mately sympathetic as they came upon ways to express the curiously double-edged iconoclasm that marks the work and character of each of them' (*DTA*, 21). This was therefore another case of Thomas being welcomed as a fellow-outsider by American poets. 'Cummings's poetry, both Dylan and I knew, had for years met with determined or out- raged resistance in England,' wrote Brinnin, adding there had even been instances 'where a book of his had been returned to its English publisher by wary reviewers, who suspected a literary hoax.' There was also genuine fellow-feeling and respect between them, intensified by the fact that Cummings 'had been so moved by Dylan's reading the previous Thursday evening ... that he had left the auditorium to walk the street alone for hours' (*DTA*, 21).

The major American poet, however, with a claim to having been the most faithful of them all in championing Thomas is undoubtedly W. S. Merwin. As late as 2001, he was considering including 'A Refusal to Mourn' in the list of five books for reading by the crew of a US nuclear submarine that carried the Trident ballistic missile! And, in 1996, he had included the same poem in *Lament for the Makers: A Memorial Anthology*.[75] Thinking back, in that volume, to when he was in his twen- ties, he paid tribute to 'all the poets who were then living/ and whose lines had been/ sustenance and company/ and a light for years to me', and he continued:

> and they would always be the same
> in that distance of their fame
>   affixed in immortality
>   during their lifetimes while around me
>
> all was woods seen from a train
> no sooner glimpsed than gone again
>   but those immortals constantly
>   in some measure reassured me

> then first there was Dylan Thomas
> from the White Horse taken from us
>   to the brick wall I woke to see
>   for years across the street from me.[76]

Son of a Presbyterian minister as Merwin was, it makes sense that his first extensive discussion of Thomas was as a religious poet, by which he meant that Thomas was 'primarily a celebrator. A celebrator in the sense of one who participates in the rite, and whom the rite makes joyful. That which he celebrates is creation, and more particularly the human condition.'[77] We can discern here the ghostly lineaments of the ecological campaigner that Merwin was to become. At this early juncture, however, his emphasis was rather on Thomas's vocation being 'to remake in terms of the celebration of the details of life, to save that which is individual and thereby mortal, by imagining it, making it, in terms of what he conceives to be eternal' (*T*, 237). He admitted he most liked the later poems, where his religious vision had matured into what Merwin termed a 'dramatic' treatment of life, a development accompanied by a deepening of his tragic vision 'and with it the power of joy' (*T*, 243).

Merwin detected in a poem such as 'A Winter's Tale' 'a mythological treatment of the re-birth of the year (of the earth, of man)' (*T*, 244), and linked this to the fact that 'in Wales until the Christian era, and among parts of the population for a long time afterwards, the presiding deity was a goddess; the mid-winter rite was in her praise; she was often represented as a bird; the all-night running of the bride-groom corresponds with the marriage labours in many legends'.[78] And he concluded that 'Dylan Thomas remains the most skilful maker of verse writing in English; the stanzaic forms which he often fashioned for his rhythms are as complex and, for him, unhampering and informative as they seem to have been among the Welsh ollaves' (*T*, 246). As the Library of Ireland explains, in the Celtic world the 'ollave' (from the Celtic 'ollamh') was in effect what in Wales came to be known as a 'bardd': that is, a poet rigorously versed in traditional poetic forms and meters who is simultaneously learned in all the lore and traditions of his people and thus the custodian, and perpetuator, of tribal memory.[79]

These references to Wales are contextualised in a letter Merwin kindly wrote to me in 2003, replying to my query about Thomas's influence on his work.[80] 'I did love Thomas's writing when I was very young,' he wrote,

> and have a more sober admiration for some of it now. And both he and [David] Jones represent for me some things integrally Welsh, and precious for that, in English. My own name, of course, is Welsh. Merwins began coming to the States from Wales as far back as 1630 (to get away from the English!). I like to imagine that my link to Wales is clearer and tighter than it is. I am proud of the Welsh persistence in keeping their language and surely wish I knew Welsh.

This reveals what one might call a powerful 'myth of origin' – Merwin's wish to feel that he was descended from the Welsh (he believed 'Merwin' had originally been 'Myrddin', the name that was changed in English into 'Merlin') – because for him Wales exists as the ancient, romantic native region of the bards, and he sees himself as an American 'bardic' poet. Merwin admitted that Thomas 'mocked the bards and all that but heavens he had learned from them', and he disarmingly added that he 'couldn't imagine what I wrote about Dylan back in the fifties. I was trying to work out what it could mean to find the allegorical dimension of existence essential while not buying any codified creed, and I probably floundered around the subject and hope I was not horribly pretentious.' He went on to explain that 'I never met Dylan at the time though our paths often nearly crossed at the BBC. I thought I should not meet him until I'd got the piece finished, which was silly in several crucial ways.' Merwin looked back to his early years, first at university and then in London, when 'I was extremely [here he'd crossed out 'greatly'] addicted to Thomas's poetry'. After that, his enthusiasm had run cold for a period, but now it seemed to him that 'A Refusal to Mourn' was 'one of the great war poems, great poems about grief, that I know in any language, and I love "In the Last Dawn Raid" etc.'. His early passion for Thomas had, he concluded, now matured into 'a more sober admiration for some of it ... and both he and Jones represent for me some thing integrally Welsh, and precious for that, in English'. He wistfully added that he 'sorely wish[ed] I knew Welsh'.

VII

Merwin's sense of Wales was powerfully operative in many Americans who listened to Thomas read and felt that here was the authentic modern incarnation of the bardic spirit. As we all know, one famous 'bardic' product of the 'alternative culture' of the 1960s actually bears Dylan's name. Did Bob Dylan, when he came to fame, indeed knowingly take the Welshman's name? He has consistently denied it, while conceding that he had indeed heard of Dylan Thomas before renaming himself – one of the aliases he adopted was that of Robert Milkwood Thomas. Scholars entertain three possibilities in his case: (1) that his choice of name was purely serendipitous, and had no connection with the Thomas phenomenon; (2) that he actually named himself after the fictional Matt Dillon of *Gunsmoke*, but later modified the spelling because of his awareness of Dylan Thomas's glamour; and (3) that he did indeed have the Welshman in mind when taking his initial decision. Why mention these possibilities – between which scholars are unable to decide?[81] Because it instances the difficulty of exactly identifying the extent and nature of Dylan Thomas's impact on the United States. It is fitting to be nervous about any tidy notions of 'tracing influence'. A looser, more sensible, imaginative and appropriate approach would be to explore a singular phenomenon, the extraordinary impact, as indubitably far-reaching in consequence as it is unquantifiable in nature, of Dylan Thomas on the postwar culture of the USA.

So let this discussion end where it began: with Ginbserg. Speaking to students in Berkeley in the 1960s, he admitted to liking 'Fern Hill', but that otherwise he didn't really 'dig' Thomas, who was too romantic: '[w]ith his kind of gift, the way to groove was to begin with bricks and build a starry tower, but Thomas *began* in a starry tower'.[82] He also disapproved of one who seemed to resort to drink in order to write poetry, rather than trusting to the natural, ordinary 'goofiness' of the mind. As Louis Simpson notes in reporting this, 'Ginsberg had a point: Thomas's obscure writings were very different from the direct expression of thought that would be the Beats' stock in trade … [T]hey had no time for imagining – they were in a hurry to live, and writing was merely one means to this end. For the Beat poets, words were not realities as they were for Thomas, they were an extension of life.' But as Simpson adds, 'though Ginsberg would write in a different way, he found the way a great deal easier because Thomas had been before him. Thomas was the icebreaker – he ended the Age of Auden.'[83] Moreover, Kenneth Rexroth, acknowledged father of the Beats, himself 'testifi[ed] to the transformation wrought in San Francisco by Thomas's public readings'.[84]

All that, or so I like to think, is what Ginsberg himself recalled, and acknowledged when, very near the end of his life, he stood up my wife and myself in order to make that pilgrimage of a detour from Aberystwyth to Laugharne, and sank on his knees in homage to a poet who, as Louis Simpson also noted, had 'looked forward to a new generation of poets who would express their emotions and adopt a prophetic stance'.[85]

Notes

Unpublished in this form. Some of this material appeared in a book chapter co-written with Daniel G. Williams, '"A Sweet Union"?: Dylan Thomas and Post-War American Poetry', in Gilbert Bennett et al. (eds), *I Sang in My Chains: Essays and Poems in Tribute to Dylan Thomas* (Swansea: The Dylan Thomas Society of Great Britain, 2003), pp. 68–79. Williams's development of this work can be found in 'Blood Jumps: Dylan Thomas, Charlie Parker and 1950s America', in *Wales Unchained: Literature Politics and Identity in the American Century* (Cardiff: University of Wales Press, 2015), pp. 47–72.

1. In the early 1950s, the San Remo was 'the restlessly crowded hang-out of the intellectual hipster and catch-all for whatever survived of Bohemianism in Greenwich Village. There Dylan was ogled, and intruded upon, and recognized with surliness or awe.' John Malcolm Brinnin, *Dylan Thomas in America* (London; Dent, 1956), p. 8. Hereafter *DTA*.

2. Gordon Ball (ed.), *Ginsberg, Journals Early Fifties, Early Sixties* (New York: Grove Press, 1977), pp. 14–16.

3. Dic Jones, a farmer, was probably the most distinguished master of the traditional strict-metre poetry of Wales since the golden age of the late Middle Ages. *Barddas* is the modern society of poets dedicated to the maintenance of the strict metre tradition (which in Welsh is known as 'barddas'). Dafydd Rowlands was an accomplished Welsh-language poet and writer.

4. James A. Davies, *A Reference Companion to Dylan Thomas* (London: Greenwood Press, 1998), p. 102. This shamefully neglected source-book includes a valuable chapter (18) on 'Dylan Thomas in North America'. Hereafter *RC*.

5. Eric Homberger, *The Art of the Real: Poetry in England and America since 1939* (London: Dent, 1972), p. 71. I am grateful to Daniel G Williams for this reference.

6. See, for example, the chapter by Daniel G. Williams mentioned above. Also his 'The White Negro?', in *New Welsh Review*, 104 (Summer 2014), 33–42. See also the relevant parts of John Goodby, *The Poetry of Dylan Thomas: Under the Spelling Wall* (Liverpool: Liverpool University Press, 2013); and Philip Coleman, 'Dylan Thomas and American Poetry: "a kind of secret, but powerful, leaven"', in Edward Allen (ed.), *Reading Dylan Thomas* (Edinburgh; Edinburgh University Press, 2019), pp. 197–214.

7. Kenneth Rexroth, 'The New Poetry', in Eric Mottram (ed.), *The Rexroth Reader* (London: Cape, 1972), p. 239.

8. Ian Hamilton, *Robert Lowell: A Biography* (New York: Random House, 1983), p. 104. Hereafter *H*.

9. Randall Jarrell, *Kipling, Auden and Co.: Essays and Reviews 1935–1964* (1980), p. 36.

10. Raymond Williams, *Culture* (London: Fontana, 1981), p. 83.

11. James Scully (ed.), *Poets on Modern Poetry* (London: Collins, 1966), p. 242.

12. Robert Lowell, 'Thomas, Bishop and Williams', *The Sewanee Review* (July–September 1947), 493–503.

13. John Crowe Ransom, 'The Poetry of 1900–1950', *ELH*, 18/2 (June 1951), 155–62 (161).

14. Saskia Hamilton (ed.), *The Letters of Robert Lowell* (New York: Farrar, Straus and Giroux, 2005), p. 96. Hereafter *LRL*.

15. Thomas Travisano with Saskia Hamilton (eds), *Words in Air: The Complete Correspondence between Elizabeth Bishop and Robert Lowell* (New York: Farrar, Straus and Giroux, 2010), p. 147.

16. Travisano and Hamilton, *Words in Air*, p. 4.

17. Paul Ferris (ed.), *Dylan Thomas: the Collected Letters* (London: Dent, 1985), pp. 747, 748–9. Hereafter *CL*.

18. William Carlos Williams, 'Letter to Stinivas Rayaprol', in Graziano Krätli (ed.), *Why Should I Write a Poem Now: The Letters of Srinivas Rayaprol and William Carlos Williams, 1949–1958* (Recencies Series: Research and Recovery in Twentieth-Century American Poetics), p. 56.

19. Ralph Maud, 'Dylan Thomas and Charles Olson', *Planet: the Welsh Internationalist*, 68 (April–May 1988), 68–72.

20. All quotations taken from Ralph Maud's article on Thomas and Olson.

21. See M. Wynn Thomas, 'A "singing Walt from the mower": Dylan Thomas and the Whitmanian [re]turn in the post-war poetic culture of the United States', *Walt Whitman Quarterly Review* 40/3–4 (Winter/Spring, 2023), 1–31.

22. Karl Shapiro, 'Dylan Thomas', in E. W. Tedlock (ed.), *Dylan Thomas: the Legend and the Poet* (London: Heinemann, 1960), p. 269. Hereafter *T*.

23. Donald Hall, *Their Ancient Glittering Eyes: Remembering Poets and More Poets* (New York: Ticknor and Fields, 1991; expanded edn 1998), pp. 46–7.

24. Patchen was one of the American poets with whom Thomas corresponded.

25. Richard Gray's phrase in *A History of American Poetry* (Oxford: Wiley-Blackwell, 2015), p. 278.

26. The review is collected in *T*, pp. 211–13.

27. For the origins of the term in Southern folk culture, see Henry Wonham, 'Character Development of the Ring-Tailed Roarer in American Literature', *Southern Folklore*, 46/3 (1 January 1989), 265.

28. Matthew Arnold, *On the Study of Celtic Literature* (1867), in R. H. Super (ed.), *The Complete Prose Works of Matthew Arnold*, 3 (Ann Arbor: University of Michigan Press, 1962), pp. 291–386. For an extensive discussion of the 'Celticism' that became immensely popular at the end of the Victorian period, see chapter 5, 'The Celtic Option', in M. Wynn Thomas, *The Nations of Wales: 1890–1914* (Cardiff: University of Wales Press, 2016).

29. Arnold, *On the Study of Celtic Literature*, p. 347.

30. See Prys Morgan, *The Eighteenth-Century Renaissance* (Llandybie: Christopher Davies, 1981).

31. Dylan Thomas, 'After the Funeral', *The Collected Poems of Dylan Thomas*, pp. 101–2. For the cultural implications of Thomas's appropriation of the role of the Welsh-language 'bard', see chapter 4, 'Dylan Thomas and the "Tin Bethels"', in M. Wynn Thomas, *In the Shadow of the Pulpit: Literature and Nonconformist Wales* (Cardiff: University of Wales Press, 2010).

32. Karl, Shapiro, 'Dylan Thomas (1955)', in *T*, pp. 269–83.

33. James E. Miller, Jr, Karl Shapiro and Bernice Slote, *Start with the Sun: Studies in Cosmic Poetry* (Nebraska: Nebraska University Press, 1960).

34. Monroe K. Spears, 'James Dickey as Southern Visionary', *VQR: A National Journal of Literature and Discussion* (Winter, 1987); online at https://www.vqronline.org/essay/james-dickey-southern-visionary#:~:text=Dickey%20is%20convinced%2C%20then%2C%20that,of%20values%20from%20one's%20ancestors%2C (accessed August 2023).

35. James Dickey, 'Introductory Remarks to a Reading'; online at http://msr-archives.rutgers.edu/archives/Issue%201/documents/Mstreet%201%20-%20essay%20-%20INTRODUCTORY%20REMARKS%20TO%20A%20READING%20etc%20-%20.pdf (accessed August 2022).

36. Quoted in Aaron Baker, 'The Strangeness of James Dickey', *Contemporary Poetry Review* (1 February 2004); online at https://www.cprw.com/the-strangeness-of-james-dickey (accessed August 2023).

37. James Dickey, 'Interview: Writer's Workshop'; online video at https://www.knowitall.org/video/james-dickey-writers-workshop#:~:text=In%20an%20interview%20laced%20with,poet%20in%20the%20English%20language (accessed 29 September 2022).

38. Elizabeth Hardwick, 'America and Dylan Thomas', in John Malcolm Brinnin (ed.), *A Casebook on Dylan Thomas* (New York: Thomas Y. Cromwell Co., 1961), 153–9. Hereafter *EH*.

39. John Kenneth Galbraith, *The Affluent Society* (1958. New York: Houghton Mifflin Harcourt, 1998), p. 4.

40. By this time, Robeson had become *persona non grata* in the States because he was a self-confessed Communist and admirer of the Soviet Union. The account of the FBI's hounding of Robeson is as disgraceful as it is harrowing. Having deprived him of his passport, the FBI then systematically set out to break him mentally. But in Wales, Robeson had been a huge hero since the 1930s. He was a staunch admirer and supporter of the International Socialism of the South Wales Miners; he was eventually to sing to the miners 'down the line' from the States at their annual eisteddfod in Porthcawl in 1957, because the FBI had deprived his means of travel abroad. Robeson had famously played the part of a black miner in a Welsh mining valley in the film *Proud Valley* in 1939. For a definitive and scrupulously balanced, account of Robeson's relationship to Wales, see '"They feel me a part of that land": Paul Robeson, Race and the Making of Modern Wales', in Daniel G. Williams, *Black Skin, Blue Books: African Americans and Wales, 1845–1945* (Cardiff; University of Wales Press, 2012), pp. 142–207. Also 'Class and Identity: Aneurin Bevan and Paul Robeson', in Daniel G. Williams, *Wales Unchained: Literature, Politics and Identity in the American Century* (Cardiff; University of Wales Press, 2014), pp. 73–92. Brinnin mentions that Thomas specifically instructed him to agree to a reading, at a much-reduced fee, for the Socialist Party of New York City: another example of his fidelity to the socialism that was the default political faith of the industrial South Wales of his era (*DTA*, p. 109).

41. Whitman's appeal to industrial Wales in the late Victorian and early twentieth-century period was based on interpretation of him (mediated by Edward Carpenter's writings) as a kind of Utopian Socialist. See chapter 9, M. Wynn Thomas, *Transatlantic Connections; Whitman US/Whitman UK* (Iowa City: University of Iowa Press, 2005), pp. 226–60.

42. John Berryman, 'After many a summer: memories of Dylan Thomas', *Times Literary Supplement*, 3 (1993), 13–14.

43. John Berryman, *Dream Songs*, excerpted in Helen Vendler (ed.), *The Harvard Book of Contemporary Poetry* (Cambridge MA: Harvard University Press, 1985), pp. 85–6.

44. Kurt Heinzelman, 'John Berryman and the American Legacy of Dylan Thomas', *International Journal of Welsh Writing in English*, 5/5; online at https://ijwwe.uwp.co.uk/article/id/498/ (accessed: August 2023).

45. 'In Memoriam', in John Berryman, *Collected Poems, 1937–1971*, ed. Charles Thornbury (London: Faber, 1990), p. 244.

46. Berryman, 'After many a summer', 14.

47. Robert Bly, *Iron John: Men and Masculinity* (London: Random House, 1990).

48. Bly, *Iron John*, pp. 200–1.

49. Some important work has been done on this subject. See, for example, Victor Paananen, 'The Social Vision of Dylan Thomas', in *Welsh Writing in English: A Yearbook of Critical Essays*, 8 (2003), 46–66; and Vic Golightly, '"Writing with Dreams and Blood": Dylan Thomas, Marxism and 1930s Swansea', *Welsh Writing in English*, 8 (2003), 67–91.

50. Kenneth Rexroth, 'Thou Shalt Not Kill', in Ann Charters (ed.), *The Penguin Book of the Beats* (London: Penguin Books, 1992). pp. 233–41.

51. Kenneth Rexroth, *The Rexroth Reader*, ed. Eric Mottram (London: Cape, 1972), p. 332.

52. Kenneth Rexroth, *An Autobiographical Novel* (London: Whittet Books, 1977), p. 161.

53. See Williams, 'Blood Jumps', pp. 48, 65.

54. See, for example, his response to a *Time Magazine* suggestion that he was the father of the Beats: 'An entomologist is not a bug!'. Sam Hamill and Elaine Kleiner, 'Introduction', *Sacramental Acts: The Love Poems of Kenneth Rexroth* (Port Townsend WA: Copper Canyon Press, 1997), p. xv.

55. John Ciardi, 'War and the Poet', *The Atlantic* (April 1946); online at https://www.theatlantic.com/magazine/archive/1946/04/war-and-the-poet/656623/ (accessed August 2023).

56. Selden Rodman, 'Two Poetic Voices of Our Time', *New York Times*, 22 November 1953, p. 5.

57. See report in *The Crimson*, 27 November 1953.

58. David Boucher, 'The price of fame: Bob Dylan, the Beats and Dylan Thomas', *Symbiosis: A Journal of Anglo-American Literary Relations*, 20/1, 75–90. Hereafter *DB*. The following paragraphs are heavily indebted to Boucher's discussion.

59. See Williams, 'Blood Jumps', pp. 47–72.

60. Letter of summer 1958, reprinted in Matt Theado (ed.), *The Beats: A Literary Reference* (New York: Carroll and Graf, 2003), p. 82.

61. Kenneth Rexroth, 'Disengagement: The Art of the Beat Generation' (1959), in *The Alternative Society* (New York: Herder and Herder, 1970), pp. 1–16. See Daniel G. Williams's brilliant exploration of this perceived affinity in *Wales Unchained*, pp. 49–64. Williams in particular sees both Parker and Thomas as representing different versions of the supposed 'primitivism' (both of African Americans and of 'Celts') that post-war white middle-class America welcomed as sources of 'revitalisation' for a jaded and satiated emergent consumer culture.

62. Lawrence Ferlinghetti and Nancy J. Peters, *Literary San Francisco* (New York: HarperCollins, 1981), p. 166.

63. Lawrence Ferlinghetti, 'Palinode for Dylan Thomas', *These Are My Rivers: New and Selected Poems 1955–1993* (San Francisco CA: New Directions Books, 1994), pp. 42–4.

64. Studs Terkel, Allen Ginsberg and Gregory Corso, 'The Studs Terkel Show', January 1959; found at The Allen Ginsberg Project, https://allenginsberg. org/2013/07/more-vintage-corso/ (accessed 27 August 2022).

65. Charles Bukowski, letter to Sten Richmon, February 1967, in Seamus Cooney (ed.), *Screams from a Balcony: Selected Letters 1960–1970* (New York: HarperCollins, 1978), p. 42.

66. Charles Bukowski, 'O, We Are The Outcasts, O We Burn In Wondrous Flame!', in *The Roominghouse Madrigals: Early Selected Poems 1946–1966* (Santa Rosa: Black Sparrow Press, 1988), p. 22.

67. Rexroth, 'Disengagement', p. 2.

68. Richard Wilbur, 'The Art of Poetry No. 22', *Paris Review*, 72 (Winter 1977), pp. 68–105.

69. Alice Quinn, 'Working Poets: Interview with Galway Kinnell and Philip Levine', *New Yorker* (23 October 2006); online at https://www.newyorker.com/magazine/ 2006/10/30/working-poets (accessed August 2023).

70. 'Philip Levine on the Legacy of Dylan Thomas', Levine interviewed by Carolyn Hitt (31 October 2014); online: https://www.wnyc.org/story/philip-levine-legacy-dylan-thomas/ (accessed August 2023).

71. All from the interview with Carolyn Hitt, see n. 70.

72. Louis Simpson, 'Walt Whitman at Bear Mountain', in Sheila Coghill and Thom Tammaro (eds), *Visiting Walt: Poems inspired by the life and work of Walt Whitman* (Iowa City: University of Iowa Press, 2003), pp. 183–4.

73. Simpson's father was of part Scottish descent.

74. Louis Simpson, *Studies of Dylan Thomas, Allen Ginsberg, Sylvia Plath and Robert Lowell* (London; Macmillan, 1978), p. 36.

75. W. S. Merwin (ed.), *Lament for the Makers: A Memorial Anthology* (Washington DC: Counterpoint, 1996).

76. Merwin, *Lament for the Makers*, p. 7.

77. W. S. Merwin, 'The Religious Poet', in *T*, pp. 236–47.

78. It seems clear that Merwin had been reading Robert Graves's fanciful study, *The White Goddess*.

79. Library of Ireland; online at https://www.libraryireland.com/SocialHistory AncientIreland/II-VII-5.php (accessed August 2022).

80. Private correspondence, 24 January 2003.

81. See Boucher's important discussion of the case; and, since the completion of this chapter, K. G. Miles and Jeff Towns, *Bob Dylan and Dylan Thomas: The Two Dylans* (Caerfyrddin: McNidder & Grace, 2022).

82. Jane Kramer, *Allen Ginsberg in America* (New York: Random House, 1968), p. 108.

83. Quoted in Simpson, *Studies*, pp. 39–40.

84. Simpson's phrase, in *Studies*, p. 37.

85. Simpson, *Studies*, p. 37.

'There's words': Dylan Thomas, Swansea and language

'Dylan loved people and loved Swansea. Even the eccentrics and odd characters were his kinsfolk be they Swansea people.'[1] The words are those of one of Thomas's closest friends, Bert Trick, and they seem to me to be a fair summary of the positive aspects of the relationship between the poet and his hometown. The negative aspects, mostly limited to that period in late adolescence when he morosely viewed Swansea as the provincial graveyard of his burgeoning talent, are lividly recorded in the self-dramatising letters he sent to his young London girlfriend Pamela Hansford Johnson. It is still possible, in one sense, to tour Thomas's Swansea. Yet in another, more important, sense it is not. That is not only because such a substantial part of what he loved about the place was obliterated during three dreadful nights of air-raid in February 1941. It is more importantly because a writer's town can be accessed by only one route – through that author's writings. We might even say that, as an inveterate writer, Thomas turned his town *into* words. But then, it was Swansea that had first set him on the way to becoming himself a figure fashioned out of language; a linguistic sign. Instead of word being made flesh, in his case flesh eventually ended up being made word.

This sobering realisation occurs to Thomas at one arresting point in his moving and grossly underestimated radio play *Return Journey*. Broadcast first in 1947, it is a haunting account of his post-war return to his hometown in a wry, comic, poignant attempt to reconnect with his youthful self. He comes 'home' in search of what (or rather who) he had once been – a search that is also a search for the Swansea that no longer is. And his first port of call, once he's left the town's High Street Station, is naturally one of the many pubs he had frequented when he'd been a young cub reporter, apprenticed to language on the local paper that became the *South Wales Evening Post*. In an attempt to describe his onetime youthful self to the barmaid, he launches into a virtuosic performance of linguistic self-portraiture:

> He'd be about seventeen or eighteen … and above medium height. Above medium height for Wales, I mean, he's five foot six and a half. Thick blubber lips; snub nose; curly mousebrown hair; one front tooth broken after playing a game called Cats and Dogs, in the Mermaid, Mumbles; speaks rather fancy; truculent; plausible; a bit of a shower-off; … lived in the Uplands; a bombastic adolescent provincial Bohemian with a thick-knotted artist's tie made out of his sister's scarf, she never knew where it had gone … a gabbing, ambitious, mock-tough, pretentious young man; and mole-y, too.[2]

And what is the barmaid's response? It is devastatingly uncomprehending. 'There's words: what d'you want to find *him* for, I wouldn't touch him with a barge-pole.'

'There's words': the phrase haunts me, because in its ambivalence it encapsulates the creative heart of Thomas's life and writing. 'There's words' is, obviously enough, Dylan's self-knowing and self-mocking advertisement of his irresistible way with language, voiced here in a naive barmaid's unconsciously wondering tribute to a poet's seductive potency of expression. And I shall return to this celebratory aspect of the phrase later. But the exclamation also carries dark, disturbing overtones. His wistful question to the girl behind the bar has in effect been 'do you remember a young Mr Thomas?' To prompt her memory he's launched into a bravura performance. And what is her response? 'There's words.' It is as if, horrifyingly, Thomas, the would-be homecomer, discovers he now has existence only in language, not only as a clever arranger of words but as a clever arrangement of them.

This is a realisation already anticipated in an earlier failure of his in *Return Journey* to conjure up memories of his younger self in Swansea people, this time by mentioning him by name. The blank reply he this time gets from the barmaid, as she turns to another customer at the bar for confirmation, is 'this is a regular home from home for Thomases, isn't it, Mr Griffiths?' (*RJ*, 75). Even the surname 'Thomas', it turns out, is not a reliable personal signifier, an identifier of self: 'Thomas' is after all the most common of surnames in Swansea, a by-word for all and sundry. It is much more common even than the familiarly Welsh 'Mr Griffiths' – a surname the barmaid can here confidently (even point-edly) deploy to denote a real, living, single person. It is as if Dylan the returnee finds himself lost in language. No wonder, therefore, that, as he walks the streets of his old town, he seems to have become a merely ghostly presence wandering among the 'blitzed flat graves' of shops, 'marbled with snow and headstoned with fences' (*RJ*, 73). Words, it is implied, have usurped and thus obliterated his living, individual human identity. This is a point underlined, as the radio play subtly emphasises, by the way the barmaid's phrase 'There's words' precisely echoes her earlier phrase 'There's snow'. As *Return Journey* makes graphically clear, the exceptionally heavy snowfall under which Swansea disappeared in the notoriously hard winter of Thomas's return to the town in 1947 is symbolic of the obliteration, during the terrible three-night blitz in 1941, of the centre of the old town which had been the heartland not just of the town but of the young Dylan too.

The war in Europe had ended only some two and half years before Thomas's return to Swansea in 1947, and so much of the town still lay in ruins. Devastated by bombing, large areas from the docks to the shopping centre remained in a derelict, devastated state. 'What's the *Three Lamps* like now?', asks the returning Thomas of the barmaid. And the reply comes from a customer leaning on the counter: 'It isn't like anything. It isn't there. It's nothing mun. You remember Ben Evans's stores? It's right next door to that. Ben Evans isn't there either' (*RJ*, 77). Buildings, places, these are now just names, just words. Whereas Thomas had once been able to take his substantial, material bearings from these buildings, and thus been able to orientate himself, now, diso-rientatingly, where there were solid shops there are nothing but 'hole[s] in space'. Those 'displaced' shops now have an existence – a 'place' – only in language. 'Eddershaw Furnishers, Curry's Bicycles ... Hodges and Clothiers ... Crouch the Jeweller, Lennard's Boots, Kardomah ... David Evans ... Burton's, Lloyd's Bank' (*RJ*, 78): 'there's words', just as the barmaid said. This vivid elegy for a Swansea town that is no more may remind us how aware, and how appalled, the post-war Thomas was that the age had turned nuclear since last he'd visited his home town. Bombed Swansea was, so to speak, his personal Hiroshima. It is as if the hopeless sense of nihilism by which he had been afflicted following the first nuclear explosions had fatefully heightened his sense that his beloved, Swansea-generated world of words and memories was itself likewise nothing but an endless chain reaction of signifiers.

After all, Swansea and language had always been so intimately interconnected in Dylan Thomas's experience as to be virtually interchangeable. It is therefore not surprising that *Return Journey* should from the very outset show us a Dylan who, in returning to Swansea, is brought face to face not with his younger self but with language itself. It was there that he had first been brought alive to words. I should therefore like briefly to consider just a very few of the many important locations and occasions of his original awakening not just to the world but to the word in his home town.

II

Let's start with one of his best-known poems: 'Do not go gentle into that good night,/ Old age should burn and rave at close of day;/ Rage, rage against the dying of the light.'[3] This famous villanelle bespeaks Thomas's awareness that his father hadn't only begotten him; it was his father, too, who had made him a poet. Because what is rarely, if ever, noticed by commentators is that 'Do not go gentle' is Dylan's despairing, taunting challenge to his rapidly ageing father to assume the role of a King Lear. Behind the poem lies the aged Yeats's recently published poem 'Lapis Lazuli', a poem Thomas would certainly have known, not least because his great Swansea friend Vernon Watkins was a Yeats fanatic.[4] In that poem, Yeats famously celebrates the defiant 'gaiety' with which the great Shakespearean heroes meet their end, 'gaiety transfiguring all that dread', a phrase echoed in Thomas's '[b]lind eyes could blaze like meteors and be gay'. Thomas is also picking up on Yeats's use of the verb 'blaze': 'Black out: Heaven blazing into the head'.

'Tragedy wrought to its uttermost ... Hamlet rambles and Lear rages', Yeats had written. And Thomas next proceeds to borrow yet another Yeatsian word: 'rage'. 'Rage, rage against the dying of the light.' Thus, in urging his father to turn 'age' into 'rage' just like Lear, Dylan Thomas is trying to provoke the sick atheist into once more roaring the disgusted cry that had characterised him in his prime: 'it's raining again, damn Him'.[5] Via Yeats, then, Thomas is implicitly alluding to the figure of King Lear throughout 'Do not go gentle'. And why is he doing so? Well, it is in part his way of confessing himself to be, as poet, the offspring of a passionate Shakespearean – his father had actually read the Bard's poetry to him in his very cradle. 'Do not go gentle' implicitly bears witness to the vivifying effect of poetic language on little Dylan at the very beginning of his life, and so the villanelle is able convincingly to claim a like power to *re*-vivify D. J. Thomas at the very end of his life. Therefore, in being a poem about Dylan's father, 'Do not go gentle' is also inescapably a poem about origins, about Swansea as a cradle of language, and about the power of words to shape personal identity.

D. J. Thomas was, by some reports, not an easy man to live with. Aloof, frustrated and irascible, he seems to have been periodically irritated by the class difference between his sophisticated educated self and his comfortably homely chatterbox of a wife from working-class Swansea east. Young Dylan was thus encouraged early to escape and make an alternative home for himself in language, which is what he memorably did in magical Cwmdonkin Park, whose true 'keeper' was not the park keeper but, of course, the hunchback. Bent out of true, 'The hunchback in the park' is the physical image of the enticingly deviant, the alluringly monstrous, the rivetingly grotesque (*CP*, 93–4). Like the poet, he is the eternal outsider. To enter his territory is to cross over to the wild side, to join the company of 'the truant boys from the town'. Truancy must have held an irresistible appeal for a schoolmaster's son who went on to revel in the truancy of words.

Tributary influences on 'The Hunchback in the Park' are many, and obviously include the film of *The Hunchback of Notre Dame* and the William books by Richmal Crompton that Thomas devoured as a boy.[6] But all influences tend towards the same conclusion; that as a poet he feels most at home with the errant life and the wild energy of words. Those are the words that, like the truant boys, once they're clearly heard can then seem to 'run on out of sound'. This truant phrase, like so many of Thomas's, is itself a hunchback, because it wilfully distorts a well-known idiom – 'run on out of sight'. In the process it reveals all poetry to be language mis-shapen, like the hunchback himself. It also reminds us that, for a poet like Thomas, a poem is a device for allowing words to 'run on out of [the] sound' of their usual, ordinary usage and meaning. A poem is a magical 'park' where words are let out to play, given their head, and allowed to go wherever their exuberant energy of life may take them. 'Run on out of sound' can mean either 'run on out of the reach of sound', or it can mean 'run on propelled only by sound' (cf. 'I did that out of spite'), just like one of Thomas's poems.

'The Hunchback in the Park' is often sentimentally read as enchanting idyll and indulgently supposed to be a poem as innocent as strawberries. But stalking the text is an incipient, because pre-pubescent, sexuality, hinted at in the description of the hunchback himself as 'the old dog sleeper' – the phrase 'old dog' (with its echo of the Welsh 'hen gi') implies a dirty old womaniser, the roguish aged twin of the 'young dog' Thomas himself boasted of being in his *Portrait of the Artist as a Young Dog*. Of course, the poor old hunchback can be such only in his sleep, and even then he is capable only of a eunuch dream of 'a woman figure without fault', the old man's pathetic twist on the Pygmalion story. The sublimated sexuality of his frustrated making is paralleled and contrasted with the activity of the incipiently sexual boys who 'made the tigers jump out of their eyes/ to roar on the rockery stones,/ and the groves were blue with sailors'. The word 'blue' there refers not only to the colour of the sea and the uniform of sailors, but also to their blue language and thus by connection to the docks from which the Cape Horners sailed in the heyday of Swansea as Copperopolis. This dockland area, with its adjacent red-light district of the Strand, was distantly visible from Dylan Thomas's window away at the far end of town from his home in the affluent genteel suburban Uplands. Indeed, wickedly hidden in that phrase 'the groves were blue with sailors' is a subversive allusion to the bourgeois neighbourhood in which young Dylan lived, because the name of the triangle of streets directly adjacent to Cwmdonkin Park is 'the Grove'. In exultantly making the groves 'blue with sailors', Thomas is therefore slyly using his power as poet to turn the respectable Grove into a district of low repute.

For Thomas, Cwmdonkin Park was both nursery of the imagination and an adventure playground for language. That it was so may have been in part due to its proximity to what in those days was referred to as a School for the Deaf and Dumb, the significance of which for Thomas was pointed out in an important but neglected essay by my late friend Vic Golightly.[7] It was awareness of signing that lay behind such phrases as 'the rows/ Of the star-gestured children in the park'. Hence, from earliest days, Thomas was aware of language not as voiced, fixed and given, but as a system of flexible signs, a nimble means of signifying.

That words could be produced in all forms, shapes and sizes would have been self-evident to one who grew up in a bilingual environment. Welsh was the first language of both his parents, and his country relatives were virtually monoglot Welsh-speakers. There were Welsh-language dictionaries, grammars and poetry anthologies on his father's shelves. And the English spoken all around him as a boy would have been colourfully influenced by the Welsh language. Indeed, the very phrase 'there's words' is a good example of this. A familiar form of Welsh English, it derives from the use in Welsh of 'dyna' (English 'there [is]') where in English an exclamatory 'What' or 'How' would be used. Hence 'There's posh', 'There's lovely', and so on. The young Dylan would also have been very familiar with code-switching – a primitive example of it in the text of *Return Journey* being the use of 'Tawe water' to denote a pint of beer – 'Tawe' being the Welsh name of the river at whose mouth ('aber') Swansea (Abertawe) stands.

To mention code-switching is to be reminded of an intriguing fact. Thomas's two closest friends at Swansea, the poet Vernon Watkins and the musician Daniel Jones, went on to work during the war at the Government's secret code-breaking centre of Bletchley Park. They seemed to share with Dylan an exceptional sensitivity to the complex patterned character of closed signifying systems such as language. Thomas's was an interestingly hybrid model of poetry. He repeatedly spoke of it in organicist and biological terms suggestive of natural processes. But he also described his poems as laboured assemblages, which is why of late they've caught the attention of the L=A=N=G=U=A=G=E school of poets. Thomas could represent poems as word machines for multiplying meaning. In the interests of the latter he did not respect the individual integrity of a single word but was happy to reduce it to its constituent parts if this served his purposes. This is most evident in the case of his only known Joycean, multi-lingual pun. His notebooks record his discovery that the Welsh word 'amser' (meaning time) could be split into the two syllables 'am' (which normally means around) and 'sêr' (which means stars). The outcome of this bizarre nuclear splitting of a word to release its arbitrary additional signifying possibilities was the line he included in 'The force that through the green fuse', about 'how time has ticked a heaven around [am] the stars [sêr].' He has treated 'amser' as if it were a code word, a miniature cipher that needed to be cracked to reveal its secret meaning.[8]

It would be interesting to explore the broad analogies between both the making and the reading of Thomas's poetry with those of cipher-construction and cipher-breaking. Central to all these processes is the construction and deconstruction of patterns of equivalence. But if Thomas can be read as a maker of codes, he can also be read as a maker of anti-codes, since while his poems operate, like codes or ciphers, on the principle of equivalence, they knowingly resist the reducibility to singleness of meaning that any code or cipher presupposes.

III

After the 'Cwmdonkin period' in Thomas's development came the period of Warmley, the substantial middle-class Sketty home of Dylan Thomas's great friend and fellow artist Daniel Jones. It was there that two lads crossing the threshold into their teens conspired to create their own theatre of the absurd out of the incorrigible zaniness of language. If Cwmdonkin Park was the nursery of Thomas the poet, then Warmley was the nursery of Thomas the comic writer – and I'd even venture to suggest that he may have had a greater natural genius for comedy than he had for poetry, because comedy allowed (and indeed positively encouraged) him to gleefully exploit the sheer glorious silliness of words. He revelled in the anarchic accidents of meaning and loved the adventitious character of words. In later years he was, after all, shrewdly and glumly to surmise that he might be more 'a freak user of words than a poet'.[9] In Warmley, Dan and Dylan (even their names conveniently rhyme) mirrored the Marx Brothers films and anticipated the Goon Show, that madcap classic of postwar British radio, by inventing characters outrageously named Miguel Y Bradshaw, Waldo Carpet, Xmas Pulpit, Paul America, Winter Vaux, Tonenbach, and Bram (*CL*, 196). Across the sky of their Warmley world there flew 'panama-shaped birds from the Suez Canal', and the 'Radio Warmley' they invented broadcast rhymes of which Lewis Carroll or Edward Lear might not have been entirely ashamed: 'a drummer is a man we know who has to do with drums,/ But I've never met a plumber yet who had to do with plums,/ A cheerful man who sells you hats would be a cheerful hatter,/ But is a serious man who sells you mats a serious matter?' (*CL*, 5). The adult Thomas was to view Warmley nostalgically as the epitome of 'the queer,

Swansea world, a world that was, thank god, self-sufficient'. And of his Warmley alter ego Percy he was to write, 'Percy's world in Warmley was, and still is, the only one that has any claims of permanence … his was a world of our own, from which we can interpret nearly everything that's worth anything' (*CL*, 197). To which I would add the question, what is Llareggub, after all, but a Warmley for grown-ups?

Cwmdonkin Park, Warmley; these were then two Swansea locales important for Thomas's evolution in language. To these can be added an unexpected third: the Paraclete Congregational Chapel, just around the bay from Swansea in Newton, a corner of the sometime fishing village of Mumbles. It was there that the boy Dylan was regularly subjected of a Sunday to a strong dose of chapel religion administered by his mother's brother-in-law, who was a local minister. And that made him aware that for more than a century in Wales, the word had been the preserve of the great preachers of the Welsh pulpit, the lords and masters of language who had been allowed the last word on every aspect of life.[10]

Realising that if he wanted to become a writer, he would have to wrestle language out of the iron control of the pulpit, he began early to wage his own war for the word. One of the most celebrated of his attempts to displace what remained of the erstwhile regnant discourse of Nonconformist, chapel-mad Wales is 'After the Funeral', sometimes sub-titled 'in memory of Ann Jones' (*CP*, 73–4). The poem openly presents itself to us as the very site of a linguistic struggle between Dylan, 'Ann's [dionysiac] bard on a raised hearth', who commands the power to 'call/ all the seas to service', and the ministers and deacons of a repressed and repressive patriarchal culture, with their 'mule praises, brays' and 'hymning heads' as they soberly preside over Ann's chapel funeral service. In this inverted version of the Old Testament story about the contest between Elijah and the pagan priests of Baal, it is the pagan champion of nature, the anti-chapel Thomas, who emerges triumphant. That triumph is variously expressed in the poem as a power to raise an 'alternative', verbal tombstone in Ann's memory, and as a power to resurrect the dead fox, so that its 'stuffed lung … twitch and cry Love/ And the strutting fern lay seeds on the black sill'. The outrageous phallic thrust of that final image is, of course, utterly unmistakeable.

It is already evident in 'After the Funeral' that, to coin an image from *Under Milk Wood*, Dylan Thomas is a Polly Garter of a poet. He defies the respectable chapel-cowed community not only by flaunting the fecund sexuality of his poetry but by delightedly indulging in pro-miscuous verbal liaisons, encouraging words to copulate and thrive so as to breed unpredictable and uncontainable meaning: 'I like contradicting my images, saying two things in one word, four in two words and one in six … Poetry … should be as orgiastic and organic as copulation, dividing and unifying … Man should be two tooled, and a poet's middle leg is his pencil' (*CL*, 182). Implicitly imaging Nonconformist discourse as authoritarian, univocal to the point of being totalitarian, this poetic Polly Garter rebels by becoming a connoisseur of polysemy, a subversive profilerator of meanings.

From the beginning Dylan Thomas consciously uses puns, double-entendres and a whole wild menagerie of suspect forms and socially proscribed kinds of 'language' to reflect on the profligate, uninhibited nature of 'language' itself. 'Llarregub/ Llarregyb' – a word he had already coined and patented as his own in the stories of the early 1930s – was always Thomas's true native place, a place made exclusively out of the potentialities of language to turn itself back to front, inside out, upside down. In his poetry topsy-turvy language proves itself to be an incorrigible contortionist and shameless shape-changer. 'Every device there is in language is there to be used if you will', he told a Texan post-graduate in 1951, 'old tricks, new tricks, paragram, catachresis, slang, assonantal rhymes, vowel rhymes, sprung rhythm'.[11] 'Poets have got to enjoy themselves sometimes', he added disingenuously. But there was always much more to it than that. To the Calvinistic minister's implicit model of human words as solidly and respectably underpinned by The Divine Word, Thomas, from his teens onwards, opposed an alternative, radically different model – of the ungovernable liquefactions of lan-guage, 'the sea-slides of saying' as he suggestively phrased it. His lifelong infatuation as poet, as short-story writer, and even as letter-writer, was with 'the procreant urge of the word', to misquote Walt Whitman, one of his poetic heroes.[12] In a poem like 'After the Funeral', Thomas adopts an openly confrontational stance towards the dominant discourse of Nonconformity and constructs what socio-linguists term an 'anti-language'; an alternative discourse of his own.

And if 'After the Funeral' is the key text in Thomas the poet's struggle for mastery of the word, then its equivalent for Thomas the comic writer is 'The Peaches', the first story in *Portrait of the Artist as a Young Dog*.[13] Based on Thomas's boyhood recollections of visiting his

relatives' farm in the rural west, it features a wonderfully comical sermon, solemnly delivered by the would-be preacher Gwilym, a twenty
year old 'with a thin stick of a body and spade-shaped face'. He has a
captive audience of one – his cousin Marlais, Dylan's alter ego, a little
Swansea towny. Obediently seated on hay-bales in the barn that passes
for Gwilym's chapel, little Marlais listens to his country cousin's 'voice
rise and crack and sink to a whisper, and break into singing and Welsh
and ring triumphantly and be wild and meek', until the sermon reaches
its grand solemn climax: '"Thou canst see and spy and watch us all the
time, in the little black corners, in the big cowboys' prairies, under the
blankets when we're snoring fast, in the terrible shadows: pitch black,
pitch black: Thou canst see everything we do, in the night and day, in
the day and the night, everything, everything: Thou canst see all the
time. O God, mun, you're like a bloody cat".' In the silence that follows
'the one duck quacked outside'. '"Now I take a collection," Gwilym said'
(*CS*, 128). Then, as the story proceeds, Gwilym's Calvinistic sermon
(the emphasis is on a humanly distant, prying, preying God) is implicitly trumped by the alternative, secular, story-weaving power of little
Marlais from Swansea town, as he plays with his Swansea friend Jack
Williams in the secret dingle on the farm: 'There, playing Indians in
the evening, I was aware of me myself in the exact middle of a living
story, and my body was my adventure and my name.'

IV

By the end of his teens, Thomas was understandably beginning to feel
distinctly isolated in Swansea. In 1933, when he was nineteen, he could
write like this, in one of his outrageously pretentious letters to Pamela
Hansford Johnson. 'In my untidy bedroom, surrounded with books
and papers, full of the unhealthy smell of very bad tobacco, I sit and
write' (*CL*, 47). In one way, his Swansea had shrunk to a single cramped
room 'by the boiler', to which he regularly retreated between 1930 and
1934 to fill notebook after notebook with remarkable drafts of poems,
steeped in adolescent eroticism, many of which, duly reworked, would
find their way into his first two published collections. By now, he could
superciliously describe his Swansea as a 'dingy hell', from which he
longed to escape, 'and my mother is a vulgar humbug, but I'm not so

bad, and Gower is beautiful as anywhere' (*CL*, 63). In a letter to the *West Wales Guardian*, he expressed disgust at 'this overpeopled breeding box of ours, this ugly contradiction of a town for ever compromised between the stacks and the littered bays' (*CL*, 142).

By this time, the Thomas who yearned to escape the confines of his home town and who had ostensibly retreated from its Philistinism into the safety of his own bedroom, was also the Thomas who had for a couple of years been a 'young dog', cutting a figure in the local pubs, on the stage of the Swansea Little Theatre, and in the mildly bohemian company of his acquaintances at the Kardomah Café. As a cub reporter on what became the *Evening Post*, Thomas was wholly unreliable and frankly irresponsible. But, as James A. Davies has emphasised, it

> increased his knowledge of Swansea and particularly of its crisis areas and low life: the hospital, the police station, the mortuary and its sad cargo, and the docks area with its sleazy pubs and loose women. He cultivated a 'reporter's image' influenced by American films; a pulled-down porkpie hat, dangling cigarette, and check overcoat. (*RG*, 21)

And it was during this period that the habit of trawling the pubs began. He captured the atmosphere of his life at this time in the last two stories of *Portrait of the Artist as a Young Dog*.

The old Kardomah Café was conveniently situated directly opposite the *Evening Post* buildings (diagonally opposite the Castle), and so at lunch times Thomas and his fellow trainee journalists like Charles Fisher could always slip across the road. Once again, he therefore occupied a frontier zone, a socio-linguistic positioning that contributed significantly, time after time, to the development of his distinctively hybrid imagination. This cultural situation is again conveniently represented for us by the Kardomah's physical location and accordingly mixed clientele at that time. It was located in Castle Street, at the bottom of High Street, adjacent to the red-light district of the Strand and the racy docks area of Swansea. But it was also in the heart of the old Swansea's downtown shopping area, next to prestigious stores like Ben Evans, and so patronised by middle-class and working-class shoppers alike.

The strong development of the Swansea Art School under Grant Murray after the First World War meant that the town was home to a young artistic set, and from the late 1920s onwards one of the favourite haunts of young artists was the Kardomah. It was to this set that Thomas the cub reporter attached himself. Those gathering periodically at the café included the two young artists Fred Janes and Mervyn Levy, a young man who spoke Yiddish at home (that frontier zone again) because he was the grandson of the refugee Russian Jew who had opened the first cinema in Swansea. Other regulars were aspiring writers Tom Warner and Charles Fisher, who was to enjoy a very colourful career as a globe-trotting journalist and died in Canada at the beginning of the twenty-first century. Daniel Jones, Thomas's boyhood friend who would go on to fame as a symphonic composer, would also sometimes join the company. The model for them all were the Viennese and South Bank Parisian cafes frequented by intellectuals and artists who had contributed so notably to the development of the modernist arts.

The Kardomah was, for Thomas, the successor to Cwmdonkin Park and Warmley – a congenial space within a comfortingly protective, intimately knowable, but ultimately Philistine town where his imagination could be allowed full play, and find stimulation in the company of others. The informal café setting also promoted cross-fertilisation between different art forms. This fluid, highly informal group consisted of painters and musicians as well as poets, many of them fascinated by the modernist experimentations that had foregrounded the formal, compositional properties of art at the expense of the old, traditional, representational paradigms. And these interests, too, chimed with those of the young Thomas, reinforcing his instinct to treat words rather as, say, the Cubist painters treated objects. He captured the flavour of their meetings in the story 'Old Garbo', from *Portrait of the Artist as a Young Dog*:

> Most of the boys were there already. Some wore the outlines of moustaches, others had sideboards and crimped hair, some smoked curved pipes and talked with them gripped between their teeth, there were pin-striped trousers and hard collars, one daring bowler [...] 'Sit by here', said Leslie Bird. He was in the boots at Dan Lewis's.[14]

'Sit by here' is an example of the young men's self-mocking affectation of the Welsh-English that was the vernacular idiom of this cultural frontier town, situated on the very edge of the thoroughly Welsh-speaking industrial Tawe (Swansea) valley. And it is obvious that the language spoken by the youths in the café was a mix of the standard 'educated' English of their grammar school backgrounds, the Welsh-English of the streets, the high 'literary' language of the modernist writers with whom they were obsessed, and the flavoursome slang of the American gangster movies they so loved. Whereas the language used by the leading English poets of the day, such as W. H. Auden, tended to be very much the limited product of an English public school, middle-class milieu, a Swansea Welshman like Dylan Thomas was early exposed to a variety of linguistic registers, class sociolects and cultural discourses that helped make him the distinctively 'hybrid' poet he became.[15] And conversations around the tables in the Kardomah obviously featured a constant switching between these many different examples of language usage. No wonder therefore that one of the places Thomas revisited so movingly in imagination, and indeed in implicit homage, in *Return Journey* was the site of the Kardomah, reduced to rubble in the blitz:

> I haven't seen him since the old Kardomah days … Him and Charlie Fisher – Charlie's got whiskers now – and Tom Warner and Fred Janes, drinking coffee-dashes and arguing the toss … [about] music and poetry and politics, Einstein and Epstein, Stravinsky and Greta Garbo, death and religion, Picasso and girls (*RJ*, 81).

V

These were also years during which Thomas was active with the Swansea Little Theatre, 'based in Mumbles … close to congenial pubs', as James Davies has astutely noted. This was a breakaway group from the Swansea Amateur Dramatic Society, interested in staging more sophisticated plays such as classics by Shakespeare, Chekhov and Ibsen.[16] During his time with the group, Thomas had roles in William Congreve's *The Way of the World*, Noël Coward's *Hay Fever* and a couple of other contemporary plays. He attracted good notices for his performances but was also criticised for his inability to adapt his accent and mode of delivery to suit the different parts he was required to play. The experiences that he gained through his acting obviously contributed very substantially to his subsequent career of public performance, both as a brilliant radio broadcaster (who first took the microphone at the Swansea studios of the BBC) and as an incomparable reader of his own poetry.

His theatrical experience enabled him to perfect his public persona – or rather, his public personae, as he actually proved far more adept in life than he did on stage at changing his personality to suit his various audiences. One of the leading figures in the Little Theatre was Thomas Taig, at that time lecturer in the English Department at the fledgling University College of Swansea, and after Thomas's death, Taig was to stress how consummate an actor he had become in the street theatre of life itself. 'I think of him as infinitely vulnerable,' Taig wrote, 'living from moment to moment a heightened awareness of sense-impressions and emotional tensions, the victim rather than the master of his environment.' It was his acting skills, Taig added, that enabled Thomas to overcome these handicaps and eventually to achieve a mastery, of sorts, of his environment – but at considerable, and eventually tragic, cost to his inner self (*DR*, 100–4).

Eerily enough, Daniel Jones was to paint a very similar picture of Thomas in one of the last interviews he gave before his death. He spoke of the Dylan he knew so well as a lost soul, one who could never reconcile public performer and inner being. Jones's Dylan is one who never really knew who he was – he's the lost soul we've already met, who in that opening passage from *Return Journey* returned to Swansea in a vain attempt to re-integrate his present with his past. Never lost for words, Daniel Jones's Dylan was consequently condemned to be forever lost in words, doomed to be a garrulous performer for all and sundry to the very last. So maybe the barmaid had indeed innocently seen him for what he was, when she'd exclaimed 'There's words.'

After his first departure for London in 1933, Thomas was never again really a native of Swansea. And then, over those three terrible nights in 1941, the centre of Swansea was razed to the ground. It's scarcely an exaggeration to claim that the erasure of his hometown's heartland was a traumatic event in Thomas's life. After it, he felt imaginatively orphaned. The umbilical cord connecting him to the richest and most dependable source of his creativity had been cut for ever. He'd always been restless, but after the war he became a displaced person. There is even a sense in which both of his most popular works – *Under Milk Wood* and 'Fern Hill' – are elegies for the lost Swansea of his boyhood. In *Under Milk Wood* he recreated, after an adult fashion, the zany world he invented with Daniel Jones during those years of high-spirited collaboration in Warmley. And 'Fern Hill', although of course a poem nostalgically recalling boyhood holidays on his aunt's west-Wales farm near Llanstephan, is also a poem directly responding to the two events that changed Thomas's world for ever. The first was the bombing of Swansea; the second was the bombing of Hiroshima and Nagasaki. In Thomas's mind they tended to merge into a single nightmare – the irreversible loss of what had remained to him of human hope and innocence. 'Fern Hill' is an elegy for such a lost world. And his radio play *Return Journey*, about his imaginary journey back to Swansea in the terribly cold winter of 1947 in search of an irretrievably lost town and an irretrievably lost self, is a memorable elegy for both self and Swansea that also darkly foreshadows his own imminent death.

Rooted in his Swansea experiences, then, are Thomas's great affirmations of language, such as the great magnificat to words he sent to an enquiring obscure Texan postgraduate in 1951. Recalling his early discovery, once more in his Swansea childhood, of 'what went on between the covers of books' (the sly insinuation of verbal sexual shenanigans is interesting), he wrote of 'such sand-storms and ice-blasts of words, such slashing of humbug, and humbug too, such staggering peace, such enormous laughter, such and so many blinding bright lights breaking across the just-awaking wits and splashing all over the pages in a million bits and pieces all of which were words, words, words, and each of which was alive forever in its own delight and glory and oddity and light' (*EPW*, 156). But Thomas was also ever aware of being 'Shut, too, in a tower of words' – a tower that could be phallically creative but could also be humanly imprisoning. It is telling, I think, that at the time of his death, one of the projects Thomas was contemplating undertaking was entitled 'Where Have the Old Words Got Me'.[17]

VI

As I started this discussion with *Return Journey*, let me also finish with it, ending with its immensely moving conclusion. It features Thomas, the returnee, wandering Cwmdonkin Park as twilight falls and the park prepares for closure. In one, final attempt at coming face to face with his young self, he asks the lugubrious Park Keeper, now turned gatekeeper of tenebrous regions, the same plaintively insistent question he had asked the barmaid earlier: does he remember a curly-haired youngster? 'Oh yes, yes I knew him well,' comes the reply, '[h]e used to climb the reservoir railings and pelt the old swans. Run like a billygoat over the grass you should keep off of. Cut branches off the trees. Carve words on the benches.' This seems promising, at last, not least that memory of a boy whose very identity yearned to take the form of words. But even as the Park Keeper goes on to fill in the rest of the picture – of a boy who used to '[c]limb the elms and moon up the top like a owl. Light fires in the bushes' – he is, we discover, preparing the way not for a revelatory disclosure but rather for an anticlimax. 'Oh yes, I knew him well. I think he was happy all the time,' the Park Keeper poignantly repeats, before fatally adding, 'I've known him by the thousands.'

> [Dylan Thomas]: We had reached the last gate. Dusk drew around us and the town. I said: What has become of him now?
>
> Park-Keeper: Dead.
>
> [Dylan Thomas]: The Park-keeper said:
>
> > (*The park bell rings*)
>
> Park-Keeper: Dead ... Dead ... Dead ... Dead ... Dead ...Dead.
>
> (RJ, 90)

That is indeed the play's very last word; the last word on the play; the last word on Thomas's search; the word that marks the end of language itself; the dead end. And behind this concluding passage we are surely meant to hear the ironic echo of yet more words, as memorable as they are ultimately futile; the words of John Donne in the great, famous, prophetic utterance that had ignited the young Swansea Thomas's imagination and helped turn his entire life into a fateful adventure in language: 'Ask not for whom the bell tolls: it tolls for thee.'[18]

Notes

This is the text of a keynote lecture delivered at an International Dylan Thomas Conference held at the University of Bordeaux in Autumn 2014. Published as '"There's words": Dylan Thomas et la langue', Pascale Sardin et Christian Gutleben (eds), *Lire et Relire Dylan Thomas, Cycnos*, 31/2 (2015), 29–56.

1. Quoted in James A. Davies, *A Reference Guide to Dylan Thomas* (Westport, CN: Greenwood Press, 1998), p. 24. Hereafter *RG*.
2. 'Return Journey', in Dylan Thomas, *Quite Early One Morning: Poems, Stories, Essays* (London: Dent, 1974), p. 76. Hereafter *RJ*.
3. Walford Davies and Ralph Maud (eds), *Dylan Thomas: Collected Poems 1934–1953* (London: Dent, 1988), p. 148. Hereafter *CP*.
4. 'Lapis Lazuli', in *The Collected Poems of W. B. Yeats* (London: Macmillan, 1963), pp. 338–9.
5. Constantine Fitzgibbon, *A Life of Dylan Thomas* (London: Dent, 1965), p. 13.
6. For the influence of Crompton, see Betty and William Greenway, 'Just Dylan: Dylan Thomas as Subversive Children's Writer', in *Welsh Writing in English: A Yearbook of Critical Essays*, 5 (1999), 42–50.
7. Vic Golightly, '"Speak on a Finger and Thumb": Dylan Thomas, Language and the Deaf', in *Welsh Writing in English: a Yearbook of Critical Essays*, 10 (2005), 73–97.
8. See Ralph Maud, *Where Have the Old Words Got Me?* (Cardiff: University of Wales Press, 2003), pp. 237–8.
9. Paul Ferris (ed.), *Dylan Thomas: The Collected Letters* (London: Dent, 1985), p. 130. Hereafter *CL*.
10. In the discussion that follows, I draw upon two earlier publications of mine, viz. the chapter entitled 'Marlais: Dylan Thomas and the "Tin Bethels"', in M. Wynn Thomas, *In the Shadow of the Pulpit: Literature and Nonconformist Wales* (Cardiff: University of Wales Press, 2010), pp. 226–55; and 'Marlais', in Hannah Ellis (ed.), *Dylan Thomas: A Centenary Celebration* (London: Bloomsbury, 2014), pp. 30–41.
11. Walford Davies (ed.), *Dylan Thomas: Early Prose Writings* (London: Dent, 1971), p. 156.
12. Francis Murphy (ed.), *Walt Whitman: The Complete Poems* (London: Penguin, 1977), p. 65.
13. Leslie Norris (ed.), *Dylan Thomas: The Collected Stories* (London: Dent, 1983). Hereafter *CS*.
14. *The Dylan Thomas Omnibus, Under Milk Wood, Poems, Stories and Broadcasts* (London: Phoenix, 2000), p. 242.
15. This aspect of his poetry has been highlighted most recently in John Goodby, *Dylan Thomas: Under the Spelling Wall* (Liverpool: Liverpool University Press, 2013).
16. Useful information about this period is detailed in David N. Thomas's edited collection of interviews by Colin Edwards, *Dylan Remembered, Volume One, 1914–1934* (Bridgend: Seren, 2003), 26off. Hereafter *DR*.
17. Ralph Maud, *Where Have the Old Words Got Me?*, p. xix.
18. John Hayward (ed.), *John Donne: Complete Poetry and Selected Prose* (London: The Nonesuch Press, 1972), p. 538.

III.
ON R. S. THOMAS

The Real Manafon

R. S. Thomas served as rector of the rural parish of Manafon, in what was then rural Montgomeryshire (now Powys), from 1942 to 1954. The importance of the period he spent there for his development both as poet and as nationalist can scarcely be overestimated. It was then that he began to apply himself in earnest to learning Welsh, not only gradually acquiring fluency but in the process opening up Welsh-language literature to his attention. His awareness of the language and his preliminary reading in its literature shaped his awareness of two aspects of Manafon: first, that only very recently had the parishioners turned from speaking Welsh to speaking English, and secondly that the farmers of the district had, up to a mere few decades earlier, been participants in a rich Welsh-language rural culture the remnants of which he could still occasionally encounter during his rambles in the surrounding upland area and the loss of which to lowland communities had, in his opinion, left them vastly diminished. All this made him sharply aware of the vulnerability of the whole of Wales to a similarly rapid and debasing shift in language and culture that, he believed, would deprive the country of any real distinctively Welsh essence. In other words, at Manafon Thomas underwent a crash course in the mentality of the Welsh Border Country (known since Anglo-Norman times as the Marches), and like other prominent products of that country, most famously including Emyr Humphreys and Raymond Williams, the experience made him very aware of the necessity first of choosing between Wales and England, and secondly, if opting for the former, of the pressing need to protect that form of Welshness that was bound up with the Welsh language and that was, as he had come to understand, very much imperilled in consequence. Manafon helped him realise that the whole of modern Wales had become border country.

And then, of course, there were the poems. Not only was it while he was at Manafon that he published his very first collection, *The Stones of the Field* (1946), but it was also during that period that he completed most of the poems that appeared in his first four published collections, including *Song at the Year's Turning* (1955) that first brought him widespread recognition. And it was also out of the upland farmers of the parish of Manafon that he fashioned the arresting, singular figure that was to preoccupy him as poet for the first half of his career: the composite, yet highly individualised, figure, so enigmatic as to seem permanently bent over his work into the shape of a question mark, to which he gave the name Iago Prytherch. The very name was a cipher for the terrible loss that he believed had befallen Manafon, the loss of the Welsh language and its culture. In 'Y Llwybrau Gynt', the sketch he wrote of his earlier years, he mentioned wishing that he had 'been able to speak Welsh when I went to Manafon, it would have been easier to get some of the inhabitants to use a language which quite a few of them still knew. Every farm and every family had a Welsh name, but most people spoke with a Shropshire accent using a strange admixture of Welsh idioms.'[1]

'Iago', a name about which some English commentators have woven remarkably Byzantine speculations, is the ordinary Welsh name for James. Prydderch is the anglicised version of ap Rhydderch, or son of Rhydderch, a patronymic in the old Welsh fashion. Yet, although his Welshness is thus blazoned in Iago's name, it is likely, given the situation in Manafon that Thomas describes, that Iago speaks no Welsh and is therefore totally unaware of what his own name signifies. No wonder that, in one marvellous phrase, Thomas describes another of Iago's breed as 'lost in his own breath'.[2] Lost indeed: in Thomas's eyes, all these Manafon farmers were the victims of a loss that had left them self-alienated in ways they themselves could not grasp and that therefore left them bereft and bewildered, 'marooned' in a 'sea of grass', as he elsewhere described their condition.[3] That physical isolation of theirs that he found so compelling was also a cultural isolation by which he was equally haunted.

Commentators have been astute enough to detect the generic, even mythic, aspects of Iago and his kind. But in the very act of exploring, as so many of them profitably have, the rich, and endlessly complex, implications of that mythic quality, they have ignored virtually completely the social, cultural and economic materials out of which that myth was cunningly wrought. They have never really bothered to enquire in detail into the actual living conditions of those upland farmers of the Manafon parish.

Valuable oblique light is thrown on those conditions in an anthropological study of a similar parish in exactly the same period that was written by Alwyn D. Rees and that has come to be accepted as a classic. It so happens that R. S. Thomas came to know Alwyn Rees later very well and to admire him immensely. But exploration of that interesting relationship must be left to another occasion.[4] Published in 1952 under the title *Life in a Welsh Countryside*, Rees's work was a scrupulously objective ethnographic analysis of life in Llanfihangel-yng-Ngwynfa, the parish that was famous throughout Wales as the home of Ann Griffiths, Dolwar Fach, the great mystical hymn-writer of the early nineteenth century, a figure to whom Thomas addressed several significant poems.[5] Situated some dozen miles almost directly north of Manafon, and still situated within the county of Montgomeryshire, 'Llan', as Rees tended to call it, was largely an upland parish like Manafon, and thus shared several important features with the latter which, as identified by Rees, throw very interesting light both on many of the aspects of Manafon that Thomas chose to highlight in his poems and on the equally numerous aspects of that parish that he deliberately excluded from his poetic attention. Rees's period of association with Llan as a professional anthropologist coincided almost exactly with Thomas's stay at Manafon. Most of his detailed field work, he reports, was undertaken in 1939 and 1940, but he continued to spend periods in residence in the parish from 1940 to 1946. His study appeared in 1953.

Rees's *Life in a Welsh Countryside* makes it very clear how Thomas carefully fashioned his memorably mythic rural poetry by severely limiting the social materials that were at his disposal. For example, it demonstrates in considerable detail how socially complex was the life of the upland farmers whom Thomas chose to represent almost exclusively as if they were isolates. As in Manafon, most of the farms in Llan were little more than smallholdings, and Rees's study emphasises that every one was its own miniature community, usually consisting of the nuclear family of a farmer, his wife, and his sons and daughters, all of whom contributed to the work. As the sons grew older, the youngest, who was expected to stay home, eventually inherited the farm, while the older siblings struck out on their own, usually having served an apprenticeship from a young age by working on neighbouring farms. There was therefore a strong inter-generational aspect to a style of living that depended on co-operative endeavour and that was strongly social in character. Moreover, far-flung though their farms obviously were, and hard though their living undoubtedly was in these 'starved pastures', as

Thomas put it, they were sustained by a rich network of relations with their kinsfolk, an intricate web that covered the whole of the parish. Though invisible to the casual visitor, these blood relations were very close and operative at many levels of their lives. These 'isolated' farmers were therefore securely nested within a strong community. But, as Rees shrewdly observes, lack of visible signs of that community life 'leads to outsiders' supposition of universal social isolation' (*LWC*, 101).

One is given some inkling of circumstances such as these in 'Y Llwybrau Gynt', where Thomas speaks warmly of his regular visits to the far-flung farms, of the lavish hospitality he encountered on their comfortable hearths, of the farmers busy about their work 'hoeing, sheep-shearing, collecting hay and cutting hedges' (*SP*, 138). He realised he was likely to catch them at home only of an evening. And he came to expect 'at a given moment, after some considerable activity on the part of the women, the formal almost curt command: Come to the table. And what a feast, for us at any rate. Their own meat, their own bread, their own butter, apple pie with a quarter of a pint of cream on it. And then back to the log fire on the open hearth' (*SP*, 141). Time after time in his essay Thomas makes clear how warm were his memories of that period, and how dearly he came to love the hill people, as well as to respect them. He also notes how inquisitive were the people of this farming community: 'since the farms were on the sides of the valley, it was obvious to everyone how his neighbour was getting on ... Their interest in each other's lives was inborn ... if a farmer with a hundred acres had given ten shillings, a farmer with fifty would give five' (*SP*, 140). But he then adds that what he nevertheless most vividly remembered was 'the lonely figures in the fields, hoeing or docking mangles, hour and hour. What was going on in their heads, I wonder? The question remains unanswered to this day.' Therefore, here in his prose Thomas offers his reader a scrupulously balanced insight into Manafon life, while in his poetry he deliberately chooses to pursue a very different path.

There he is willing to respect only the ruthless dictation of his poet's imagination. Identification and explication of the psychic determinants of the raw shaping-force that drove that imaginative process lies beyond the purview of this article.[6] But it is clear that it is by isolating that image of the solitary farmer in his high fields that Thomas the poet was able to cunningly fashion his unforgettable image of existential loneliness and unremitting life-or-death struggle; a heroic vision positively

Hemingway-esque in character. This fashioning begins with the very first poem in *Stones of the Field*. There Thomas describes the farmer come to town 'out of the hills' as one whose mind is slow to escape the environment within which it has for so long been imprisoned: 'The shadow of the mountain dwindles', he writes, 'his scaly eye/ Sloughs its cold care and glitters'.[7] Almost reptilian, the image effectively dehumanises its subject. What Thomas is actually describing here is the bringing of store cattle to a border market, a process that had by this time become 'archaic', as one agricultural historian has pointed out in a classic study.[8] So many farmers had been forced by economic circumstances to become unskilled dealers that they had swamped the market and caused monopolistic 'rings' to be formed that drove down prices. And the strongest dealers bought directly from the farms, so that all the animals that were actually brought to market were scrawny beasts, reflective of the 'starved pastures' Thomas mentions in the poem. Agricultural historians have also had much to say about the backward and neglected state of Welsh upland pastures, as we shall see later in this discussion. This is the sort of complex socio-economic circumstance that Thomas completely filters out from the poetry, but that is worth recalling in order to sharpen awareness of the special, peculiar, conditions of his poetic world.

His Iago Prytherch is similarly a loner, whether elementally described as a creature of 'the bald Welsh hills' (that 'bald' neatly conflates features characteristic both of humans and of bare uplands), and statically viewed as forever penning 'a few sheep in a gap of clouds', or at home of an evening, slumped 'vacantly in his chair' (*CP*, 12). He often seems to have no interiority, because he is not a social being at all. His condition is succinctly summarised in 'The Last of the Peasantry', whose 'face is lit always from without,/ The sun by day, the red fire at night;/ Within is dark and bare' (*CP*, 67).

In 'A Peasant', therefore, Iago is seen as having no human ties whatsoever. By contrast, 'Country Child' is a portrait of a young man caught in the common situation described by Rees, as 'maturing in his place against his parents' ageing' (*CP*, 5). He has no life or character that he can really call his own, having been destined from birth to be tied to the farm as his father's successor. *Life in a Welsh Countryside* elaborates on the life of such and singles out two consequences in particular of such an upbringing. Rees points out that it was exceedingly rare for a Welsh upland farmer ever actually to retire, regardless of age, a situation that contrasted strongly with the custom in England. 'The postponement of marriage until late middle life,' which was one consequence of this Welsh practice, 'can be understood only in the light of filial duty and the custom whereby the paternal holding and stock are inherited' (*LWC*, 66). This Rees saw as a fascinating example of continuity with the social system of Medieval Wales – 'the Welsh tribesman retained control of his share of the land of his kindred until his death' (*LWC*, 71). 'Although the old tribal society has long since passed away,' Rees adds, 'something of its spirit lives on in the cohesion and paternalism of the present-day family' (*LWC*, 72).

One consequence of this was that farmers' sons tended to delay marrying until they were in their late twenties or early thirties. No wonder, therefore, that in 'Country Child' Thomas grimly imagines the boy as having been 'dropped without joy from the gaunt womb', intended from the beginning only to fit the role of heir, and he then proceeds to imagine the sexual frustration attendant on his long awaiting of marriage. It inclines him to eroticise an ash tree so that it 'wantons with sensuous body and smooth,/ Provocative limbs to play the whore to his youth' (*CP*, 5). And then, once he has indeed married a wife, she is imagined as 'half wild, half shy of the ancestral bed,/ The crumbling house, and the whisperers on the stairs'. In other words, she is very aware of being ghosted by the past, and of being haunted by those elders whose spirits seem still to hover in the air invisibly determining every detail of her life. She is trapped in a Gothic nightmare.

Very few commentators, if any, have paid attention to Thomas's admittedly sporadic depiction of the wives of hill farmers in his Manafon poems. When he does admit them into his vision his treatment of them is sympathetic, after a fashion, but they are always represented as marginal. And here again he departs sharply from Alwyn Rees's account of the centrality of the place of women in the rural Welsh economy, partly no doubt because Thomas was creative fabulist enough to realise that the distinctive world he had fashioned in his poetry needed to be self-consistent in its every particular, unswervingly true to its basic premises. In his cool, dispassionate analysis of the disposition and operations of the family unit that was central to the maintenance of the rudimentary economy of the rural uplands Rees emphasises that the farms were by necessity co-operative enterprises:

Women and girls may be seen working in the fields during the hay and corn harvest, but on the whole they participate less in such tasks as planting, weeding and harvesting rootcrops than they did a generation or so ago. Normally there is now a fairly clear division of labour between the sexes, the activities of the women being largely confined to the house and the farm-yard. The success of the family farm depends a great deal upon the resourcefulness of the farmer's wife. In addition to her household duties she looks after the poultry, collects the eggs, makes the butter and sells all these products. In this she may have the assistance of a daughter or a domestic servant, but at nearly half the farms, as well as at the smallholdings, all the work was done by one woman.

From the sale of her domestic products – locally defined as the things taken to market in a basket – the wife derives the house-keeping money with which she buys the groceries, clothes herself and the younger children and replenishes the stock of household equipment. The wife's budget is thus largely independent of that of her husband, and she is usually rather secretive about it. This separation of moneys is even more marked in parts of southern Montgomeryshire where the farmer's wife starts her married life with a separate banking account based on a dowry of a few tens or hundreds of pounds according to the circumstances of her parents ... In this connection it is interesting to recall that under medieval Welsh law the wife of a freeman might dispose of her clothing, her meal, her cheese, her butter and milk 'without advice of her husband'[.] (*LWC*, 62–3)

This picture is startlingly at odds with the impression that Thomas chooses to give in his poetry, where the hill wife is likely to be depicted as a poor drab, entirely subject to her husband's will, little better than a brood mare, and a source of unpaid labour. Thomas repeatedly describes her as one robbed entirely of her own identity, her femininity as good as erased. In the gallery of family portraits staring from a farm wall, images of previous generations, John All appears accompanied by

> his lean wife,
> Whose forced complicity gave life
> To each loathed foetus. (*CP*, 90)

In 'Age' Thomas imagines a farmer who, when young, had met and married a mate who 'grew to the warm woman/ Your hands had imagined/ Fondling soil in the spring fields' (*CP*, 78). She also proved to be fertile, giving birth to 'four strong sons' who 'stood up like corn in June about you'. But he had failed to 'cherish' her, so that in the last verse Thomas broods on opportunity wasted, on the farmer's failure to lavish on her, even for a single day, the loving care he had squandered on his land, so that 'she lay fallow/ Drying, hardening, withering to waste'. In 'The Airy Tomb', Twm's mother is so dependent on her husband that his death leaves her nothing but a 'pale, spent woman, who sat with death/ Jogging her elbow through the hot, still days/ Of July and August, or passed like a ghost/ By the scurrying poultry' (*CP*, 19). When Thomas launched into his jeremiad against his ignorant parishioners in the blistering opening of 'A Priest to His People', he attacked the 'Men of the hills, wantoners, men of Wales,/ With your sheep and your pigs and your ponies, your sweaty females' – a listing that contemptuously ends by implying that the hill farmers' wives are nothing but another, and lesser, kind of beast (*CP*, 13).

The one exception where Thomas's depiction is closer to that of Rees is 'Farm Wife'. The impression given there is closer to the account he himself gives in 'Y Llwybrau Gynt' since she is seen as queen of her hearth, in a 'clean apron, good for fire/ Or lamp to embroider, as we talk slowly/ In the long kitchen, while the white dough/ Turns to pastry in the great oven,/ Sweetly and surely as hay making/ In a June meadow; hers are the hands/ Humble with milking' (*CP*, 94). Here she is a fully realised human being, evidently wholly at one with her environment, both domestic and natural, and very much in control of her own particular domain. And by mentioning the milking and choosing to make her baking 'rhyme' so to speak with hay making Thomas is subtly acknowledging this woman's crucial contribution not just to home-making but to the whole economy of her farm, exactly as Rees had pointed out.

Just as R. S. Thomas chooses for the most part to depart from that image of a wife's life on a hill farm offered by Alwyn Rees, so too does his representation of farm labourers differ from the same author's account, and for much the same reason: a concern to maintain the internal consistency of his overall image of life in the uplands of Wales. Rees points out that in Llanfihangel – and the same was undoubtedly true of

Manafon – the majority of the upland farms were in truth little more than smallholdings, that required no labour additional to that the family could comfortably supply. Labourers were therefore relatively few and far between, although they might be needed on the larger farms of over fifty acres. In those cases, many of the labourers were in fact sons from the smallholdings that were serving an apprenticeship before searching for farms of their own. Of these, therefore, many were related in some way to the farmers for whom they worked, and were usually 'youths in their teens and young men in their twenties' (*LWC*, 61) – merely temporary labourers so to speak, who 'live under the same roof as the employer and his family eat at the same table' (61). It was only in lowland areas that the tendency was growing to discriminate between farmers' sons and labourers. Relations between employers and these employees were strictly governed by regulations set by the Agricultural Wages Board that determined both such employers' requirements as were acceptable and the wages that labourers were to be paid. Not that these regulations were rigidly adhered to, since labourers could easily obtain more generous terms than those stipulated. So 'under present conditions the employee usually receives more than the minimum wage' (*LSW*, 62).

Contrast this state of affairs with the condition of 'A Labourer' in Thomas's poem of that name, which opens by enquiring 'Who can tell his years/ for the winds have stretched/ So tight the skin on the bare racks of bone/ That his face is smooth, inscrutable as stone?', and continues in the same vein (*CP*, 2). Consequently the overall impression is of a character resembling such an ageless archetypal figure as Wordsworth's old Leech Gatherer or Old Cumberland Beggar much more than the labourer of Alwyn Rees's description, which is meticulously faithful to contemporary realities. And Thomas's labourer is condemned to perform, to all eternity it seems, the same back-breaking, demeaning labour of pulling 'reluctant swedes' so that he has ended up so bent in two that when 'his back comes straight' it is as if 'an old tree [were] lightened of the snow's weight'.

And Thomas uses the same rhetorical devices to identical effect in another poem that is this time entitled 'The Labourer' so as to make it seem even more definitive of its subject. Here again the figure is completely removed from time and change, forever clad in 'the same garments, frayed with light/ Or seamed with rain' that 'cling to the wind scoured bones' (*CP*, 39). It is an image as remarkably monumental as, say, that found in Jean-François Millet's famous painting of 'The Sower' (1850). This labourer has become entirely the creature of habit, one who has completely shed his human nature so as to seem entirely of a piece with his environment and to have been fashioned out of it, having begun as a 'vague/ Movement among the roots of the young grass'. That is strongly suggestive of a creature from some ancient Greek myth, a spirit of the soil that has emerged out of the very earth.

'Hireling' simply gives alternative expression to the same vision. Thomas describes meeting him 'wandering a road/ Fenced with rain …/ The wind feathering his hair'. He is left unnamed because he seems to lack all human identity, just as he has no claim whatsoever to social living since 'Nothing is his, neither the land/ Nor the land's flocks'. He seems to have gone completely feral:

> sharing his hearth
> With cats and hens, he has lost all
> Property but the grey ice
> Of a place splintered by life's stone. (*CP*, 109)

That use of the word 'property' is neat, because while here it means '[human] characteristics', it also refers back to the opening of the stanza which makes it clear that the hireling is literally property-less, employed simply to guard the property of others. At the same time, of course, it strongly suggests that it is this feature that has set him free to become entirely a tough, resilient being of his demanding and unyielding environment. The whole complex issue of property ownership exercised R. S. Thomas, averse as he was to modern voraciously acquisitive society. As a priest of the Church in Wales, he had himself throughout his life been something of a 'hireling', a property-less man on principle as well as by virtue of his vocation. His regret, when he decided to retire, was that he lacked means to buy a house that would allow his artist wife to keep and hang some of her paintings. Instead, he settled for living in a simple, small old cottage, a grace and favour arrangement for which he was indebted to his 'patrons', the Keating sisters of Plas-yn-Rhiw. The last of life's little ironies – to adopt Thomas Hardy's sardonic phrase – in Thomas's case was that at the very end he married a very wealthy woman, and through her was introduced to some of the luxuries of life. But he remained wedded in principle to what today would be called an 'alternative' minimalist lifestyle.

II

The second consequence noted by Rees of the extended adolescence that was the fate of a farmer's son was that of the chronic lack of social interaction with his peers. The oldest son would have been the worst affected, since farming duties always trumped socialising:

> The farmer's son has to serve a long apprenticeship, and it is my impression that the psychological effect of this prolonged boy-hood may be observed in the reticence and subdued behaviour of farmers' sons as compared with labourers' sons as well as an element of immaturity which seems to persist in the character of many an adult farmer. (*LWC*, 63)

This identifies for us the social origin of that silence and inarticulate-ness that Thomas made such a signature feature of his 'peasant' figures. The 'country child' is long used to 'moulding his mouth to silence', as Thomas has it, and time after time he broods obsessively on this defin-ing characteristic from the point of view of one whose own exceptional articulateness found itself called thereby into question as suspect and glib. So 'Affinity' memorably opens with a Biblical invitation for us to 'Consider this man in the field beneath/ Gaitered with mud, lost in his own breath', a being seemingly 'without joy, without sorrow,/ Without children, without wife' (*CP*, 9). Thomas may initially suppose him to be 'stumbling insensitively from furrow to furrow', but by the poem's end he has learnt better, and acquired the humility not to 'be taken in/ By stinking garments or an aimless grin'.

Very much a loner himself, and scarcely given to garrulousness, Thomas found himself irresistibly drawn to Wordsworthian charac-ters like this so typical of the upland parishes of Wales. So, he opens 'Peasant Greeting' with 'No speech; the raised hand affirms/ All that is left unsaid/ By the mute tongue and unmoistened lips' (*CP*, 12). And by the end of the poem, Thomas has come to realise that such char-acters are listeners, not speakers, attuned as they are to the sounds of their environment, so that when the peasant 'slips/ To his long grave under the wave of wind,' that element still 'breaks continually on the brittle ear' (*CP*, 12). Into that adjective 'brittle' is compressed Thomas's acknowledgement of the human faculties that, as any peasant well knows, are so necessary for surviving in a harsh environment and are yet so frail and so vulnerable. Speech is not the faculty that matters most in such testing circumstances as these. Instead, as Thomas acknowledges in 'A Priest to His People', much more important are 'your eyes' that become penetrating and discerning enough to 'detect like an ewe or an ailing wether,/ Driven into the undergrowth by the nagging flies,/ My true heart wandering in a wood of lies?' (*CP*, 13)

The similarity of this image to one of the many parables in which Christ draws on the natural world to illustrate His meaning is not only unmistakeable but pointed, because Thomas goes on to dismiss the relevance of the 'devices of church and school' to the 'unhallowed movements' of peasant life. And he next identifies another of the non-verbal faculties that are essential to such an existence: 'Why should you come like sparrows for prayer crumbs/ Whose hands can dabble in the world's blood?' In his Notebooks, Thomas confesses to his sense of inadequacy at Manafon because he simply could not bring himself to 'dabble in the world's blood', even when for instance it might have resulted in putting a poor wounded creature out of its misery. 'The animals had to be looked after for the profit that came from doing it,' Thomas remembered (*SP*, 139). 'There was not the least bit of sentiment or tenderness involved. If a lamb died, the only thing to do was to throw it into the hedge for the crows' (*SP*, 140). It is only having foregrounded and prioritised these skills and faculties that Thomas concludes by realising that 'your speech has in it/ The source of all poetry, clear as a rill/ Bubbling from your lips'.

There are many instances where Thomas shows how aware and appreciative he is of the way in which the relative absence of speech has led to the heightening of other senses in the case of the reticent hill farmers. In one poem, Iago Prytherch is endowed with 'sharp eyes,/ Bright as thorns' that are well used to 'watching the sunrise/ Filling the valley with its pale yellow/ Light' (*CP*, 29). As for poor Thomas the school dunce in 'The Airy Tomb',

> he was stone blind
> To the print's magic: yet his grass-green eye
> Missed nor swoop nor swerve of the hawk's wing
> Past the high window, and the breeze could bring,
> Above the babble of the room's uproar,
> Songs to his ear from the sun-dusted moor,

> The grey curlew's whistle and the shrill, far cry
> Of circling buzzard … (*CP*, 17)

Of course, such portraits are counterbalanced, in typically contradictory Thomas fashion, by others. In 'Valediction', another farmer figure is bitterly censured for his insensitivity to his environment:

> The beauty
> And grace that trees and flowers labour to teach
> Were never yours, you shut your heart against them.
> You stopped your eyes to the soft influence
> Of birds (*CP*, 38)

But even then, Thomas grudgingly acknowledges that the senses of such a being are alternatively attuned to the rough music of the labour of ordinary farming life. The 'slow heart beating', as another poem has it, 'to the hidden pulse/ Of the strong sap, the feet firm in the soil' (*CP*, 39). At such moments, Thomas recognises that the priorities of the farming community are totally at odds with his own, just as the language they speak is essentially unintelligible, grating, and inaccessible to his cultivated ear.

Alwyn Rees, by contrast, was trained to pay respectful attention to that language, and so was able to parse utterances of the kind that so repelled Thomas, because they sounded in his ears like 'the dull tone/ Of the thick blood, the loud, unlovely rattle/ Of mucus in the throat, the shallow stream/ Of neighbours' trivial talk' (*CP*, 39). Thomas recalls 'An Old Woman', who, 'if neighbours call she leans and snatches/ The crumbs of gossip from their busy lips' (*CP*, 40). At such moments he is on the brink of registering, like Rees, the lively social life of the community in which he is living, but in such instances he unfailingly recoils, re-establishing that protective distance essential for the maintenance of the majestic governing myth of his 'Prytherch' poems; that the upland farmers essentially live an isolated, solitary, lonely and inexhaustibly enigmatic existence. In 'Temptation of a Poet', he writes self-revealingly of the 'lost poetry' of his old talk with Iago Prytherch, of 'that world/ We built together' (*CP*, 73). Of course, that 'talk' had been far less conversation than monologue, conducted almost exclusively on Thomas's terms. Yet his description of it is still a just one, because the marvellous poetry of the Manafon period had indeed been the product of a 'dialogue' of sorts – since Thomas's eloquent words had been the product of his encounter with Iago Prytherch's silence.

Time after time Thomas resorts to images suggesting that the existence of Prytherch and his kind is hermetically sealed, safely wrapped in the insulating materials of their peculiar environment. So in 'Out of the Hills', his farmer comes to town wrapped in 'Clouds of cattle breath' (*CP*, 1); in 'Song at the Year's Turning' (*CP*, 59), 'Light's peculiar grace/ In cold splendour robes this tortured place/ For strange marriage'; the hill farmer acknowledges 'The pig is a friend, the cattle's breath/ Mingles with mine in the still lanes' (*CP*, 31); and in 'Invasion on the Farm', Iago yearns to recover 'the old farm/ Warm as a sack about me', as he feels 'the cold/ Winds of the world blowing' (*CP*, 60). When Thomas encounters 'The Poacher', he realises that 'The robed night, your dark familiar,/ Covers your movements' and adds that 'the slick sun/ A dawn accomplice removes your tracks/ One by one from the bright dew' (*CP*, 61).

As an experienced anthropologist, Alwyn Rees was very alert to any indication – however invisible to modern inhabitants – of a much older pattern of life that still lurked just under the surface of contemporary communal practices. Throughout *Life in a Welsh Countryside* he points to evidence of beliefs, habits, customs and social arrangements in Llan that had survived not only from the pre-Conquest Wales of the earlier Medieval period but from the much earlier society of Celtic times. One of the most arresting examples of such residual traces related to the character of a Welsh rural village when compared with an English village of similar size and location. Whereas in the case of the latter, the village was the unmistakeable hub of local social, spiritual, cultural and economic life, the same was not true in Wales, where for instance village greens – those prominent symbols of the centrality of the village as a communal centre in England – were virtually unknown, whether quaint or otherwise. A typical Welsh village consisted simply of a drab straggle of nondescript houses, haphazardly arranged, and their social function consisted of little more than a perfunctory provision of a few basic services. 'Manafon lay in a hollow', Thomas wrote in 'Y Llwybrau Gynt'. 'There was no proper village there, just a church, a school, a shop and a public house' (*CP*, 139). In Wales, towns, Rees pointed out, were a relatively recent alien import (*LWC*, 100). The Celts had never been an urban people, because their whole view of the world was a radically decentred one – divergent rather than convergent – a view of the world that appealed greatly to Rees himself.

Thomas captures some sense of this in the one and only poem he addressed to an anonymous village:

> Scarcely a street, too few houses
> To merit the title; just a way between
> The one tavern and the one shop
> That leads nowhere and fails at the top
> Of the short hill, eaten away
> By long erosion of the green tide
> Of grass creeping perpetually nearer
> This last outpost of time past. (*CP*, 57)

But then, having established the desultory character of such a banal, characterless settlement, Thomas executes one of his familiar rhetorical about turns to end by emphasising, again just like Rees, the lively character of the local rural community for which the village simply provides an arbitrary centre of occasional convenience:

> Stay then, village, for round you spins
> On slow axis a world as vast
> And meaningful as any poised
> By great Plato's solitary mind.

In *Life in a Welsh Countryside*, Rees analyses at some length the 'alternative', decentred forms of social activity that were actually based in and on the farms themselves and that therefore remained invisible to a casual visitor or uninstructed observer. It was the farms that acted as the real social centres, closely inter-related as they were by their ancient habits of periodic collaboration both in work and in leisure activities. But Rees was every bit as conscious as was Thomas that this form of spontaneous, ostensibly unstructured, community life was under serious threat from the incursions of the outside world.

Rees's observations on the unexpected survival over a period of some two thousand years in Wales of the decentred model of society is again strikingly illuminating of other aspects of Thomas's Manafon world that are featured in his poetry. Particularly relevant are Rees's comments on the distribution of religious institutions in mid-Wales parishes such as this. 'Behind the reasons of the dispersal of the chapels', he writes for instance, 'is the independent tradition of the scattered farms' (*LWC*, 105). After all, denominational worship had originally taken place simply as 'groups of people meeting in one another's houses' (*LWC*, 105). It was therefore natural for the chapels to follow the same pattern. The familiar Welsh word for a chapel service was 'y cwrdd', which means 'the meeting' and corresponds to the term 'meeting house', which was the old term for a chapel commonly used by English Dissenters. 'The House of God became an isolated building like the houses of His people, and the community was divided into a number of smaller communities with different geographical centres' (*LWC*, 105). Elsewhere, Rees notes how 'the chapels strengthened the social self-sufficiency of the countryside', although, he adds, 'other modern institutions have had the effect of drawing it more into the orbit of the hamlets' (*LWC*, 106). But even then, the real centre of modern gravity lies not in the hamlet or village but in the towns, not least because they tend also to include marts. 'Thus, generally speaking, the native way of life in upland Wales has retarded the growth of nucleated settlements, despite their antiquity in a great many cases' (*LWC*, 108).

Such comments as this foreground for us several salient features of Thomas's important long poem 'The Minister'. The scene is set from the very beginning in the Narrator's prologue:

> In the hill country at the moor's edge
> There is a chapel, religion's outpost
> In the untamed land west of the valleys,
> The marginal land where flesh meets spirit
> Only on Sundays and the days between
> Are mortgaged to the grasping soil. (*CP*, 42)

Thomas here unconsciously betrays his own bias as priest of a parish that is centred on a village church which makes a clear distinction, which no Nonconformist would recognise, between consecrated and unconsecrated ground. And in choosing this setting he may well have been influenced by his own experience when he had first begun to learn Welsh. 'Four miles up the valley, on the edge of the moorland, there was a chapel, the main language of whose congregation was Welsh. I called on the minister the Reverend D. T. Davies, and I got a warm welcome in his house' (*SP*, 139). He came to associate the moorland very closely with the Welsh language, as he again remembered years later:

> Sometimes after a meeting or a whist-drive in Manafon, I would hear some of the people standing in the darkness talking in Welsh, and I knew they had come down from the small farms around Adfa and Cefncoch. I thought of them going back to their homes on the edge of the moor. My dream would reappear after a time, and the following day I would go for a long walk on that moorland and meet some sheep-farmer doing the round of his flock. (*SP*, 139)

The passage perfectly encapsulates the fractured nature of the life Thomas was to live until the end. On the one hand the genteel English middle-class world of 'the whist-drive', on the other the strange, mysterious, 'dark' world of Welsh Wales.

As 'The Minister' develops, there are several passages that make it quite clear that, far from dominating, as a church would, the land that surrounds it, the chapel is itself dominated, to the point of seeming to be overwhelmed, by its wild natural environment. And looking down from such a remote outpost 'the valleys', in which the churches are situated, 'are an open book/ Bound in sunlight'. By implication, the dark hill country by which the chapel finds itself surrounded is a closed book. Here the words spoken from the pulpit 'are blown/ To pieces by the unchristened wind' and worship is 'riddled by the inhuman cry/ Of buzzards circling above the moor'.

Once the poem really gets into its stride it soon becomes clear that the narrative, like the chapel, is going to be dominated not by the voice of the minister but by the contending voices of his deaconate, who are the real governors of the place, used to choosing 'their pastors as they chose their horses'. 'The Minister' is a priest's appalled exercise in imagining himself into a situation where a chapel minister is entirely in thrall to his congregation, represented by the all-powerful deaconate. Such, of course, is the realpolitik of every chapel governance. Because every chapel is in essence a wholly unhierarchical and totally democratic body. Independent chapels are particularly so, since every individual chapel is completely self-governing, entirely in charge of its own affairs, linked to other chapels in its denomination only in voluntary occasional and purely temporary loose association. Thomas seems to shudder as he imagines overhearing the voices in the chapel vestry, 'where Davies is using/ The logic of Smithfield' (*CP*, 43). So the 'unchristened sounds' that rudely invade the chapel from without are matched by what, for Thomas, are the equally 'unchristened sounds' of the human voices of a crudely worldly deaconate. No wonder the poem proceeds by degrees to Gothic extremes of horrified imaginings. No wonder either that the voice of the Reverend Elias Morgan, BA (that degree being a kind of pathetic badge of impotent learning, an ineffectual shield against the affrontery of vulgar ignorance) is not heard until the deaconate have first had their cynical say; after all, the Minister – initially so young, green and enthusiastic – is never more than a cipher in these surroundings.

The congregation is briefly energised by the novice's preaching, enthused by his ardour, 'except for the elders', and 'even they were moved/ By the holy tumult, but not extremely./ They knew better than that', as Thomas mordantly comments (*CP*, 47). They knew that the real common currency of their society, in chapel every bit as much as on the farm, 'was sex, sex, sex and money, money'. That reference to money takes on further irony in the light of Alwyn Rees's disclosure that in the Welsh uplands chapel ministers were paid only half the wages of ordinary farm labourers (*LSW*, 118). At such moments as this, one begins to suspect that in condemning the chapel members in these unsparingly harsh terms Thomas is cleverly licensing himself to give indirect voice to all the animus he feels against his own parishioners and that he would never dare express in propria person. 'I began a Bible class', poor Morgan complains, 'but no one came .../ I opened the Bible and expounded the Word/ To the flies and the spiders, as Francis preached to the birds'. Thomas himself, as we know, was no stranger to such despair.

Throughout the poem the chapel's isolation, standing as it does on the edge of the moorland that seems to threaten to come in by every window, is contrasted with life in the valley below. Morgan is a minister under permanent siege, so that with the coming of night he makes sure that 'the blinds [are] all down', as Davies the deacon savagely advises, not only 'for fear of the moon's bum rubbing the window' (*CP*, 51) but so as to avoid seeing the gross bestial conduct of his chapel members. In its cumulative squalor and bleak hopelessness the poem is quite harrowing to read as Morgan grows ever more isolated, ground down and resigned, while 'the Welsh hills looked on/ Implacably' (*CP*, 53). Having begun as a complete innocent he has become far too knowing, and thus in his way Morgan ends up complicit in the life he knows he is utterly powerless to influence let alone change.

Thomas clearly ends up sympathising with him, having partly turned him en route into an alter ego whose tragic decline serves Thomas himself as salutary warning. But at the very end, he steps away, suddenly blaming Morgan's fate not on his congregation, nor on the malignancy of the moorland, but on the minister's own insistence on dictating terms to nature instead of entering into meaningful reciprocal relationship with her. 'He chose to fight', Thomas concludes, 'With that which yields to nothing human./ He never listened to the hills'/ Music calling to the hushed/ Music within' (*CP*, 54).

The unmistakeable implication here is that Thomas has escaped Morgan's fate by learning to listen to that music, and that as valley priest of a parish, rather than isolated chapel minister, he represents a church whose relationship to nature, whether that be human nature or non-human nature, is altogether much more accommodating than that adopted by the chapel and its membership. So Thomas's epitaph for Morgan, with which the poem ends, comes not in the form of words engraved on a gravestone, but in the form of

> The wind's text
> Blown through the roof, or the thrush's song
> In the thick bush that proved him wrong.
> Wrong from the start, for nature's truth
> Is primary and her changing seasons
> Correct out of a vaster reason
> The vague errors of the flesh. (*CP*, 55)

Reverting then to the points made by Alwyn Rees, we might say that 'The Minister' is a commentary on that crucial aspect of Nonconformity that is symbolised by the siting of chapels as isolated lonely outposts at a distance from the mixed life of community that is, for Thomas, naturally centred on the village and its parish church. By thus setting itself apart, and admitting to membership only those worshippers who regard themselves as the 'called' and the 'faithful', a chapel is inviting trouble, because it is actually predicated on the exclusion of all and of everything that does not conform to its own particular iron religious

creed. Its stance is therefore an inherently adversarial one. Its geographical isolation, intended as a signifier of purity and the self-sufficiency of
spiritual integrity, is in the end its undoing.

The view R. S. Thomas takes of Welsh Nonconformity in 'The
Minister' is strikingly similar to that taken by William Carlos Williams
of the Puritan settlers of New England in his maverick 1925 study of
American history, *In the American Grain*, which has long been accepted as
a classic.[9] The spent 'flamboyant force' of 'Tudor England's lusty blos-
soming' became in them, said Williams, 'hard and little'. They regarded
the New World as a wild, barren wilderness, the Devil's own kingdom,
and were driven by an iron determination to subdue it and bend it to
their own will. 'The emptiness about them was sufficient terror for them
not to look further. The jargon of God, which they used, was their dialect by which they kept themselves surrounded as with a palisade' (*IAG*,
63). They pitted all their energies remorselessly against the foreign and
threatening forces of a natural world they regarded with horror and
suspicion. For Williams, the Puritans, retreating fearfully into themselves, called their barrenness a plenitude of spirit. So 'today', Williams
grimly concludes, 'it is a generation of gross know-nothingism,' life has
become dominated by 'the horrid beauty of … great machines', and in
'blackened churches … hymns groan like chants from stupefied jungles'
(*IAG*, 68). R. S. Thomas could not have put the case better.

It is not only in the scatter of chapel buildings across the countryside that Alwyn D. Rees finds evidence in Llanfihangel-yng-Ngwynfa of
the survival of Celtic and early Welsh practice. More surprisingly, but
equally convincingly, he finds it too in the case of the old rural churches
of Wales, such as that of Manafon itself, that were established before the
Anglo-Normans introduced the alien ecclesiastical order of the modern parish. Llanfihangel-yng-Ngwynfa means 'St Michael's Church in
Gwynfa' – Gwynfa being the old Welsh name for that particular locality. Thus, the name is 'the reverse of the more recent nomenclature
whereby a tract of country takes its name from the church and becomes
"the parish of Llanfihangel." When reference is made to "the parish of
Llanfihangel-yng-Ngwynfa" to distinguish it from other Llanfihangel
[St Michael] parishes the name has the confused meaning of "the
territory of a church in a territory"' (101). The situation in Manafon
was comparable, as Thomas himself intuited when he wrote 'Country
Church, Manafon'. 'Manafon' means 'place by the river', and thus,

as was common in traditional Welsh practice, the name refers to natural local features. Whenever Thomas wrote about the church or its
Rectory he always associated them intimately with water and stone,
and never with the patron saint. Although, as at Llan, the church in
Manafon is dedicated to San Mihangel, and so should, strictly speaking,
be described as San Mihangel ym Manafon, nowhere does Thomas ever
call it by that name. Instead, he prefers to emphasise that it was built
out of the river stone. This makes it not only 'a place by the river' but
'a place made out of the river', so to speak.[10]

The contrast with the chapel in 'The Minister' could therefore
scarcely be more pointed. The former is at war with its natural environment, whereas the church is so much a part of its environment that
it is actually fashioned out of the materials of the natural world. Time
after time, in those poems in which he records his experiences in various
unnamed country churches, Thomas registers the intimate presence –
by turns a benediction and a curse – of a natural world to which the
church's walls prove welcomingly pervious. Thus a Thomas kneeling
and beseeching in prayer in such a church laments that 'no word came/
Only the wind's song' and hears 'the dry whisper of unseen wings,/
Bats not angels, in the high roof' (*CP*, 67). In 'Chapel Deacon', Davies
heads 'this fine morning/ For the staid chapel, where the Book's frown/
Sobers the sunlight' (*CP*, 76). And as for the moor, that is such a sinister,
dark, deathly, encroaching presence in 'The Minister', contrast that
with Thomas's poem on the subject which begins 'It was like a church
to me./ I entered it on soft foot,/ Breath held like a cap in the hand'
(*CP*, 166). It is only by approaching it in that spirit that Thomas comes
to realise that 'What God was there made himself felt'.

III

Manafon was 'in some ways an old-fashioned district', Thomas remembered. 'When I went there in 1942, there was not a single tractor in the
area. The men worked with their hands, hoeing, sheep-shearing, collecting hay, and cutting hedges. The horse was still in use. There was a
smithy there; I can hear the sound of the anvil still, and see the spark
flying' (*SP*, 139). It is immediately after this that for the first time Thomas
registers in his recollections 'the lonely figures in the fields' that became

his great obsessive subject. In other words, they were representatives of an old-fashioned kind of farming and way of living, and in that, for him, lay their significance and relevance, as the poetry makes very clear.

In his study, Alwyn D. Rees places the arrival of the tractor in such districts in its appropriate context. 'The concentration of the present economy upon animal husbandry', he writes – and the same was true of Thomas's Manafon – 'is in a way a reversion to the ancient mode of life in the Welsh hills after a long interval in which the plough was more widely used':

> [i]n the hungry (eighteen) forties, when corn prices were soaring, much of the richer lowland was still retained as meadow and pasture while the newly-enclosed *ffriddoedd* were extensively ploughed. This was picturesquely described as *rhoi croen newydd ar yr hen ffriddoedd* (giving the old *ffridd* a new skin). The response to the food scarcity of the two World Wars of the twentieth century has been broadly similar. The farmers have been readier to plough the poorer than the richer lands and, in Llanfihangel as elsewhere in Wales, it is the rough *ffriddoedd* and not the cultivated fields that have been given a 'new skin' by the tractors of the War Agricultural Executive Committee. (*LSW*, 23)

As that last sentence makes clear, the Second World War was bringing significant changes to the agricultural economy of Manafon at the exact moment that Thomas first arrived there. The explicit aim was to mobilise the countryside for war, to mount a battle of the land that corresponded to what became the famous Battle for the Air. Thomas was profoundly opposed to this. As a pacifist, he objected to the militarisation of the land; and he also deplored the way in which the approach adopted by government agency was strictly functional and utilitarian. Land was to be treated simply as a national asset; the aim was to vastly increase 'returns' and to maximise 'profits'. No attention at all was to be paid to the effects of such an approach on local cultures.

One of the most successful of the government's home front campaigns was that which exhorted the people to 'Dig for Victory'. Back gardens, and every spare bit of park and common land throughout the country, were to be turned into allotments and used to produce food. Government intervention in the countryside was in a way no more than this 'Dig for Victory' campaign writ large. When, therefore, in one of his earliest (1942) Manafon poems, Thomas addressed the condition of 'A Peasant', he ended with the following well-known passage:

> Yet this is your prototype, who, season by season
> Against the siege of rain, and the wind's attrition,
> Preserves his stock, an impregnable fortress
> Not to be stormed even in death's confusion.
> Remember him, then, for he, too, is a winner of wars,
> Enduring like a tree under the curious stars. (*CP*, 4)

Those concluding lines are obviously intended as a thrust against the wartime conditions that were beginning to prevail in the countryside. In protest against the government's clamorous insistence that the agrarian economy needed to be changed before it could become 'a winner of wars', Thomas insisted that it had been such down the ages, but that the real war in which it had been involved was the unchanging one of timeless heroic struggle against the elements.[11] Nor did he change his mind with the passing of the years. Fifteen years after 'A Peasant' appeared, he opened 'To the Farmer' with the lines: 'And the wars came and you still practised/ Your crude obstetrics with flocks and herds' (*CP*, 97).

The government management of the rural economy that was to become a feature of the Second World War period was trialled during the Great War, when County War Agricultural Executive Committees were created in an effort to 'produce more food from home resources' (*FD*, 177). During the post-war period, a worldwide food surplus drove down prices, and the situation in agriculture was further aggravated by increasing competition due to overseas imports. The resulting economic impact was only partly off-set by exchequer-funded subsidies, that included a flat-rate subsidy for cattle, and the passing of Agricultural Marketing Acts in 1931 and 1933. In spite of such protectionist measures, foreign imports accounted for 65% of UK food by 1937. On the other hand, dramatic improvements in food production were beginning to be driven by the improvement of crops enabled by key developments pioneered in the agricultural departments of the University of Wales Colleges of Aberystwyth and Bangor, and in particular as a result of work done at the Welsh Plant Breeding Station at Aberystwyth.

The work of the latter, in particular as it related to dramatic improvements in the grazing potential of the rough pasture of the Welsh uplands, was conducted in full awareness of the steady process of depopulation of those areas that had been under way ever since the nineteenth century. And among the counties that were hardest hit, R. S. Thomas's Montgomeryshire was at the very top of the list. No wonder, therefore, that he devoted an important article, 'Depopulation of the Welsh Hill Country', published at the very end of his period of stay at Manafon, to this very subject.[12]

Alwyn Rees opened *Life in a Welsh Countryside* by emphasising that animal husbandry, rather than arable farming, was at the heart of the rural economy of the parish of Llan. Cultivation of crops was largely confined to roots and green crops that were produced strictly for home use and consumption. Thus Thomas's portrait of a farmer bent double docking swedes was an accurate reflection of the rural realities of the district. Historians note the irony of the fact that grassland husbandry in Wales had changed very little in a hundred years, while transformative methods 'in grass breeding and grassland management' at little economic cost to the farmer were being pioneered right under the noses of the hill farmers at the Welsh Breeding Centre. Stubborn local neglect of these innovations meant that 'many parts of Wales still retained a distinctly neglected and desolate appearances' (*FD*, 183) at the end of the Second World War, as R. S. Thomas recorded in his seminal essay. And 'Welsh livestock men had little alternative but to continue to produce store cattle'. Thomas's Iago Prytherch should therefore partly be seen as a representative of the Manafon farmer profoundly reluctant to change his old ways. He should also partly be seen – and here Thomas gives an accurate picture of social realities – as an embodiment of the truth noted by agricultural historians, that 'for the hill farmer' in Wales, 'the inter-war decades represented a period of largely unrelieved and physical struggle' (*FD*, 187). The situation only began to change with the new government policies, backed up by new Acts and investments, that were first introduced by the post-war Labour government of Clement Attlee.

As hill populations in Wales 'fell to 0.5–0.8 persons per 100 acres by 1940, periodic farm tasks became increasingly difficult to perform. Reflecting both the human population decline and the declining ration of cattle to sheep, the botanical composition of upland swards began to deteriorate as bracken began its insidious spread across the hills'

(*FD*, 187). The 'depopulation of the Welsh hill country' that Thomas so lyrically and memorably lamented in his essay was therefore not only a phenomenon of the past but an urgent reality of the present. As the economic pressures of upland farming had grown ever more severe, so hard-pressed farmers had to sell up and move out, frequently to urban and industrial centres that offered greater economic promise. And more often than not, they sold their properties to slightly more affluent neighbours who, as Thomas sardonically put it, 'live[d] somewhat nearer civilization', and who were, he added, 'probably a mere bailiff for some-one in the richer more fertile lowlands' (*SP*, 20). Time after time in his essay, Thomas mournfully notes that whereas farmhouses had become abandoned and derelict, farm buildings, once neatly maintained, had been turned into unkempt structures serving as crude stables or barn. They were sad memorials to a distinctive and culturally rich way of life that had as good as passed away.

In poems such as 'Death of a Peasant' (*CP*, 34), therefore, Thomas is recording the ending of a whole way of life, once so vital, that had by then become stale as the air trapped in Davies's 'stone croft/ On the Welsh hills', where he lies 'under the slates .../ Lonely as an ewe that is sick to lamb/ In the hard weather of mid-March'. It is a disturbingly claustrophobic poem, the poet's underlying visceral terror at helpless imprisonment suggested in 'the trapped wind/ Tearing the curtains, and the wild light's/ Frequent hysteria upon the floor'. What Thomas doesn't mention here, or in any other of his poems about traditional life in the Welsh uplands, is that as late as 1936 'in rural Wales some two-thirds of cottages were considered unfit for human habitation, with vermin infestation rife'.[13] There was no piped water, and no electricity.

Another grim elegy for the end of an era is 'Ninetieth Birthday' (*CP*, 107) that begins by describing the long uphill track leading beyond the tree line up into 'the green bracken,/ The nightjar's house', and then further again up the steep path. That journey upwards is a journey backwards, to the earlier age into which the old woman had been born long ago. As Thomas poignantly puts it, she 'waits for the news of the lost village/ She thinks she knows, a place that exists/ In her memory only'. And the sadness deepens as Thomas registers the woman's personal, social, and cultural isolation, her situation as a living anachronism, equipped with life skills that have become completely redundant:

All you can do
Is lean kindly across the abyss
To hear words that were once wise.

Contrasting with such a figure, however, is Job Davies, in 'Lore' (*CP*, 114), a portrait of a tough, indefatigable survivor, robustly vulgar ('Miserable? Kick my arse'), whom Thomas half envies and half despises for the persisting crude vitality suggested by 'the great perch' of his laugh, and his 'paunch full of hot porridge': 'What's living but courage?' is his straightforward motto. He attracts Thomas's admiration because he embodies a defiant determination to continue with his old ways, and to hell with the new ones, even if it is to them that the future will belong:

What to do? Stay green,
Never mind the machine,
Whose fuel is human souls,
Live large man, and dream small.

That last phrase is in part a rebuke uttered by Thomas to himself. He very well knew he was an incurable dreamer, inclined to dream large, to dream of a different Wales that could come only from a revitalisation, albeit in different form, of the rural life the remnants of which he had seen up in the hills. And Thomas summed up everything that was for him inimical to that way of life, and symbolic of the new that was destroying it, in that one word: Machine.

The arc of Thomas's thinking on this crucial subject is clearly outlined in his essay. There he makes it perfectly clear that in regretting the depopulation that left so much of the Welsh uplands abandoned and derelict he is not so much deploring economic waste as inveighing against the destruction of a priceless and irreplaceable way of life. That distinctive rural lifestyle had been Welsh in speech, and had sustained a sophisticated culture that had poetry at its very heart. Thomas lovingly calls to mind the 'nosweithiau llawen' (spontaneous community entertainments), the 'noswylio' (social gatherings of an evening), and above all he recalls the folk poetry, some of it conforming to the complex, requirements of the strict metre tradition. Such skills had been sharpened by regular competition in local *eisteddfodau*. He records the very recent passing at the age of eighty-three of a man who had no

English. 'A terrible condition for a Briton of the twentieth century?'
Thomas ironically enquires. 'No, he was as merry and much more
interesting than the crickets which sang to him from his hearth' – a
form of phrasing that clearly betrays the naivety and sentimentality
that so often vitiates and unfortunately invalidates Thomas's writing
in this particular vein. It is evident again when he heard one upland
farmer 'recite a poem he had written about the searchlights during a
raid on Merseyside':

> I looked up at him with wide, blue air around him, and a strange
> emotion came over me. He was haloed with the clear light and
> his face was alive, his eyes keen. In his rough shirt-sleeves and
> his old cap he had all the beauty of a bog flower or a tree, or
> anything that had grown out of the grassy moor. And I realized
> very clearly that it was because he belonged there and was happy
> there. (*SP*, 23)

To a reader of today, this kind of passage is likely to seem nothing but hooey, and to be an irritating embarrassment to read. And
Thomas waxes equally lyrical about rural crafts and the skills that
could make small haystacks 'as primitively beautiful as a painting
by Van Gogh' (*SP*, 23). So obviously selective is this as an account
of the past rural life of Wales that agricultural historians would be
perfectly justified in dismissing it without a second thought. But it was
a version that enabled some very powerful and memorable poetry to
be written, because the poems retained inviolate an enigmatic and
ambivalent quality, and did not lend themselves quite as easily to a
crude reductionist rhetoric.

It is at least worth noting that Alwyn Rees does offer, from a more
detached anthropological perspective, a picture very similar indeed
to that outlined by Thomas of life in the parish of Llanfihangel-yng-
Ngwynfa, except that there, unlike Manafon, the culture he was
describing was still very much current. Moreover, even dispassionate agricultural historians recognise that consequences such as those
deplored by Thomas were in cold historical fact an important, and
regrettable, by-product of the emergence of a modern rural economy; and they also recognise that these consequences were very much
resented and lamented by rural communities right across Britain. 'There

may be some grounds', Moore-Colyer readily concedes, 'for arguing that the decay of indigenous rural industry had important psychological effects which framed attitudes towards farming and rural life':

> As the closely-knit and cohesive fabric of rural society, with its reciprocal duties and obligations began to disappear, it carried with it the quiet pride and satisfaction characteristic of local-ism. In so doing, it may have helped to usher in 'the make do and mend' and rather ramshackle approach so characteristic of the 1930s; the view that a derelict bedstead would fix a gap in a hedge as effectively as an hour's work with a billhook and hedge knife. Perhaps it was not economic circumstances alone which led to the creeping dereliction spreading inexorably through Wales and much of England so deplored by R. G. Stapledon and his disciples? (*FD*, 180)

The interesting case of Stapledon will be considered later in this essay, but at this point it's worth noticing how strikingly close Moore-Colyer's remarks about the ramshackle use of a bedstead to fix a hedge is to Thomas's acid disapproval of the way old farm buildings had been allowed to become unkempt storage spaces.

As Thomas emphasises, his concern to save and strengthen the way of life that had been practised in the uplands of Wales was at bottom very much a cultural concern, and central to it was a campaigning effort to preserve the Welsh language. He therefore ends his essay by offering a rudimentary blueprint of the practical steps he believes need to be taken by government:

> Certain efforts are being made, I know, to revive the country districts of Wales by encouraging small, rural industries, and that is all to the good. But that will hardly benefit or even touch the uplands. What we want there are good roads and grants or loans to put the houses and buildings in repair and a revival of the type of trade such as the wool trade, which would benefit these people. But the outer world is in chaos and the rule of the day is planning and uniformity, and small districts such as these are in danger of being completely overlooked owing to the more serious or spectacular nature of other problems. (*SP*, 24)

At the time he was writing, the Attlee government was actually in process of addressing the needs of upland areas, as of other rural regions
throughout Britain. In 1946, for instance, a Hill Farming Act was
passed. And moreover, similar steps, measures and initiatives had been
forthcoming throughout the war years from a British government very
concerned to improve food production. Attention now needs to be paid
to those, beginning by noting that one common element in them is the
assumption that the introduction of machinery into the modern rural
environment would be very highly beneficial, and it was to this, of
course, that Thomas was so adamantly opposed.

IV

In his important study of farming in Wales before the Second World
War, R. J. Moore-Colyer records that '[i]n May 1929, the *Carmarthenshire
and Teifiside Advertiser* covered a demonstration of the new International
"Farmall" tractors, held at Synod Inn, Cardiganshire, an event which
seemingly "caused a great stir"' (*FD*, 188). He goes on, however, to note
that 'this lightweight machine, capable of turning on its own length,
failed to make any significant inroads on the primary source of farm
tractive power, the horse, in the years preceding the Second World
War'. Consequently, 'by 1939 there were only 1,932 tractors in the
Principality'. No wonder Thomas remembered Manafon as almost a
tractor-free zone when he arrived there first. Farmers' stubborn attachment to their horses was not only due to their innate conservativism,
or to their fond memories of the horse as a tried and tested companion
(although in Wales, unlike England, the horse actually only began to be
used for farm work in the early nineteenth century: previous to that it
would have been done by oxen, the horse being regarded as an 'aristocratic' beast, the preserve of the gentry). Farmers were also suspicious
of investing precious capital in new-fangled machines of dubious reli-
ability and usefulness. And in any case, 'the work range of the tractor'
at that early juncture 'was severely limited prior to the invention of the
hydraulic three-point linkage system in 1934–5 and, indeed, there were
only some 2,000 of these machines in operation in Britain by 1939'
(*FD*, 188). But the shape of things to come was clearly evident in the
form of the caterpillar tractor that the Welsh Plant Breeding Station

used in their dramatically successful experiment on Cahn Hill, near Aberystwyth, that utilised the latest advances in grass production to produce results that astonished Welsh farmers (FD, 185).

There is, therefore, an interesting back-story to Thomas's poem 'Cynddylan on a Tractor', which encapsulates his feelings at the arrival in Manafon of the new, 'machine age' of modern farming (*CP*, 108). Its opening line, 'Ah, you should see Cynddylan on a tractor', is dripping with sarcasm, only for the sentence to modulate into Thomas's vulnerable anxiety at the disappearance from the farmer's face of 'the old look that yoked him to the soil'. 'Yoked' captures Thomas's bewildered confusion at the spectacle, because it suggests a recognition on his part that those traditional farmers of the past whom he so admires were in fact enslaved to the very soil they worked. There are related dualities running right through the poem. First Cynddylan is roundly and confidently dismissed as a mere mutant, a sinister cyborg; but then the line about the clutch of the tractor cursing, even as 'the gears obey', suggests a grumbling acceptance of what is in fact implicitly accepted as inevitable.

The remainder of the poem seems to be settling into a briskly dismissive satiric mode, but it then modulates into vulnerable melancholia, as the roar of this strange new beast, the tractor, empties 'the wood/ Of foxes and squirrels and bright jays'. The late insertion there of the adjective 'bright' suggests that light as well as sound have been expelled from the scene, and thus anticipates the next line where reference to the sun 'kindling all the hedges' allows Thomas to exploit the pun ('kindling' means not only 'lighting a fire' but also the materials used to start a fire) so as to conclude that the primal source of life, light and energy is 'not for him/ Who runs his engine on a different fuel'. And the last lines are poignantly effective, as Thomas succinctly recognises that not only the sounds of the natural world, but by implication all voices of protest as well, are doomed to be silenced by this new intrusive racket:

> All the birds are singing, bills wide in vain,
> As Cynddylan passes proudly up the lane.

The patness and glibness of the full, masculine, rhymes in this concluding couplet, very unusual in Thomas, points back to the very beginning and to the ineffable smugness of the tractor driver who rides high in all his newly acquired power and glory. Cynddylan offers an image of impenetrable self-satisfaction that augurs ill for any attempt to challenge and undermine it. The couplet thus becomes a poet's impotent revenge on a world that he knows is moving steadily beyond his reach and his control. But, as we shall see, ten years later Thomas returned to his tussle with the tractor in a poem called 'Too Late', where he employed a different, more fruitful, line of attack (*CP*, 108).

By the time 'Cynddylan on His Tractor' had appeared in 1952, Manafon, like the rest of rural Wales, had seen a dramatic increase in the number of tractors, as the spread of these was vital for the work of the County War Agricultural Executive Committees (CWAECs) that the central government had established right across Britain, in what turned out to be a successful effort to boost the production of vital food supplies. Such committees had first been introduced for the same purpose in 1915, but as a Second World War loomed it soon became obvious to the Ministry of Agricultural and Fisheries that a similar decisive intervention by the State in managing the rural economy of the country was needed, and so a country-wide network of 62 CWAECs was established, of which 13 were in Wales. The membership consisted of influential local figures in the rural communities who oversaw the implementation of radical progressive initiatives. Above these were placed land commissioners tasked with guiding and supervising the work of the committees. And above those were liaison officers, who provided the link with central government. The overall manager of the network was the Chief Agricultural Advisor, assisted by separate co-ordinators for Scotland and for Wales.

Sir Cadwalader Bryner Jones was appointed to the latter role, and became a powerful force in the world of Welsh Agriculture. He had been appointed Professor of Agriculture at Aberystwyth in 1906, then Welsh Secretary to the Ministry of Agriculture and Fisheries in 1919, and subsequently became Agricultural Commissioner for Wales who promoted developments such as the Plant Breeding Station. During the war, his responsibilities as Liaising Officer related to Merioneth, Glamorgan, Monmouth and Montgomeryshire. It soon became apparent to Westminster that the social, and cultural character of rural Wales was very different from that of rural England, and the issue of the Welsh language immediately began to loom large. As one historian has noted, 'Welsh farmers were among the strongest upholders of Welsh language and cultural identification, the most conservative and more prone to anti-English sentiments' (*BF*, 145). R. S. Thomas would undoubtedly have strongly approved. Nevertheless, Alwyn D. Rees recorded that in Llanfihangel-yng-Ngwynfa, farmers readily began to take advantage of the tractors that the CWAEC provided.

The case of the Welsh upland areas, such as that in the vicinity of Manafon, provided the CWAECs with a particular problem, because they consisted mostly of grasslands used as rough pasture for grazing by sheep and cattle. But wartime food shortages related primarily to dairying products and arable crops. Moreover, under the straitened conditions of wartime the economic cost of feeding animals had become a significant burden. The emphasis of the committees therefore was on the ploughing up of upland grasslands, which meant exactly the kind of radical transformation of the character of the land to which R. S. Thomas took such vehement exception. And where upland farmers proved either unable or unwilling to co-operate, the CWAECs were legally empowered to take over their smallholdings. Recognition was, however, given to the fact that landscapes such as the moorland tops that were often peat covered could not be reclaimed, and also that the work of reclaiming even some of the lower slopes of the hills could prove too costly for it to be economically justifiable in wartime. But the CWAECs in Wales relied heavily on guidance from the Welsh Plant Breeding Station that had such an impressive record of improving rough upland tracts into high-quality pasture. The comments of a leading agricultural historian are arresting:

> Apart from forestry, there is no one single process that has done more to alter the historic upland landscape than improvements based on Stapledon's research (at Aberystwyth), which encouraged a massive programme of ploughing, fertilising and reseeding among the Welsh hills. (*BF*, 240)

While R. S. Thomas nowhere acknowledges this, it is obvious that such a dramatic process of change as this in his immediate locality did in fact provide a challenging and disturbing background to his responses to the hill country around Manafon. While his poetry therefore specifically involves a suppression of this context, it haunts his texts as potentially subversive subtext, imbuing them with the tensions that are everywhere palpable in the language.

In fact, R. S. Thomas's Montgomeryshire came to be admired as 'the best-known example of wartime reclamation' (*BF*, 240). The county easily exceeded its ploughing quota. And this initial ploughing was followed first by the planting of kale, rye, or ryegrass for sheep or bullocks, and then by the growing of potatoes. Dairy cattle could be grazed on the improved upland pastures, and the areas for traditional sheep grazing was significantly extended. But all this work was made possible only by the use of new heavy machinery, including prairie busters and a range of different tractors:

> The Ministry provided 13 track-laying tractors, including five huge lend-lease super-charged Allis-Chalmers HD7 tractors, the largest used in Europe at that time. There were also nine wheeled tractors (Ford-Fergusons and Fordsons), seven ploughs, including a Massey-Harris prairie buster, together with cultivating implements, manure distributors, trailers, storage tanks and a van. (*BF*, 241)

No wonder that, as his Manafon poetry testifies, R. S. Thomas felt so beleaguered. And such were the requirements of these projects that additional labour was needed, which was supplied either by school-boys or by evacuees. It is worth noting, however, that historians have come to doubt the long-term efficacy of these ambitious reclamation schemes, not least because a constant, unremitting war had to be waged against the return of 'encroaching heather and bracken'. As has been pointed out

> It is hard not to see the enormous effort expended in Montgomeryshire as being as much about symbolism and morale as about sensible upland reclamation. The former was important of course, but the inputs might have been more wisely diverted to friendlier environments where the opportunities for good returns were more promising. (*BF*, 245)

Thomas would undoubtedly have felt vindicated by the delayed revenge of the violated and ravaged uplands, whose natural character had been so violently and unsympathetically altered.

One of the ironies of the situation is that George Stapledon, whose work at the Breeding Station had inspired and enabled these ambitious, exciting but ultimately ill-advised reclamation schemes, was in fact a great believer, like R. S. Thomas, in respecting the natural character of the environment, and, again like Thomas, was no great enthusiast for the powerful new machinery that could be so easily used to destroy it. As well as being an innovative scientist, Stapledon was a nature mystic, committed pastoralist, passionate environmentalist, and early conservationist who published several influential books advancing a vision of country living that is strikingly similar to that of R. S. Thomas. Moreover, Stapledon specifically looked to poets and fiction writers for guidance. Thus he endorses the work of D. H. Lawrence, and his advocacy that people 'seek out the land and associate it at least to some degree with nature uncontaminated and unspoiled'. How else, Stapledon asks, 'is man to feed his pre-mental sides and ... ensure that the branches of his intellect are sustained by emotions whose roots draw their nourishment from sources that are natural, pure, and utterly devoid of perversion?'[14] And it was to T. S. Eliot he looked when deploring the way that 'today men are too immersed in detail, too taken up with machines and machinery to react to their whole experience'. Accordingly, he hated the intellect-made din and screeching of modern streets and factories and 'the hum even of a moderately placid machine', and yearned to recover 'the sounds of nature, the sea on the shore, the babbling brook, the wind in the willows' (WL, 64). The reference to Graham's famous book is, of course, deliberate.

Stapledon was also like Thomas in denying that his was a reactionary philosophy, although he did yearn for an England of a bygone age, as Thomas was prone to do in the case of Wales. Stapledon regarded his vision rather as representing a challenge to the modern State to ensure that, alongside all it was beginning to do in such realms as those of the economy and health, it also fostered the many different spiritual needs and creative potentialities of individuals and enabled the development of fulfilled and contented communities. But such a development could only happen, he added, if due care was given to protecting the natural environment within which alone such advances could eventually happen. He saw the protection, preservation and sensitive improvement of rural England as of the essence for a healthy national identity, and this could only be accomplished by recognising the centrality of the small farm. All this, however, depended on the introduction of improvements into the countryside, such as hot and cold water, electric light, and sanitation in farmhouses and cottages, along with the guarantee of a living wage.

Thus far his views closely coincided with those of R. S. Thomas, who likewise protested that his was a civilised vision for the future not a campaign for a return to the past. And in addition to advocating small farms, Stapledon specifically commended upland areas: 'hill men', he wrote, 'are grand men and worthy any price to the [English] nation to keep and to hold'. But unlike Thomas, Stapledon naturally emphasised that land improvement in hill country and the opening up of that landscape to urban visitors was very much part of his blueprint for the future. He went so far as to say that 'hill-farming and national parks seem to me to go absolutely hand in hand', and foresaw the arrival of holiday camps, hostels, summer schools 'and all the amenities demanded of a national park' (*WL*, 110). And departing further from Thomas, he added that for him machinery very much had its crucial place in the picture: 'the lorry and the tractor have a great national service to perform if judiciously employed on selected areas scattered over the whole of our eighteen million acres of rough and hill grazings' (83). As was to be expected, Stapledon prioritised the improvement of grasslands, emphasising the importance of doing so not only for the country at large but for those who actually lived in those areas, who deserved to enjoy the benefits of progress every bit as much as did urban dwellers. And here again, his emphasis was somewhat different from that of R. S. Thomas. But, like him, Stapledon emphasised that his fundamental concern was the welfare of the nation (England of course in his case), whose very heartland was for him the country.

V

It is fruitful to juxtapose Stapledon's writings and those of R. S. Thomas not only because they both base their similar visions on their respective experiences of much the same upland area of Wales, but because the attempts made in Stapledon's vision to reconcile tradition with modernity can sharpen our awareness of cognate tensions in Thomas's poetry. These surface most clearly in his Iago poems of the post-Manafon era, probably because distance, both physical and psychological, enabled Thomas not only to view his creation Iago Prytherch in a slightly different light, but also now for the first time to see clearly his own position in relation to Prytherch. Of course, there had been contradictions involved from the very first in Thomas's response both to Prytherch and to Manafon, but those had related to his chronic uncertainty of what exactly to make of them both. These later contradictions and tensions, however, relate to Thomas's new uncertainty as to what exactly to make of his own earlier self's relationship to these subjects.

It is confession of this that makes 'Invasion on the Farm' such a particularly affecting Iago poem. As the poem appeared a mere half dozen years after war's end, the use of the word 'invasion' in its title would have reminded its first readers of the threat that had haunted the coastline counties of southern England for so long, thus investing the word with an urgent, ominous charge that is missing today. It is one of the rare occasions when Thomas grants Iago his freedom of speech, and in it he captures the awkwardness in speaking and the disarming diffidence characteristic of a Welsh farmer confronted with someone from an entirely different class, background and culture. 'I am Prytherch. Forgive me. I don't know/ What you are talking about' (*CP*, 60). And it also touchingly conveys Prytherch's sense of being hunted and cornered, as he actually attributes to the outside visitor that merciless, destructive visual acuity Thomas had so often attributed to Iago himself and his kind: the poems about him, he complains, have left him 'exposed/ In my own fields with no place to run/ From your sharp eyes'.

The whole poem records a moment of self-awakening, when Thomas becomes aware, like a postmodern anthropologist, that he has all along been a rude, insensitive intruder into a culture and an environment to which he is in the end just an outside observer; that he has objectified the inhabitants of his parish, treating them as 'other to himself' and examining them as if they were exotic creatures in some human zoo; that he has unwittingly condescended to them; and that his very presence has not only involved a violation of their way of life but has been the means of altering it even as he sought to protect it.

Prytherch's last words bring home to Thomas that he has himself been the unintentional means of opening this previously closed world up to that other, modern, world that is certain to cause its destruction: 'I', says Prytherch with more sadness than anger, 'who a moment back',

> Paddled in the bright grass, the old farm
> Warm as a sack about me, feel the cold
> Winds of the world blowing. The patched gate
> You left open will never be shut again.

It is a tragic self-indictment by Thomas of everything he had no doubt previously thought he'd achieved in his Manafon poems. And it makes one realise that the use of the word 'Invasion' was not by any means as overblown and inappropriate as might have appeared at first reading. What has happened to Iago Prytherch and his world is, in its way, a reminder of what might have happened to southern England had the Nazis indeed managed to cross the channel: obliteration.

In 'Too Late', another post-Manafon poem, Iago Prytherch appears as one who has already been irrevocably changed by the very changes foreseen in 'Invasion on the Farm', and this time Thomas blames himself for having failed in his project to spare him such a debasing indignity, while at the same time admitting that he had infantilised Prytherch – 'You were like a child to me' (*CP*, 108). Prytherch has acquired material means, but for Thomas at the terrible cost of having become

> A servant hired to flog
> The life out of the slow soil
> Or come obediently as a dog
>
> To the pound's whistle.

And above all, he has become the creature of the machine. Thomas's helplessness at witnessing all this is again bitterly expressed in 'Movement' (*CP*, 141), in which he also acknowledges that his Manafon poems have already become completely anachronistic and irrelevant.

But most interesting of all are those two poems where Thomas begins to fear that his desire to see Iago Prytherch as representative of an unchanging world may have been demeaning and self-serving after all. 'A Welsh Testament' has Prytherch angrily aware of having been treated as a spectacle by privileged outsiders who enjoyed comforts they were anxious to deny him, simply because they wanted him to retain his ancient primitive 'authenticity':

> I saw them stand
> By the thorn hedges, watching me string
> The far flocks on a shrill whistle.
> And always there was their eyes' strong
> Pressure on me: You are Welsh, they said;

> Speak to us so; keep your fields free
> Of the smell of petrol, the loud roar
> Of hot tractors; we must have peace
> And quietness. (*CP*, 117)

This is a rare moment of acknowledgement by R. S. Thomas that the dreaded Machine, in the form of the tractor, could and did bring real benefits to the farmers of Wales. And the poem goes on to a further devastating indictment of the poet and his kind by Iago:

> Is a museum
> Peace? I asked. Am I the keeper
> Of the heart's relics, blowing the dust
> In my own eyes?

As R. S. Thomas was very well aware, a few years before these lines were written, Iorwerth Peate, a renowned ethnographer of the rural culture of Wales whose work closely paralleled that of Alwyn Rees and Thomas, had succeeded in establishing the National Folk Museum of Wales at St Fagans just outside Cardiff, a project modelled on similar ventures in several of the Scandinavian countries.[15] And so Iago Prytherch is here protesting that he has in effect become just another exhibit in a Welsh museum such as that, curated by the affluent middle-class of Wales who were nostalgic for the rural past from which they had themselves escaped into the comforts of urban living.

Thomas actually shared with Peate an enthusiasm for traditional rural crafts and the implements employed in them. Celebrating the residual culture of the hill farmers he came across on his excursions up to the moorlands, Thomas noted in 'The Depopulation of the Welsh Hill Country' that 'most of the people are good with their hands too. Apart from the traditional craft of cutting peat, much more difficult than it looks, many of them made their own implements, such as scythe or axe handles and wooden spoons. And then there is the man whose small stacks, thatched with reeds, are as primitively beautiful as a painting by Van Gogh' (*SP*, 23). As we shall see, in due course he became a patron of traditional craftsmen, and his wife Mildred Eldridge, herself an ardent advocate of such crafts, and indeed a practitioner of related skills, no doubt educated his tastes.

And there are further pointed contemporary allusions in this poem that are worth glossing. Iago speaks of having been sought out and prized because of 'my high cheek-bones, my length of skull'. The reference here is to those ethnographers, such as the distinguished and influential geographer H. J. Fleure at University of Wales Aberystwyth, who were fervent believers that the ethnic origins of individuals could be determined by the measurement of their skulls, and who further claimed that such researches amongst the population of Wales had proved that the descendants of the original, aboriginal, pre-Celtic inhabitants of the country continued to live in the uplands of mid-Wales and constituted the 'true', ur Welsh.[16]

Another moving poem of self-doubt is 'Which'. It famously opens with the anguished question 'And Prytherch – was he a real man?' (*CP*, 119), before going on to wonder whether Thomas's wish to see him as he did was in fact 'responsible for his frayed shape'. The suggestion here is not only that Prytherch may have been a figment of his own imagination, created simply to satisfy his own needs, but also that Thomas may have been responsible for making him 'frayed', that he had been complicit in the continuation of that poverty from which Iago and his kind suffered but which for Thomas and his kind was picturesque and noble.

Suggestive overlaps between the vision and writings of Sir George Stapledon and those of R. S. Thomas have already been noted. But one last intriguing little detail may further illuminate that relationship. Stapledon was absolutely delighted when one of his assistants, Gwilym Evans, drew to his attention the famous story of Olwen from *The Mabinogion*. As her names indicates (Ôl-wen: white trace or white trail), she was a young woman in whose footsteps clover sprang up wherever she went. Stapledon was very pleased to hear this, because it exactly conformed to botanical fact. Human footsteps do indeed encourage the growth of clover. As Stapledon observed, there had been no clover growing in the USA until white settlers arrived there. Hence the Native American name for clover was 'white man's footsteps'. This detail is an instance of how the practical and scientific were intimately informed, in Stapledon's temperament, by the poetic. The creative vision he outlined in his writings were akin to those advanced by poets and other creative writers in their works, as is very evident from his liberal reference to their works. One wonders, therefore, what use Thomas would have made of that insight into the Olwen story: there can be little doubt that he would have been intrigued and delighted by it.

This affinity between the two men is easy to explain, once one realises that both were to some extent instances of that extensive, multi-faceted, endlessly complex, and sometimes highly controversial phenomenon that was the English ruralist movement of the first half of the twentieth century, a movement that could trace its origins way back to the period of the great English Romantics. Thomas's awareness of this movement was undoubtedly enriched by his relationship with Mildred (aka Elsi) Eldridge, whose artistic work is evidently steeped in the spirit of it. Indeed, it was their shared enthusiasm for it that initially brought Eldridge and Thomas together, and that continued to underpin their relationship throughout their long married life. The work of both has sometimes been contemptuously dismissed by recent critics, condemned as instancing the conservative, reactionary and even at times malign and sinister, aspects of English pastoralism. Such reactions are a gross simplification and distortion of their fascinating output.

The literature on the socio-cultural and political aspects and consequences of the English pastoral movement is necessarily vast, and far too extensive to be considered here. It highlights the spectrum of enterprises and initiatives involved, ranging from the establishment of solid, conventional conservationist bodies such as the National Trust, the Council for the Preservation of Rural England (1926), and the Council for the Preservation of Rural Wales (1928), to assorted communitarian experiments in holistic living some of which showed distinct fascist sympathies (Stapledon expressed a disquieting, if naive, admiration for the 'visionary leadership' of Mussolini) and even advocated eugenics. And in some corners of the vast, variegated movement there was a decided Imperialist streak. The idea of an 'imagined organic *gemeinschaftlich* community' (*WL*, 47) was particularly attractive to middle-class urban dwellers. Common to the movement as a whole, whether in its benign or malign, progressive or reactionary, manifestations was the supposition that the 'true' England was the traditional England of the countryside, supposedly immemorial and unchanging – a countryside they very largely associated with the shires and southern counties. Industrial England was, of course, well beyond the pale, as was the political progressivism and radicalism it fostered.

I have already explored at length elsewhere the work Eldridge undertook during the war under the auspices of the government's *Recording Britain* project to chronicle visually various locations in rural Wales that were deemed at risk, and the relationship of that work to Thomas's Manafon output.[17] Eldridge was particularly interested in the 'arts and crafts' wing of the ruralist movement, that dated back to William Morris and that was famously instanced in the varied products of the Ditchling community under Eric Gill. 'Modernity' was anathema, urbanism a blight, industrialism, along with the mass production it enabled, nothing but a nightmare, and popular democracy in many ways regrettable for its vulgarity. The ambitious mural Eldridge completed for Gobowen Hospital is a perfect compound image of the various intertwined strands of her wistful pastoralism. And Peter Lord has pointed out that she even flirted briefly and unwittingly with fascism when she undertook to illustrate a work by Henry Williamson, who had joined Oswald Mosley's British Union of Fascists in 1937.

Obviously encouraged and instructed by Eldridge, Thomas became an enlightened patron of Alan Knight (1911–2011), 'one of the great artist-blacksmiths of the post-war period, and one of the last generation of makers who upheld the values of the most traditional practice and technique of their craft'.[18] Knight worked for the National Trust, and renovated the spectacular ironwork at Powis Castle and Erddig, but he specialised in church work and specimens of his ironwork can be seen in the cathedrals of Chelmsford, Worcester, Hereford, Gloucester and Truro. It was from him that Thomas commissioned first a corona chandelier for Eglwys-fach and then another such chandelier for Aberdaron. He also commissioned a cross and candlesticks for his own domestic use.[19]

Influenced although Thomas undoubtedly was during his Manafon period by the English ruralist movement, his interest was inflected and significantly altered in his work by different, cognate, enthusiasms. It was, for instance, a 'Celtic' strain of primitivism that first brought R. S. Thomas and Mildred Eldridge together. Greatly enthused by his visit to the west of Ireland, and his exposure to the 'peasants' there – an exposure that led both to enduring connections with the Irish intelligentsia in Dublin and an influential encounter with Patrick Kavanagh's masterwork *The Great Hunger* – Thomas took Eldridge up to the Highlands and Islands of Scotland, since both were enthusiasts for the work and vision of 'Fiona Macleod'. That mistily romantic nom-de-plume suggestive of a Gaelic heroine was the ingenious escapist invention of a mono-glot Lowlander, William Sharp, who was actually a product of modern industrial Scotland. Far therefore from being the authentic products of an ancient Gaelic culture, all the rhapsodic nature writing of Macleod was every bit as spurious, as synthetic, and as escapist, as had been the 'epic poetry' of 'Ossian' (in reality Thomas Macpherson) that had galvanised the imagination of Europe at the end of the nineteenth century. But W. B. Yeats, one of R. S. Thomas's great models, had been an enthusiast for Macleod, deeming 'hers' to be the voice of a Celtic Scotland as in his view that of Ernest Rhys was of Celtic Wales.[20]

Far more significant, however, was Thomas's exposure to the Welsh version of ruralism following his acquiring a fluency in the Welsh language while at Manafon. This ruralism was every bit as complex as its English counterpart, and likewise had its roots in a strong antipathy to industrial culture, which in the case of Wales had become the majority culture of Wales during the final decades of the nineteenth century as the valleys of the south steadily developed into one of the earliest and greatest industrial centres of the modern world. A full examination of Thomas's relationship to this movement would extend this discussion interminably, so two manifestations alone of it are considered here.

Central to the Welsh ruralism that had developed during the second half of the nineteenth century was the concept of a pious, naturally cultured peasantry: the *gwerin*. It was a myth assiduously cultivated by leading figures in the culture, including ministers, politicians and writers. And it originated as a response to the slandering of the society of rural Wales in a notorious 1847 report by the British Government into the state of education in Wales. Thomas's engagement with the *gwerin* myth is complex, and involves a bifurcated response. On the one hand, his wistful, highly idealised, description of the vanished Welsh-language culture of the upland farmers in 'Depopulation of the Welsh Hill Country' is very much in line with the myth. On the other, his depiction of Iago Prytherch and his kind is so savagely different from the myth as to constitute a demolition of it comparable in ferocity to that of Caradoc Evans in his landmark collection of short stories *My People*. In particular, Thomas depicts the Welsh peasantry as completely devoid of any spiritual awareness. In both cases, it is fair to suggest that in his poetic construction of a distinctive and highly controversial portrait of the farmers of Manafon parish Thomas in part took his bearings from the myth of the *gwerin* he would have come across in his new readings during that period of Welsh-language literature.

As for the second feature of early twentieth-century Welsh ruralism that is relevant to Thomas, it is hinted at in a few remarks in the depopulation essay that have been completely overlooked. In registering his fear that post-war development of the uplands seemed set fair for the implementation of 'plans for recultivating the uplands and running them from large lowland centres', Thomas adds that this is his great nightmare, because it would result in 'the end of these people'. And, he adds, that would be a national disaster, because here, 'however faintly, beats the old heart of Wales'. He then goes on to add the following remarks:

> That is why we are all Welsh Nationalists deep down within us, even if we do not subscribe outwardly to the policy of *Y Blaid* (24) ... The land is sacred and the people who live close to it belong there and must be kept there, and some who have left it must be induced to return. It is useless to try to settle strangers there ... Certain efforts are being made, I know, to revive the country districts of Wales by encouraging small, rural industries, and that is all to the good. But that will hardly benefit or even touch the uplands. (*SP*, 24)

He then goes on to specify that what those uplands need 'are good roads and grants or loans to put the houses and buildings in repair and a revival of the type of trade such as the wool trade, which would benefit these people'. And he ends by confessing that given 'the outer world is in chaos and the rule of the day is planning and uniformity' the hope of seeing any such investments as he is advocating is extremely slim.

These comments by Thomas need to be set in the context of the policies and plans that had been advocated by Plaid Cymru throughout the 1930s under the auspices of its leader, Saunders Lewis, who remained a hero for Thomas throughout his long life – so much so that I have elsewhere dubbed him a 'Son of Saunders'.[21] As aghast as R. S. Thomas was at the industrial society of south Wales, and appalled by what had become of it by the 1930s, Lewis advocated a policy of sustained, structured deindustrialisation, and partly taking his cue from the (frequently right-wing) thinkers of the English Distributist movement, he worked in close conjunction with the Plaid economist D. J. Davies to draw up plans for the establishing and fostering of small-scale rural enterprises envisaged as co-operating with each other within specific localities. Davies, who took the lead in refining this socio-economic model, had been heavily influenced by the time he'd spent in Denmark, where similar initiatives were already well established.[22] It may have been partly with such Plaid Cymru blueprints in mind that Thomas concluded his essay on depopulation by praising efforts to encourage small, rural industries before proceeding to warn that such were unlikely to benefit the hill farmers of areas like Manafon.

Thomas's concern to protect such small-scale rural communities very much chimed with concerns voiced by Alwyn Rees in his conclusion to *Life in a Welsh Countryside*. In the concluding pages of that study, he comes off the anthropologist's fence firmly on the side of advocating support for the society he has been examining, while warning that it is a mistake for 'modern society to instil new life into the countryside by commending to it its own specialisms' (*LWC*, 170). Then, in the final paragraph, Rees makes it clear that he believes modern mass society to be in a state of disintegration:

> The failure of the urban world to give its inhabitants status and significance in a functioning society, and their consequent disintegration into formless masses of rootless identities, should make us humble in planning a new life for the countryside. The completeness of the traditional rural society – involving the cohesion of family, kindred and neighbours – and its capacity to give the individual a sense of belonging, are phenomena that might well be pondered by all who seek a better order. (*LWC*, 170)

As is clear from this, Alwyn D. Rees and R. S. Thomas already shared at this early point in their careers a very critical view of modern urban, and industrial society, and several years later their views were to converge even further and their paths to cross at interesting points. Alwyn D. Rees completed his researches for his book during the war, when he was working as a full-time tutor in rural Powys for the University of Wales Aberystwyth's Department of Extra-Mural Studies. In 1950, he was appointed director of that department, a post he continued to fill with increasing distinction until his untimely death in 1973. After Thomas and his wife moved to Eglwys-fach from Manafon, Elsi Eldridge was employed by Rees as a part-time tutor in art. It was also during this time that he initiated two steps that R. S. Thomas was to admire. First, he began to emerge as a formidable public intellectual and polemicist for a number of causes, most specifically the Welsh language and its culture, that were very close to Thomas's heart. Secondly, he began to establish around him a circle of like-minded friends who together began to explore a viable model for 'alternative living', at the very centre of which lay the counter-intuitive argument that the smaller the social and economic unit the greater its productivity by every significant measure.[23]

By the end of the 1960s, Rees had found a very persuasive advocate of this vision in the person of his friend and kindred spirit Professor Leopold Kohr, who had retired from a Chair in Economics and Political Science at the University of Puerto Rico to settle in Aberystwyth in 1968. As an Austrian of Jewish descent, Kohr had first-hand experience of the sinister dehumanising consequences of a regimented society, regardless of its political persuasion. A period spent in Spain during the Spanish Civil War – where he became an acquaintance of George Orwell, André Malraux and Ernest Hemingway – had made him aware that regimes of the Left could be every bit as humanly destructive as regimes of the Right. Once settled in Wales, Kohr became an unofficial adviser to the leader of Plaid Cymru, Gwynfor Evans, to whom he dedicated a book entitled *Is Wales Viable?*, to which Rees provided a typically succinct foreword. For Kohr, Rees pointed out, 'provincial prosperity in the prosperity of a large political unit diminishes with the distance between the provinces and the centre of government' The only remedy for such 'inbuilt inequality' was 'the division of large states into their more manageable component parts', and this diagnosis predisposed Kohr 'favorably', as Rees said, 'towards "separatism" wherever it manifests itself' (*LK*, 11). As stated in his lucid little book, his preference was for Welsh 'separatism', but within the framework of an economic 'common market' that would include the other nations of the United Kingdom.

Thanks initially to the link provided by Elsie Eldridge and subsequently to the powerful and controversial crusading essays published by Rees in his capacity as editor of the cultural periodical *Barn*, Thomas became aware from the late 1960s onwards of the thinking of this group that coincided so strikingly with his own. Both Thomas and Rees could date the origins of their cognate convictions way back to the time they had spent in rural Montgomeryshire, and so it is unsurprising that Thomas should express dismay at hearing around Christmas time in 1973 that Rees had suffered a stroke that led to his premature death in 1974, at the age of 63. 'I heard a rumour that Alwyn Rees had suffered a stroke. Such a necessary person in Wales; we can ill afford to have him hors de combat.'[24] And fifteen years later, he continued to regret the premature removal of Rees from the scene:

> One can't ignore the fact that there are more nationally con-
> scious elements in countries like Hungary and Czechoslovakia,
> as well as more politically informed ones, than we can boast yng
> Nghymru. Who have we to compare with Saunders and Alwyn
> Rees? (*LG*, 184).

By then, the fruitful rapport between the thinking of the two men, the beginnings of which can be dated way back to Thomas's Manafon days, had lasted for some quarter of a century.

Notes

Text published for the first time in the present volume.

1. R. S. Thomas, 'The Paths Gone By', in Sandra Anstey (ed.), *R. S. Thomas: Selected Prose* (Bridgend: Poetry Wales Press, 1983), 139. Hereafter *SP*.
2. R. S. Thomas, 'Affinity', in *Collected Poems, 1945–1990* (London: Dent, 1993), p. 9. Hereafter *CP*.
3. R. S. Thomas, 'The Face' (*CP*, 178), 'Evans' (*CP*, 74).
4. Alwyn Rees was my uncle, and for a personal estimate of his career, see my article 'Yr Heriwr Anhepgor, Alwyn D. Rees', *Y Traethodydd* (Ionawr, 2020), 37–51.
5. Alwyn D. Rees, *Life in a Welsh Countryside* (Cardiff: University of Wales Press, 1950). Hereafter *LWC*.
6. One of the earliest commentators to remark on the striking disparity between the real character of Manafon and the impressions of the district provided by Thomas in his poetry was Brian Morris. In an article first published in 1980, Morris shrewdly observed that 'Manafon is not an exposed hill-village, sur-rounded by moors and mountains, and peopled by peasants more isolated than the sheep they tend. It lies very snugly in a small river valley, the fields are hedged, the pasture reasonably rich, and the hills which lie around it are no more than a few hundred feet.' He adds that 'the village is strung out on both sides of a minor

road'. Brian Morris, 'The Topography of R. S. Thomas', in Sandra Anstey (ed.), *Critical Writings on R. S. Thomas* (Bridgend: Seren Books, 1992), p. 113.

7. R. S. Thomas, 'Out of the Hills', *CP*, p. 1.

8. R. J. Moore-Colyer, 'Farming in Depression: Wales between the Wars, 1919–1939', *Agricultural History Review*, 46/2, 177–96 (186). Hereafter *FD*.

9. William Carlos Williams, *In the American Grain* (1925) (New York: New Directions Paperback, 1956). Hereafter *IAG*.

10. As Brian Morris pointed out in his *Critical Writings* article mentioned above, '[t]he little church of St Michael and All Angels, which Mr Thomas served, is an ancient structure, stone-built with a good timber roof. But it was heavily restored in 1898, its rood screen is uncompromisingly modern and the overall effect is of a well-kept but quite undistinguished piece of Victorian ecclesiastical rural architecture' (114). Thomas hated the Victorian aspects of the Church and did whatever he could to 'remedy' them, often to his parishioners' uncomprehending disapproval.

11. For a fuller discussion of Thomas's response to the war in his earliest Manafon poems, see 'War Poet', in M. Wynn Thomas, *R. S. Thomas: Serial Obsessive* (Cardiff: University of Wales Press, 2013), pp. 13–36.

12. R. S. Thomas, 'Depopulation of the Welsh Hill Country' (1945), in Sandra Anstey (ed.), *Selected Prose* (Bridgend: Seren Books, 1983).

13. Brian Short, *The Battle of the Fields: Rural Community and Authority in Britain during the Second World War* (Woodbridge: The Boydell Press, 2014), p. 43. Hereafter *BF*.

14. Sir George Stapledon, *The Way of the Land* (London: Faber and Faber, 1943), p. 64. Hereafter *WL*.

15. For this enterprise, see M. Wynn Thomas, *Eutopia: Studies in Cultural Euro-Welshness 1850–1980* (Cardiff: University of Wales Press, 2021).

16. This a subject that I pursue in greater depth in 'War Poet'.

17. See 'For Wales see Landscape', in Thomas, *Serial Obsessive*, pp. 37–66.

18. David Whiting, 'Alan Knight: Obituary', *Independent*, 22 October 2011.

19. I am very indebted to David Whiting for this information in personal correspondence, 14 July 2021.

20. See M. Wynn Thomas, *The Nations of Wales: 1890–1920* (Cardiff; University of Wales Press, 2018), pp. 154ff.

21. See Thomas, *Serial Obsessive*, pp. 93–116.

22. See Thomas, *Eutopia*, pp. 166–78.

23. See Thomas, 'Yr Heriwr Anhepgor'.

24. Jason Walford Davies (ed.), *R.S. Thomas: Letters to Raymond Garlick, 1951–1999* (Llandysul: Gomer, 1999), p. 137. Hereafter *LG*.

Bury my Heart:
R. S. Thomas and Native America

I

In 1978, R. S. Thomas published an illuminating review in the periodical *Planet* of a book that was attracting attention worldwide to the tragic history of the Native American peoples of the United States. Evocatively entitled *Bury My Heart at Wounded Knee*, it laid bare the long and complex historical foreground of that final, fateful episode in aboriginal history. The review makes it clear how deep was Thomas's sympathy with the Indian peoples. But the approach he adopted – which was demonstrably at variance with historical realities in many respects – also laid bare the grounds of that sympathy; in what had happened to Native Americans he saw clear resemblances with 'his' Wales – the Wales of Welsh-language speakers. This aspect of the review is well worth isolating for contemplation, not least because it offers a clear view of Thomas in his role as 'warrior poet'. But before we come to that, it may be useful to examine the long foreground to Dee Brown's seminal publication.

II

Thomas opened his review by recalling his childhood days in Holyhead, when he was lured to the cinema by the romance of the great Westerns of the era, featuring 'exciting battles with the Indians'. With chagrin he admitted that he, like his friends, had tended to identify with the 'tough, honest cowboy[s]', who seemed engaged in mortal combat with the 'savage varmits'.[1] Indians were seen as 'savages, launching unprovoked attacks on the white men'. His confession of adult guilt – in the light of which the review may be read as an attempt at making amends – is slightly offset by the memory of 'how I used to identify secretly with the Indians. They were the expert horsemen. They were the ones who were free and lived closest to nature.'

But Thomas's divided sympathies were not shared by his young friends, whose reactions were representative of their Welsh society at large. Indeed, some Welshmen had actually served with the US Cavalry in the Indian Wars. In 2015, an interesting discovery was reported by Mike Lewis, a Pembrokeshire journalist on the *County Echo*.[2] It was a cache of letters in English sent home to his family by a young Pembrokeshire man from Pen-cnwc Farm in Dinas, just east of Fishguard, which at the time would have been an overwhelmingly Welsh-speaking area. In content they are unremarkable – mostly requests for funds from his brother and complaints that the latter did not write to him. But they also include a request that his mother not be informed of the step her distant son has taken of joining the US Cavalry, lest she worry. It turned out that she had very good cause to do so, because the unfortunate William James had in fact joined the Seventh Cavalry troop, commanded by General George Armstrong Custer, and he, like most of that troop, was duly killed in June 1876, at what became known as the celebrated Battle of the Little Bighorn. It seems that he was the only Welshman to be unlucky enough to be serving under Custer on that disastrous occasion, and where and when he fell during the course of the fight will now never be known.[3] To appreciate the impact of Dee Brown's book when it first appeared, it is necessary to understand the role played by this battle, and the resulting valorisation of Custer, in shaping white people's views of the 'Indians', right down to the late twentieth century.

Initially convinced – thanks to a typically reckless failure to reconnoitre the ground carefully – that he was attacking a small, largely defenceless, Sioux settlement, and intent on winning for himself further glory, the charismatic, colourful and impulsive Custer had split his troop into three companies. One was led by Major Reno, another by Captain Benteen and the third by Custer himself. The first attempted to attack the village from the south, and was duly repulsed with several casualties. It retreated in pell mell panic to what became known as Reno's hill, where the troops dug in best they could and managed to hang on until eventually reinforced by Benteen's troop that had been advancing on their western flank. Custer had meanwhile proceeded to the north end of the village, realising with mounting dismay in the process that it was in fact unimaginably huge – probably the largest ever seen on the Plains, and consisting of some 8,000 people. These included a very substantial number of warriors as well as leaders of the legendary calibre of Sitting Bull and Crazy Horse. En route, Custer divided his reduced company into three units. Two of these were wiped out alongside the river while Custer was driven to attempt a last stand (far less glorious than is popularly imagined) on what became known as Custer Hill, a site which ended up littered with corpses. William James could therefore have met his sad end at any one of these points and junctures.

The defeat – the greatest ever inflicted up to that point on the US Army – was met with incredulity and anger in all the cities of the east. Press reports, unfailingly inaccurate, dwelt with lascivious outrage on the scalpings and mutilations visited upon the corpses by the 'savages'. What they failed to mention, however, was the pent-up fury and disgust that the Northern Cheyennes and the Lakota Sioux peoples had felt in the wake of the latest egregious example of betrayal by the invading whites of a significant peace treaty. In 1868 at Fort Laramie, Red Cloud (whose attacks had forced the Army to close its forts along the Bozeman Trail to the far North West) and Spotted Tail, prominent chiefs among the Plains Indians, had signed an agreement that had included a guarantee on the part of the white government that the Black Hills, sacred to the Indians, and the vast neighbouring regions of South Dakota, Wyoming and Nebrasksa that served them as important hunting grounds, would be safe from incursions by white hunters.

The agreement had of course no sooner been signed than it was immediately broken, but a step-change had occurred in 1874, when prospectors, protected by a cavalry troop that had actually been led by Custer, confirmed previous rumours that there was gold in the Black Hills. A gold rush ensued immediately, strongly supported by a Washington government in desperate need of bullion because the country was in the grip of a serious economic depression. It was also under pressure from the powerful investors of the Northern Pacific Railroad, who had heavily borrowed money to finance their costly and ambitious project of a transcontinental railroad and now could no longer afford to service their colossal debts. In consequence the Government set about 'clearing' the land of the free Indians, who had refused to settle on either of the two reservations that had been set aside for their use. When harassment failed to work, direct enforcement, implemented by the Army, had to be resorted to, and Custer's expedition was one instrument of that policy.

The Cheyennes, in particular, also had one further personal griev-
ance against Custer. He had gained his reputation during the Civil War
for reckless courage in the dashing charge, and it had been augmented
by his flamboyant showmanship. By the time, therefore, that he had
taken to 'Indian-hunting' post-war he had become a personality with a
reputation to live up to. Given to waywardness in his own conduct, he
required discipline of his troops, to whom he proved a very hard task-
master. The kind of lucky break for which he was always famous came
in November 1868 when he stumbled on a small camp of Southern
Cheyennes wintering on the Washita river in Oklahoma. Not only were
they peaceable, but their chief, Black Kettle, had actually been given
a large US flag by the army to display in the event of any threat of a
cavalry attack. Consequently, he rushed out into the snow displaying the
flag alongside the white flag of surrender, only to be gunned down as
he attempted to flee, as were most of his followers, women and children
as well as a handful of old warriors.

A century later, the events on the Washita came to be viewed by
Native American sympathisers as a massacre rather than a battle, and
were compared with the My Lai massacre by US troops in Vietnam. It
therefore came to be bracketed with the notorious Sandcreek massacre
of 1864 in Colorado, when a division of cavalry led by the bloodthirsty
Methodist preacher John Chivington, a hulking brute of a man,
attacked and destroyed a Cheyenne village, leaving somewhere between
70 and 500 Indians dead. The first to be killed was Lean Bear, a peace-
chief who had just returned from a month in Washington where he'd
met President Lincoln and been presented with a medallion as a token
of peace. The instigator of the attack had been Governor John Evans,
who could very well have been of Welsh descent. When, therefore, the
Cheyenne women had fallen on the bodies of the dead after the Little
Bighorn battle they had been animated by a burning desire to avenge
their distant relatives, whose corpses had been mutilated by the white
troops in the very same ways. The Little Bighorn warriors would also
have in mind the 1870 massacre at the Big Bend of the Marias river
in Montana of a defenceless band of Blackfeet, most of whom were
women, children, and old people.

Despite all this, for the best part of a century, the Battle of the
Little Bighorn continued to be generally known as Custer's Last Stand,
because to the non-Native population of the United States the event was

of significance only because of the supposed heroics of the General. Two silent movies – *The Scarlet West* (1925) and *Custer's Last Stand* (1926) – ensured that the Custer myth was disseminated to early twentieth-century audiences worldwide. As recently as 1993, the documentary filmmaker Paul Stekler could regretfully note that

> The Battle of the Little Bighorn, Custer's Last Stand, is the single most reproduced event in all of American history. It has inspired scores of Hollywood films, over a thousand documented paintings, and countless books, cartoons, and advertisements. Hundreds of thousands of people still trek to the battlefields in south-central Montana every summer, many of them busloads of tourists from throughout the world. Staged reenactments in nearby Hardin, Montana, featuring Crow Indians playing Sitting Bull and the Sioux – revisionist role-playing, as their ancestors were scouts for the 7th Cavalry that day – and a blond plumber from Michigan playing Custer, regularly sell out to large, appreciative crowds … The story of Little Bighorn is always cast with Custer at its center, a handsome young officer in buckskin with long blond hair. (*KC*, 291)

In fact, Custer had cut his hair short before the battle, and the hundred degree temperature that day would certainly have ruled out the wearing of buckskin. But American showbiz triumphs over all such mere obstacles of fact. Precedent was set extremely early.

> On 19 July 1876, the *New York Daily Graphic* featured a dramatic, full-page illustration by William de la Montague Cary … *The Battle on the Little Big Horn River – The Death Struggle of General Custer*. It showed Custer and his troopers bravely resisting an overwhelming, savage foe. Though outnumbered and doomed, each soldier still struggles to get off a parting shot as the Indians, armed with rifles and bows and arrows and war clubs, and some wielding scalping knives, close in for the kill. The situation is hopeless, but there, in the midst of chaos, stands Custer, tall and calm, a peculiar light falling on him through the heavy clouds and dust, illuminating the moment of imperishable glory. Sabre drawn back, blazing away with a pistol, he scrambles over a

fallen horse to get at the enemy and defy death itself. Civilization, never more glorious than in defeat, was never more certain of ultimate victory.[4]

The perspective only began to change in the 1970s, when the Native American view of the battle gradually came to be recorded and respected. It marked the beginning of what has become known as the Native American Renaissance in the Arts that accompanied the gradual formation of a movement, increasingly militant, to ensure full recognition of the rights of the indigenous peoples of North America. This came in the immediate wake of the Vietnam War protests, the great Civil Rights marches in the American South, Lyndon Johnson's historic Civil Rights legislation, a new burgeoning wave of feminist struggle, and an incipient movement to secure the rights of gays.[5] 'The Indian political scene,' one of its most prominent associates later reflected, 'was a fine blend of the first large generation of college-trained Indians and the entrenched veterans of the New Deal who had served most of their lives in tribal government.'[6]

Politically, the most significant development by far was the formation in 1968 of the American Indian Movement (AIM) that, under the controversial leadership of Russell Means (an Oglala Sioux born on the Pine Ridge Reservation) and Dennis Banks (Ojibwe), organised a number of spectacular protest events, including an eighteen-month occupation of Alcatraz (1969), the seizing of a replica of the Mayflower (1970), a takeover of Mount Rushmore (1971), an occupation of the Bureau of Indian Affairs (1972) and, most arresting of all, an occupation of Wounded Knee (1973) that culminated in an armed standoff. Another significant activist linked to AIM was Leonard Peltier, who was controversially imprisoned in 1977 for the murder of two FBI agents on Pine Ridge Reservation in 1975, and remains in prison despite prominent public campaigns to secure his release.[7]

Coinciding with these activities were significant developments in the arts. Arthur Penn's landmark 1970 film *Little Big Man* (based on a novel of the same title published by Thomas Berger in 1964) is generally recognised as an important landmark, the first revisionist Western. But it was another quarter of a century before a popular successor appeared in the form of Kevin Costner's *Dances with Wolves* (1990), which was also adapted from a book and featured genuine Lakota Sioux speaking their native language (albeit in a somewhat stilted fashion for the most part, as only one of them was a native speaker). Equally momentous was the beginning of an important literary movement, heralded by a remarkable historical study by Vine DeLoria Jr (Sioux). Entitled *Custer Died For Your Sins: An Indian Manifesto* it was a book as notable for its witty self-awareness as for its trenchancy. Its opening sentences set the tone: 'Indians are like the weather. Everyone knows all about the weather, but none can change it ... [I]f you count on the unpredictability of Indian people, you will never be sorry' (*FDYS*, 1). And later, he mockingly observed, '[w]e often hear "give it back to the Indians" when a gadget fails to work. It's a terrible thing for a people to realize that a society has set aside all non-working gadgets for their exclusive use' (*FDYS*, 2). A couple of decades later, DeLoria was to single out Richard Nixon's administration as the best by far of all administrations with regard to the Indian policy it implemented. His comments on the Wannabe Indians among the American whites of his generation are particularly funny. 'At times I became quite defensive about being a Sioux when these white people had a pedigree that was so much more respectable than mine.' And he noticed how many of those who claimed there was an admixture of Native American blood in their veins, traced its origins back through their grandmother. 'I once did a projection backward,' DeLoria commented, 'and discovered that evidently most tribes were entirely female for the first three hundred years of white occupancy' (*FDYS*, 2).

In 1968, *A House Made of Dawn*, a great novel by N. Scott Momaday of the Kiowa people, was awarded a Pulitzer Prize. Then hot on its heels came *Winter in the Blood* (1974), the first novel of James Welch (Blackfeet/A'anin [Gros Ventre]) (1974) – later, his *Fools Crow* was to prove a notable effort to write a fiction which attempted to be entirely faithful to Blackfeet experience of traditional living by reproducing their own singular view of the world – and poetry and fiction by Leslie Marmon Silko (Laguna Pueblo), as well as work by the influential theorist Gerald Vizenor. A second wave of writers followed, including Louise Erdrich (Chippewa/Ojibwe), Simon Ortiz (Acoma), Joy Harjo (Muscogee/Cherokee), and later Sherman Alexie (Spokane/Coeur d'Alene). He has probably become the best known of them all, due to the profile he enjoys in popular culture thanks to such initiatives as the first all-Indian film, *Smoke Signals* (1998), and the first Native American thriller *Indian Killer* (1996). But probably the most influential contribution to the initial Native American Renaissance was Dee Brown's *Bury My Heart at Wounded Knee*, a non-fiction account of the late-nineteenth-century history of Native Americans that, appearing in 1970, went on to worldwide success. Never out of print, it has been translated into seventeen languages.[8] And it was this book that excited R. S. Thomas's attention and prompted him to publish the review in *Planet*.

III

Thomas was very far indeed from being alone in the warm enthusiasm of his response. The back cover of the 1975 Picador reprint of Brown's memorable dissection of the 'dark myth' of Indian savagery carried a quotation from the *Times* reviewer: 'Calculated to make the head pound, the heart ache and the blood boil.' And the essence of Brown's narrative was epitomised in another quotation that appeared on that cover. 'The white man,' said the Teton Sioux chief Red Cloud (who ironically ended up compromising with the whites) with bitterness, 'made us many promises, more than I can remember, but they never kept but one; they promised to take our land, and they took it.' As for the title of the book, it was part of a quotation from Stephen Vincent Benét: 'I shall not be there. I shall rise and pass./ Bury my heart at Wounded Knee.' In fact Benét's entire, attractive poem ('American Names') is relevant to R. S. Thomas's outlook. It begins with the confession 'I have fallen in love with American names/ The sharp names that never get fat', before moving on to admit that 'There are English counties like hunting-tunes/ Played on the keys of a postboy's horn,// But I will remember where I was born'. He proceeds to list examples of the American names he loves, such as Medicine Hat, Tucson, Deadwood, Calamity Jane, Salem, Boston, and so on. Then he concludes by resonantly declaring:

> I shall not rest quiet in Montparnasse.
> I shall not lie easy at Winchelsea.
> You may bury my body in Sussex grass,
> You may bury my tongue at Champmedy.
> I shall not be there. I shall rise and pass.
> Bury my heart at Wounded Knee.

There is therefore a decided irony in Brown's use of Benét's concluding phrase, because in context it comes at the end of a poem that glories in the 'renaming' of the Continent by the whites who now occupy it, having more or less eliminated its native peoples and their many utterly different languages. Whereas R. S. Thomas would no doubt have endorsed Benét's deep attachment to place, he would equally certainly have deplored his implied total indifference to the aboriginal language(s) of what had become, by force, 'his' country. His understanding of the significance of aboriginal names was very similar to that of the other great Welsh poet of the modern era, Waldo Williams ('Anglo-Welsh and Welsh'):

> To feel that a language is a great manifestation of the human spirit is to feel its loss as a real deprivation. 'Life is only half itself; its other half is expression.' One hears the wind moaning through the ruins of a noble habitation when one hears a Welsh place-name in the tongues of people to whom it means nothing. You who are concerned about ancient buildings and rural scenery, cannot you also hear the real things that I hear, and see the real things that I see? [9]

Brown is acutely conscious of this problem, particularly as the foreign place-names imposed on the North American continent are the legacy of a white supremacist stance. Starting with Columbus's (mis)treatment of the 'natives' and similar atrocities committed from Jamestown Virginia to Plymouth, Connecticut, he proceeds to chronicle with remorseless grimness the appalling consequences for the natives of the inexorable white conquest of their entire country, culminating in the final dreadful phase of Native American suppression that stretched from the end of the Civil War to the dawn of the twentieth century and that concluded with the killing of Sitting Bull in 1890, followed by the coup de grâce of the final massacre in 1890 at Wounded Knee Creek, South Dakota, of a group of Lakota Sioux led by Spotted Elk, who were heading for the Pine Ridge Agency after concluding their Ghost Dance. As for the present, Dee Brown makes excruciatingly clear in his Introduction that for the remnants of the native peoples of his time it consists almost entirely of 'the poverty, the hopelessness, and the squalor of a modern Indian reservation'. More recent

facts subsequently bear testimony to the fact that little had changed in
the interim:

> The National Academy of Public Administration reported in
> 1999 that 31 per cent of all Indians lived below the poverty line,
> compared to 12 per cent within the US population as a whole.
> Again in October 2002 the Census Bureau reported that the low-
> est US median household income of all was at Buffalo County,
> South Dakota, home of the Crow Creek Indian Reservation.
> The recent economic and social factor of Indian gaming has
> not displaced poverty as the specter haunting Indian America ...
> The historically large disparities in the health statistics between
> Indian and non-Indian populations persist, with Indians much
> more likely than non-Indians to die from tuberculosis, liver dis-
> ease, diabetes, pneumonia, and influenza and from accidents,
> homicides, and suicide. (*CC*, 39–40)

While those statistics were current twenty years ago, the situation is
much the same on the reservations even today, except on those that
have succeeded in opening highly lucrative gambling casinos (which is
one reason why such an unexpectedly high percentage of Americans
now claim Native American descent). But by now, 70% of the First
Peoples live outside the reservations, many of them in the great urban
centres. A figure of 5.1 million Americans claim to be Native American,
either in part or in full. Of these 2.9 million are registered as wholly
Native American, while 2.7 million are registered as being part-Native
American. And in 2009, 'an apology to Native Peoples of the United
States' was included in the Defense Appropriations Act which stated
that the US 'apologizes on behalf of the people of the United States
to all Native Peoples for the many instances of violence, maltreatment,
and neglect inflicted on Native Peoples by citizens of the United States'.

Dee Brown's book may modestly claim to have played some part
in the radical change of attitude, at least, on the part of white America
to the history and situation of the Native American peoples of their
country. *Bury My Heart* reads more like a narrative fiction, as pitiful as
it is gripping, than a studiously impersonal historical analysis and it
deserves to be recognised as a kind of 'alternative', painfully tragic,
epic of the Native American West. It does not, of course, include the

entire appalling history of the mistreatment of native peoples in North America for over three hundred years since Columbus's arrival, and it begins too late to address the notorious Cherokee 'Trail of Tears' exodus – a forced march in harsh winter conditions – to distant Oklahoma in 1838, which cost the lives of a quarter of the tribe. But it covers the history of the Navaho of the South West, the Apaches (first under Conchise and later under Geronimo) of Arizona,[10] the Kiowas under Satanta, the Pocas of Missouri under Standing Bear, the Modocs of northern California and Oregon under 'Captain Jack', the Nez Percés under 'Chief Joseph',[11] the Santee Sioux, formerly woodland dwellers, forced to move out onto the plains of Minnesota and Colorado, the Arapahos of the same area, the Northern Cheyenne in their last struggles under Dull Knife, and the many different tribes of the great Sioux People[12] forced back into Montana and South Dakota, resisting all the way, before being terminally defeated. By 1900, fewer than 250,000 Indians remained, and by 1920 some 6% of them were already living in urban environments – a development that accelerated rapidly after the Second World War.

The US soldiers possessed howitzers and the modern breech-loading repeating rifles. The Indians had only bows, arrows, lances, clubs and knives, along with the occasional ancient bore-loading gun they'd acquired from traders. It was a gross mismatch of firepower. Even though the advantage in manpower was always overwhelmingly on the Indian side, because the Washington government always elected to send only minimal forces. R. S. Thomas was struck by this aspect of the case, because for him the mismatch in raw power was similar in effect, if not in kind, to that between Welsh-language Wales and the English and their language, and also between the political power of the Anglo-British state and that of stateless, and therefore relatively powerless, Wales. The few chiefs who visited Washington and other great cities of the East realised early that their fate was sealed, but fought stoically on; and long before the end even a figure as unyielding and as utterly extraordinary as Crazy Horse knew there was no hope and fought only to secure one more summer of traditional living for his people on the tiny areas of free land still remaining.

It is a sorry tale indeed, with a pattern that is numbingly repeated: forced removal and resettlement, corrupt, conniving Indian agents, double-crossing military commanders, promises broken, treaties

regularly violated (some 367 were signed between 1778 and 1868), voraciously land-hungry whites, the evil genocidal ideology of Manifest
Destiny, gold-rush frenzies, fearful, lying interpreters, corrupt agents,
exploitative traders, vengeful settlers and ranchers, callous railroad
moguls, and all the time the native peoples were being steadily wiped
out by smallpox (sometimes deliberately delivered to them in infected
blankets; an early form of germ warfare) and the many other diseases
(including cholera and syphilis) that the aggressively invasive Europeans
brought in their wake. And then the Plains peoples, who lived by hunting, were slowly starved as buffalo were cavalierly slaughtered *en masse*
(some four million between 1872 and 1874 alone), sometimes just for the
entertainment of visitors from Europe and the East.

Thankfully, there were also some whites who were fair-minded and
fair-dealing, and even a few who showed an honourable if impotent
empathy. One such was the trader Major Edward Wynkoop, founder
of Denver, who did his level best to protect Black Kettle's Southern
Cheyenne before the infamous attack by Custer on the village camped
on the Washita and resigned in protest against the massacre. Dee
Brown's account also includes such delightful details as the passion the
great Brulés Sioux Chief Spotted Tail developed for strawberries and
ice-cream on his visit to Washington in 1870. And there is the remarkable 'success' story of Donehowaga, the Iroquois who adopted the white
name of Ely Parker, became a civil engineer and a friend of Ulysses S.
Grant, and ended up appointed in 1870 as the first Indian to serve as
Commissioner for Indian Affairs, lasting only for a short term before
resigning in disgust.

In 2016, Peter Cozzens published a study of nineteenth-century
Indian history that included a partial correction of the (salutary) pro-
Indian bias that had been displayed by Brown.[13] Cozzens, for instance,
drew attention to the fact that even top US Cavalry figures such as
General Crook, who was involved in the Little Bighorn campaign, felt
conflicted about government treatment of Native American peoples. 'I
do not wonder,' he remarked to a journalist,

> and you will not either, that when Indians see their wives and
> children starving and their last source of supplies cut off, they
> go to war. And then we are sent out there to kill them. It is an
> outrage. All tribes tell the same story. They are surrounded on all

sides, the game is destroyed or driven away, they are left to starve, and there remains but one thing for them to do – fight while they can. Our treatment of the Indian is an outrage. (Prologue)

Cozzens also drew attention to the poisonous divisions that existed between Indian peoples who warred interminably on each other, and pointed out how many of these peoples had in effect attempted to enlist the whites and their powerful cavalry on their side in their interne-cine campaigns. So 'the Shoshones, Crows, and Pawnees all proved invaluable army allies in war, following the adage that the enemy of my enemy is my friend'. 'There was no sense of "Indianness",' Cozzens sadly concludes, 'until it was too late, and then it came but dimly through a millennial faith that brought only bloodshed, horror, and broken hopes.' R. S. Thomas repeatedly attempted to draw attention to a similar, potentially fatal, division in Wales, particularly between the Welsh-speaking and English-speaking regions of the country, and between the country and the city.

A blow as cruel and damaging as any was that inflicted on Native American peoples not by the US Army but by a 'well-meaning' Washington government that, by the late nineteenth century, had been persuaded there could be no future for them outside of modern white society. But in order to be thus 'civilised' the children who could become tractable American citizens needed first to be culturally re-educated at Indian boarding schools, run by good Christian denominations, that were usually located at an immense distance from their homes – a policy that has been described as one of 'education for extinction'. In 1891, a government law was duly passed that made 'compulsory attendance' at such schools, where of course no Indian language was permitted to be spoken, a legal requirement.[14] A similar policy was pursued north of the border in Canada. In late May 2021, BBC news reported that the remains of 215 indigenous children had been unearthed at the former Kamloops Indian Residential School in British Columbia that closed its doors as late as 1976.

Interestingly enough, from R. S. Thomas's perspective, a devel-opment not unlike although incomparably less evil was by then also well underway in Wales. The infamous 1847 'Blue Books' report to government of the State of Education in Wales had concluded that the (Nonconformist) Welsh of the period were largely illiterate and disgracefully licentious. Westminster consequently became anxious to extend into Wales the 'civilising' state system of primary school education that was being set up in England. Tuition was to be solely through the medium of English, just as the world was to be viewed entirely through an English lens. Over the decades, this fateful step came to threaten doom to the Welsh language, as R. S. Thomas realised.

Had it ever occurred to him, therefore, William James from Pembrokeshire might have realised that there were parallels, admittedly faint but unmistakeably tragic, between his original situation at home and that of the poor Sioux he was preparing to attack. Not only were there broad comparisons between their respective cultural situations, but both parties were also in constant danger of falling victim to avaricious land-grabs. The Pembrokeshire farmers of William James's day were tenant farmers virtually to a man and they had to deal with fickle distant landlords the worst of whom didn't scruple to evict them from their land if they couldn't pay rents that could be extortionate. It was an acute awareness of such parallels – but in his case particularly those concerning language and culture as much as land – that prompted R. S. Thomas, over a century later, to identify with the Native American peoples of North America in the review he wrote for *Planet*.

IV

As Thomas made clear at the very beginning of his review, '[t]he sufferings of the Welsh are not to be compared with those of the Indians, although the decline of the Welsh has been going on for centuries'.[15] There were nevertheless many interesting comparisons, he suggested, to be drawn between the history of the First Peoples of the United States and that of his own people – by which he primarily meant, as he explained, the members of the Welsh-speaking community with whom he specifically identified. 'For instance', he explained, 'Wales was conquered by the English and our best land taken' – although, he facetiously added, not by violence: 'Our land today is being taken over by the English completely legally, according to English law, namely by means of money, and most of our fellow Welshmen [*sic*] do not care at all, as long as they make a profit' (*SP*, 179).

On R. S. Thomas

That comment is a useful reminder of the historical context of Thomas's review. It appeared in the leading Welsh periodical *Planet* in 1978. The year of campaigning for a Yes vote in the 1979 Referendum on a Welsh Assembly, it was also the year when the campaign to establish a Welsh-language television channel was moving towards its climax. The review appeared towards the end of a period of extraordinary civil turmoil in Wales that had largely been driven by acute concern about the status and future of the Welsh language. (It is interesting to note that more than 70 indigenous languages are spoken in Northern America, products of 18 different language families – Europe has only four.) Central to the mood of civil disobedience were the campaigning activities of Cymdeithas yr Iaith Gymraeg (the Welsh Language Society) that were strongly and publicly supported by R. S. Thomas. Cymdeithas yr Iaith was a young people's movement that had emanated in 1962 from the university colleges (and most particularly the University College of Wales Aberystwyth) largely in response to the aged Saunders Lewis's extraordinary and apocalyptic radio lecture *Tynged yr Iaith*, which forecast the imminent disappearance of the Welsh language unless immediate drastic steps were taken to prevent it. For the first decade or so of its existence, Cymdeithas yr Iaith concentrated first on gaining official recognition for the language, and second on ensuring that legal parity with English, once granted, was actually implemented in the form of bilingual road signs, bilingual forms and the like. Some of its energy was also spent on protesting the Investiture of Charles as Prince of Wales at Caernarfon Castle in 1969.

While a campaign for a Welsh-medium television channel (strongly supported by Thomas) occupied most of the energies of Cymdeithas yr Iaith throughout the 1970s, it also slowly began to focus attention on the rapidly increasing threat to the western rural heartlands of the language that came in the wake of a dramatic expansion of second home ownership. An urgent awareness of this crisis and its implications for the language and its culture led to the emergence in 1979 of a shadowy organisation called Meibion Glyndŵr (Sons of Glyndŵr – a name also chosen for its distant echo of 'Merched Beca', 'Rebecca's Daughters', the famous jacquerie of the 1830s in rural west Wales aimed at destroying the hated toll-gates that had been placed on country roads). While protesting it had no intention of harming any individuals, Meibion Glyndŵr embarked on what turned out to be a ten-year arson campaign

257

against holiday homes – and that led to popular cartoons appearing in the Press with the caption 'Come Home to a Real Fire'. Pressed for comment on this movement, Thomas invariably condemned its methods while adding that he fully understood and shared the feelings of outrage that had called it into being – a response that the Press equally invariably condemned as hypocritical prevarication. He also recognised the similarity between the young protesters of Cymdeithas yr Iaith, and those involved in youthful grass-roots protests across the Western world against inequalities and injustices. And one such movement, as he pointed out in the review, was that of the Native American insurrectionists in the United States.

In 1979, the Meibion Glyndŵr campaign was just the latest in a series of campaigns involving various forms of peaceful civil disobedience that had punctuated the history of Wales for almost fifty years, and R. S. Thomas himself had been an active participant in most of those that had been waged since the Second World War. They were all protests by a politically disadvantaged population against the appropriation of Welsh land either by various different arms of a Westminster Government or by public corporations in England. Thomas's involvement with so many of these protests deserves not only to be fully acknowledged and studied in depth but also to be understood as intimately linked with many of the poems he produced throughout the first quarter century and more of his career. It is high time that his stature as a 'Warrior Poet' was properly appreciated. This would better enable the perception of him as the heir to a distinguished Welsh tradition of 'Warrior Poets' of the twentieth century, because so many of the outstanding figures in the culture were, as Thomas himself was very acutely aware, as politically conscious and as politically active as himself. In their case, too, poetry provided them with a powerful vehicle for protest and served as an instrument for inciting action. And like him, virtually all the Welsh warrior poets were committed pacifists, totally opposed to any form of violence against persons, although not necessarily against property.

Thomas never wavered in his pacifism, but he did confess to a secret sympathy with the great early fourteenth-century resistance leader Owain Glyndŵr and admitted that had he been alive at the time he could not swear that he would not have taken up arms and joined his followers. This tacit condoning of violence is found again in his review of Dee Brown's book, when he egregiously misrepresented the Indians as an inherently peaceful people, inclined to compromise and coexistence but driven to violence as a desperate last resort. 'Their sufferings were beyond description. When they saw there was nothing else they could do, they fought bravely, and at times successfully. But they had no real chance. Their weapons were bows and arrows and some old cannons' (*SP*, 179).

It was this kind of romantic fantasising that lay behind 'The Rising of Glyndŵr', a poem that appeared in his first collection *The Stones of the Field*, vitiating its opening, where phrases like 'Thunder-browed and shaggy-throated/ All the men were there' are embarrassing rhodomontade unfortunately reminiscent of the early twentieth-century England and Empire poetry of Henry Newbolt et al. Fortunately, the last stanza has just about enough real poetry in it to mitigate the disaster:

> Beasts gave tongue and brown-owls hooted,
> Every branch grew loud
> With the menace of that crowd,
> That thronged the dark, huge as a thundercloud.[16]

Thomas found himself repeatedly drawn to the exploits of Glyndŵr. 'Hyddgen', for example, is a poem addressed to a place that lives on in legend as the site where a small armed body of the Welsh, led by Glyndŵr, famously saw off a much larger contingent of English troops, thanks probably to the manoeuvrability of the lightly-armed former that gave them an advantage over foes that were encumbered with much heavier armour. Thomas was always readily attracted to strong, charismatic leadership – Glyndŵr provided him with an instance of such, as, in his own time, did Saunders Lewis. And a like hero-worship appears in his treatment of Indian chiefs in his review. 'What strikes the reader,' he writes, 'is their wisdom, their moderation, and the soundness of their reasoning. Much of what the other side said, on the other hand, is stupid, deceitful and completely unreasonable' (*SP*, 179). In his visit to the Hyddgen site, five centuries after the battle had occurred, Thomas typically contrasts the heroics displayed there at the beginning of the fourteenth century with what he regards as the supinely quiescent conduct of the twentieth-century Welsh. Thus, he muses sardonically, the battle of Mount Hyddgen has proved in the end to be but 'a barren victory'. Whereas Welsh farmers now earn world renown for the quality of their lamb, their product is largely reserved for export, leaving the 'hireling shepherd' with next to nothing (17). And, again in typical fashion, Thomas reflects that the verdict of history on the battle of Hyddgen is recorded not in human documents, nor in human memories, but on the rocks, covered with lichen, that measure the passage of time by the aeon and not by the feeble calendar year of humans.

Thomas's ambivalence on the use of violence to effect a national revolution in Wales is again betrayed in the two different versions of the conclusion he wrote for 'Welsh History', which opens with a vision of the warrior Wales of the distant past – 'We were a people taut for war; the hills/ Were no harder' – and is infused with a nostalgia for the spirit of armed insurrection in a bygone age. Thomas was attracted to such warfare, viewing it as more romantically heroic in character. Hence his emphasis in his review on the contrast between the destructive modern weapons of the whites and the bows and arrows of the Indians. Echoes of the latter may even be heard in some of his poems. 'To live in Wales,' he claims in 'Welsh Landscape', is to 'be aware/ Above the noisy tractor/ And hum of the machine/ Of strife in the strung woods,/ Vibrant with sped arrows' (*CP*, 37). And there are further hints at an Indian-like presence in his mention of 'cries in the dark at night/ As owls answer the moon,/ And thick ambush of shadows,/ Hushed at the fields' corners'.

The original version of 'Welsh History', as printed in *An Acre of Land*, ended with the assertion that 'We will arise,/ Armed, but not in the old way' (*SYT*, 61). In subsequent printings, however, the wording was changed to read 'We will arise/ and greet each other in a new dawn'. Among the factors that determined this change, I would suggest, were two in particular that gave Thomas more heart, by the time he came to revise his original wording, and thus disinclined him to the fantasy of armed insurrection. First, the dramatic change in the political climate in Wales at the beginning of the 1960s following the highly controversial decision by Liverpool Corporation to drown Tryweryn, a valley in mid-Wales that contained the small working community of Capel Celyn, and the city's refusal to reconsider its reservoir proposal in the light of the huge wave of protest that followed. Frustrated popular outrage eventually led to an explosives attack on the pipeline that was under construction, and a few years later the Investiture of the Prince of Wales gave rise to a bombing campaign that caused the death of two of the young extremists involved. In such a context, any mention of a resort to arms, however metaphorically intended, could have unfortunate consequences. Then second, Thomas's own spirits had been boosted from the mid-1960s onwards by the non-violent activities of Cymdeithas yr Iaith, and by the courage of its young members, many of whom faced periods of imprisonment for their actions. These were for the previously disillusioned and jaundiced Thomas promising signs of a meaningful national awakening – a 'new dawn' indeed.

V

Bury My Heart at Wounded Knee was a text all the more attractive to Thomas because at its heart lay a people's struggle for their land, and he had always seen the condition of modern Wales in like terms. The first governmental depredations of Welsh land came courtesy of the Forestry Commission, a government department established in 1919 because the First World War had highlighted a shortage of timber in Britain that threatened to prevent the production of the wood alcohol that was a crucial component of the cordite on which the great guns depended. By 1939, 28,000 hectares of prime Welsh farmland had been purchased by the Commission; another 20,000 was acquired between 1946 and 1951, and by 1975 the Forestry Commission owned 134,000 hectares of woodland in Wales.[17] The reverse situation applied in the Native American case, but with like effect. 'Much of the forest was cleared or burnt,' Thomas noted, 'just so as to put an end to the Indians' way of life, and force them to go and live in the completely unsuitable areas which had been provided for them' (*SP*, 178).

So serious had the consequences of all this manic plantation programme in Wales become for the rural communities that provided the backbone for the Welsh language and its culture, that Gwenallt, one of the most prominent and distinguished of Welsh warrior-poets, was left aghast. One of his most notable poems was written in the wake of the destruction of 'Rhydcymerau', the rural area just south of Lampeter that had for centuries been home to his family and that had become for him such an important refuge and source of strength, in order to create the Brechfa forest. It opens with the apocalyptic warning that

'The saplings of the third world war were planted/ On the land of Esgeir-ceir and the fields of Tir-bach/ Near Rhydcymerau'.[18] This war reference was anything but a rhetorical gesture. It resonated with the pain that was permanently lodged within the inner core of Gwenallt's being. When still but a teenager growing up within the remarkable industrial community of the lower Swansea Valley, he had refused to answer the summons to conscription, on the grounds that he was a conscientious objector. A member of the ILP at the time, he adhered to their view that the war was in essence one being waged between two aggressive powers, both of which were malign instances of an imperialist capitalism. Fleeing the authorities, he had sought refuge amongst his people in Rhydcymerau, but had been tracked down, and was subsequently sentenced to several periods of incarceration on Dartmoor. Back then, it seemed as if peaceful Rhydcymerau existed in a different world entirely from that of the Somme. But by 1951, to his horror he realised that this region, too, had been appropriated by the sinister war machine.

After the body of the poem has explored the richness of the historic culture that has been obliterated, the final section resumes the work of registering Gwenallt's opening nightmare, this time in terms of the nuclear war that seemed impending in the wake of Hiroshima and Nagasaki and the dangerous armed hostility between the West and the Soviet Union. It begins with a specific lament for all that has been lost:

> And now there are only trees there,
> With their impudent roots sucking the old earth:
> Trees where there was a community,
> Forest where there were farms …

The vision then darkens towards its sombre conclusion:

> In the darkness at its centre
> Is the den of the English Minotaur;
> And on trees, as on crosses,
> The skeletons of poets, chapel elders, ministers and Sunday
>   School teachers
> Bleaching in the sun,
> And being washed by the rain and dried by the wind.

For Gwenallt in 1951 it must have seemed as if he were about to relive his dreadful youthful experience during the First World War.

In his poem 'Afforestation', R. S. Thomas seems to me to be conducting a conversation with Gwenallt's poem, with which he was undoubtedly familiar.[19] He, too, emphasises that now 'It's a population of trees/ Colonising the old/ Haunts of men.' As the next lines ('I pre-fer/ Listening to their talk,/ The bare language of grass/ To what the woods say') seem to imply, Thomas, like Gwenallt, is very conscious that these pinewood forests, foreign invaders as they are, are 'colonisers' not only because they have displaced native species of woodlands but also because they have been planted to serve the needs of an 'alien' popula-tion and are effectively displacing Welsh-speaking communities. 'I see', he continues, adopting the tones of a Cassandra, as he so frequently did when speaking of the condition of Wales,

> The cheap times
> Against which they grow:
> Thin houses for dupes,
> Pages of pale trash,
> A world that has gone sour
> With spruce.

Not only is his notorious anti-modernism on shameless display here, but his adoption of the metaphor of print and books (he is of course thinking of the process of making paper out of wood pulp) turns that trope into an attack on all the different, debased and debasing, products of the 'foreign' English publishing industry of his time. These it is that have effectively destroyed the widespread Welsh rural culture of local verse, that Gwenallt recalls sentimentally and elegiacally in his poem by quoting popular lines written by a relative of his about a scratching little cockerel that had become proverbial in the Rhydcymerau area. And officials at Westminster were arrogantly open about their intention to alter the entire landscape of Wales. A spokesman for the post-war Attlee administration could unabashedly state that '[w]e intend to plant 800,000 acres in Wales. We know that there will be opposition but we intend to force this thing through.'[20]

With the process of afforestation already very well established in Wales by the beginning of the Second World War, the War Office next turned its attention to putting further acres of the rural Welsh landscape to 'useful' military use. This was the equivalent for Thomas of the situating of forts on the frontier of the United States in order to regulate the Indians, a development that prompted many conflicts during the Indian wars. In 1938, the Ministry of Defence acquired what were eventually 6,000 acres of land in south Pembrokeshire as a training area. This was abandoned after the war, but was then reinstated in 1951 to meet needs arising from the Korean war. Then in 1961, it became an important training area for the British Army of the Rhine, whose tanks were sent there for target practice. Eventually, further sites in the area were also acquired, including the Royal Artillery Range Manorbier, Penally Training Camp and Templeton Airfields – air defence systems. At nearby Aberporth, 2,000 square miles of Cardigan Bay are reserved for the use of a Royal Aircraft Establishment used for testing guided missiles. Aberporth is also home to an Early Warning System.

All these developments have happened within a stone's throw of the ancient Preseli Mountains – an area that has historically functioned in Welsh culture in ways not wholly dissimilar to the sacred significance of the Black Hills for the nineteenth-century Sioux peoples. The great poet of that area, and one of the greatest of the twentieth-century poets of Wales, was Waldo Williams, a pacifist and poetic genius and one whose unworldliness found paradoxical expression in an activism powered by an astonishingly sensitive conscience. He was imprisoned in the early 1950s for refusing to pay taxes part of which, he knew, would go towards supporting the British war effort in Korea and, somewhat later, towards supporting troop deployment to Cyprus. So ashamed was he of his initial inactivity in these connections that he found himself unable, for days, even to venture out of doors because he was afraid to look his neighbours in the face. Eventually, he was taken to court for his actions and briefly imprisoned in Swansea gaol.

Waldo Williams had grown up in the shadow of the Preseli, a range of hills he revered for their aura and history, and for the honourable tradition of conscientious dissent and civil disobedience that they had nurtured. It was they, he wrote, that had provided him with backbone for his every assertion of dissenting independence of judgement. In 1939, with Britain on the brink of war, he published 'Daw'r wennol yn ôl i'w nyth' ('The swallow will return to its nest'), a lovely, haunting elegy for a corner of Pembrokeshire, traditionally providing winter pasture for upland Preseli farmers, that had been appropriated by the War Office. Slightly tempering the melancholy meditation on a local population deprived of their land is the refrain with which the poem begins and ends and that finds consolation in the annual return of the swallow to its nest, regardless of human interference.

Waldo returned to this theme in 'Preseli', a wonderful, dignified poem of 1946 that protested against the announcement by the War Ministry that they planned to commandeer a large part of his beloved Preseli range and surrounding land.[21] In it he celebrates the hills that had served his childhood as protective wall, evokes his community as composed of the offspring of wind and rain and mist and sword-grass and heather, and imagines them as handing on the sun from their labouring crouch to their children. And then, as they straighten their poor backs, their giant laughter rises to the clouds in unison. It was this land and its community, he concludes, that had served him as the window through which he could glimpse the grand palatial order of human solidarity worldwide. But now, the rape of devastation advances through the windowless forest, and so the final line is a pacifist's call to arms: 'Cadwn y mur rhag y bwystfil, cadwn y ffynnon rhag y baw' ('let us man the wall against the monster, let us preserve the spring from the filth').[22]

For R. S. Thomas, the occupation of the land by the military was implicitly, and sadly, endorsed in St Davids Cathedral, the very ancient seat of the spiritual authority of the Church in Wales. This is a feature of the cathedral only obliquely alluded to in his poem 'A Line from Saint Davids', but, as I have pointed out at length elsewhere,[23] Thomas himself specifically drew attention to that covert allusion in a radio lecture he delivered: 'We have no empire to defend,' he there wrote, 'so little are our needs. So, peace is our cry … It was not the banners and [*sic*] the battalions hanging in limp magnificence, nor the bejewelled roof, that brought these thoughts to me, but the little fern that grew from the stones.' He was here directly alluding to a detail in his poem, where he had noted that

> The wall lettuce in the crevices
> Is as green now as when Giraldus
> Altered the colour of his thought
> By drinking from the Welsh fountain. (*CP*, 123)

It is a ringing affirmation that the Welsh landscape possesses a tenacity that assures its survival of every human attempt to dominate and destroy it.

Both Waldo Williams and R. S. Thomas shared an almost mystical belief, broadly analogous to that of Native American peoples, that the landscape of Wales was imbued with the living spirit of the people that had inhabited it for at least two millennia. 'Dan haul a chwmwl ein profiad a'i prynodd;/ rhed yr arial trwom ni' ('Under sun and cloud our experience purchased her;/ Her vigour courses through us'), wrote Waldo in 'Daear Cymru' (*WWC*, 215). And again, even more famously, 'Dyma'r mynyddoedd. Ni fedr ond un iaith eu codi./ A'u rhoi yn eu rhyddid yn erbyn wybren cân' ('Here are the mountains. No language can raise them save one/ And set them free against a firmament of song') (*WWC*, 330). That language, he adds with an eye partly on the on-going invasion of Pembrokeshire and the growing ascendancy of a foreign tongue, has always been a 'merch perygl', 'the daughter of danger'. As Jason Walford Davies has noticed, Thomas seems to borrow the image of the language raising up the mountains in *Neb*.[24]

Dorian Llywelyn's seminal study *Sacred Place, Chosen People* enables us not only to understand the cultural parameters of that sense of place shared by Waldo Williams and R. S. Thomas but also to place it in relationship to the sense of place (and time) common to deeply traditional native communities such as those of the American Indian peoples.[25] In his review, R. S. Thomas makes clear that his sympathy for the latter rests in large part on his empathetic understanding of the centrality of the concept of belonging to a place in their world-view. Llywelyn writes of there being 'two species of … soteriological landscape … the other-worldly, extra-historical heaven, and the intramundane sacred place' (*SCCP*, 1). And for exploring the latter in its various modern ramifications, he draws on the work of major scholars in the fields of anthropology and sociology. 'In traditional societies,' he points out, 'the individual is defined, among other things, by his or her belonging to a specific place. Only in modern, Western, industrialized society is such a relation absent, and it is perhaps Wales's rural and generally conservative society which has allowed the sense of place to survive there' (*SPCP*, 15). This is a remark that throws light on R. S. Thomas's deep suspicion of the kind of modern society that had been developed by industrialism in the south of Wales in the second half of the nineteenth century.

For inhabitants of the latter kind of society across the West, Llywelyn points out, all space is homogeneous – a 'comparatively new concept' (*SPCP*, 15). Such a model conceives of space as a kind of 'anti-place', an existential vacuum. By contrast, traditional societies conceive not of space but of place, 'locations which are charged with human significance and positive values and associations' (*SPCP*, 16). These locations are sites of the sacred.

One suggestive aspect of such, mentioned by Dorian Llywelyn, is particularly well suited, as he points out, to understanding the nature of colonial invasion of space (*SPCP*, 18). He quotes the American theologian Beldane Lane's observation that '*Sacred place can be tread upon without being entered. Its recognition is existentially, not ontologically discerned.* The identification of sacred places is thus intimately related to states of consciousness' (*SPCP*, 18). It is precisely this distinction that is central to understanding the mystification of the Sioux peoples, for example, at the treatment by the whites of their sacred site of the Black Hills, as of the whites' curious insistence on arbitrarily carving the land up into different sections, to most of which they then proceeded to claim 'possession'. It is also the very distinction that Thomas chooses to exploit in his poem 'Welcome'. It begins by conceding territory to invaders – 'You can come in./ You can come a long way;/ We can't stop you./ ... You can walk this country/ From end to end' (*CP*, 134). Then it reveals the catch: 'But you won't be inside;/ You must stop at the bar,/ The old bar of speech.'

Then the second stanza opens with Thomas deliberately practising a linguistic duplicity that simultaneously advertises his mastery of the English language and his use of that mastery for purely subversive reasons: 'We have learnt your own/ Language, but don't/ Let it take you in.' The final phrase plays wickedly on its two meanings – 'don't be deceived' and 'it won't get you anywhere'. The poem then moves on to contrast the incomers' treatment of place as exchangeable for money, just like any other commercial goods (exactly the commodified view taken of the land of the Sioux, for example, by the whites), with Thomas's sense of the secret, sacred significance of place: 'You must travel back,' he brusquely informs the incomer, 'To the cold bud of water/ In the hard rock.' That 'cold bud' is the core, or essence, or presiding spirit, of place, sole custodian of which is the Welsh language. It is the growing point of national identity. Thomas was writing his poem against a background not only of exponential increase in tourism and in second home or holiday home ownership, but also of a mass migration whereby some half a million people native to Wales moved over the border while a corresponding half a million, mostly English, people, entered the country. It was the equivalent at the time of some eight million French people settling in England.

It may be argued that one difference between Sioux and Welsh sense of place arises from their different sense of time, of their relationship to the past. For the Sioux, that sense is largely synchronic; for the Welsh it is largely diachronic – there being a strong sense of chronology and the operations of cause-and-effect, although with some elements of synchronicity, in that the historical past is recognised, and indeed felt, to have a continuing 'presence' in national life. Indeed, to lose such a sense of 'presence' is also to lose an indispensable element in the experience of 'place', and Thomas's poetry is full of angry and anguished reflection on this process in connection with the modern land of Wales.

One poem on this subject is 'A Land' – the use of the indefinite article, even though it is obviously Wales that is being referred to, is a measure of Thomas's sense of alienated distance from his own country in its modern aspect. The opening sets the gloomy tone: 'Their souls are something smaller/ than the mountain above them' (*CP*, 465). The next couple of lines – 'They are not touched/ either by the sun rising at morning/ or the sun setting at evening' – involve a caustic recasting of famous lines from T. S. Eliot's epochal *The Waste Land*:

> (Come in under the shadow of this red rock),
> And I will show you something different from either
> Your shadow at morning striding behind you
> Or your shadow at evening rising to met you:
> I will show you fear in a handful of dust.

While Thomas does not explicitly reference that handful of dust, he does produce an equivalent nihilistic image of life reduced to meaninglessness: 'They are all in shadow/ pale and winding themselves about each other/ inhibiting growth.' 'Death lives in this village,' he continues, and people look out at the world 'through the eternal downpour/ of their tears.' His revulsion at the spectacle then gives rise to an image of Grand Guignol levels of bestiality as he describes 'hard hands that money adhere/ to like the scales/ of some hideous disease, so that they grizzle/ as it is picked off'. And then finally, no doubt recalling how in the south Wales valleys, even as the chapels declined the hymns sung in them survived in debased form to be sung in pubs and in rugby grounds, he listens to these people

> sing, not music
> so much as the sound of a nation
> rending itself, fierce with all the promise
> of a beauty that might have been theirs.

The whole poem is a devastating indictment of a culture-less popula-tion who have thus in effect becomes a dis-placed people even while remaining *in situ*. His own term elsewhere for them is 'an evicted people' (*CP*, 70). And he repeatedly recoils from Welsh names (such as Olwen, Beuno, Ceridwen, Arthur) that have become, when used by non-Welsh speakers, mere sad vestiges of their original selves. They are, he wrote in 'Welsh', '[n]ames that are ghosts/ from a green era' (*CP*, 129). 'I want', is his response, 'the right word/ For the gut's trouble/ When I see this land/ Empty of folk', and his poetry could be read as consisting of his search for those 'right words'. Thomas wrote an essay on the difference between 'Wales' and 'Cymru', and in 'A Country' he speaks rather poignantly of venturing out only at night, because only then could he imagine 'the dark country/ Between the border and the coast/ Was still Wales' (*CP*, 137). Because at all other times, 'the land/ Had no more right to its name/ Than a corpse had; self-given wounds/ Wasted it'.

Thomas was always very aware that in the eighteenth century this process of colonisation, by commodification, of the Welsh landscape had been reflected in the picturesque tradition, paintings of Welsh land-scape carefully absented of people, language and culture. A similar fate befell the mid- and far-West of the United States (originally the territory of the Plains Indians) during the second half of the nineteenth century, as talented artists of huge popular appeal such as Albert Bierstadt began to produce landscape paintings that could sometime be on the monu-mental scale deemed appropriate to their subject matter.

No better example could be found of the acquisitive eye and the highly individualistic and proprietorial approach to landscape that char-acterised nineteenth-century white American society than the superb wood- and steel-engravings lavishly scattered throughout the two volumes of *Picturesque America* (1872–4). Edited by William Cullen Bryant, and catering for bourgeois pockets and tastes, the three volumes were lavishly bound in leather and adorned with brass fittings and clasps. 'Our country borders on two oceans,' the distinguished editor wrote, and comprises within the vast space that lies between them 'a variety of scenery that no other people can boast of ... No country in the world possesses a succession of such varied pictures.'[26] The use of the little word 'possesses' speaks volumes. These huge albums confirm that the advent of the cross-continental railways had made it possible by 1872 – four years before the Battle of the Little Bighorn – to treat the whole continent as nothing but a single tourist area. No single mention is made in their pages of the Native American inhabitants of those vast regions; nowhere is a Native American place-name. They have been totally effaced from the scene, as the Welsh were effaced, no doubt for analogous reasons of 'good taste', from the English eighteenth century's picturesque (or, in Turner's case, usually sublime) depictions of Welsh mountain scenery.

Thomas, who was married to an English artist, wrote his landscape poems in full awareness of this English tradition.[27] His are therefore conscious textual exercises in the reclamation of landscape. Time after time he not only flaunts Welsh place-names but rubs his readers' noses in their culturally occluded meanings, associations and implications. But his most celebrated direct confrontation with the English picturesque tradition undoubtedly comes in 'The Welsh Hill Country' (*CP*, 22), where he mocks the cultivation of vista, involving separation from the scene, that was integral to picturesque landscapes. 'Too far for you to see', he writes,

> The fluke and the foot-rot and the fat maggot
> Gnawing the skin from the small bones,
> The sheep are grazing at Bwlch-y-Fedwen,
> Arranged romantically in the usual manner
> On a bleak background of bald stone.

The poem proceeds in resolutely anti-romantic manner, making sure the reader registers all the grim details of a physical, social and cultural reality that had been effaced in traditional landscape painting.

Analogously, 'Welsh Landscape' (*CP*, 37) begins by placing the reader, not, as might have been expected from the title, at a comfortable viewing distance from the subject, but directly within the scene, with the resulting shocking adjustment of consciousness to the stark realities of Welsh experience, both past and present: 'To live in Wales is to be conscious/ At dusk of the spilled blood/ That went to the making of the wild sky,/ Dyeing the immaculate rivers/ In all their courses.' And as the poem proceeds, it makes it explicitly clear that to be truly exposed to the Welsh landscape is to be fully involved in it, so that its eternal inexorable pastness is felt as pressing present experience. There is therefore a sense in this poem of a land and a people's zombie existence. The Welsh are nothing but the living dead. Place is no longer a connective, a kind of conduit between present, past and future, but only a terminus. Wales has become an un-place.

VI

The War Office did not rest content with appropriating huge chunks of Pembrokeshire. In 1940, it requisitioned 30,000 acres of the Epynt Mountains, north of Brecon, turning it into what is known as the Sennybridge Training Area and in the process destroying 54 farms and a pub, and evicting a total of 200 men, women and children. Welsh names were obliterated overnight – 'Mynydd Bwlch y Groes' became 'Dixies Corner'. The community had been Welsh-speaking, their place-names included Llwyn Coll, Gilfachyrhaidd, Waunlwyd, Abercriban, Cwm Car. But with the community's dispersal, the language became lost to subsequent generations.

By then there was already a history of Welsh dispossession. The most famous example of such had been just four years earlier, when, in spite of nation-wide protest, the Westminster government pressed ruthlessly on with its plans to establish a bombing school in the Llŷn peninsula, on a site whose cultural significance for the Welsh stretched right back to the fifteenth century. This prompted three prominent members of Plaid Cymru to take direct action by mounting an arson attack on the building site. The first trial before a non-Welsh-speaking judge resulted in a hung jury, so the case was moved to the Old Bailey in London. This time the trio were sentenced to nine months in prison. It was this event that awoke a talented generation of young Welsh writers that included R. S. Thomas and Emyr Humphreys to national consciousness. And some thirty years later, it was a similar assault on Welsh land, this time in Cwm Tryweryn, that provided the catalyst for a similar reaction, radicalising a new young generation of Welsh literary talent. Nation-wide protests against the development of a reservoir having once more proved in vain, some young people took it into their hands to mount attacks on the pipeline that was under construction. While the publicity surrounding this gave rise to mixed response, another young generation of Welsh writers underwent an education in the woeful lack of effective Welsh representation at Westminster.

It was this incident that gave rise to one of R. S. Thomas's best-known poems, with its memorable opening:

> There are places I don't go:
> Reservoirs that are the subconscious
> Of a people, troubled far down
> With gravestones, chapels, villages even (*CP*, 194)

Then, as the poem unfolds, Thomas's mind begins to find an ironic association between this landscape, entirely emptied out, as it has been, of all human and cultural content, and the English tradition of treating the landscape of Wales simply as fodder for picturesque representation. The still waters of the reservoir, he bitterly concludes, are 'a pose/ For strangers, a watercolour's appeal/ To the mass, instead of the poem's/ Harsher conditions'. It is hard not to feel that there is another word – 'appall' – hiding within 'appeal' at this point. And once this train of thought is started it leads to Thomas, his eyes newly opened, noticing that the whole land of Wales has become subject to the same colonising treatment:

> There are the hills,
> Too; gardens gone under the scum
> Of the forests; and the smashed faces
> Of the farms with the stone trickle
> Of their tears down the hills' side.

So the 'harsher conditions' that his poem provides has enabled him to detect and voice the truth about the state of his over-run country, so

that by its conclusion he finds that wherever he turns he is confronted
by the same ghastly vision:

> I have walked the shore
> For an hour and seen the English
> Scavenging among the remains
> Of our culture, covering the sand
> Like the tide and, with the roughness
> Of the tide, elbowing our language
> Into the grave that we have dug for it.

It is deeply discomfiting writing, and meant to be such. No wonder
that explosively splenetic writing of such dark bleak accusatory
hopelessness by Thomas has come to embarrass several generations
of his compatriots sufficiently for it to be safely buried in anodyne
poetic anthologies.

Thomas's mention in this poem of 'the smashed faces of the farms'
should remind us of how often, during the years he spent at Manafon,
he had deplored what in one striking poem he called 'The Depopulation
of the Hills'. There were many factors involved in that process, most
obviously migration to the towns and cities, first to centres of industry
then to centres of commerce, and it was a movement that had begun in
Wales up to a couple of centuries before it came to Thomas's attention.
But during his time of service in a border parish another development
was under way which was radically changing the practice of farming
in parts of Wales in ways of which he deeply disapproved. And this
development, too, was being orchestrated by the wartime Westminster
government. Its most visible instrument was the tractor, a machine that
Thomas deeply mistrusted and disliked, as is evident in 'Cynddylan on
his Tractor', a poem whose extensive cultural implications have never
really been appreciated.

We might best prepare ourselves to understand those implications
by exploring the implications of the name 'Cynddylan'. Of no obvious significance to any English-speaking reader, to a Welsh-speaker it
is a name that carries with it very important associations. Because it is
the name of a medieval prince of Powys the defeat of whom, followed
by the complete destruction of his palace, is famously elegised in a
great medieval poem 'Ystafell Cynddylan'. The speaker in the poem is

Heledd, Cynddylan's sister, and she it is who gives voice to the famous dirge with which the poem opens:

> Stafell Gynddylan ys tywyll heno,
> Heb dân, heb wely;
> Wylaf wers, tawaf wedy.

> (Dark is Cynddylan's hall tonight
> With no fire, no bed.
> I weep awhile, then am silent.)

As immediately becomes clear, then, the poem with which the name of Cynddylan is indelibly connected is a lament for land irrecoverably lost to invasion. For R. S. Thomas, it would have been doubly resonant because it is a poem associated with what later became known as the Marches and with that part of the region where land once belonging to the Welsh had been permanently occupied by the English. Later mention is made in the poem of Eryr Pengwern, the Eagle of Pengwern, feasting on the corpses of the dead, and it is to this that Thomas makes reference is resonant lines in 'Border Blues':

> *Eryr Pengwern, penngarn llwyt heno...*
> We still come in by the Welsh gate, but it's a long way
> To Shrewsbury from the Welsh border (*WA*, 11)

Giraldus Cambrensis had (probably mistakenly) identified Pengwern with modern-day Shrewsbury, thus underlining the fact that the land on which the town now stands was once in Wales. In short, in Thomas's poem the name Cynddylan stands for dispossession – appropriately so, because in the poem he is a figure who is presented as doubly alienated: first because he seems wholly unaware of the cultural implications of his name, probably because he speaks no Welsh – as seems also true of Iago Prytherch (Iago being Welsh for James); and secondly, because he is alienating himself from the long traditions of his farming background by riding so proudly on his tractor.

As for the tractor, it would have stood for Thomas not only as a vague signifier of the evils of a machine age (as many have narrowly supposed) but as a signifier of the agrarian revolution, overseen by the wartime Ministry for Agriculture, that was blatantly afoot in the very hills surrounding him in Manafon. This has entirely escaped notice by Thomas's numerous critics and commentators, but it throws interesting light on the body of work he produced while he was based there. Detailed attention has already been paid to this in an earlier discussion, suffice it for now to note that the clamour for increased agricultural production during the wartime years greatly accelerated the process of introducing machinery into the farming industry in Britain. To facilitate this development, government grants were made available to farmers to encourage them in this direction. Moreover, rural Montgomeryshire was a rural region that became particularly well known and generally admired for the wartime steps it took to reclaim upland land for use as new, additional, sources of valuable food production. What Thomas was seeing happening all around him in Manafon was therefore what he came to regard as yet another example of foreign interference; the appropriation and manipulation of Welsh land for English purposes; and central to the process was a machine like the tractor. It was yet another experience that prepared him, in due course, to write his empathetic review of *Bury My Heart at Wounded Knee*.

No wonder, therefore, that he adopts the tone of the mock-heroic in 'celebrating' – in consciously perverted 'bardic' fashion – the 'achievements' of his Cynddylan: he is 'the knight at arms breaking the fields'/ Mirror of silence, emptying the wood/ Of foxes and squirrels and bright jays' (*CP*, 30). And as for Cynddylan, he is not so much man as cyborg, the perverted modern-day equivalent of the Centaur of old (to whom horsemen had frequently been compared): 'He's a new man now, part of the machine,/ His nerves metal and his blood oil.' In his way, therefore, he is for Thomas an essential part of the machinery of war itself, a warrior of the soil, so it turns out that there was a truth in his earlier mocking depiction of Cynddylan as a knight at arms after all, even though his 'victory' is won not over the enemy but over the land itself and its creatures.

Perhaps because of the tractor's particular significance in the context of the wartime revolution in upland rural Montgomeryshire, Thomas seems in 'Cynddylan on a Tractor' (published in 1952) to have anticipated by a few years the widespread use of that machine by Welsh-language poets of the 1960s as a short-hand for the astonishing, and partly regrettable, transformation of Welsh farming practice by modern methods. The tractor had apparently begun to be introduced into Wales during the early 1920s, but it was some forty years later before its impact began to be registered by a generation of poets increasingly inclined to elegize the rapid passing in its wake of an old rural way of life rich in idioms, practices and traditions. One notable example of the poetry that was produced by the 'beirdd gwlad' (the local, rural poets some of whom were highly talented, and whose own ancient role in their societies was itself under threat from these new 'alien' developments) was Isfoel's 'Cywydd y Tractor', published in 1965: 'Upheaval and transformation/ rang out clear across the countryside,/ No horse will be tethered, with his abundant mane,/ again to tread the field …'.[28] And another such poet, J. R. Jones, wrote of involuntarily recalling one fine May day, while driving the tractor towards a gap in a hedge, an old horse churning up the clay, and registering how much more than two old nags his father had sold when shaking hands with a dealer on the sale of two faithful old horses (*BC*, 18). Likewise, Alun Jones, another of the best of such poets, nicely captured his ambivalence at the passing of the Age of the Horse in agriculture, when on the one hand (and not entirely without irony) he praised the un-companionable tractor in the very act of cursing it, and on the other he wrote an eloquent epitaph for the two broad-shouldered 'Clydesdales', ready for any challenge however hard, who had been sent to the knacker's yard once the tractor had arrived in the farmyard (*BC*, 19). What all these poets were also elegising was the loss, with the horses, of an entire, vast poetic vocabulary in the form of the wealth of rural images generated by traditional farming methods, that had been such a vital part of the currency of the poetry of the past. And for all the benefits that they recognised this new agrarian revolution was bringing, they all also saw it clearly, like R. S. Thomas, as ushering in a 'foreign' way of life that was certain to destroy the Welsh-language societies that had from time immemorial been bedrock of Welsh identity. For them, too, like the Plains Indians, the passing of the age of the horse unmistakeably meant the end of their world.

VII

It is obvious enough, I'm sure, that the account R. S. Thomas offers of Native Americans in his review, mediated as it is by Brown's narrative,

is very partial (in both senses of that word), sentimental and highly ten-
dentious. When, for instance, he writes as follows he is misrepresenting
both American and Indian history:

> Some held that the best thing was to do as the white man wished.
> The future was his. Some went so far as to serve as scouts to the
> soldiers, showing them the hiding-places of the other Indians.
> You see the comparisons. As long ago as Glendower, there were
> Welshmen who believed that the future lay with the English.
> That was why he failed. (*SP*, 180)

It is extremely misleading to suggest that Glyndŵr would have triumphed over his enemies had he not been betrayed by his own men.
The truth is that he never really stood much of a chance once the
English, freed of obligations elsewhere, were able to concentrate their
overwhelmingly superior forces on suppressing his rebellion. As for the
comment on the Native Americans, it betrays a complete ignorance of
the fact that, far from being a homogeneous 'national' body, they were
in fact a collection of dozens of totally distinct peoples, most of them
at least as different from each other as are the French from the English,
and not a few as different as the English are from the Chinese. It also
shows that Thomas was unaware of the history of inter-tribal conflict
– or disinclined to acknowledge it, since it undermined his thesis as it
had long predated the coming of the whites. In serving as scouts for
the Americans in their campaigns against the Sioux, for example, the
Crows were simply trying to take advantage of the power of one enemy
to defeat another enemy who, to them, was even more of a threat.
He also shows no awareness of how relatively recent was the Plains
Indians' occupation of the lands they claimed had been theirs from
time immemorial, just as he seems unaware that it was only early in the
eighteenth century that they first acquired horses, celebrated though
they subsequently became as peerless horsemen.

A somewhat less egregious example of Thomas misreading and
misleading is his treatment of the relationship of Native Americans to
the natural world, which he summarises as follows:

> The redskin respected the earth. Although he hunted, he did
> so for food and clothing. He never killed for the sake of killing.

He would never damage the living earth. To an age such as our own which is beginning to wake up to the need to look after the environment, the Red Indians appear in a new light, as environmentalists. (*SP*, 178)

He then goes on to contrast the Indians' treatment of the bison with that of the invading whites. There is obviously a considerable degree of truth in his reservations, but their effect is to create a picture of a 'primitive' world, pristine and Edenic until the coming of white civilisation brought the Fall in its wake. This is American pastoral – a genre practised by several prominent American writers of the past – and as such there is an irony attached to it, since the R. S. Thomas who owed his early reputation to the Iago Prytherch poems had been consciously and scathingly attacking versions of English and Welsh pastoralism. He himself attributed this body of poetry to his personal awakening, during his period in Manafon, to the hard realities of a farming life he had previously idealised and romanticised. There is, however, no doubt that the Plains Indians were deeply shocked by the callous slaughter of wild animals by the whites, as the Blackfoot writer James Welch makes clear in his notable novel *Fools Crow*. There the eponymous young warrior is visited by his friend and mentor Raven, because the old crow is so appalled by the trail of devastation being left by white hunters:

> For three more sleeps I followed this strange Napikwan [white man] that leaves his meat. He killed a long-tail, a bighead, three real-dogs and five wags-his-tails. He even tried to kill your brother, Skunk Bear, but I flew ahead and warned him. In anger the Napikwan took a shot at me, scared the shit out of me, so I left. But for many moons now the hunter kills animals until they become scarce. I fear he will kill us all off if something isn't done.[29]

But closer reflection quickly reveals the fissures in Thomas's picture of Native American life. It is entirely true that the peoples of the plains had no concept of property that allowed them to make sense of the white society by which their territories were being mercilessly invaded, and so theirs was not a possessive relationship to their land, nor was it an exploitative one, as it inevitably was for the whites whose outlook and practices all flowed from the commercialism of their acquisitive culture. Clearly the plains Indians did regard the earth both as a source of food and also as a great spiritual entity to be respected, revered and worshipped, and its creatures were to be treated in like manner. True, too, that they did not hunt the bison to extinction, nor did they kill the beavers for their lucrative furs. They certainly valued skills developed in hunting – an essential activity in their cultures that not only provided food and clothing, but also afforded opportunities for sport and for training the warrior skills that led to social prestige within the tribe. But they were not above treating animals such as the bison on occasion in a manner that did not strictly conform to modern environmentalist ideals. For instance, before the coming of the horse to the plains, the hunters had relied on collective tribal effort to drive whole buffalo herds over the edge of a precipice, a highly effective method of hunting that inevitably resulted in a carnage that left far, far more buffalo dead than the tribe could possibly 'need' or make use of. As for their limiting the number of animals they killed, it should be remembered that even after acquiring horses they remained primarily reliant on bows and arrows that, by definition, were incapable of mass slaughter on anything like the scale known to the whites. Even when tribes began to acquire guns, they remained relatively few in number, and were old, antiquated weapons that were both unreliable and often wildly inaccurate, so that the buffalo were spared mass slaughter.

All that said, there is no denying the vast gulf between the values of a Native American society that placed the highest premium on collective experience and that of a white America formed by a belief in a competitive and acquisitive individualism. One of the most affecting details in the extraordinary story of Sitting Bull concerns the brief time he spent touring some of the Eastern cities as the most prominent 'specimen' on offer at Buffalo Bill's Wild West Show. Paid, no doubt reasonably handsomely, for his participation, Sitting Bull nevertheless ended up as penniless at the end of the tour as he was when it had begun. He had given all his money away en route to the poor people he'd seen crowding the urban streets. And he confessed himself completely baffled that such could exist within such an obviously wealthy society.

In other words, Thomas is using Brown's account as a launch-pad for his own convictions, and he certainly had a strong record as a Welsh environmentalist. From the beginning his concern with defending the land of

Wales as the great repository of history, culture and language overlapped both with his activities as a CND Cymru activist who travelled the length and breadth of Britain to participate in protests, and with his anxiety to protect the landscape itself, along with its creatures and plants. As a CND activist, he was present at protests conducted at the site of what became Trawsfynydd nuclear power station in the 1950s, and again in Carmarthen, where the local council, egged on by Thatcherite policies, embarked on the expensive construction of a nuclear bunker. And as environmentalist, he played a key role, for instance, in the campaign to save Ynys Enlli (Bardsey Island) as a sanctuary and was a leading member of Cyfeillion Llŷn, an organisation of locals of which Thomas was both founder member and secretary for eight years. Its aim was to protect the peninsula from the depredations of second-home ownership and the holiday trade.[30] The bird-watching for which he became well known also obviously had its environmentalist aspects, and to the end of his life he bitterly lamented that the people of Wales were so obviously careless of their own environment and that it was left to incomers (such as his good friend Bill Condry, the distinguished naturalist who first served as Mid-Wales Field Society Officer before becoming Warden of the RSPB Ynys-hir Reserve, north of Aberystwyth) to do their best to defend the environment of their adopted land.

Simplification – stemming both from ignorance and from tendentiousness and leading to distortion – is, then, a recurrent feature of Thomas's essay about *Bury My Heart at Wounded Knee*, a piece that is, as he himself as good as admits, at least as much autobiography as objective review. And in an autobiographical essay, he speaks of the enthusiasm of his boyhood friend, Rhodri, for cowboy films, and his hero-worship of Tom Mix in particular: 'It was he who taught me that the rows of fox-gloves were not flowers but wave after wave of Red Indians to be felled by our weapons: stones thrown – by Rhodri at least – with devastating effect' (*SP*, 13). As the adult Thomas well knew, such was not only an Anglesey schoolboy's reactions at the beginning of the twentieth century but that of the Welsh people as a whole, never better exemplified than in the hysterical enthusiasm with which Buffalo Bill Cody's travelling Wild West Show toured the towns of Wales in the 1890s and again at the beginning of the last century.

An online blog for BBC Wales, posted by Phil Carradice on 12 January 2012, vividly sets the scene: 'There is a smell of gunsmoke in the air, the thunder of horses hooves echo down the roadway, Buffalo Bill and his Wild West Show have come to town.' Carradice notes that it consisted of some 500 people (they could be as many as 1,000 in some places): cowboys, Indians (some of them Sioux and Cheyennes who had participated in the Battle of the Little Bighorn), backstage workers, grooms and so on. The Show boasted 180 horses, 18 buffalo and numerous other animals, including elks and Texas longhorn cattle. When Buffalo Bill set up camp in Sophia Gardens, Cardiff, he 'created an arena 175 yards long and 70 yards wide'.[31] Sitting Bull had been part of the cast when the show originally toured the US (as had Geronimo), and Annie Oakley, the prodigious sharpshooter whom the Indian chief greatly admired for her skills, was actually part of the troop that visited Britain, as too was Young Sitting Bull, the chief's son who was to play a fateful part in his father's assassination by one of his own people at Wounded Knee. Nearly 130,000 people paid to attend during the time the show was in Cardiff, and during its final visit to Wales (there were several) the tour took in innumerable small towns and lasted from 1902 to 1904. When the show came to Swansea, almost half the town's population had flocked to see it. Needless to say, the cowboys (who were partnered at times in the show by gauchos and 'Arabs' and Cossacks under the banner of 'Rough Riders of the World') were always the victorious heroes of the various scenarios enacted (such as the attack on the Deadwood Stage), while the Indians, who enthralled all visitors, were always the colourful but despised and defeated enemy – except in the re-enactment of the Little Bighorn battle, when the focus shifted of course to the heroic last stand of Custer. The correspondent of the *Aberdare Times* wrote as follows about the show's visit to the town on Saturday, 25 September 1886:

> It is well worth seeing, and is not unlike a military camp, with its headquarters under canvas and its grouped tepees savagely orna-mented with scalps and feathers. Picturesque Indian children are playing under trees. The uncouth, extemporised comfort and prevailing air of organisation give it a novel interest. There are no restrictions upon visitors, who are allowed to enter the tents and chuck the Indian babies under the chin, watch the squaws at work, and interview the patriarchal chief who sits grim and stoical on his blanket.[32]

As well he might, one could add, given that his people were being treated as specimens to be examined like exotic animals in some grisly human zoo.

VIII

According to records, Buffalo Bill's Wild West Show visited Holyhead on 3 May 1904. A mere fifteen or so years later, if Thomas's reminiscences are to be believed, a little boy watching cowboy movies in that town 'used to identify secretly with the Indians', as if intuiting the exploitation and degradation that had been attendant on that spectacle earlier in the century. Thankfully, there were also examples of a very different approach to Native American history. In 2016, S4C screened a three-part documentary, fronted by Professor Jerry Hunter, about Evan Jones, a draper from Powys, who followed his widowed mother to Pennsylvania, settling in an area known by the Welsh name of Duffryn (*sic*) Mawr, where, having joined the Baptist congregation, he became a missionary among the Cherokee. He learned their language, taught their children to read, and began a Cherokee newspaper. According to Hunter, the people appreciated Jones's work amongst them sufficiently to make him and his son a full member of their tribe. When the Federal Government took the infamous decision to remove the Cherokee to the distant region of Oklahoma, and decreed they undertake their journey there in the depths of winter, Evan decided to accompany them, to alleviate their sufferings best he could. As a result, he continues to be remembered and respected by the Cherokee people.[33]

A more nuanced summary of Jones's work amongst the Cherokees may, however, be found in John Ehle's *Trail of Tears*. He makes it clear that Jones's primary concern as a Baptist missionary was to effect the conversion of the people to Christianity, and that his role as mediator with the white government was somewhat mixed in character. He certainly protested against the forced removal from North Carolina to distant, alien Oklahoma and withstood pressure on him from the authorities to try to persuade the people to accept the unjust Treaty of New Echota (that was aimed at removing the Cherokees to the Indian territory in the West), but also, rather than blaming the Andrew Jackson administration for the condition of the Cherokees, he chose to attribute it instead to their sinfulness, particularly emphasising their involvement in slavery.³⁴ A visiting English 'gentleman' and geologist, George W. Featherstonhaugh, a fervent anti-Jacksonian who was deeply sympathetic to the plight of the Cherokees, went so far as to claim that the 'Englishman' (*sic*) Jones was 'detested' by the Cherokee nation (*TT*, 314).

Evan Jones's story was of course unknown to R. S. Thomas, but there can be little doubt that he would have been deeply encouraged by at least the more favourable account of his exploits among the Cherokee. In his review he is uncompromising in his total identification, as a Welsh person, with the American Indians. And towards its conclusion he explains why. Beginning by mentioning the acquisition of land and the effective erasure of a people, he then proceeds to link the Indian story with his own early 'dream of a different society in Wales' (*SP*, 180). Back then, he recalls, the language still seemed vibrant, while industrialism, although already widespread, seemed limited to the southern regions, so there was still 'space', as he put it. But then, his dream had begun to fade in the face of a reality that saw the industrial outlook spreading throughout the country, the language in retreat, the countryside being covered by forests, the cottages and smallholdings taken by Englishmen. But now, as of the time of writing the review, he finds his early dream is slowly reappearing, and he concludes with what, for him, was quite an unusually upbeat passage that is also a sonorous call to action:

> The Welsh nation is not finished yet. The language is still alive. We have not yet been put into a reservation to scrape a living there. There are intelligent, sensible people among us. Our air and our streams have not yet been polluted. Right is on our side. Rise up, you Welsh, demand leaders of your own choosing to govern you in your own country, to help you make a future in keeping with your own best traditions, before it is too late (*SP*, 180–1).

What exactly prompted such an unexpected upsurge of optimism is not clear, and in retrospect it seems particularly ironic, since a mere year after the review appeared a Government proposal to devolve powers to a limited Welsh Assembly would actually be rejected by the people of

Wales, a negative vote that at the time seemed to signify for many of Thomas's persuasion the end of any independent sense of national pride in difference. It was the collective suicide of the Welsh as a nation; their self-inflicted Wounded Knee. But since the review was presumably written during the campaigning that was prelude to the vote, it could just be that Thomas, along with so many like-minded of his compatriots, might at that time have reasonably anticipated a vote in favour that would have long last secured an extremely modest degree of self-government. It could also be that in writing his conclusion Thomas had very much in mind the brave campaigns of the young people of Cymdeithas yr Iaith Gymraeg, of which he was a fervent public supporter.

Be that as it may, there is no mistaking the spirit of affirmation with which an otherwise bleak review concludes. And in this respect it invites illuminating comparison with the famous lecture on Abercuawg that R. S. Thomas had delivered at the National Eisteddfod of Wales just two years previously. Because that remarkable lecture is, in essence, an outlining of a dream such as Thomas mentions in his review, and to which he there gives the name Abercuawg. It is a denial of the common 'modern' supposition that dreams are mere 'eunuchs' (to adopt Dylan Thomas's description); that they bring nothing into being; that they can offer only the dangerous consolation of illusion. The whole lecture is about the inexplicable magic for him of a name which he had come across in a line from a renowned medieval poem traditionally attributed to Llywarch Hen that simply states 'Yn Abercuawc yt ganant gogeu' ('In Abercuawg cuckoos sing').

This prompts him first to meditate on the nature of language and in particular its strange capacity to conjure up something out of nothing – a place out of mere sound – and to give that place a reality, albeit it does not actually exist. This, in turn, leads him to ponder why humans indulge in this kind of naming; why it is that they seem to need to mobilise language in order to imagine, or to conjure up, something or somewhere that seems to have no ordinary earthly being. For him, Abercuawg is the product of exactly such an act of language, of naming. It names a purely imaginary 'place', and he spells out what exactly that word and that place mean for him:

Whatever Abercuawg might be, it is a place of trees and fields and flowers and bright unpolluted streams, where the cuckoos continue to sing. For such a place I am ready to make sacrifices, maybe even to die. But what of a place which is overcrowded with people, that has endless streets of modern, characterless houses, each with its garage and television aerial, a place from where the trees and the birds and the flowers have fled before the yearly extension of concrete and tarmacadam; where the people do the same kind of soul-less, monotonous work to provide for still more and more of their kind? (*SP*, 159)

He proceeds from this to explore the paradox of language, a medium so powerful that in the hand of masters (*sic*) 'it can create figures which are more real than reality itself' (*SP*, 159). This leads to an interesting rumination on the emergence of his own 'creature', Iago Prytherch, a 'being' conjured out of nothing who also was nothing, yet had nevertheless been given 'life' in the poetry. All such matters, he adds, relate to the mysterious powers of the imagination, which the modern age is all too ready to equate with mere fantasy and to which it is keen to deny any substantive 'reality'. By way of response, he recalls the high function of the imagination as understood by the greatest of Romantic writers, such as Blake and Coleridge. Frequently, those who trust to the imagination, he states, are accused of failing to face up to reality and of wanting to 'turn the clock back'. But that is to adopt a false model of time, which is an endless changefulness, an endless becoming, as Henri Bergson had pointed out, an irreversible process at the very heart of which lies the enigma that we can never possibly tell exactly when 'now' becomes 'then'. For him, Thomas adds, Abercuawg too exists in exactly such a limbo-world, between potentiality and actuality. (In his strange 'autobiography' *Neb*, Thomas had likewise explained how he chose its title because that one word in Welsh could mean both 'no-one' and 'someone'.) All this leads him to emphasise that 'we shall have to build and rebuild Abercuawg anew, as a proof of the fact that it is something which is forever coming into existence, not something which has been frozen once and for all' (*SP*, 164). The labour of building will take imagination, sacrifice and effort, and the materials can only be those of the Welsh language.

It should therefore be clear that R. S. Thomas's lecture on Abercuawg is a seminal statement that has been unaccountably overlooked and underestimated by commentators. It is the definitive *apologia pro vita sua* of one who had taken upon himself the burden of being the national poet of Wales. And buried so deep within it as to have gone virtually unnoticed is his answer to the many nationalist critics who had been savaging him for more than a decade. Young cultural and political turks, they prided themselves on pragmatically accepting that their national aspirations had to be based on the 'realities' of bilingual contemporary Wales as they seemed to them to be, not on pipedreams such as those of the ageing R. S. Thomas. They accused him of having withdrawn from the heat of the struggle, of having retreated into antique fantasies, and in effect of having betrayed the younger generation. For them, he was divisive and obstructive. But above all, he was deeply reactionary; he had retreated to the imaginary Wales of a long distant past.

Thomas explicitly confronts this final accusation in his lecture. Indeed his long digression on the nature of time is related to that very issue. Time after time he repudiates any fixed, static, 'Platonic' view of the ideal he is outlining, a view that is wholly at odds with what Bergson has shown to be the nature of time, and therefore with existential human reality. He places his faith specifically in the eternal changefulness of things, and accordingly places his Abercuawg in the flow of time. It is a place that can be moulded only out of time and that can exist only in time. And it is a reminder to his compatriots that an alternative, infinitely better, future can indeed be fashioned in time but only through an immense timely effort both of imagination and of will – and here Thomas is obviously meaning to implicitly acknowledge the activities of the young people of Cymdeithas yr Iaith, and underlining that in actively and publicly supporting them he had in face taken a direct part in their struggle, rather than retreating to his dream world as his critics had asserted. He also implicitly asserts that a poet such as himself may have a vital role to play in this process of transformation, because Abercuawg is also a name for that imaginative power that poets uniquely possess, and for the potentialities of language that they are uniquely empowered to deploy.

It seems to me that 'Abercuawg' is crying out to be read alongside the review of *Bury My Heart at Wounded Knee*, because taken together they represent the positive and negative poles of Thomas's temperament, of his poetics, and of his view of Wales. The review is in essence a product of his tragic vision. A bleak picture is there offered of the present and future of Wales. Although then, as has already been noted, there is a sudden and somewhat unexpected turn for the better at the very end. Thomas knew that the heroic story of the Sioux peoples had come to a bloody end at Wounded Knee, an occasion which virtually marked the final extinction of a whole people. He also knew that the final act had been precipitated by a last great collective act of dreaming, known to history as the Ghost Dance. While he obviously feared that the common collective desires of his Wales could very well end up producing much the same outcome, in that final section of the review he summoned up confidence enough in his own different dream of Abercuawg to allow for the possibility, at least, that it might be turned into a redemptive reality. And he recognised that that could happen only if that dream were translated into radical, revolutionary, positive action. It is at this point that his review connects with his Abercuawg lecture. Because opposites although they may be, the two statements are nevertheless joined at the hip like some Siamese twins. From beginning to end the lecture is an insistent assertion that dreams have the power to alter the established order of things, since that 'order most Plantaganet', to quote Wallace Stevens's phrase for the apparently regal, unchallengeable majesty of existent conditions, is merely masquerading as inalterable 'reality'. Abercuawg is, then, Thomas's supreme attempt to convince his people that it is still open to them to avoid ending up at Wounded Knee.

IX

Many times during his final years, R. S. Thomas made it unambiguously clear that he wanted no grave, no monument; he wanted only to be cremated, to be thus committed to earth and scattered to the winds. Had it, however, proved possible to salvage his heart, at least, from that final conflagration, there is surely only one place where it could have been buried. And if some day a plaque, however modest and inconspicuous, is unveiled in memory of one of Wales's greatest warrior poets, then clearly the epitaph engraved on it should simply read: 'Bury my heart at Abercuawg.'

Notes

1. R. S. Thomas, 'Review of *Bury My Heart at Wounded Knee*', in Sandra Anstey (ed.), *R. S. Thomas: Selected Prose* (Bridgend: Poetry Wales Press, 1983) pp. 178–81 (176). Hereafter *SP*.

2. *County Echo and St Davids City Chronicle*, 18 December 2015; republished in the *Cambrian News*, Cardigan and Newcastle Emlyn edn, 30 December 2015. Delwyn Sion released a CD of songs about William B. James, titled *Chwilio am America* (Recordiau Dies, 2015). Evans was the subject of a BBC Wales documentary, *Little Big Welshman*, aired in 2002.

3. Innumerable books have been written about the battle. Among the most interesting is Stephen E. Ambrose, *Crazy Horse and Custer* (London: Simon and Schuster Pocket Books, 2003). The first modern Native American account is Vine Deloria Jr's epochal study *Custer Died For Your Sins: An Indian Manifesto* (New York: Macmillan, 1969), followed by James Welch (with Paul Stekler), *Killing Custer: The Battle of Little Bighorn and the Fate of the Plains Indians* (New York: Norton, 2007). Hereafter *KC*. A fascinating study of the strangest warrior leader of the Sioux is Larry McMurtry, *Crazy Horse* (London: Orion, Phoenix, 1999). For Custer, see Evan S. Connell, *Son of the Morning Star: General Custer and the Battle of the Little Bighorn* (London: Pan Books, 1986).

4. Brian W. Dippie, 'The Visual West', in Clyde A. Milner II, Carol A. O'Connor and Martha A. Sandweiss (eds), *The Oxford History of the American West* (Oxford: Oxford University Press, 1994), p. 676.

5. An invaluable overview of the Native American scene is Joy Porter and Kenneth M. Roemer (eds), *The Cambridge Companion to Native American Literature* (Cambridge: Cambridge University Press, 2005). Hereafter *CC*.

6. Vincent DeLoria Jr, *Custer Died For Your Sins: An Indian Manifesto*, Preface (New York: Macmillan, 1969). Hereafter *CDFS*.

7. See Peter Matthiessen, *In the Spirit of Crazy Horse* (New York: Viking, 1982).

8. Dee Brown, *Bury My Heart at Wounded Knee: An Indian History of the American West* (1971. London: Picador, 1975). See also the same author's *The American West* (London: Simon and Schuster Pocket Book, 2004).

9. Waldo Williams, 'Anglo-Welsh and Welsh' (1953), in Damian Walford Davies (ed.), *Waldo Williams: Rhyddiaith* (Cardiff: University of Wales Press, 2001), pp. 157–8.

10. For some reason, Brown has very little to say about the Comanches, the most formidable of all the peoples of the South West and the Mexican border, whose confrontation with the Texas Rangers has acquired legendary status in that part of the country. For the history of the Comanches, see T. R. Fehrenbach, *Comanches: the History of A People* (London: Pimlico, 2005). A fictional version of the response of the Rangers is Larry McMurtry's Lonesome Dove quartet (*Lonesome Dove* (1986), *Streets of Laredo* (1993), *Dead Man's Walk* (1995), *Comanche Moon* (1997)).

11. See Brian Schofield, *Selling Your Father's Bones: The Epic Fate of the American West* (New York: HarperCollins, 2008).

12. Originally woodland dwellers in the upper Mid-West, the Sioux divided as they moved westward into three different groups: the Dakotas (semisedentary), the Nakotas, and the huge contingent of Lakotas, who were the horse-riding Plains riders *par excellence*. In turn, the Lakotas became subdivided into seven tribes: the Oglalas, Brulés, Miniconjous, Two Kettles, Hunkpapas, Blackfeet, and the Sans Arcs. Between them the Oglalas and the Brulés outnumbered all the non-Lakota on the northern plains. The Sioux gradually formed (frequently tense) alliances with the Arapahos and the Cheyennes, particularly when confronting the Crows and the Pawnee, driving both peoples eventually into alliance with the invading whites. As the pressures on them increased, the Cheyennes split into the Southern Cheyennes, who moved south to escape the Lakotas, and the Northern Cheyennes who co-existed with them. Further South, the Kiowas retreated under pressure from the Sioux and entered the territory of the Comanches, sparking conflict that eventually led to uneasy alliance.

13. Peter Cozzens, *The Earth is Weeping: The Epic Story of the Indian Wars for the American West* (New York: Alfred Knopf, 2016).

14. For a full account of the education initiative see Alan Trachtenberg, *Shades of Hiawatha: Staging Indians, Making Americans, 1880–1930* (New York: Hill and Wang, 2004).

15. *SP*, p. 179.

16. 'The Rising of Glyndŵr', *Song at the Year's Turning* (London: Rupert Hart-Davis, 1965 edn), p. 23. Hereafter *SYT*.

17. For a full, excellent discussion of this issue and the response of Welsh writers to it, see 'The Battle for the Hills: Politicized Landscapes and the Erasure of Place', in Kirsti Bohata, *Postcolonialism Revisited* (Cardiff: University of Wales Press, 2004), pp. 80–103.

18. 'Rhydcymerau', trans. in Donald Allchin, D. Densil Morgan and Patrick Thomas (eds), *Sensuous Glory: The Poetic Vision of D. Gwenallt Jones* (Norwich; Canterbury Press, 2000), p. 114. Hereafter *SG*.

19. 'Afforestation', in R. S. Thomas, *Collected Poems, 1945–1990* (London: Phoenix, 1993), p. 130. Hereafter *CP*.

20. Quoted in Matthew Jarvis, *Welsh Environments in Contemporary Poetry* (Cardiff: University of Wales Press, 2008), p. 30.

21. Robert Rhys, 'T. Gwynn Jones and the Renaissance of Welsh Poetry', in Geraint Evans and Helen Fulton (eds), *The Cambridge History of Welsh Literature* (Cambridge: Cambridge University Press, 2019), p. 377.

22. Waldo Williams, 'Preseli', in Alan Llwyd and Robert Rhys (eds), *Waldo Williams: Cerddi 1922–1970* (Llandysul: Gwasg Gomer, 2014), p. 253. Hereafter *WWC*.

23. See '"Yr Hen Fam": R. S. Thomas and the Church in Wales', in M. Wynn Thomas, *All That Is Wales* (Cardiff: University of Wales Press, 2017), pp. 165–84.

24. Jason Walford Davies, *Gororau'r Iaith: R. S. Thomas a'r Traddodiad Llenyddol Cymraeg* (Caerdydd: Gwasg Prifysgol Cymru, 2003), p. 144.

25. Dorian Llywelyn, *Sacred Place, Chosen People* (Cardiff: University of Wales Press, 1999). Hereafter *SPCP*.

26. W. C. Bryant (ed.), *Picturesque America*, 2 vols (D. Appleton: New York, 1872).

27. For a full discussion of this subject, see 'For Wales, See Landscape', in M. Wynn Thomas, *R. S. Thomas: Serial Obsessive* (Cardiff: University of Wales Press, 2013), pp. 37–66.

28. Quoted in Alan Llwyd, *Barddoniaeth y Chwedegau: Astudiaeth Lenyddol-hanesyddol* (Caernarfon: Cyhoeddiadau Barddas, 1986), p. 19. Hereafter *BC*.

29. James Welch, *Fools Crow* (London: Penguin, 2011), p. 166.

30. The best insights into Thomas's activities as an activist during his Aberdaron period may be found in Gareth Neigwl Williams (ed.), *Cofio R.S.: Cleniach yn Gymraeg?* (Caernarfon: Gwasg y Bwthyn, 2013), p. 42.

31. Phil Carradice, 'Buffalo Bill in Wales' https://www.bbc.co.uk/blogs/Wales/ entries (accessed 20 June 2021).

32. 'Buffalo Bill Show', *The Aberdare Times*, 25 September 1886, Welsh Newspapers Online: https://newspapers.library.wales/view/3026975/3026978/24/ (accessed 4 October 2023).

33. See Jerry Hunter, *Llwybrau Cenhedloedd: Cyd-Destunoli'r Genhadaeth Gymreig i'r Tsalagi* (Caerdydd: Gwasg Prifysgol Cymru, 2012).

34. John Ehle, *Trail of Tears: The Rise and Fall of the Cherokee Nation* (London: Doubleday, 1988), pp. 299–301. Hereafter *TT*.

IV.
INTERVIEWS

Interview with Rita Dove

Born in Akron, Ohio in 1952, Rita Dove was US Poet Laureate at the Library of Congress from 1993 to 1995. She was awarded the Pulitzer Prize in 1987, and was recipient of the 2022 Ruth Lilly Poetry Prize. Her publications include *Thomas and Beulah* (1986), *Grace Notes* (1989), *Mother Love* (1995), *Sonata Mulattica* (2009), *Collected Poems 1974–2004* (2016). She edited the *Penguin Anthology of 20th-Century American Poetry* (2011). This interview took place in Swansea on 12 August 1995, and was published as 'Rita Dove Talks to M. Wynn Thomas', *Swansea Review*, 19 (1995), 158–63.

MWT: You're coming to the end of your term as Poet Laureate of the United States. Clearly it's an honour and has involved ceremonial duties, does it seem to you that it has also served a more serious purpose?

RD: The ceremonial duties for the American Poet Laureate are not that onerous or defined. I rarely felt that I was being forced to 'popularise' poetry, or in any way make it simple or tailored for some kind of ceremonial rite. Since I wasn't required to write occasional poems, if I was ever asked to 'say a few words' at an event, I had the freedom to do whatever I wished: either to talk, or to recite a poem if I already had a poem appropriate to the moment. I was very careful not to compromise the art itself. A lot of what I've done these past two years has involved educating young people in matters of poetry, and bringing real poetry into real life – and by that I mean serious and difficult poetry. My experience has been that as soon as people are relaxed, even very difficult poetry becomes accessible. It's when someone is told: 'This is great literature: you should appreciate it' that they get uptight and don't do very well with the poem. So by helping introduce people to poetry and widening the audience for poetry, I do think my term has served a more serious purpose.

MWT: You're a poet: you're also African-American. Are you an African-American poet?

RD: I've never been sure what exactly it's supposed to mean, to be called an African-American poet or a woman poet. I'm a woman, I'm an African-American. My poems often reflect these two aspects of myself. With some of my poems, obviously, you can't tell race or gender. A recent poem called 'Evening Primroses', for example, is about that particular flower. How can one tell who wrote that? My own reluctance with being labelled an African-American poet comes from battling the assumption that this means writing in a racially programmatic way. As far as I'm concerned, no programmatic poetry, no matter how well meant the ideology, can be truly as free. So long as we agree that that's not what you mean, I'll say yes, I'm an African-American poet; I'm a woman poet; I'm an American poet: all those things. But I'm a poet first.

MWT: Could I ask a similar question, but in a different way. Have you got a sense of your place, vis-à-vis other American poets, Langston Hughes, for example, Gwendolyn Brooks, Michael Harper, Robert Hayden – or, for that matter, to think differently about you, James Wright, and his poetry relating to Ohio. Is that the way you place yourself?

RD: I don't try to place myself. I'll leave that up to the critics. That sounds corny, but I feel a part of a literary family, a community of both living and dead poets. In the way of families, I may argue vehemently with other relatives sometimes, but the empathy – the fact of inclusion – is always there. I feel a deep affinity with Langston Hughes, and Gwendolyn Brooks and Richard Wright – indeed, with what one could call the African-American canon of literature. I remember discovering Langston Hughes in an anthology when I was in my teens and reading a poem like 'Dream Boogie', where the language just hops and leaps all over the page, and recognising a part of my life that I hadn't ever encountered in a poem before That recognition is incredibly vital to my personal and spiritual identity. I don't know if my own work reflects this, but I know the influence is there. I don't think anyone's ever mentioned James Wright as a possible influence before, but I do feel an affinity to him as well – because Ohio is my home state and I recognise, in his work, a certain attitude and inflection – that Midwestern, flat, no-nonsense tone – that's part of me, too.

MWT: What about that other side of Wright that interests me, the sense you have that he speaks for the socially mute, as you might say; that his is a poetry flaring out of deprivation. I get that in *Thomas and Beulah*, for example. Is that a fair comment?

RD: That's more than fair. One of the things that attracts me to James Wright is his way of speaking for the mute. I've been fascinated by what I've called before 'the underside of history', the dramas of ordinary people – the quiet courage of their actions, all which buoy up the big events. In *Thomas and Beulah*, for instance, I had great fun with the chronology at the end, because it gave me the chance to intersperse important historical events with the things that never really stand a chance of appearing in history texts, such as the birth of a grandson. Putting these private events on equal footing with historical occurrences is a way of saying that the personal and historical are equally important.

MWT: I think the question comes partly out of my own Welsh background, and by the way, a feature of Welsh poetry in Welsh and English has been its sense of responsibility for the collective. Now that, up to a point, has been absent from American poetry, where the ethos of individualism has been very strong. I sense it in you, though, and I wonder whether that comes from a black tradition – you get it in Hayden, for example.

RD: You certainly get it in the black tradition, yes. You get it in Robert Hayden, and in Michael Harper – when he writes those homages to blues musicians, it's as if he's saying: 'And remember this person in the community … and remember this one, too.' He's paying his respects. The ethos of collective responsibility is present not only in the poetry, but in real life. One is always conscious that everything one does can reflect on the community, and every decision made is not entirely one's own to make. But I've never felt this to be oppressive;

rather, the tenor is more: 'Do what you have to, but just understand what effect it will have, what legacy you will leave.' That's all. But that's enough! As for me – I never think of my audience when I write a poem. I try to write out of whatever is haunting me; in order for a poem to feel authentic. I have to feel I am treading on very danger- ous ground, which can mean that the resulting revelations may prove hurtful to other people. The time for thinking about that kind of guilt or any collective sense of responsibility, however, occurs much later in the creative process, after the poem is finished. At that point, I must decide what I will do with it – publish it, or put it away.

MWT: You also seem to me to explore relationships in your poetry – *Mother Love*, for example, deals with this in a very complex way, and in a way that suggests to me you may feel relationships are constitutive of a woman's being to a degree greater than they are of a man's. Is that fair?

RD: I haven't thought it through on a rational level yet, because this book is still very fresh. I do find relationships to be kaleidoscopic and infinitely changing; no relationship is ever clear or safe, no matter how intrinsically wonderful it is and all that. The relationship between mother and daughter, for me, is incredibly rich ground. But, simply because I am both mother and daughter, I can't speak for the male relationship in the same way. For instance, I've been working on a group of poems about the black soldiers in the First World War, who fought under the French command. They're in voice – that is, they're persona poems – and I find them to be some of the hardest poems I've ever written. Those poems are taking a long time; I will finish them eventually, or they'll finish me. But I'm finding great difficult with entering that masculine world, that particular sensibility. Sometimes it feels presumptuous even to attempt it.

MWT: Although you did it in *Thomas and Beulah*, didn't you? There you manage to even-up the relationship.

RD: Yes, that's true – and though I didn't write the poems chrono- logically, I did begin with the Thomas poems. I think one of the differences sprang from the fact that Thomas was based on my maternal grandfather, so there was a feeling that I was writing about family, and I felt that I knew him well enough. The chief difficulties with the soldier poems lie in the different period – all the poems occur during the First World War – plus the fact that each poem is about a different soldier, so I can't simply spend the entire book exploring the thoughts and emotions of one character. Each soldier is represented by one short persona poem, and each man is discovered in a situation that for centuries has been considered the domain of the masculine. All these factors make the writing quite challenging.

MWT: Again, and related to what I've been asking you about, it seems to me you alternate between the subjectivism of the lyric, as you might say, exploring your own world very intensely, and on the other hand a generously empathic sense of other people's lives. Is this, to use Whitman's expression, the systole and diastole of your imagination?

RD: Mm … That's kind of nice, isn't it? Because that's what our heart does all the time … that rhythm, that push-and-pull, feels natural to us. For me, it goes back again to the community. The storytellers from my childhood basically told stories about other people – eccentrics in the family, neighbourhood. What made these stories effective, and what qualified someone as a great storyteller, was the degree of intimacy the story conjured – which meant in another sense, how metaphoric and lyric the stories were. It wasn't about getting to the point: 'What did Uncle Bob do with that broken-down car?' Rather, the journey of the narrative was interesting, and therefore the telling of that journey was paramount. So you see that even before I began to read, I had discovered the delight of shaping life with words. I think I'll never want to be rid of this delicious tension between the telling and the tale – which, when translated into the lyric and the narrative, is part of the systolic and diastolic of the poetry. In *Thomas and Beulah*, for instance, I was consciously trying to put a narrative into short lyric poems – stringing the lyric moments one after the other like beads on a necklace; I was working the lyric moment against the narrative impulse, so that they would counterpoint each other. In the States, there has been an unfortunate division between narrative poetry and lyric poetry; frankly, I've never felt that much of a difference. A good poem usually has both. A lyric may not have a traditional narrative

line, but it all depends what you define as story. Even a leaf falling
from a tree is a pretty dramatic story … to the leaf!

MWT: Now I'm going to hazard another generalisation! It seems to me
that in your poetry a recurrent dialectic is that between the attraction
towards the safety of closure, on the one hand, and impulse to surrender to 'the lack of conclusion / the eternal dénouement' on the
other. And your stance as a poet is for me captured in the opening
stanza of 'The Other Side of the House':

> I walk out the kitchen doors
> trailing extension cords into the open
> gaze of the Southwest.

RD: This was especially interesting – exactly this tension – when I
was working on the poems in *Mother Love*. Most of them are some
variation on a sonnet, so even while they are encaged, they felt very
dangerous to me.

MWT: And yet you don't write processual poetry, do you? You're
attracted to the closed forms.

RD: I'm attracted to them, but I think they're ultimately false. The
temptation of being charmed by a well-made box is very great. To
me, the pleasures to be gotten from a well-made box are not as great,
ultimately, as opening the box and letting the stuff out. I love boxes
– I'm a crossword fanatic – but I realise that no box is ever that
perfect. Maybe that's why I like playing around with them! While I
was writing the sonnets in *Mother Love*, I worried incessantly, because
I didn't want to be lured into an end line that only sounded right,
an ending that underscored complacency. Sometimes you can trick
yourself into thinking that something – a line, a rhythm, an image –
is really interesting, when all it really does is complete a predictable
or clever fit. In a review which included *Thomas and Beulah*, Helen
Vendler speculated what each of the poets might be tempted to try
next. I loved that gesture – because to the writer, all that's important
is what comes next. Anyway, she wished for me an attempt at looser
poems. But what did I do but head right for the sonnet! And yet …

even in this book of sonnets there is a seven-part poem in free verse, set in contemporary Paris, called 'Persephone in Hell', which ranges all over the place in terms of voices, dialogue, rhythms, dictions. I had so much fun writing that poem; the freedom was exhilarating. Though it *was* very frightening not to have my box!

MWT: Another way in which you tighten not form but sound, is through exploring the musicality of language. I know *Grace Notes* is itself a musical expression, but I was thinking beyond that. In that collection particularly, again as a Welshman I suppose, I was very aware of the play of sounds going on there. Now you're an accomplished musician. Does that carry over, or is it something quite different? Music, music and poetry – are they something quite different from each other?

RD: I don't think they're much different from each other. In my case, at least, they complement each other. I played the cello from my tenth year all the way through college and a little beyond, and then I switched to the viola da gamba, which I still play. I also sing – opera, strictly amateur. Consequently, I have a good sense of phrasing, the movement of the musical line both within and across measure bars. I guess it's true to form that I prefer Mozart over Beethoven. Music and poetry have much in common: the sense of a poem moves in and out of sync with the music of its language, which creates a marvellous kind of vibration – a *frisson* – and all unsaid things between those two poles keep a poem churning. And for me, if a poem doesn't have a sense of music, its own cage of sound against which the denotative struggles ... then that poem probably won't move me very much. There's a corollary to my music connection: when it comes to learning a foreign language; I tend to be very empathetic. I hear the music of the language first: cadences in phrasing, predominant sounds – fricatives, sibilants and so forth. Then I pick up the intricacies of that language as if learning a piece of music. There are definite drawbacks to this empathy; for instance, my husband claims that I adjust my speech, chameleon-like, to imitate the person I'm speaking with. When we're in Germany, and I meet somebody who speaks a different dialect – like Swiss-German, which has a distinctive lilting cadence – after about an hour's conversation, I'm using the same inflections, and my husband is nudging me, because he's afraid they'll think I'm making fun of their speech. Incidentally, I've had a lot of trouble here in Wales trying not to talk with a Welsh accent!

MWT: So you're very receptive to rhythm and pitch of speech, and that helps you presumably when you dramatise, when you're speaking in voices.

RD: Yes, I think so.

MWT: An apparently new interest of yours in myth surfaces in *Mother Love*. On the other hand, you've always been fascinated by the way humans live in a highly coloured and phantasmagoric reality, by the way, for example, that silos can look like cigarettes if we're middle-aged, or like a fresh packet of chalk when we're children. You've said earlier that this may be related to your earlier background. Is there any other way you'd account for it?

RD: I was reminded, when you referred to a 'highly coloured and phantasmagoric reality' – among the black oral tropes are the traditions of Signifying and Toasts. Toasts are improvisations on standard tales which are orated in a kind of doggerel. The Toast revolves around a semi-mythical character and his or her adventures, which are always wildly exaggerated versions of what possibly could happen. The point is to improve upon the story, adding incidents, embroidering the death-defying feats. In many ways, Toasts are allegories, and their legendary figures, Shine or Stag-o-Lee, are the black equivalents to Odysseus or Perseus. Signifying, on the hand, is the art of speaking sarcastically about someone while they are listening; but you must be creative and sophisticated in this verbal abuse, or you'll have failed. A sub-genre of Signifying is called 'playing the dozens', where the point is to malign your opponent's mother, and to do so with insults that are absolutely outrageous and gorgeously creative, for example: 'Your mother's so ugly, you could put her face in a bowl of dough and make gorilla cookies.' Now in a manner similar to Toasts, a myth stays the same and yet always changes. We know the story-line of most myths; the Greek myths have been rammed down our throats for centuries. So why do we still like to hear them told? Because even though we know every detail of their plots, they're still ultimately mysterious; their meaning deepens. As we grow and learn to traffic in the world, we can bring our experiences to the template of this or that mythic allegory, and it will provide both a grid upon which to batten our own emotional confusion and a frame – an aperture setting – through which to contemplate our inner selves.

Interview with Jorie Graham

Born in New York City in 1950, Jorie Graham is the author of numerous collections of poetry, including *Hybrids of Plants and Ghosts* (1980), *Erosion* (1983), *The End of Beauty* (1987), *Region of Unlikeness* (1991), *The Dream of the Unified Field: Selected Poems 1974–1992* (1995) (winner of the Pulitzer Prize for Poetry), *Never* (2002), *Sea Change* (2008), *Place* (2012) (winner of the Forward Poetry Prize for best collection), *From the New World* (2015), *Fast* (2017), and *Runaway* (2020). She has taught for many years at Harvard University as the Boylston Professor of Rhetoric and Oratory, the first woman to hold this position. This interview took place in Swansea on 31 March 1995. It originally appeared in *Swansea Review*, 16 (1996), 1–8.

MWT: It strikes me that in your poetry, cinema – one way or another – is given a prominent place. It's either a location, as in the first poem in *Region of Unlikeness*; or you make mention of it, as if you had found a correspondence between what you are doing and certain techniques in film; or film is for you a trope or analogy for some mode of our being or state of our existence. Could you help me understand it further than that?

JG: I would imagine the ways in which things are connected via editing in film had a great influence on the way I perceived cause and effect – at least at a certain point in my life. You have to understand, I didn't speak English very well until I was eighteen and came to school in the US. I enrolled in a cinema studies programme – partly because it seemed to me the programme where a universal language was being spoken.

　　I was in New York, eighteen years old, and spoke broken English with a French accent. I didn't think I was going to do very well unless I could find a language in which I could communicate rather quickly. And I became very interested in editing. Now it's all done with a computer on a console, it's all on tape, but in those days we actually shot film and spliced it and glued little bits of tape on it – on what was called a moviola. You had to determine where one shot ended, where the next shot began. Visually. There was no devising alternative methods for cutting – so the sense of *what* was juxtaposed to *what* was, I think, really important to me.

Of course, the film editing techniques that come to us through the theories of Eisenstein, and which are first manifested in the famous Potemkin step sequence in his movie by that name, taught us a great deal about how a collision of conflicting images could give birth to an alternative reality, an imaginative reality, in which a cause and effect are linked which might not be evident in the actual place the poem (or film) attempted to record. And too, Eisenstein said he developed his theories by simply trying to transfer onto celluloid what Dickens did in his novels; so I'm not sure that these are such avant garde techniques. But they do have to do with the illusion of continuity, and how it's manifest in a poem. I'm interested in leaps that hold together, and, as I move from book to book, I think I've become more interested in how far one can leap, how great the juxtaposition can be between two images or gestures, or statements, and still attain coherence. I'm not interested in a reader-based activity, in which the coherence is radically different for each reader. I'm interested in a coherence which can come about through juxtaposition.

I tried to read some poems tonight in which things were rather far apart from each other, but in which either the music of the poem could tell you the ways in which the things were connected, or in which inherent information in the images pulled them together. So that a meaning which might not be a rational meaning, which might not be a logical meaning, which might not be a meaning which could be grasped through exposition or even through thematic description, can still be gleaned. It seems to me that *that* meaning is why we read poetry, that intuitive sense of 'I'm not sure what this means but I can feel it' – that sensation of meaning. It's not alternative to knowing, it's just a form of knowledge that we tend to otherwise degrade in the culture.

MWT: There's a lovely phrase in one of your poems where you talk about a 'cadenza of gaps'. Is that in line with what you're talking about? Is that a way of talking about your poetics?

JG: Yes, but if you think about some of those gaps and those link-
ages, one of the most prevalent places in which they are used in our
culture is advertising. More and more, you might have noticed, for
example, narratives are collapsing out of television commercials,
and the sellers, the ad-people, are trying to create dizzying associations between objects and contexts that are supposed to lead you
to a sensation of desire, one that will lead you to acquire a given
object. It seems to me important that such leaping, which is the
province and signature activity of a great deal of human intuition, not be allowed to degrade to such uses as it is put to by our
consumer culture.

    If you read Julian of Norwich's – or Teresa of Avila's, or St John
of the Cross's – description of deity (in their case the Christ before
them), what you will notice are the gaps, the incredible intuitive leaps,
that take place. Dream-life takes place within such illogical sequences.
Again, this is not an alternative to knowledge; it is merely the form of
intellectual knowledge that we tend, in this culture, most to distrust –
a culture that tends perhaps to over-privilege rational or scientific or
certain kinds of mechanistic knowledge.

    Of course, when I use the term 'scientific', I instantly have to
hesitate, because the advanced science of our day is in fact a leaping
dance – more intuitive and more mystical and more filled with the
kinds of lies-that-tell-the-truth, the great imaginative lies, than probably any other current province of knowledge outside the arts. We
have survived the great schism between religion and science. And
though nobody knows all that much about either, they're starting to
use the word God again when they try to describe what is expanding
out there. It's interesting.

MWT: How much personal belief do you have?

JG: I have what I would call 'belief'. I believe in God: I'm not sure what
I would mean by that, other than a sensation which is not its opposite. I'm not sure about most things, except that I'm sure that I don't
know, and that I couldn't live without the sensation of an immanent
presence in the world. I can't imagine spending a single day in the
physical universe without believing very quickly that something much
more complicated than the human mind is at work; something much

more complicated and profound than anything the human mind can really, in the end, approach – something numinous.

I don't like religious institutions – mostly I don't like the human intermediaries between me and the sensation we would call the sacred, or the numinous, which you can approach via not-knowing. I don't like priests, ministers or rabbis, although I think they're fine if they're doing a good job. I don't feel sin is a useful concept except on a personal level. At any rate, I don't like the intermediary; I have a hard time with organised religion. But I love the buildings that organised religion has built for us, because they *are* sacred – the ways in which cathedrals in Europe, in particular, are often the products of six, seven, nine hundred years of anonymous work … I mean, one might recognise a Signorelli fresco, or a Piero della Francesca fresco, but the amount of human energy, and belief, and devotion, and hard work and craft and intelligence and sheer passage of time, and death, that has built those buildings is as awe-inspiring an idea to hold in the mind as anything in the cosmology of the universe. Who are all the people who built the cathedral in Orvieto? Think of all their work, every hand-laid, hand-carved, hand-quarried stone … It took six hundred years to complete that church. Such a huge, sacred, amount of labour, in itself, for me, constitutes a form of belief.

MWT: In reading your poem 'From the New World', you said that the capital 'Y' was important at one point in the word 'You'. Is that where you call God to witness, or indeed call God to account in that particular poem?

JG: I imagine that gesture, by the speaker of the poem, to be a some-what helpless attempt to bring the sensation of that level of witness into the purviews the poem inhabits. The fact that the text 'you' is not capitalised, but actually addressed to the audience, or to the reader, was an attempt on my part, in writing that particular book of poems, to feel the simultaneous presence of two different kinds of witnesses: human witnesses (readers) and the larger witness, in which one is, also, accountable – God, time, and history, whatever.

When I wrote *The End of Beauty* I began to feel – or imagine – how very much people were exhausted by books, how the amount of space, time, solitude, and deep loneliness, involved in the act of solitary reading, is being threatened by our culture. In many different ways, I kept trying to image, for myself, someone – a total stranger – picking up this thing of pages and words, summoning up that ghost, attempting to make contact with that figure. That imaginary figure was correlative, of course, for any kind of imaginary listener – including God I guess ... All poems, it seems to me, being a form of invocation or prayer, attempt to clear the space, so that one can hear, not just be heard.

MWT: I was very intrigued by your description of your background. Can I ask you whether nostalgia has any part in your writing?

JG: Well, in each of the books I essentially had an encounter with something I would consider 'other', something that resists the will of the speaker. In the first book I read from tonight, *Erosion*, the encounter was primarily with paintings – and what intrigued me about visual representations was their apparently eternal nature, the ways in which the events could not be altered and yet were always taking place, not unlike what is undertaken (obviously much more brilliantly and succinctly) by Keats in 'Ode on a Grecian Urn' ... At any rate, in the next book, *The End of Beauty*, the place of paintings in that dynamic was taken by myth. I went primarily to Greek and Roman myths (and some other myths as well), attempting to engage in a dialogue with them.

In the book after that, *Region of Unlikeness*, I tried to use the kind of fact we think of as autobiographical as the texture against which I was testing my sense of what knowing, or thinking, or feeling is. In many ways, I used autobiographical fact in those poems as a kind of tuning fork by which to gauge the sense of reality in what I was saying. I'm not sure I would consider them 'confessional' poems, or poems that are interested in using autobiographical detail to explain anything about how the speaker of the poem has ended up being who she is. But autobiographical fact was so intoxicatingly resistant to me in the writing of that book, in the way the myth of Daphne and Apollo is resistant. You know, certain things took place in it. She doesn't turn around and say, 'Gee, I don't want to be a tree after all, I'll marry you' – she turns into a tree, and that's that, just as in the first book, the painting by Lucas Signorelli is forever the way it's going to be.

That interested me. I was trying to find those places in my auto-biography where the facts were unalterable (uninterpretable really): these people were put in a nursing home; he needed a telephone; her pocket-book was white ... I did something that is difficult for me: I didn't change facts. There are certain details in it about my father's and mother's life for example, that I might have altered slightly 'to protect the innocent', as it were, but I didn't. I layered them in – the way at a certain point the Cubist painters felt compelled to have an actual piece of newspaper in there; it couldn't just be a painted representation of a newspaper. I tried to understand what can swirl about something so resistant; what the imagination is; what it's capable of; what you can invent, once you have the tuning-fork of something as stable as an autobiographical fact in there ... It was an imaginative vertigo that was very useful for me, at that time. Obviously, if I believed that facts were truly real I would just write out the narrative! Rather, because I believe that the thing that can be invented by the presence of the facts – what swirls around them, the cloud-chamber if you will – is real, much more so, perhaps, than the who-did-what-to-whom – I used it in that book.

Whether that involves an act of nostalgia I don't know ... perhaps nostalgia for a time in which one believed the stories that one was told were true, a nostalgia we all share. Nostalgia for the descriptions the Science of our childhoods gave us for the infrastructure of matter, for example. Remember? It was so simple. There were not fifty different kinds of quarks with strange names, being born as they disappeared, material and not-material at the same time ... Just think what that's doing to all of us. We used to have little wooden models of how the atom was, and we were told that's what the table was made of. I have no idea what that table's made of now; nobody else does either. And they keep going deeper and deeper into it, finding stranger and stranger things. And yet I think *that* relativity is an experience I now want to have in the act of writing the poems; I want the poem itself to keep slipping for me – so that I'm compelled to keep inventing – until I bump into something which might be stable enough to 'feel true'.

MWT: Here in Wales, a great deal of poetry has been written that is a poetry of place – for various reasons we won't go into. In one of the early poems you say we've now got texture instead of place, instead of history. That seems to me to be quite close to the sense I get reading your poetry; that when you go back, what you really recover is a sense of texture, of density, of atmosphere, of feel? Is that right?

JG: The book entitled *Materialism* in fact tries to use physical place as the resistant material. Many of its poems are extended acts of description. And a great deal of the drama for me in writing those poems was feeling the degree to which, the minute an adjective was introduced, for example – the minute the noun itself came to be coloured, pushed into a syntax, into a sentence – the place you think you could possibly touch in language – or evoke or approach – is already invaded, colonised, dangerously trespassed-upon. And, for me, in that book, the act of description becomes a metaphorical place in which I can undertake sensations that we might otherwise call 'colonial' or 'imperialist' – landings of all kinds on the shoreline of the visible.

The way in which intellectual America decided to 'reverse' its position on Columbus in 1992 got a little tedious, and the accompanying exclusive notion of genocidal Europeans who had inflicted vast amounts of savagery upon a completely innocent continent got tedious. We descend from human beings, who, among other things, inflicted savagery upon a continent of people already inflicting savagery upon one another. We were yet another wave of human desire. And so on.

At any rate, the insatiable destructiveness of human curiosity got acted out, for me, in that book, in the very act of description itself. I mean if I'm going to see this or that – the minute I have an adjective, or simile, or metaphor in mind – I'm really beginning to be a Columbus of the imagination.

MWT: You've touched on the literature of ancient Greece and ancient Rome, but the tragedy is that only a tiny percentage of what those ancient people wrote, what they believed, what they thought, has come down to us … so it's as if they were writing a message in a bottle, with a small chance of being washed up on the shore of a distant epoch. Think of Sophocles: he wrote 128 plays, and we have only seven.

JG: Well, there are more recent examples. Do you know the poems of the British poet Thomas Traherne, who wrote in the early seventeenth

century? As I understand it, only one thing was published in his lifetime, and it was published under the name of the woman who ran
the abbey he lived in. In 1892, a bookseller in London sold a volume
to someone, a volume that had handwritten poems in it. They were
the first evidence that a poet named Thomas Traherne had lived, but
no-one really knew who he was. They connected him up with that
poem by the Abbess, but it took until 1968 for his poems to be truly
brought to light.

That happened when someone bought a house (somewhere in
England), and while emptying out the attic of the house, burning the
unwanted contents of the attic, the man tending the fire, admiring
the leather on a couple of volumes that were in the fire, pulled them
out to get the leather off. Those volumes held in handwritten form
most of the works of Thomas Traherne (some much modified by his
brother Philip). Some of those manuscripts haven't even been tran-
scribed yet ... they're still in manuscript form at Yale and Princeton, I
think ... Traherne is, to my mind, as great as Henry Vaughan or John
Donne, yet but for the little greed coursing through the heart of that
groundskeeper (you see, greed is such a good thing!) – his curiosity,
his desire for that leather – we would have no Thomas Traherne.

Who knows what else has vanished? I couldn't agree more; the
whole thing is messages tossed in bottles that very well might not get
anywhere. But it's the act of doing it, the act of believing in it – and
what it is you believe you can make out of words – that counts. Just
think, you can make things no-one can own! That's one of the loveli-
est things about a poem. It's one of the strangest characteristics that
attaches to something made out of words. When I'm holding a copy
of 'Ode on a Grecian Urn', who does it belong to? If it vanished in
a great fire, and no-one every saw it again, would it have vanished?

MWT: For me, one of the most powerful poems in your work is that
one about the two paintings of Klimt. Can you tell us any more about
the resonance of that poem for you? For instance, the extraordinary
fact (I take it to be) of that painting on Klimt's easel. What it was, as
you say, is the naked woman he was then going to cover with design
and fabric. The meanings of that for you must have been multiple;
would one of them have been expressive of your own ambiguous
feelings towards art, and what it does? To what extent it creates a

'shapeliness' (one of your words), the 'click shut' of closure (you talk about), the form which can distort, obscure and occlude? Is that part of it, or is it not?

JG: Yes, you should just keep talking, it sounds great! I think it was fascinating to discover that the pornographic attention in the painting, which was accidentally made visible to the world, apparently exists beneath Klimt's paintings of women in general. And that he was painting what comes to be known as his signature surface, his covering – a somewhat violent activity. It seemed very true to me. It seemed a great intuition, an action which had, embedded in it, an intuition as the nature of beauty – or the surface of things that create the sensation of beauty – the surfaces that creates a sensation of meaning – the coherence of the visible over the violent core of desire.

It's such a complex image, I think I've been unpacking it for twenty years, but it definitely has to do again with a form of desire: we see its positive effects in art and we see its negative effects in people putting gas in the subways of Japan. Desire is not necessarily vectored towards the positive or the negative – it's just a fuel that burns in us – and figuring how to experience it, make it shapely (not destroying it through the act of shapelessness), how to make it meaningful (but not destroying it through the attempt to impose meanings), how to keep it alive and yet not letting it overwhelm us, seems to me embedded in that activity of Klimt's. And so I find it very moving.

Interview with Helen Vendler

Helen Vendler was born in Boston, Massachusetts, in 1933, and passed away in April 2024. At the time of her passing, she was A. Kingsley Porter University Professor Emerita at Harvard University. Her voluminous body of work includes *On Extended Wings: Wallace Stevens' Longer Poems* (1969), *Wallace Stevens: Words Chosen out of Desire* (1986), *The Given and the Made: Strategies of Poetic Redefinition* (1995), *Our Secret Discipline: Yeats and Lyric Form* (2007) and *The Ocean, the Bird, and the Scholar: Essays on Poets and Poetry* (2015). In 2004, the National Endowment for the Humanities selected her for the Jefferson Lecture, the federal government's highest honour for achievement in the humanities. She speaks of how she got to know M. Wynn Thomas in the 'Foreword' to this volume. The following interview took place at Swansea on 28 May 1995, and first appeared in *Swansea Review*, 16 (1996), 1–8.

MWT: These days, students at university seem to be positively afraid of poetry. Have you any advice to offer as to how that fear may best be allayed, or overcome?

HV: I agree that they haven't seen enough poetry to feel comfortable with it, so the first thing they need to do is to hear a poem read in the human voice, making it sound like an utterance that a genuine human voice might utter. The other thing I think needs to be done, in order to get on to more interesting discussions of the poem, is that the teacher should say, 'This is a poem about somebody who's very upset because he's just been jilted. These are his responses. Now let's talk about how the author has decided to present it.' That is, not by saying, 'What do you think the first line means?', and then, 'What do you think the second line means?' An inchworm progress through the poem leaves the students without a view of the whole. You don't understand what the first line means until you've understood the whole.

So it seems to me that to present them with the import of the poem is the right thing to do first. Then to say: 'Now you see it falls into three stanzas: why is it? Why do you suppose this is the way experience is arranged? If this is the arrangement of the experience here, can you think of a different way to arrange it? What if stanza two came first? Or what if stanza two had come last instead of stanza three being last?' The poem has to be made comprehensible as a human utterance. There shouldn't be any problem about knowing what it's about, and then you can go on to see it as a work of art comfortably, rather than having the students feel puzzled.

MWT: Does that mean you have no objection whatsoever to treating poetry as if it were the voice of experience – as if the author were present, at the level of experience, in what was written on the page?

HV: It depends very much on the poem that you're starting with. If you're starting with something that is a widely accepted common experience – love, death, what-have-you – it seems that you must meet it first at that level. But there are poems that are about odd, marginal experience, or nonsense poems, or something where it seems the right way to begin would be to notice something in the play of language. 'What if a much of a which of a wind?' or 'Anyone lived in a pretty how town' – the first thing you notice is that it's not the way someone would speak, and there I think you have to address head-on the fact that it's written in some species of idiolect that isn't normal utterance. It depends very much on the poem, I think, whether you begin with some ground-level of human experience or whether you begin with the nonsense language of poetry.

MWT: To pursue further this question of poetry and the university. The Anglo-Welsh poet John Tripp once famously said that a poet would be about as welcome in an English Department as a cow would be in United Dairies. And as you know, there are few creative writing departments in Britain. It's very different in America. What's your view of the way poetry has been brought into the academy?

HV: When I was growing up, there weren't creative writing classes as such, at least not in most universities. So it was rather an anomaly to me, when I went to teach at Cornell, to find that there were creative writings being offered there in 1960. I didn't know what to think of them – I had never been in one myself, I had never assisted in the creation of such things. I had never been present at a creative writing class. But I soon noticed that among the students I was teaching, in a survey of British Literature, there were those who, when they wrote a paper, seemed to have some understanding of how a poem was put together, and others who didn't have a clue. And I finally began to ask them, 'Well, how did you get this understanding of poetry? How did you come to know that this was what a poet might or might not do with such a kind of poem?' And they would always say, as if it were the total explanation, 'Oh! I had a creative writing class.' And that's when I decided that this was very valuable for people even if they weren't going to be poets. They got out of it a sense of poetry as something connected with mortise and tenon, and joints, and planks, and wedges, and it was much better than people who saw a poem simply as a statement, or as something on which they were supposed to perform information retrieval.

MWT: What do you think of Dana Gioia's criticism of that whole set-up? I think he describes it as a sort of sub-culture that now monop-olises American poetry. Is that a fair comment on the situation?

HV: Well, of course, it can be done badly, like anything else. There are very depressing aspects to creative writing classes when they are done badly. There was a recent book put out by two creative writing teachers, who had collected assignments from other creative writing teachers and put them all together in a book. And whereas I can see that an assignment may make sense in the evolution of a particular class's work, when the assignments were all put together huggermug-ger from many different ways of teaching writing, it looked like a bag of tricks, and was very depressing to me.

On the other hand, when you have an inspiring teacher who can bring forth from a student what the poem is trying to be – I've seen Seamus Heaney do it – the workshop can elicit further imaginative acts from a student to bring the poem to its best development. This seems to me to be a kind of training that the student is not getting in other classes – where the imagination is not asked to press further, to develop itself more, or widen its glance. I remember that one of Heaney's exercises was to write a letter to an unborn child. Now that's a very weighty and consequential thing for an imagination to do. No other class that a university student would be taking would be asking for such a cast of the imagination, and that seems to me very useful to be doing, even for people who aren't going to be poets.

In a nation of 270 million people, there's bound to be a lot of mediocrity, and I think Dana Gioia was at that point trying to address failings in a system that he would like to see improved. But it's also possible to see the originalities in that system that are not being evoked elsewhere in the education of our students.

MWT: To return to the problem of teaching students poetry: I find that British students still feel American poetry to be foreign to them. Is that feeling reciprocated? For example, do you feel British poetry – particularly twentieth-century and contemporary British poetry – to be foreign to you as an American, in any significant way?

HV: I think the cultures have split further apart than they were when I was growing up, when the basic training that an American would receive in literature would be a training in British poetry. My education might be closer to the education of somebody in England of the same age. Now I think the cultures have split, so that the training of Americans is in American poetry – Whitman, Dickinson, Stevens, Frost etc. – rather than Marvell, Shakespeare, Milton. And that's bound to make a difference in culture.

Also, manners have split far more widely. England possesses a more inhibited set of manners than America, and manners dictate the way utterances go. I feel when I read British poetry that it's much less free-wheeling, on the whole (I mean the kind of British poetry that has made it into anthologies or that appears in the *TLS*). I know that there are other kinds being written, but the written poetry – by contrast with the oral poetry of Britain – seems to me still better mannered, you might say, and less loose-limbed than American poetry. More of it's written in form. American poetry is most often written in free-verse, it seems to me; the colloquial is admitted more widely. Think of Allen Ginsberg: that sort of poetry wouldn't have been written in Britain by a man of his generation. I do think that the gap is widening, and the cultural differences are greater than they used to be.

MWT: You've written with particular sensitivity about Seamus Heaney. Are there any other poets from the British Isles who attract your interested attention?

HV: Heaney has, of course, taught in America, and been my colleague for years, so there's a natural reason why I would be interested in his work, though I became interested in it long before he was my colleague, when I first heard him read from *North*. It was *North* itself that convinced me. I don't know of another book written by anybody in the British Isles that has been as powerful to me as *North*, which seems to me one of the great books of twentieth-century poetry. I read Larkin; I read Hughes; but neither of them appealed to me as strongly as Heaney. And I don't think that anyone else has since. I read with interest people like Michael Hofmann, Mark Ford, Paul Muldoon, and yet I don't feel I know the whole scene, because so many of the books are published only on one side of the water, and don't make it to the other side.

MWT: Then to turn to what might be called your reading of American poetry – the reading of the poetry as a body of work that's implicit in your anthology, for instance. I remember Charles Tomlinson describing that anthology as a kind of empire building, by which he meant you had emphasised the line running from Stevens to Ashbery, at the expense of what he regarded as other, alternative traditions. And he instanced such poets as the Black Mountain group (Olson particularly), the Objectivists (Oppen), poets like Duncan, and Bly, and implied that yours was therefore a rather exclusive reading of American poetry. How would you respond to that criticism.

HV: Well, of course, in writing about the contemporary we all stake a wager. And you may prove to be very wrong. The history of criticism is full of error. When you think of some things that Dr Johnson said – that 'Lycidas' was 'easy, vulgar, and therefore disgusting' – it seems a scarcely credible judgement to us now. But if Dr Johnson could be wrong, I can certainly be wrong!

On the other hand, the poets that Tomlinson mentions tend to be the followers of Pound. At least, Olson and Black Mountain were, along with Duncan, Creeley, and so forth. I don't think of Oppen as so much a follower of Pound. He's *sui generis* truly, and he's someone I don't know well enough. But the others seem to me to be doing less well what Pound did, and in fact Pound himself seems to me to have done less well later what he did better earlier. And they seem to be following the most unpromising aspects of Pound – Olson and Duncan especially. In Olson there's an overplus of historical material that seems rather undigested. And in Duncan, the soft side of Pound – the archaisms, the 'what thou lovest well remains' side of Pound – seems to have gotten softer than it ever was in Pound. All I can say is that they seem to me less original than their founding-father, Pound himself, and that they don't seem to me to have had such a depth of influence as others of their generation.

MWT: Tomlinson made the additional observation that you seem to be privileging the lyric; and he points out it's a term that has become central to your whole discussion of poetry over the last few years. He mentioned other forms of poetry, such as the narrative poem, the long poem, the didactic poem, the burlesque, the satire, and wondered how sensitive you were to them.

HV: Well, I think the narrative poem has been dead for a long time. There are periodic attempts to revive it – Vikram Seth has attempted to revive it, and recently Craig Raine has attempted to revive it. But finally, fiction has taken over the function of the long narrative poem. I don't know why that should have happened, necessarily, but it seems to have happened. The weight of broad social commentary and broad social representation which we find in Chaucer, or the long cosmology that we find in Milton, seems to have been taken over by the novel more successfully than by the narrative poem. It's too bad that we've lost epic poetry and narrative poetry, but there's no point crying over spilt milk in that respect.

I think of James Merrill's *The Changing Light at Sandover*, for instance, which is the most recent attempt at epic. For me, it doesn't stand except its first book, *The Book of Ephraim*, as nearly so successful as Merrill's other work. It may be that my taste is restricted to lyric, but I certainly find that Merrill and others have succeeded better in the short form than in the long form.

Now I don't know whether we've had any extended satiric poems of any great success – I can't think of one offhand. We've had the extended historic poem in Olson and others, but that is done in the Poundian manner, where you substitute phanopoeia for the expository sentence, and I am still too attached to the sentence to like non-sentence poetry. You give up a great deal when you give up syntax, and do image, image, image, in successive montages in the Poundian manner. That, too, may be a judgement that will prove to be flawed: I don't know.

MWT: Again, it's been commented about your choice of poets that you seem to favour the cerebral, that there is a lack of blood and guts and of director sensory and emotional experience in the poets you're attracted to.

HV: Unfortunately, the blood and guts poets are often sentimental. That is, when you think of the 'Iron John' movement in American poetry, there's a vein of poetry that I do find sentimental in its wish to be bodily rather than cerebral. I think that all of the successful poets of the past have had an enormous intellectual component, and I include poets such as John Clare, who had pronounced political views, pronounced topographical and ecological views. Behind even the simplest poem there's a powerful mentality. Think of the mentality that's behind *Songs of Innocence*.

The division into the cerebral versus the blood and guts is in the first place wrong. There's no complex art that doesn't have a great amount of intellectuality in it – no complex verbal art anyhow. It isn't that the complex mental poets or the complex cerebral poets can't write simply. They often do – Shakespeare did in the songs – but there isn't such a thing as a simple mind writing poetry out of its simple heart.

MWT: In the introduction to the Faber/Harvard anthology of contemporary American poetry, you talk interestingly about the way it seems to you the poetry of the second half of the century in America involves a rewriting in many respects of the poetry of the first half of the century, by way of reaction against it, or critique of it, and also incorporation, adaptation, modification of it. Is that a process that's now completed do you think, or do you see it as ongoing even with the younger, emergent generation of writers?

HV: I think the process is substantially complete. Modernism seemed such a powerful force: it broke with so much of the past – the free verse break, the Surrealist break, the abstract break, those were all significant breaks with the past. And I do think it took a second generation to absorb it and do something else with it. Mainly the second generation Freudianised modernism, which of itself was not a Freudian movement. In Plath, Lowell, Berryman, Sexton and many others – even in somebody like Robert Bly (the 'Teeth Mother' and whatnot) – there is a reprocessing, a Freudianising, of the first wave of Modernism.

At the moment there is no way ahead, and the New Formalism is an experiment that has not been notably successful, in my view. It seems inhibited, prissy, and schoolmarmish; and there are various other deliberately conservative, reactionary, moves that it has made. And I don't mean only that they are doing non-free verse. I mean their whole mentality is a kind of conservative turn-away from avant-garde and subversive movements towards a centrist culture. There's an attempt to praise the suburban, if you want, that seems to be a wrong path, partly because it's not volatile enough to make a very interesting poetry.

I don't know where the next impulse of energy will come from, except that it probably will come from the hybridising of different cultures. The increasing presence of educated writers from the different minority groups will eventually affect the face of poetry a great deal. There's a powerful surge of rather untrained writing, and that may eventually contribute something, but I do think it takes high training to produce high poetry, a terrifically complex mastery of both language and syntactic patterns. That will not come immediately from the new linguistic groups but it will come eventually.

MWT: A commitment to the contemporary in poetry is relatively unusual in an academic. Equally unusual is the use of the review as a means of substantially addressing poetry. Why do you think you are different?

HV: Some have the disposition to live in a particular century. I think many scholars live in another historical period: they have a great imaginative grasp of the Middle Ages, or of the eighteenth century. They know a period down to its memoirs and its letters and its newspapers; and that's a powerful motive for scholarship. I don't have that sort of historical imagination. There is no other century I live in with the same vivacity with which I live in my own. What I want is poetry in any century where I find it, but I don't live in any century except my own day-by-day: I don't have a parallel life in another century, the way that the historically imaginative have. Maybe that's why I've stuck with poetry of my own century, as well. I like poems of all sort wherever they exist, and they exist in the journals and newspapers and publishing houses of America. It seems to me that if you like Renaissance poetry you also like twentieth-century poetry: it seems natural.

MWT: You've also written very thoughtfully about the language of criticism. You've made the point that a critic needs to interrogate his, or her, own language – to take a lesson both from contemporary theory and from the example of poets in so doing. Does this mean that you think that a critic can only be as good a critic as he is a writer?

HV: That's a hard one. I don't know that there's any definition of a good critic: there are so many different kinds of good critics. Some are highly normative, like Dr Johnson or Yvor Winters: some of them are more sympathetic, like Randall Jarrell, who imagined himself into the very body of the poem; others are more rhapsodic, others are more scientific. It's a temperament that creates a critic; some critics are polemical and fiery, and others are more meditative, more empathetic. I don't think there's any one definition of a good critic.

It simply has to be somebody who finds a way of conveying his or her own experience to someone else – criticism is a teaching function essentially, or else it's an evangelical function. Some people preach, some people teach, some people show, some people hum along. I don't think there's any prescription that you can give, except that you want to find words that are somehow adequate as a bridge from the poem to the more ordinary language of experience. You end up, in so far as possible, reproducing the words of the poem in hundreds of extra words, but your aim is somehow to give a simulacrum of the poem in another language.

The most important thing for me, when I was first reading critics, was that the critic be decisive. I wanted someone to say something strong about the work. I didn't much care whether I agreed with it or not, but I wanted to have a point of view and a strong aspect of the work exhibited, and strong things said about it. I like uncompromising language, and clear language. I remember, when I first began to write, taking Northrop Frye as a model. I didn't always agree with Frye, but I always knew what he had said, and he always said it in a very vivid and decisive language. I like that more than anything else.

MWT: I wonder then whether that is tantamount to agreeing with somebody who said that you as a critic are at your best when you're being argumentative. This also implies that you may not always be at your best when you talk about poets you like very much.

HV: I myself think that I am at my best when I am most sympathetic to the work. I see best into the works I am most sympathetic with. And to the extent that I have reservations about moral positions, political positions of sentiment in a work, I feel I see into it less well than into work I'm completely in sympathy with. I feel I'm seeing deepest when I love the poems best, that is to say with poets like Herbert, or Stevens, or Keats.

Now it may be that other people like it better where there's an edge. People enjoy polemic; they feel energised by polemic. I don't particularly feel energised by polemic. I like the sort of empathetic criticism that Jarrell did very much, but he was far wittier than I could ever be. I do feel that people love argument, and find it more exciting on the page than they find sympathetic exposition. I understand that point of view, but it's not my own.

MWT: Poets that are overlooked – either poets from earlier centuries or poets of our time – are there such that come to mind?

HV: I think the poets I'm least sympathetic to are the ones who write about hunting deer with their grandfather, because it doesn't overlap particularly with my experience. It's rural poetry, perhaps, of a kind of raw or savage life that I have never had. I am a city person, and I am an intellectual person. Perhaps somebody who had more experience with swamps and foxes than I had would look very strongly for a different kind of poetry. I'm not hunting that poetry, so there's probably poetry like that I haven't found. I don't feel there's a lot of poetry to my taste that I haven't found.

MWT: Poets that are undervalued – poets that you would like to bear witness to and for – can you think of any?

HV: Well, I feel that in America the entire British tradition has been lost. There are virtually no requirements any longer for our students, and I constantly meet graduate students in English who have no acquaintance with the British tradition of poetry. I've had students come up to me and ask, 'Why didn't anyone tell me before about George Herbert, or Vaughan, or Marvell, or Sidney, or Raleigh?' It seems terrible that someone should grow up not knowing about 'The Passionate Man's Pilgrimage', or 'What if this present were the world's last night', or any number of other things.

That being said, I also think a great deal of American poetry has vanished from the schools. A little Whitman, a little Dickinson may be read, but the subversive tradition of American poetry – Melville's poetry about the Civil War, for instance – is never seen by anyone. Nor are the subversive poems about the First World War or the Second, or the Vietnamese War. There's a whole strain of subversive poetry that is essentially censored out from the schools. And that seems to me a great pity.

V.
SELECTED REVIEWS
(2007–2012)

Dannie Abse

THE HEART OF THE MATTER
Dannie Abse, *New Selected Poems:*
Anniversary Collection, 1949–2009 (**Hutchinson, 2009**)
The Guardian, 30 May 2009

With Dannie Abse, 'we are always on the haunted brink of what might
be revealed'. So wrote his friend, the fine poet John Ormond, almost
half of Abse's long writing lifetime ago. And as this new selection of his
poems confirms, his best work has always seemed to materialise almost
spontaneously, a tangible yet ghostly presence at the interface between
different realities. These realities are sometimes crudely represented by
readers as binaries: Welsh-Jewish; London-Ogmore; doctor-poet. But
that is to misconstrue the ABC of Abse's distinctive alphabet. Virtually
from the beginning, sixty years ago, his writing has been much more
subtly liminal in character. And now, as he closes steadily in on his
ninetieth year, his poetry, while still stubbornly rooted in scepticism,
seems more insinuatingly soul-haunted than ever. 'The final letter of
the alphabet,' he mordantly writes, has always seemed to him to be 'on
its knees praying/ with its back to the abyss.'

He is, of course, the most congenial, the most dangerously disarming, of poets. Many of his poems seem modestly to aspire only
to the condition of anecdote; and that is the very precondition of
their extraordinarily durable power. Yet to describe their cumulative
effect best one has ultimately, however uneasily, to reach for that currently unfashionable noun 'wisdom'. A good poem, he has written, is
like clear water: it tempts one to suppose the bottom can readily be
touched with a stick. Included in this selection are many old favourites
already quietly lodged in public consciousness, ready to disturb complacency at any moment: 'Return to Cardiff', 'In the Theatre', 'Not
Adlestrop', 'White Coat, Purple Coat', 'The Pathology of Colours',
'In Llandough Hospital'. His poetry has lost nothing of its unnerv-
ing power to reveal its unexpected side. The doctor in him can still

unpredictably trump the poet: 'Darkest tulip her head bends,/ face white as leukaemia.'

He has retained all his power deep into old age because the enigma of existence still remains his faithful Muse:

> Now I'm old, I'm credulous. Superstition clings.
> After the melting eyes and devastation
> of Hiroshima, they say butterflies, crazed,
> flew about, fluttering soundless things.

Just as Abse has always refused to condescend to life, so he has distained to 'bully language', the vice of the swaggering, swearing youngsters who invade his beloved Ogmore. A magician of ordinary speech, he has from the first enjoyed the finest ear for the elusive pitch of perfect meaning. He is constantly wary of how much more liable poetry is than prose to stray from what Wallace Stevens called 'the music of what happens'. Abse's Sleeping Beauty suffers 'from profound anaemia', while his 'Jill who tumbled down has wrecked her back'. Humour has ever been his safeguard. It keeps his vision and his expression honest. Some might unkindly remark that a sense of humour has been a necessity for one who, ever since childhood, has stubbornly supported Cardiff City, even repeatedly celebrating that strange addiction in verse. But then, as he recalls his 'scruffy, odorous Uncle Isidore/ (surely one of the elect)' saying a lifetime ago, 'Little boy, who needs all the lyric strings?/ Is the great world perfect?' And the very arrangement of poems in this selection seems designed to advertise that fact: relatively slight poems alternate with meaty ones and humour barges unceremoniously in on seriousness.

In choosing to include his youthful elegy for Dylan Thomas in this volume, Abse may surprise a few who might have expected him to cover his early tracks when, like many another Welsh poet of his generation, he seemed wrong-heading towards becoming a Thomas clone. But such a move is as revealing as it is honest, because it highlights one of the most important continuities in Abse's writing. Tutored early by Thomas, he has remained committed to poetry as song, a commitment that led to his spat in the fifties with some of the luminaries of 'the Movement', to whom his poetic shift towards the conversational no doubt seemed a sign he was one of them. His unique achievement has been to fashion a genuinely lyric art out of a relaxed, colloquial, deceptively desultory style of writing. It remains a potentially devastating combination, as the wonderful poems wrung from him by the tragedy of his wife Joan's recent death in a road accident testify:

> Shades
> Lengthen in the losing sun.
> She is everywhere and nowhere
> Now that I am less than one.

This achingly moving poetry of loss is all the more memorable because it here shares space, and therefore after a fashion time, with some of the marvellous love poems born of the Abse's long and happy marriage.

Years earlier, he had presciently written 'what ends happily is never the end'. And he'd added that 'the secret is/ there's another secret always'. By scrupulously honouring that truth for sixty years, his own poetry has continued to retain its own mystery, and it has done so without ever resorting to vulgar mystification because his poems have always 'advocated// the secret of lucidity'. For rosary he has mentally fingered '[k]eepsake pebbles, exiled shells,/ looted from some holiday shore,/ this mysterious giant key/ that opens no familiar door'. As he adventures ever further into his eighties, Dannie Abse is a continuing wonder. And he is so because, as this fine selection makes so arrestingly clear, he has never ceased wondering.

Charles Bukowski

Charles Bukowski, *The Pleasures of the Damned,*
Poems 1951–1993, ed. John Martin (Canongate, 2010);
Howard Sounes, *Charles Bukowski: Locked in the Arms*
of a Crazy Life (Canongate, 2010).
Acumen, 67 (May 2010), 103–6

Sounes's biography, a revised version of the 1997 original, follows his subject's crazy picaresque career from his brutalised, blue-collar boyhood to his late notoriety, when fans used to party outside his home just to be able to boast they'd got drunk at Bukowski's house. Reading this life is like viewing a screwball black comedy, a Tom-and-Jerry cartoon for adults, with lashings of booze, sex and violence, where all the knockabout stuff is for real and people get hurt. The text is adorned with the poet's own doodles, resembling James Thurber on acid. Not that Bukowski ('Hank' to his friends) was into dope. He despised the Beats and Hippies, who were white collar softies. In like spirit, he dismissed Bono, a huge fan, as a middle-class creature of the establishment. He himself was a bruiser, a red neck, a drifter with attitude and a soft spot for Hitler. Since his careering life could have been measured out in smashed bottles, it's not surprising that reading some of his poems is like picking up shards of glass. Yet some of them were written to the accompaniment of Mozart and Beethoven, a genuine passion. His roaringly macho, lock-up-your daughters character is difficult to like. Sometimes it seems one of his few endearing features was his readiness to pick a fight with Arnold Schwarzenegger.

For much of his life, Hank was a walking disaster area. When one of his girlfriends died, even her fish committed suicide by leaping out of its bowl. Bukowski was devastated. A friend's sympathetic comment on the incident could have come straight out of *The Godfather*: 'He was a very tender-hearted guy – not towards people necessarily, but towards goldfish.' Goldfish feature in three of his poems, and battle-scarred cats in four more. Dogs are plentiful, including the white dog whose exceedingly brief friendship he memorably celebrated, and the beagle upon whose portrait he lavished a Rembrandt-like love and attention, noting how it 'spreads a paw,/ the lamp burns warm/ bathed in the life of his/ size'.

Take away the legend, as Sounes rightly advises, and there's still plenty of the black comedy of excess left in Bukowski's shenanigans for a single lifetime. Just as there were always more than enough mean streaks in his character to feed the devil in his writing. And his drunken sprees would have made Dylan Thomas look like 'an amateur drunk.' From beginning to end, his chaotic career was colourfully spattered with examples of what Thomas Hardy called life's little ironies. In adulthood, he was saved by a transfusion of blood from the sadistic father who had turned his childhood into domestic hell. Stricken in old age by a mysterious disease that baffled LA's best doctors, he discovered it was TB only thanks to the chance intervention of his vet.

Sounes's life is vivid without being lurid, but he has little to say about the poetry or about Bukowski's literary debts – his poems readily acknowledge the uninhibited vigour of other artists and writers, including Hemingway, Henry Miller and the chill, spooky William Burroughs, and their sometimes obscenely carnal lyricism recall poetry at least as old as the ribald tales and fabliaux of the Middle Ages. But we do learn that, having been banned by an exasperated landlord from banging noisily away on a typewriter after 9.30 pm, he developed a talent for speedy writing in hand-printed block capitals, a facility that seems to have been uncannily well suited to his poetry in all its loud, laconic haphazardness. As a youngster, he used to scribble in the margins of newspapers, and his writing never lost that electric connection to the desultory concerns of the moment. And he had a mastery of demotic language to match.

Terming his poems 'only bits of scratchings/ on the floor of a cage', he drew attention to the sardonic philosophy of life implicit in his seemingly disposable writing. There were few better than he at spitting out all the butt-ends of modern America's days and ways. A poetic Joseph Cornell, he was an assiduous collector of the quotidian detritus of objects, people, experiences and feelings. But reading his poetry in bulk, as one is encouraged to by the Canongate collection which is some five hundred pages, what becomes apparent is that these often casual fragments seem spontaneously to cohere into a tragi-comic persona of some power. Tucked away in the heap of random impressions are unexpected moments of louche delicacy, as in his gustatory registering of a woman's naked body, 'buttered toast with the butter/ melted in', and his parody of butch maleness: chatting up a girl, he taps 'my cigar ashes into my beer to give me/ strength'. He's good on body language and, for my taste, his scribblings get better the closer he draws to 'the common verity of dying'.

As Sounes makes clear, there was never any danger of Bukowski underestimating his own gifts, and in his poem to Sherwood Anderson he seems to be inadvertently describing some of the best features of his own performance. In Anderson's fiction, he shrewdly notes, 'one felt space between his lines, air', as 'he told stories and left the meaning open/ and sometimes he told meaningless stories/ because that was the way it was'. I'd like to think that Bukowski also implicitly acknowledged his own limitations when, referring to Bruckner, he wrote 'there are times when we should/ remember/ the strange courage/ of the second-rate/ who refuse to quit/ when the nights/ are black and long and sleepless/ and the days are without/ end'. But, however finally modest Bukowski's achievements, many poets greater than he would have been proud to hit, in old age, upon lines as quietly and serenely luminous as these that pay such perfect, poignantly sensuous tribute to 'woman on the street':

> her shoes themselves
> would light my room
> like many candles.

> she walks like all things
> shining on glass,
> like all things
> that make a difference.

> she walks away.

Jorie Graham

FULL FATHOM FIVE
Jorie Graham, *Sea Change* (Carcanet 2008)
The Guardian, 3 May 2008

For W. H. Auden, 'the crack in the tea-cup opens/ A lane to the land of the dead'. Jorie Graham's poetry is all about the vertiginous (and sometimes heady) experience of falling through the cracks – in reason, in consciousness, in time. Ever since she was inspired as a poet by editing tape at film school, she has been fascinated by the disconcerting alterations in perception that can be produced by little hiccups in the confident flow of mundane experience. Consequently, her writing, she once pungently suggested, is never more than a 'cadenza of gaps'.

Graham's new collection confirms her to be a cerebral shaman for our age, a time-traveller in a shape-shifting mental universe. The human mind, she writes, is 'open and oozing with/ inwardness'; a process her poetry registers. Her intensely focused, sensuously inflected meditations are both entranced and entrancing. A poet for whom thoughts are sensations and sensations thoughts, she is perfectly equipped to capture, as she does in 'Loan', the rapt instant when heavy rain suddenly stops:

> ... & the stillness
> of brimming & the
> wet rainbowing where oil from
> exhaust picks up the light, sheds glow,
> then
> echoes in the drains where
> deep inside the
> drops fall individually, plink,
> & the places where birds
> interject, & the coming-on of heat, & the girl looking sideways
>   carrying the large
> bouquet of blue hydrangeas, shaking the water off

Her recollection of how 'the faucet flared [with water] like a glare/ of open speech' is a further example of her capacity to step casually into another dimension.

Given Graham's preoccupation with the phenomenological and the metaphysical, it might seem tempting to accuse her (like Wallace Stevens) of ignoring the social and political catastrophes of the day. But such an accusation would be groundless. In her new work, as ever in her poetry, 'the cadaver' is always threatening 'to show through the skin of the day'. Her imagination is fearfully sensitised by the threats of climate change and global pollution, while memory never allows her to forget mankind's reliable talent for war. In addition, she is aware that the collapse of belief systems has left us vulnerable to the seduction of nihilism as we contemplate eventual annihilation. In the face of all this, the affirmations of poetry can seem no more than a primitive ritual to quell existential fear, the textual equivalent of burning incense – 'always smoke rising to propitiate the stars that might turn black'. Significantly, this volume's title points us not to the redemptive vision of *The Tempest* but to Shakespeare's play as ominously refracted through Eliot's 'The Waste Land'.

Nevertheless, humankind's unfathomable will to hope is explored in one of the most arresting poems in this collection, 'The Violinist at the Window, 1918 (after Matisse)'. Graham imagines the painter's gaunt instrumentalist to be willing, even in the immediate aftermath of the great war, 'to take up whatever it is/ the spirit/ must take up'. He becomes for her an emblem of 'obligatory hope', a figure from whom she can 'plagiarize humanity' even as 'history starts up again'. The music she imagines him preparing to play 'is what hope forced upon one's self sounds/ like – this high note trembling'. Occurring as it does at the centre of *Sea Change*, the poem highlights the fact that this is a collection pivoting tremulously on the impulse to hope, repeatedly probing its occasions and credentials while weighing the 'good' against the 'ugly'.

Graham is most certainly not a poet to everyone's taste. Many find her difficult, elusive, cerebral, bloodless, and they are unlikely to be won over by this new volume. She remains much more Rothko than Rembrandt. But for her admirers, Graham's voyages through strange seas of thought will seem as singular, unpredictable and seductive as ever. These poems again demonstrate her gift for enabling us to see change, a gift that places her unexpectedly in the company of such writers as Virginia Woolf. And once more she is preternaturally alive to every sign in her present of the sheen of the numinous. She finds it, memorably, in 'Positive Feedback Loop':

we
shall walk
out on the porch and the evening shall come around
   us, unconcealed,
blinking, abundant, as if catching sight of us,
everything in and out under the eaves, even the grass seeming
   to push up into this
our world as if out of
homesickness for it,
gleaming.

But hers is a very modern sense of the sources of the numinous, embedded in an awareness of a universe only briefly troubled by human presence. Her imagination constantly registers the end of human time: 'And always the absent thing, there, up ahead, like a highway ripped open and left hanging in/ the void.' We live not in a 'city on the/ hill', but in a 'city of dis/ appearance'. The mid-word line-break, and the gulf that follows, instances Graham's use of using spatial form to emblematise psycho-spiritual experience. Her masters in this technique were no doubt Donne, Herbert, Vaughan, and Traherne, the great Metaphysical writers from whom she confesses herself to be distantly descended.

Graham's poems act as the sonar devices of contemporary western consciousness, probing the depths of human existential experience. But they are also radio telescopes, restlessly scanning, as the last line of this collection tells us, to pick up 'the sounds the planet will always make, even if there is no one to hear them'. The ability to translate that combination of concerns into singular poetry makes her a remarkable poet of our time.

Geoffrey Hill

Geoffrey Hill, *Oraclau/Oracles* (Clutag Press, 2010)
The Guardian, 16 October 2010

'For the Oracle, turn off at next junction' reads the M4 sign. In this new volume, invoking the vatic tradition of *barddas* and featuring its key genres of panegyric and elegy, Geoffrey Hill offers us rather different guidance for the road ahead. A 'prophet of the past', like Hazlitt's Scott, Hill (for whom '*milk of Lethe* remains our poison') here turns his oracular eye on the Welsh and their history. As he disarmingly observes, 'Great shame/ I cannot speak or sing/ This language of my late awakening.'

This is a sequence of 144 poems based on one of the ingenious metric patterns of Hill's fellow Metaphysical, John Donne (descended from the Dwnns of Kidwelly, whose gravitation to London and Englishness provided an early example of how 'Tudur uchelgais [ambition] raised our common spivs'). The fainthearted and weak of stomach may choose to treat it as an elaborate bagatelle, the self-indulgent whimsy of an ageing eccentric. But intemperate dismissal would be unwise. As Hill resonantly affirmed in *Mercian Hymns*, King Offa is the regnant Muse of his tormentedly English poetry, and this latest work – a counterweight to that classic early volume – is very much a product of the border country of which that early aspirant to a definitive Englishness was lord and master. In this sequence, Hill walks his own crumbling mental Dyke, anxiously beating the bounds of his modern identity. As its bilingual title indicates, *Oraclau/Oracles* is a complex meditation on his wanly bicultural inheritance; an internal dialogue between the dominantly English and recessively Welsh elements in the genetic make-up of this great grandson of Pryce Jukes, Llanllwchaiarn.

Milton's *Comus* is situated in metamorphic border country, and in Hill's learned work, in part a kind of modern Masque in honour of Wales, the antique figures range from the Fifth Monarchist Vavasour Powell and Behmenist Morgan Llwyd to the Siamese pairing of Parry-Williams and Williams Parry; spectacle is provided by Alfred

Janes's portrait of fellow Kardomah-boy Dylan Thomas, with his 'belladonna eyes', and by Ceri Richards's Jungian painting *Afal du Bro Gŵyr*, the alchemy of its black sun rhyming visually with the hermetic philosophising of Henry Vaughan's twin brother, Thomas – a key figure in this baroque theatre. And the text glitters dangerously with wit. The fictions issuing from the crabbed, malevolent genius of Caradoc Evans are characterised as 'cribbed saturnalia/ Of dead reckoning'.

A spirit akin to that of Masque seems appropriate to a Wales that is partly close to Hill's heart because 'Fantastic logic found unreason here'. Lightly citing Russell's old-age retreat in north Wales and Williams-Ellis's Italianate folly at Portmeirion, he also has in mind the tragic case of the innocently ludic B. S. Johnson, a martyr to language like Hill himself, whose stay at Gregynog proved terminal. But industrial Wales is also given careful attention, the country of Idris Davies and *How Green Was My Valley* being for him still haunted, even in its post-industrial state, by the spirits of Lord Bute and Nye Bevan. And the closest this Warwickshire writer comes to simple, raw emotion is in his angry tribute to the miners: 'How did any man twist away/ Soul-free from that shining,/ rise undamaged into the raw day/ With his black minstrel's face absurdly grinning,/ Travestied as was Jude that drole of learning?' For a moment, a poetry embossed with erudition, stiff with multilayered multicultural allusion, its every torqued phrase resistant to syntax, and its rhythm staccato, seems to find its free lyric voice.

Normally, style seems inauthentic to Hill unless it bears the stigmata of suffering, but his expression clears again briefly in a moving elegy to the God-intoxicated Ann Griffiths of Dolwar Fach, in whose '[i]ntelligence new made of late/ By paradox and oxymoron pressed' he implicitly recognises a consciousness akin to his own, but more securely blessed. 'Your Calvinisms gnaw me. I recuse,' Hill tells a Wales from which he constantly seeks to measure a guilty, uneasy distance, even as he beseeches his alter ego, Saunders Lewis (his 'beaklike head' crowned with 'belated laurels' now that his 'litanies' have been betrayed), to 'teach me how to be received/ By people amongst whom I have not lived.' But 'this is a strange country, the words foreign', the sequence confesses at one point, and, as ever with Hill, the issue of language – which for him inevitably means the condition of England – is what is primarily at stake. 'True Welsh, I would be monoglot', he ambiguously observes, while remonstrating – tetchily and indulgently by turn

– with 'language [the] old reprobate' because of its 'eccentric loves' and errant ways.

Many have been the English writers – Gerard Manley Hopkins, Edward Thomas, Cowper Powys, Kingsley Amis – who have found it useful to create a Wales in their own image, using it to backlight their variously troubled Englishness. In adding himself to their number, Hill – like that other English Cymrophile, David Jones – provides us with the means of constructing a much more radically inclusive sense of Britishness. But even while registering that 'Resurgent Wales gripes for its Easter Rising', Hill is honestly English enough to express deep unease at the upheaval that would be involved in culturally reconfiguring a stubbornly anglocentric Britain: 'Could you fit *Y Ddraig/Goch* on the old union flag/ Without ruining the design?/ I would not sacrifice/ The Cross of St George merely to be nice.' We Welsh speakers were right to be wary. *Oraclau/Oracles* is indeed a troubling and challenging volume of 'devices', a remarkable emblem book for our times by one of the most considerable, and accordingly formidable, poets of our age.

Gwyneth Lewis

Gwyneth Lewis, *A Hospital Odyssey* (Bloodaxe 2010)
The Guardian, 17 April 2010

'If a man could see/ The perils and diseases that he elbows,/ Each day he walks a mile,' wrote Thomas Lovell Beddoes almost two centuries ago, 'then would he know that Life's a single pilgrim/ Fighting unarmed amongst a thousand soldiers.' Gwyneth Lewis's remarkable long poem, an epic for our time, tracks such a pilgrim's progress, as Maris, her heroine and surrogate, takes on both disease and the National Health Service in her fight to save her cancer-stricken husband, Hardy. The result is a kind of surreal morality tale.

On her psychosomatic quest, she encounters a bewildering plurality of creatures, landscapes, situations stranger far than any imagined in *Lord of the Rings*. In this universe of ill health beyond the looking glass that comfortingly mirrors our normality, she faces up to a matronly Greater Spotted Woodpecker. Next comes a consultant, a latter-day Knight Templar, keeper of the sacred sites of the human body, who is stiffly strait-jacketed by the armour of his medical authority. Along the way she picks up friendly allies, companionable guides like Wilson the lugubrious and at times lupine greyhound, named after a legendary superhero of the *Wizard*; and Ichabod, the statuesque image of glowing good health. Their numerous adventures include attendance at the Grand Ball where the microbes, clothed in all the sinister glamour of their beautiful shapes and exotic names (*Bordetella pertusissis, Trypanosoma, Streptococci, Vibrios, Varicella zoster, Giardia lambia, Spirogyra* ...), perform the mad dance of life and death and gorge on all manner of matter. The heroes narrowly avoid entanglement in the web of an insinuatingly predatory spider, escaping partly through Maris's expertise at identifying and destroying cancer in a computer game where cells proliferate like paint on a Jackson Pollack canvas.

We may no longer all believe in God, but by God, we all believe in the NHS, with the desperate fervour of anxiety otherwise invested in religion. Hospitals are the great sacred sites of our secular world, dedicated to the cult of health, requiring votive offerings to the gods of disease, staffed by a revered priesthood of doctors and consultants, supplying ministering angels in the form of nurses. As Lewis brilliantly shows, no other places in the modern world are more unnervingly revealing of the bewildering blend in our natures of the rational and irrational, the sophisticated and the primal; the head, the heart and the gut.

Serious, life-threatening illness sucks not only Hardy but also his loving partner Maris into a deadly, Dante-esque whirlpool of seemingly interminable physical suffering and psychological struggle. What form but that of the epic, where the questing hero battles with monsters, pins down shape-shifters, solves riddles, makes impossibly difficult choices, avoids seductresses and visits the underworld, is suited to the exploration of this ghastly, madcap, phantasmagoric world of our worst nightmares?

But what poet of our time would dare take on the challenge of such an august and demanding form? As Lewis makes clear in a work that constantly reflects on its own processes and proceeding, writing an epic was for her not a result of choice but of sheer necessity, its creation a matter of life and death. Behind her poem lies the author's recent experience of her husband Leyton's successful fight against cancer, shadowed in turn by her father's earlier unsuccessful battle with the same disease. Her epic of 'health and loving' is not only about the struggle to rescue her partner, it also re-enacts the mental effort to save him by saving her own sanity and sharpening her intelligence into a counter-aggressive weapon: 'It's a hospital,/ this place I'm constructing line by line.'

From beginning to end, this long poem is an attempt to prevent the fear and despair in Maris's imagination from metastasising: 'Words are my health,' she stubbornly declares, 'the struggle to hear and transcribe the tune/ behind what I'm given by word of mouth.' Omnivorous as cancer itself, this outrageously capacious poem is, for her, the unique, and therefore indispensable, means of gaining that deep understanding of self, relationship and situation through which the salvation of physical and mental health may alone come. 'I use rhymes,' she elsewhere writes, 'to catch stray dreams that happen to float past me.' Adventitious rhyming, such as the supple verse form allows, is the natural ally of Lewis's remarkably resourceful wit and her gift for metamorphic imagination.

Together they enable her to wrong-foot the plodding reason on its journey down what the circumstances might prove to be all too literally the dead end of thought. They provide her with the energy and agility of intelligence that alone can trace the fluidities of psychosomatic events. And through the almost hysterical joie-de-vivre of the writing, with its desperate inventiveness and manic resourcefulness, one seems to live the thousand and one nights of a soul striving to ensure its own survival by willing the survival of its beloved.

This, therefore, is virtuoso writing whose end, mercifully, is not self-display but the healthful mobilisation of the will. Accordingly, the legend that might be inscribed over the gates to Lewis's particular hell is not '[a]bandon hope', but rather – given the hybrid character of her sources and resources – '[b]e of good cheer, Snoopy'. Of course, since in this text she, like her fictional Maris, is constantly living by her wits, there are occasional less successful passages where the strain inevitably tells. But overall, this is a performance that more than confirms Gwyneth Lewis's reputation as one of the most exhilaratingly gifted poets of her generation.

W. S. Merwin

WRITTEN IN WATER
W. S. Merwin, *Selected Poems* (Bloodaxe, 2007)
The Guardian, 2 June 2007

The work of more than five decades, gathered from fifteen volumes, is here compressed into a selection that is more luminous than voluminous. Bulk is not Merwin's style. A fastidious, elegant writer, he is a calligrapher of consciousness, a fine penman aware that he is writing not on parchment but in water. His deliquescent verse 'sways/ Like hair', as if drifting in 'the soft wash of the air'. Concerned always to go with the Heraclitean flow, the writing bypasses punctuation, so that since 'none of the sentences begins or ends there is time'. And there Merwin is in his element: some of his finest poems are the textual equivalent of Turner's late paintings, turning the world into a mirage of form momentarily coalescing out of light, and air, and moisture:

> In the unmade light I can see the world
> as the leaves brighten I see the air
> the shadows melt and the apricots appear
> now that the branches vanish I see the apricots
> from a thousand trees ripening in the air

Fifty years is a long time in poetry, and can be a dead weight of history for any writer to carry. Yet, although Merwin has always been averse to the direct transcription of his age, the best of his poems bear the faint, delicate watermark of their period. Concerned with 'knowing the tone of falling', the early 'Dictum: for a Masque of Deluge', with its 'tales of distended seas, continents/ submerged, worlds drowned', and its even more sinister 'drowning/ In mirrors', is a product of the post-war terror of nuclear annihilation. The desolate fables, disordered dreams and dark elegies of *The Lice* come from a mind prostrated by the

shame of American predations as they extend from Vietnam throughout
South East Asia:

> I am not ashamed of the wren's murders
> Nor the badger's dinners
> On which all worldly good depends
> If I were not human I would not be ashamed of anything.

The later poetry is aghast at globalised living's carelessness of both
natural bio-systems and cultural eco-systems, and in dead languages
and disappeared creatures Merwin finds ominous analogues for the
endangered species of poems. In lines characteristically ghosted by gentle meanings, he charges himself with a like thoughtlessness, a lack of
fidelity to what really matters:

> Only I never came back
>
> the gates stood open
> where I left the barnyard in the evening
> as the owl was bringing the mouse home
> in the gold sky
> at the milking hour
> and I turned to the amber hill and followed
> along the grey fallen wall
> by the small mossed oaks and the bushes of rusting
> arches

If, decades earlier, his younger self had expressed the hope of finding
'words for departure', then the ageing Merwin becomes a plangent
master of that lexicon.

True, the shine of text is, in a very few cases, not that of mellow
inner radiance but of threadbare materials, like the sheen of clothing
worn thin at knees and elbows. But the signature failures of important
poets serve only to highlight the risks taken to achieve their distinctive
successes. The supreme poet of fallings from us, vanishings, misgivings,
Merwin is a Romantic phenomenologist, an evident (older) contemporary of Jorie Graham's, but sensuous where she is cerebral – Keats is not
only mentioned in one poem but a spectral presence in many passages:

> it was the turning of autumn and already
>   the mornings were cold with ragged clouds in the hollows
> long after sunrise but the pasture sagging like a roof
>   the glassy water and flickering yellow leaves
> in the few poplars and knotted plum trees were held up
>   in a handful of sunlight that made the slates on the silent
> mill by the stream glisten white above their ruin …

From *The Vixen* (1996), the most elegiacally sumptuous of his volumes and one of the most important poetry collections of recent years, these lines reveal the unorthodox narrative impulse in Merwin's writing – he draws us into the mysterious world of story, which is the ancient and modern world of the human mind as it adventures through time. And, starting with *The Vixen*, his writing seems to become more gloriously, richly, sensuous, as if, advancing into old age, imagination's fading eyesight were ever more ravenous for sensation, and ever more haunted by the fragile substantial beauty of the world.

Merwin is the unmistakeable heir of the Emerson and Whitman who so ecstatically hymned flux. Like them he wonders constantly at how 'all that I did not know went on beginning around me'; and like them he possesses a rare gift for pristine sensation. Yet between him and them there is a difference, evident from the minor key of his psalms, written as they mostly are in what can only be called the 'passing tense'. That difference is the measure of the history of the American century and of the present American world. As much American Noah as American Adam, post-modern Merwin is aware of launching a porous ark of language. Behind even his most serene raptures lies always the quiet imagination of apocalypse:

> I hope I make sense to
> you in the shimmer
> of our days while the world we
> cling to in common is
>
> burning.

To which one can only gratefully answer: 'yes, indeed, this volume does make very good sense'.

Sharon Olds

FLESH KNEW ITSELF AND SPOKE
Sharon Olds , *One Secret Thing* (Cape Poetry 2009)
The Guardian, 21 March 2009

In 'Diving into the Wreck', one of the signature poems of the women's movement, Adrienne Rich saw women writers as burdened with 'a book of myths/ in which / our names do not appear'. For several decades, Sharon Olds has been fascinating readers by weaving the myth of her own female existence into a Nessus shirt of flaming sensuousness. Like Whitman, she is a remarkable mythopoeic poet of bodily identity and in the latter stages of this striking new collection explores ageing through the cases of both herself and her dying mother, to whom she addresses movingly conciliatory elegies at the last.

But she opens with a dozen meditations on war photographs that have slashed her imagination open to the quick. One of her own mythic personae, it appears, is that of war baby, one brought disturbingly alive by the universal struggle for existence. Her sensibility is erotically excited by violence and danger. A brave pilot, having bought his crew time to parachute from his burning bomber, turns its nose to the ground and sees 'the earth coming up towards him,/ green as a great basin of water/ being lifted to his face'. Parents stand appalled as a thuggish soldier picks up the 'amber/ torso-shape' of their child's cello, and breaks it against a fireplace where 'the brickwork crushed/ the close-grained satiny wood'. Olds can read like a thrill junkie at times.

This character trait is traced back to source in the second section and attributed to the harshly inhibiting punitive background of her Puritan upbringing. But rebellion is not only bred in her changeling's genes – to her mother she seems demonically possessed, even as a baby. Even more importantly for a poet, it is invitingly present in the very language she is given to speak. A remarkable poem has Olds explore, with baroque wantonness, the dictionary meanings of her maiden name of Cobb. It's the heady verbal equivalent of splitting the atom – identity is multiplied exponentially through a chain reaction. There is deep pain at the root of this verbal saturnalia, however. 'Dear Dad,' she writes, acknowledging perhaps the most problematic of all her relationships, 'I search for how/ to be your daughter.' In that moment, she also reveals herself to be, in part, the poetic daughter of another great risk-taking American, John Berryman.

It is, though, the question of how to be her mother's daughter that most consumes her in this volume. Much of her life, it seems, has been engaged in devising strategies of liberation from that oppressive tie. One of the most remarkable poems in this collection has her metamorphose into a fly on the wall of her Puritan family home: 'in each of the hundred/ eyes of both of my compound eyes,/ one wallpaper rose'. It's an astonishing image for the terrible fixity of a pathological obsession. And the opposite of it is the kind of freely licensed and licentious vision Olds tries to develop in herself through her poetry: 'a looking/ primed … a looking to the power of itself'.

Her great ally in this enterprise of self-liberation is, as always, the body. It has an uncontrollable animal life of its own which she relishes with a libertine delight. Another of Old's mythic personae is Diana the huntress, because she, too, seems most fiercely happy when surrounded by the bestiary of her own being. Witness Olds's memory in one poem of the fantastic creatures that decorated her nightie as a child, a scene reprised in another when her teenage daughter chooses an 'Animal Dress' to wear when first leaving home for college:

> And then she was on the train, in her dress
> like a zodiac, her body covered with
> the animals that carried us in their
> bodies for a thousand centuries
> of sex and death, until flesh knew itself, and spoke.

Those last two phrases could well serve as epigraph for all of Olds's writing.

The poems about her mother's decline and death in the last sections are all the more powerful because Olds's acute powers of empathy are the mature expression of the fiercely sensuous young imagination that had so frightened and appalled her parents. So, glimpsing her mother paralysed in the light of the ambulance that is carrying her second husband away, she sees her 'so vivid,/ like a woman motionless at the moment of orgasm,/ pure attention …/ every cell of her body was looking at him'. Hearing her loneliness speak down the wires of a phone is, for Olds, to hear in her voice 'the low singing/ of a watered plant long not watered'. The brain tumour that claims her is the final revelation of that feral life of the body that Olds has always so uninhibitedly known. And then, when it's over, the cremation done, her mother no more than 'the pint of her hearth-stuff', Olds holds all that is left of her in her hands for the last time:

> And my mother
> was violet-gray, she was blue spruce,
> twilight, fur, I ran my hand into the
> evening talcum of her absent action,

It is a remarkable conclusion to a memorable collection.

Keidrych Rhys

THE BEST SORT OF CRANK
Keidrych Rhys, *The Van Pool*,
ed. Charles Mundye (Seren 2012)
Agenda 47 (Summer 2012), 82–3

The name William Ronald Rees Jones: it doesn't have the swagger
of 'Keidrych Rhys', and in its prime the career of this raffish drifter
(1913–87) was rarely short on swagger. Self-promoting, he was an impre-
sario of genius, circus barker and ringmaster of a generation of striking
talent – the 1930s generation of Dylan Thomas and his contemporaries.
His greatest invention proved to be not himself but the 'Anglo-Welsh
brand' as he set out to create a modernist aesthetic distinctively Welsh,
but resolutely anglophone.

Wales, the brash, in-your-face 'house journal' he established in
1937, not only encouraged a group of disparate writers to recognise
in itself a groundbreaking cultural collective but also aggressively
'sold' its individual talents to a metropolitan London market that Rhys
affected to despise, even as he frequented the bohemian haunts of Soho
and Fitzrovia. Taking its cue both from the loudly opinionated Little
Magazines of the Modernist movement and cutting-edge journals like
Life and Letters Today, *Wales*, with its penchant for controversial snippets,
spiky reviews and general aggro, was always happy to start a textual
riot. No wonder the piece by Dylan Thomas that fronted its opening
number was entitled 'Prologue to an Adventure'.

Skilled at turning sacred cows into minced meat, Rhys produced
marginal comments, manifestoes and editorials that still make for entertaining reading. 'British culture,' he grandly announces, 'is a fact, but the
English contribution to it is very small … There is actually no such thing
as "English" culture; a few individuals may be highly cultured but the
people as a whole are crass.' An eccentric nationalist, he had a wicked
eye for the wilder reaches of anti-Welsh prejudice: '… the Welsh are
a nation of toughs, rogues, and poetic humbugs, vivid in their speech,

impulsive in behaviour, and riddled with a sly and belligerent tribalism'
(V. S. Pritchett, *The New Statesman*).

But behind the calculated bombast and the outrageous assertions
lay a shrewd, calculating mind, an ability to spot genuine creative poten-
tial, and a readiness to encourage it. Hospitable to Dylan Thomas, Glyn
Jones, Rhys Davies, Idris Davies, Vernon Watkins, Lynette Roberts,
Margiad Evans and others, his *Wales* provided a platform for the young
Emyr Humphreys, R. S. Thomas (whose first collection, *The Stones of the
Field*, was published by Rhys's Druid Press) and 'Davies Aberpennar';
Welsh-language writers such as R. Williams Parry, Gwenallt, Alun
Llywelyn Williams and Aneirin Talfan Davies were featured alongside
Hugh MacDiarmid, Norman Macleod, George Barker, James Findlay
Hendry – and Kafka. Even today, it can seem like a heady mix, a
magical crucible of creativity. And Rhys's exceptional gifts as literary
midwife were also manifest in a number of important poetic anthologies
he proceeded to edit.

Charles Mundye may well be the first scholar to have patiently
untangled the skein of Rhys's self-mythologising. Particularly concerned to rehabilitate his subject's poetic reputation, Mundye
correctly sees the uncovering of new, accurate biographical facts as
contributing to the process of taking his life and creative work more
seriously. We learn not only of the bizarre episode when Rhys, short
of cash, was arrested for menacing women with a gun, but also of
his probable nervous breakdown and his curious relationship with
the 'progressive army psychiatric hospital' in South Birmingham.
And in Rhys's personal appropriation of the name of his natal
Carmarthenshire valley (the Ceidrych), Mundye persuasively per-
ceives an attempt to 'ground' his complex, conflicted personality
on his own terms. Alienated from the stuffy chapel background of
his background, Rhys was nevertheless devoted to the cultural and
political liberation of a Wales whose legacy of myth excited his modernist, experimental imagination and whose economically depressed
social condition angered him. One outcome of Mundye's excellent,
measured introduction is that it challenges future scholars of Welsh
Writing in English to revalue Rhys. He emerges from this sympathetic revisionist study as a compelling example of the confused,
dislocated, but creatively fruitful, cultural condition of Anglophone
Wales in his time.

But what of his poetry? 'The best sort of crank' was Dylan Thomas's characteristically dismissive verdict on a man he also cruelly characterised as 'a turnip' and as 'consciously queer and talking little magazines until the air was reeking full of names and nonsense'. He had been banned from the Rhys household by Lynette Roberts (Rhys's wife), Thomas added, 'because I tell him bad things about poetry, such as that his isn't poetry at all'. Was Thomas right? Was Rhys only a wannabe poet, a 'period' curiosity? Mundye believes not, arguing cogently for the humanity of wartime poems characterised by 'clear-sightedness and journalistic currency', appreciating his experimentalism, commending 'his engagements with myth and legend', and approving of 'his committed investment in the poetry of the natural world'. He ends by proposing that Rhys significantly 'continued a distinct Anglo-Welsh poetic tradition'.

Whereas Mundye is a steady admirer of Rhys's poetry, I can summon up only an intermittent interest, and that primarily for verbal collages such as the following, where he assembles phrases to form a striking textual landscape:

Long tails sheared; highland blood easy in red paint pools.
The butting dog linked in the barn, old veteran; a bantam
  pecks
At the big morning fowls' corn leavings; the yard's a little
Smeared with fluid;

I also respond to the sharp shards of phrasing – a technique partly borrowed from the Welsh 'englyn' – that serve to capture the heightened, febrile atmosphere of wartime experiences:

Sun comes gleaming
thru wall window
of ice-barred temple
punishment enough

Alternating with his desultory records of wartime service, the home front poems ('Differences between home and bare barrackroom') are interesting historical documents (to be set alongside the work of Alun Lewis, Lynette Roberts and Brenda Chamberlain) of a period when

Wales struggled to resolve its position in a world at war. In grimly no-nonsense poems like 'Death of a Hurricane Pilot', he brutally elegises mangled young flesh: 'Whole scalp attached to a Comper Piccadilly helmet.' As for his copious experimentalism, it is altogether too consciously kin to the appreciably superior work of Dylan Thomas, David Jones, Lynette Roberts and Glyn Jones. Largely deaf, it seems, to rhythm, Rhys was inclined to modishly court the obscure and to strain for effect.

But while I remain reluctantly unpersuaded of Rhys's notable gifts as a poet, this admirable annotated edition of poems published, uncollected, and unpublished has significantly altered my estimation of his career, stimulating a wish to explore perspectives unexamined in the introduction – Rhys's interest in the Welsh-language literary renaissance and promotion of inter-cultural relations; his eccentric nationalist activism and admiration for Saunders Lewis ('Fire was forced on the three' was his verdict on the 1936 Penyberth episode in 'The Fire Sermon or Bureaucracy Burned'); and the links between *Wales* and its progressive Welsh-language counterpart, *Tir Newydd*. In these as well as other respects, his now appears to have been a much more complex and compelling case than I had supposed, and Dylan Thomas seems after all to have captured the enigma that was Keidrych Rhys very precisely (albeit unintentionally) when he described him as 'the *best* sort of crank'.

Anne Stevenson

AGE, THE EQUALISER
Anne Stevenson, *Stone Milk* (Bloodaxe 2007)
The Guardian, 13 October 2007

Old Age – there seems to be more of it about these days, highlighting a neglected sub-genre of writing. The poetry of age has always been with us. Ben Jonson wailed over his mountain belly, Yeats celebrated the res-erection of waning sexual energies, Hardy was penetrated by wind oozing thin through the thorn from nor'ward, and, following his stroke, Carlos Williams demonstrated that Eliot was indeed right: old men should be explorers. The last forty or so years has seen a significant increase in writing about the experience of the process of ageing and Anne Stevenson's latest collection is an absorbing addition to this rapidly growing body of work. Hers is no mere bid, however, to become the laureate of the wrinklies. For her, age is the great equaliser, bringing the gift of a levelling, communitarian vision.

The opening poem, 'Lament for the Makers', has for epigraph lines from Dunbar's celebrated poem, with its shuddering refrain 'Timor mortis conturbat me'. But Stevenson flinches from such rawness of confession. Following her early model and mentor, Elizabeth Bishop, she habitually practises a scrupulous urbanity. Such temperature-controlled writing has its dangers; the temperate can become the tepid, as appears in some passages and poems in *Stone Milk*. If the anxiety of influence drives some young writers to parricidal or matricidal assault on giant predecessors, in ageing one may feel companionably close to the mighty dead – more so than to youthful contemporaries: 'I-pod is a hideous word'. 'Lament for the Makers' is gently ghosted by a throng of great poets, some long dead others recently departed, and is thus informed by a Poundean vision of 'one raft on the veiled/ flood of Acheron,/ Marius and Jugurtha together'. Stevenson consciously joins the visionary company of the great poetic explorers of the underworld in order to create a compound elegy, marrying elements from Dante's terza rima with Eliot's Dante-esque *Four Quartets*. Such a grave salute to the soul of poetry serves to remind us that every age is equidistant from eternity. Through the tribute of allusion and of imitation as much as through statement, Stevenson's collection persistently values 'this resurrection of the dead that represents/ The life in us, the strangeness of it all'. Writing of the heirlooms left by her grandmother, she notes 'the adhesiveness of things/ to the ghosts that prized them'. Her poetry is suffused with an awareness of how words and phrases, too, can remain faithful to their favourite poets.

To affirm commonalty, to escape from the clamour of a 'self-propelled, vicious' obsession with asserting one's uniqueness – a swaggering characteristic of our age – is one of the most consistent, and attractive, features of this volume. In her seventies, Stevenson quietly celebrates, through her poetic practice, her love for 'the milk of stones' in preference to that of human kindness. Stones comfort her 'with the pristine beauty of my almost absence'. Another powerfully affirmative figure for the quiet virtues of self-abnegation is harmony: 'Bach at the organ/ tossing sunlight between/ voices'. This prevailing vision makes for an attractively modest, self-effacing collection, that is nevertheless perhaps a trifle underpowered at times and given to occasional lapses: 'I am alive. I'm human./ Get dressed. Make coffee./ Shore a few lines against my ruin.'

Counter to this dominant tendency, however, there runs another current of poetic energy. With her strong Scottish connections, Stevenson seems to have acquired a taste for flyting, and her poetry is periodically liable to violent disturbances of its peace. The targets are several. She indulges in 'acronymonious' raging at TESCO and ASDA, disgust at '*Apocalypse London*', contempt for 'proliferating theory' and 'sycophant' PhDs. Those stones whose milk she so prizes are here rudely grabbed and hurled at an array of enemies, as Stevenson turns Savanarola. It's invigorating – few can resist the appeal of a good punch-up – but she rather risks sounding less like an enraged prophet than a peevish Old Grump, especially irritated at the infidelities of her oldest and dearest friend, language: 'Should I "download" the messages I'm "text'd?"' What road-rage is to the young, digi-rage is to the old. In such a context, her otherwise admirably generous practice of writing poems to honour departed poet friends can unfortunately seem a bit like circling the wagons.

The collection ends with 'The Myth of Medea', a modern 'take' (as we nowadays say) on the great ancient classic. It is a spirited, witty burlesque that makes play alike with feminist and patriarchal readings of the tragedy. Euripides is reduced to spluttering protest as his play dissolves back into the fertile polysemy of myth. So much for all ingenious human devices of meaning. It is as futile for any individual, whatever his or her genius, to seek to have the final word as to say or to do something completely new. What art does is to allow us access to the deep, inexhaustible common source of our human story:

> Those plummet lines of language, free of fashion,
> Reach to your deepest layer and won't let go.
> There, every minute tells you lightly, gently,
> *The still sad music of humanity*
> Is all we know, and all we need to know.

One of the privileges of growing older is to feel 'free of fashion', and at its best *Stone Milk* provides us with a knowledge, given to some in age, that is needed by our own time.

Afterword

Kirsti Bohata

Nations are often divided into the cultural and the political, the ethnic and the civic, not least by those benefitting from the cultural hegemony within a nation-state. Yet as Benedict Anderson demonstrated, the nation as imagined community is dependent on cultural and material institutions – mass produced and efficiently distributed print culture in his foundational example.[1] In the colonial model, this imagined community is harder to create because the institutions and networks upon which it depends are fractured or missing, or the arterial infrastructure runs towards a distant imperial heart. Cultures need institutions and in colonised or decolonising nations these structures have to be created in often unfavourable conditions. The Cymru Fydd (Young Wales) movement grasped this and in the face of political failure of home rule in the 1890s, pivoted towards cultural construction with the aid of the Liberal party for whom their cultural vision remained a 'potent influence', as M. Wynn Thomas explains in *The Nations of Wales: 1880–1914*, and 'a series of nation-building initiatives [were] enabled by the Liberal victory in the 1906 General Election: a Welsh Department of the Board of Education, a National Library, a National Museum, a Welsh Insurance Commission and a National Council for Wales for Agriculture'.[2] Plaid Cymru (the Party of Wales), founded in 1925, initially prioritised cultural nationalism over political independence and a newly devolved Welsh Government certainly did not regard Culture as an inconsequential brief, as is the tendency of the UK government.

As Wynn Thomas showed in *The Nations of Wales*, literature and print culture has played a defining role constructing a 'usable past',[3] expressing Welsh identities and imagining Welsh futures. And literature itself is of course dependent on the institutions that commission, edit, print, publish, distribute, conserve, fund, lend, promote, sell, teach and discuss this writing. Indeed, in her literary history of post-war West Indian and Commonwealth writing, Gail Low argues that we need 'to investigate literature not only as "text" in the narrow sense of the word, but also as "institution"'. We must recognise the networks of 'social, cultural and discursive relationships' that underpin this (post)colonial literature which was largely written and published in London. In particular, we need to recognise 'the connections between publishing, cultural, educational, [commercial] and literary institutions and individuals'.[4] As a public intellectual, Thomas has helped to build and sustain the material and cultural institutions needed to sustain a national literary culture, drawing on his networks and experiences on both sides of the Atlantic.

In his introduction to *All That is Wales* (2017), Thomas has provided a detailed and important history of the intertwined cultural and academic development of Welsh writing in English, but the focus was mainly on academia and its structures. In this afterword, I turn the spotlight back on some of those crucial civic and cultural bodies – the Arts Council, Books Council, and the Learned Society of Wales among them – which Thomas has laboured to support and which he has used to ensure the growth and diversification of the literary culture of Wales in both languages. What follows draws on interviews with Wynn Thomas, supplemented by published commentaries on the changing literary, cultural and publishing landscape in Wales from the 1980s to the present.[5] The framing and interpretation is mine, however, since Thomas's own accounts, whilst vividly conveying the development of academic and civic structures, tend to downplay his own contribution at the centre of cultural networks and institutions often initiated and sustained by him.

His first institutional role outside academia coincided with the publication, in 1984, of his first book. Preceding his landmark volume on Walt Whitman by a few years, it was a slim volume on the seventeenth century mystical Welsh-language writer and Puritan activist, Morgan Llwyd. It was published in the 'Writers of Wales' series established and co-edited by Meic Stephens, and thus Wynn Thomas was brought into contact with one of the most indomitable advocates and influential architects of anglophone Welsh literary culture. Stephens, as the Arts Council's inaugural Director of Literature since 1967, used his considerable power and influence to support writers and publishing in both languages. Literature funding and policy was overseen at the Arts Council by an independent Literature Committee, which Stephens invited Thomas to join. After just two meetings, Thomas was asked to become chair, replacing the outgoing Walford Davies. Stephens, in Thomas's estimation, 'was a powerful man and he knew that I was an absolute novice and therefore he could do what he liked'. Working with Stephens and the Literature Committee provided an accelerated introduction to the literary world of Wales in both languages, and to chairing a high-powered committee that included major names in Welsh literature, including Emyr Humphreys. Thomas rapidly set to work to acquire the necessary skills that would later make him such an effective and strategic player. As Chair of the Literature Committee, Thomas was responsible for advocating for literature at the highest level of the Arts Council itself. This was a generative time for anglophone Welsh literature, and though funding had fallen from its earlier heights, the Literature Committee nevertheless oversaw the ambitious policy Stephens was implementing to nurture writers, forge international relationships, and develop a publishing infrastructure for the nation, offering anglophone Welsh writers the potentially transformative opportunity of being published and edited in Wales rather than London.

His tenure as Chair of the Literature Committee was not without controversy and demonstrated Thomas's readiness to make difficult choices, including the decision to withdraw funding and thus effectively close *Y Faner*, the Welsh-language weekly paper that had been an influential cultural and political presence since the nineteenth century.[6] Once a commercial success, it was now performing very poorly, according to a review commissioned by Meic Stephens, and, after a debate at committee level, the decision to defund the journal was carried. With a characteristic sense of responsibility and perhaps a naivety about what was expected of the Chairman, Thomas duly stepped forward into the ensuing outcry to account for and publicly defend the decision. It would be his first experience of such hostility, and it left its mark, bringing into sharp relief the fissured and fragmented cultural landscape of Wales, including the often fraught relations between the two languages both of which relied on Arts Council support.

Thomas left the Arts Council to go to Harvard as Visiting Professor, for the second time, in autumn 1991. Some years later, in 2004, he would be appointed to join a five-person group established by the recently devolved Welsh Assembly Government to review the mission of Arts Council of Wales in response to a new furore – this time over Rhodri Morgan's plans to take arts funding in-house. The First Minister's plans were developed in the wider context of abolishing quangos (unelected agencies), but in the case of the Arts Council this policy would risk politicising arts funding in Wales. The report produced by Thomas and his four colleagues ensured the essential arms-length policy was preserved, saving and remodelling the Arts Council for a devolved Wales.

On returning to Swansea from America in the early 1990s, Thomas resumed his service to national literary culture by working directly with publishers, joining the Board of Seren Books alongside Dannie Abse, and later the Board of University of Wales Press (UWP), both of which were, and are, in their different ways pivotal to the vitality of Welsh writing in English. At Seren and UWP, and in his earlier capacity at the Arts Council where he oversaw the work of Peter Finch at the Oriel Bookshop, Thomas learned more about the processes and pressures of publishing and the book trade, and thus about the material dimensions of a literary culture which, particularly for a small nation in the shadow of a powerful neighbour, are so crucial for the expression of a distinctive national literary culture.

Thomas left UWP after the departure of Susan Jenkins as Director, and was invited to Chair the English-language Publishing Grants Panel of the Welsh Books Council (since renamed the Books Council of Wales). This was a new Panel, necessitated by the transfer at the behest of Tony Bianchi, Literature Director at the Arts Council of Wales, of responsibility for supporting literary publishing from the Arts Council to the Books Council. The handover was a response to the diminished status of literature funding in the Arts Council's portfolio but it was also an inspired act which concentrated support for publishing within a unique Welsh institution.[7] The transfer of funding to the Books Council was nevertheless viewed with a degree of suspicion and misgiving by the English-language publishers who would now be reliant on an organisation which, though already providing some services and distribution for English-language books, had been founded to promote and protect Welsh-language writing. The early involvement of figures such as Wynn Thomas was key to demonstrating the Books Council's commitment to anglophone Wales.

It was a timely transfer that came into effect in April 2003, and by September of that year the Welsh Assembly's Culture Committee had launched a policy review into 'English-Medium Writing in Wales'. Their recommendations were published as *Welsh Writing in English: A Review*, in March 2004.[8] Thomas had been instrumental in bringing about the review, having lobbied the Minister for Culture and the Assembly since its inception, and the argument was further leveraged by the precedent of a boost in funding for Welsh language publishing the year before.[9] Suddenly, the co-location of publishing support for the two languages at the Books Council was proving a distinct advantage to English-language funding. The review was wide-ranging in its remit and, having studied the recommendations, Minister for Culture Alun Pugh ultimately prioritised a series of recommendations to boost publishing – not least due to the concerted behind the scenes efforts of the Books Council and its astute Director, Gwerfyl Pierce Jones. The sum granted was modest, £250,000 in additional funding per annum, but that represented almost a 50% increase on existing grants for English-language literary publishing inherited from the Arts Council. Much of this new funding would ultimately be directed towards improvements in infrastructure, including staffing, and for commissioning a wider range of titles to enable publishers to balance their lists. What had caught the Minister's imagination, however, and had arguably led to the total increase in funding, was Wynn Thomas's evidence to the Committee in which he recommended the Government create a high-profile series of Welsh classics to present the anglophone literary heritage of Wales to the world: the Library of Wales.

Thomas drew his inspiration from his transatlantic connections: the model and the name were based on the Library of America, that 'popular monument to the literary achievements of the USA',[10] and on Thomas's inside knowledge of that prestigious series as a close friend to one of its founders, Professor Daniel Aaron. Brandishing a copy of the Library of America edition of *Whitman: Poetry and Prose*, Thomas gave an impassioned account of the importance and interconnectivity of publishing and education in supporting Welsh writing – new and old – inviting the Committee to accord the 'rich and varied' literature that Wales had produced the same stature as that other non-English but anglophone body of writing celebrated by the Library of America.

The idea for the Library of Wales was enthusiastically taken up by the Committee, winning warm cross-party support in the chamber when the recommendations were published. Recognising that Wales had its own English-language literary tradition was hardly new (Seren had long published a series of classics as well as key titles for schools, such as Emyr Humphreys's novel, *A Toy Epic* (1958), edited by Thomas, and Honno's Welsh Women's Classics were already changing the academic and cultural landscape), but for politicians concerned with their own legacy and for those whose sympathies did not primarily lie with Welsh-speaking Wales, this was an opportunity to celebrate and promote a specifically English-language Welsh culture. Whatever the different and sometimes doubtful motivations of the politicians who supported and ultimately funded the series, it not only raised the profile of Welsh writing in English, it provided the hook on which support for the more mundane – but crucial – investments in infrastructure and commissioning would be secured.

The Library of Wales was ultimately rather different from its model, the Library of America. Edited by Dai Smith and published by Parthian, it was aimed at a more popular market with short impressionistic introductions, but it has delivered on its promise to raise the profile and availability of Welsh writing in English. An international launch in New York on St David's Day 2005 was accompanied by a mass promotion in American bookstore chain Barnes & Noble. The poetry anthology commissioned by the Library of Wales and edited by Meic Stephens was adopted as a set text by the Education Department when it reviewed the GCSE English Literature Curriculum in 2014 – the first time any Welsh writing in English formed a compulsory part of the qualification. The profile of the series means the existence of a substantial body of English-language writing from Wales is visible even for those who don't read it (much as Oxford Classics functions as a marker of an English canon), and the series continues to expand and diversify under a new editor. As Thomas himself has described it, the Library of Wales 'was an ambitious exercise in the transmission of culture, and its inauguration furnished a dramatic instance of the identity politics being practised by a fledgling, nation-building Assembly. It was a development publicly endorsed, in due course, by the First Minister Rhodri Morgan, as the single most important imitative of his long period in office.'[11]

Having joined the Books Council as Chair of the English-language grants panel at around the time the new funding schemes were being created, Thomas went on to chair the whole of the Books Council of Wales at a time when it was consolidating its role at the centre of the publishing industry of Wales in both languages. Established in 1961, a year before Saunders Lewis's galvanising 'Tynged yr Iaith' (Fate of the Language) lecture, to support the distribution and publication of Welsh-language literature, the Books Council offered a range of editorial, design, marketing and distribution services for publishers, and developed a major programme for children's books and schools. It already offered significant grants for Welsh-language publishing before it took over the funding of English-language literary publishing in 2003. It is hard to overstate the significance to the print culture of Wales of this unique organisation, which combines functions delivered elsewhere in the UK by Arts Councils and Publishers Associations. Dedicated now to supporting an indigenous publishing industry in both languages, expanding the range of texts available and their reach, the Books Council is also a privileged interlocutor with the Welsh Government, ensuring the literary history and future of Wales is placed high on the cultural agenda. As Chair, Thomas worked with successive directors through periods of expansion and crisis, drawing on his considerable skills in diplomacy, and passionate commitment to both literatures of Wales, in bringing together sometimes mutually suspicious sectors in Welsh publishing.[12]

The focus of this afterword is on Thomas's generative work in civic and cultural life beyond the academy, but I want to include one final example of his institution building, as co-founder and inaugural vice-chair of the Learned Society of Wales (LSW). This initiative drew on both the insights of his long service on public bodies as well as his understanding of UK and international academic structures. The Learned Society was created in 2010, with the aim of promoting and enabling research, recognising its societal and civic benefits, and providing independent policy advice. At Thomas's instigation, LSW identified 'Wales Studies' as a key area for development, thus establishing a new multi- and inter-disciplinary field of research 'about Wales, for Wales',[13] and raising the profile of this research as a priority area for the Higher Education Funding Council Wales (HEFCW) and Welsh Government. LSW was instrumental in creating a Celtic Academies Alliance of national academies in Wales, Scotland and Ireland, and contributes to foregrounding the four nations landscape of the UK, which UK Research and Innovation (UKRI) and its funding councils are beginning to take on board.

Co-founding the Learned Society of Wales was the culmination of a long-term programme of institution building, which included the co-foundation in 1982 of the University of Wales Association for Welsh

Writing in English (AWWE), and establishing the Centre for Research into the English Literature and Language of Wales (CREW) at Swansea University. The creation of LSW also drew on Thomas's experience at the British Academy, to which he had been elected Fellow in 1996, the highest honour for an academic in the Humanities and Social Sciences in Britain, and where he was involved in governance and oversight as a member of the Council (2006–10). His experience of the anglocentric focus of the British Academy and other organisations designed to support and fund the arts and humanities in Britain fuelled the drive to create a Wales-centred and outward looking academy.

Wynn Thomas has been acutely aware of the need of institutions to support a distinctive Welsh culture, and acutely alive to the potential for political devolution to enable cultural re-definition. He has used his transatlantic networks to mobilise connections between publishing, cultural, educational, commercial and literary institutions, and he has taken politicians, academics, students and writers along with him, creating opportunities for change. In his discussion of Raymond Williams's *The Long Revolution* (1961) and Rudi Dutschke's 'long march through the institutions' concept (1967), David Frost reminds us of both the radical dimensions and the drawn-out, uneven nature of the inter-related cultural, industrial and institutional revolutions that Williams mapped and analysed:

> The process of the 'long revolution' is neither a triumphant and linear climb to a peak, nor a leisurely stroll along the slopes of history. It is trudging out with a sense of our destination in mind, never forgetting the importance of placing one foot in front of the other, of knowing where our next step must fall, fully cognisant of our surroundings and of the sacrifices involved in coming this far. And it is doing so together.[14]

Wynn Thomas has been unstinting and far-sighted in his institution building, and has been willing to undertake the long hours of unglamorous work required to sustain and transform them. Prioritising the literary culture of Wales in both languages, he has never lost sight of the political dimensions of this work, nor the institutional structures necessary to both nation and culture. The arts and humanities face constant challenges in Brexit Britain, and funding for the arts in an under-resourced Wales is precarious. But the networks and institutions nurtured and created by Thomas give the broader culture and future leaders a significantly elevated starting point for the next stage of the march.

Notes

1. Benedict Anderson, *Imagined Communities: Reflections on the Origin and Spread of Nationalism* (London and New York: Verso, 1983).

2. M. Wynn Thomas, *The Nations of Wales; 1890–1914* (Cardiff: University of Wales Press, 2016), p. 6.

3. The term is perhaps best described by Robert Crawford in *Devolving English Literature* (Oxford: Clarendon Press, 1992).

4. Gail Low '"Finding the Centre?" Publishing Commonwealth Writing in London: The Case of Anglophone Caribbean Writing 1950–65', *The Journal of Commonwealth Literature* (2002), 21–37; DOI 10.1177/002198940203700203, pp. 21–2.

5. M. Wynn Thomas, *All That is Wales: The Collected Essays of M. Wynn Thomas* (Cardiff: University of Wales Press, 2017); Gwen Davies (ed.), *Two Rivers from a Common Spring: The Books Council at 60* (Aberystwyth: Books Council of Wales, 2021); Alumni Profile https://www.swansea.ac.uk/alumni/alumni-profiles/wynn-thomas/.

6. *Baner ac Amserau Cymru* was a weekly paper established by Thomas Gee in 1859 (by combining two newspapers, *Baner Cymru* (published from 1857) and *Yr Amserau* (published from 1843)). It was renamed *Y Faner* in 1972, and ran until 1992 before 'folding after 135 years'. Laurel Brake and Marysa Demoor (eds), *Dictionary of Nineteenth-Century Journalism in Great Britain and Ireland* (Ghent and London: Academia Press and British Library, 2009), p. 38.

7. Support for writers remained at the Arts Council, via the Welsh Academy/Yr Academi Gymreig, subsequently the Academi before being renamed Literature Wales.

8. Culture, Welsh Language and Sport Committee, 'Welsh Writing in English: A Review' (2004). See senedd.wales/media/xgubog00/bus-guide-n00000000000 00000000000000019390-english.pdf.

9. Gwerfyl Pierce Jones, 'The Growth of the Mustard Seed: From the sixties to 2010', in Gwen Davies (ed.), *Two Rivers from a Common Spring: The Books Council of Wales at 60* (Aberystwyth: Books Council of Wales, 2001), pp. 62–83 (78).

10. See Meeting Documents, Culture Welsh Language and Sport Committee, Second Assembly, Wednesday, 15 October 2003, Document CWLS(2)-04-03 (p. 3) Professor M. Wynn Thomas Paper at https://business.senedd.wales/CeList Documents.aspx?CommitteeId=564&MeetingId=7692&DF=15%2F10%2F20 03&Ver=2 (accessed 27 June 2024).

11. M. Wynn Thomas, 'Two Rivers from a Common Spring', in Davies (ed.), *Two Rivers*, pp. 92–113 (100).

12. Elwyn Jones, 'Cloudbusting', in Gwen Davies (ed.), *Two Rivers from a Common Spring: The Books Council of Wales at 60* (Aberystwyth: Books Council of Wales, 2001), pp. 86–9.

13. Learned Society of Wales, 'What is Wales Studies', https://www.learnedsociety.wales/wales-studies/what-is-wales-studies/.

14. David Frost, 'Long marches, long revolutions', *Red Pepper* (8 April 2022). This version, https://mronline.org/2022/04/13/long-marches-long-revolutions/ (13 April 2022), accessed 21 November 2023.

SELECTED ROLES AND HONOURS

1982
Founding Member and Secretary, University of Wales Association for the Study of Welsh Writing in English (until 1997)

1984
Member, Wales Arts Council Literature Committee (until 1985)

1985
Member, Yr Academi Gymreig
Chair, Wales Arts Council Literature Committee (until 1991)
Council Member, Wales Arts Council (until 1991)
Member, Wales Arts Council Finance and Policy Committee (until 1991)

1989
Member, Saunders Lewis Memorial Committee

1990
Member, Executive Committee West Wales Arts Association (until 1991)
Member, Executive Committee, WJEC (until 1993)
Chair, Rhys Davies Trust (until 1993)

1992
Chair of Adjudicators, National Eisteddfod Daniel Owen Prize
Member, Board of Management Swansea UK City of Literature (until 1996)

1993
Vice-Chair, Friends of Welsh Books Council
Nominator, Arts Foundation
Member, Welsh-medium HE education committee, HEFCW (until 1996)

1994
Member, editorial committee, *Oxford Companion to the Literature of Wales* (until 1996)
Member, Board of Management, Seren Books (until 1997)
Member, Yr Academi Gymreig Executive Committee (until 1998)

1995

Chair, Saunders Lewis Memorial Committee

Member, R. S. Thomas Nobel Prize for Literature Committee

1996

Fellow, British Academy

Member, Advisory Board, Welsh Studies Centre, University of Tübingen

Member, Adjudicator Panel, David Cohen Prize for Lifetime Achievement (until 1997)

Chair, Yr Academi Gymreig Welsh Section Executive Committee (until 1997)

1997

Acting Chair, Yr Academi Gymreig (until 1998)

Member, Board of Management University of Wales Press (until 1999)

Member, Standing Committee, Modern Languages and Literature Section, British Academy (until 2001)

1999

Chair, Board of Management University of Wales Press (until 2003)

Chair, Literary Publishers Wales/Welsh Books Council Committee (until 2004)

2000

Admitted to the National Eisteddfod Gorsedd

Chair of Adjudicators, National Eisteddfod Literature Medal

2002

Member, editorial board, Gregynog Press (until 2005)

Member, Welsh Assembly Government Committee to review Arts Council of Wales (until 2007)

2004

Awarded OBE

Member, Advisory Board, British Library (until 2008)

Chair, Welsh Books Council English-Language Publishing Grants to Panel (until 2017)

2005
Vice-Chair, Welsh Books Council, Council
Chair, editorial Board, Gregynog Press (until 2010)
Chair, Books Council of Wales, Council (until 2022)

2006
Member, Council, British Academy (until 2010)

2009
Chair of Adjudicators, National Eisteddfod Crown

2010
Founding Fellow and Vice-President (Arts, Humanities, Social Sciences),
    Learned Society of Wales Council (until 2015)

2012
Honorary Fellow of Coleg Cymraeg Cenedlaethol

2013
Trustee and Member, Board of Centre for Advanced Welsh and Celtic
    Studies, University of Wales (until 2019)

2017
Chair of Adjudicators, National Eisteddfod Crown
Chair, R. S. Thomas Society (until 2019)

2021
Chair of Trustees, Books Council of Wales (until 2022)

Bibliography of
M. Wynn Thomas 2004–2024

A full bibliography for the years 1970–2003 was compiled by Rhian Reynolds, and can be found in Alyce von Rothkirch and Daniel Williams (eds), *Beyond the Difference: Welsh Literature in Comparative Contexts. Essays for M. Wynn Thomas at Sixty* (Cardiff: University of Wales Press, 2004).

Books

Transatlantic Connections: Whitman US/Whitman UK (Iowa: Iowa University Press, 2005).

Emyr Humphreys (Cardiff: University of Wales Press, 2009).

In the Shadow of the Pulpit: Literature and Nonconformity (Cardiff: University of Wales Press, 2010). Longlisted for Welsh Book of the Year Prize, and shortlisted for the Roland Mathias Prize.

R. S. Thomas: Serial Obsessive (Cardiff: University of Wales Press, 2013). Shortlisted for a Welsh Book of the Year Prize.

The Nations of Wales, 1890–1914 (Cardiff: University of Wales Press, 2016).

Cyfan-dir Cymru: Ysgrifau ar Gyfannu Dwy Lenyddiaeth Cymru (Caerdydd: Gwasg Prifysgol Cymru, 2017).

All That is Wales: Collected Essays of M. Wynn Thomas (Cardiff: University of Wales Press, 2017). Winner of 2018 Welsh Book of the Year Prize for non-creative writing.

Eutopia: Studies in Cultural Euro-Welshness, 1850–1980 (Cardiff: University of Wales Press, 2021).

The History of Wales in Twelve Poems (Cardiff: University of Wales Press, 2021).

From R. S. Thomas to Rowan Williams: the spiritual tradition in modern Welsh Poetry (Cardiff; University of Wales Press, 2022).

A Map of Love (Cardiff: University of Wales Press, 2023).

Poems from the Soul (Cardiff: University of Wales Press, 2024).

Contributions to books

'All lenient muscles tensed: the poetry of Roland Mathias', in R. Minhinnick (ed.), *Poetry of Wales Press: Forty Years* (Bridgend: Seren, 2005), pp. 168–77.

'Whitman and the Labouring Classes', in Donald D. Kummings (ed.), *A Companion to Walt Whitman* (Malden, Massachusetts: Blackwell Publishing, 2006), pp. 60–75.

'*The Stones of the Field* and the power of the sword: R. S. Thomas as War Poet', in Tony Curtis (ed.), *Wales at War: Critical Essays on Literature and Art* (Bridgend: Seren, 2007), pp. 142–64.

'United States and States United: Whitman's national vision in 1855', in Susan Belasco, Ed Folsom and Kenneth Price (eds), *Leaves of Grass: the Sesquicentennial Essays* (Lincoln and London: University of Nebraska Press, 2007), pp. 62–83.

'R. S. Thomas and Modern Welsh Poetry', in Neil Corcoran (ed.), *The Cambridge Companion to Twentieth-Century English Poetry* (Cambridge: Cambridge University Press, 2007), pp. 159–72.

'R. S. Thomas, Denise Levertov and the poetry of contemplation', in Christopher Meredith (ed.), *Moments of Earth* (Aberystwyth: Celtic Studies Publications, 2007), pp. 248–302.

'R. S. Thomas: Claf Abercuawg?', in Tegwyn Jones and Huw Walters (eds), *Cawr i'w Genedl* (Llandysul: Gwasg Gomer, 2008), pp. 245–64.

'Whitman, Tennyson, and the poetry of Old Age', in Stephen Burt and Nick Halpern (eds), *Something Understood: Essays and Poetry for Helen Vendler* (Charlottesville and London: University of Virginia Press, 2009), pp. 161–82.

'"The grammar of the night," ekphrasis and loss in Lucie Brock-Broido's *Trouble in Mind*', in Jane Hedley, Nick Halpern and Willard Spiegelman (eds), *In the Frame: Women's Ekphrastic Poetry from Marianne Moore to Susan Wheeler* (Newark: University of Delaware Press, 2009), pp. 6–7.

'Perilous freedom of speech: the politics of Gary Geddes's poetry', in Robert G. May (ed.), *Gary Geddes: Essays on his work* (Toronto-Buffalo-Lancaster: Guernica Press, 2010), pp. 178–2020.

'"A Huge Assembling of Unease": readings in *A Man's Estate*', in Katie Gramich (ed.), *Mapping the Territory: Critical Approaches to Welsh Fiction in English* (Cardigan: Parthian, 2010), pp. 185–216.

'Cotton Mather's *Wonders of the Invisible World*: some metamorphoses of Salem witchraft', in Sydney Anglo (ed.), *The Damned Art: Essays in the Literature of Witchcraft* (London: Routledge, 2011; first published 1977), pp. 202–26.

'Margiad Evans and Eudora Welty: a confluence of imaginations', in Kirsti Bohata and Katie Gramich (eds), *Rediscovering Margiad Evans* (Cardiff: University of Wales Press, 2013), pp. 86–106.

'Morgan Llwyd and the foundations of the Nonconformist nation', in Stewart Mottram and Sarah Prescott (eds), *Writing Wales: From the Renaissance to Romanticism* (Surrey: Ashgate Publishing Ltd, 2012), pp. 111–30.

'Marlais', in Hannah Ellis (ed.), *Dylan Thomas: A Centenary Celebration* (London: Bloomsbury, 2014), pp. 30–41.

'Chwarae Rhan yng nghynhyrchiad Cymru Fydd', in Anwen Jones (ed.), *Perfformio'r Genedl: Ar drwydd Hywel Teifi Edwards* (Caerdydd: Gwasg Prifysgol Cymru, 2017), pp. 91–111.

367

'The Scarlet Woman: Lynette Roberts', in Siriol MacAvoy (ed.), *Locating Lynette Roberts* (Cardiff: University of Wales Press, 2018).

'"Ei luniad yn oleuni": R. S. Thomas ym myd lluniau', David Meredith (ed.), *Kyffin Dan Sylw / In View* (Llandysul: Gomer, 2018), pp. 168–82.

'From Nonconformist nation to Proleterian nation: writing Wales, 1885–1930', in Helen Fulton and Geraint Evans (eds), *The Cambridge Companion to the Literature of Wales* (Cambridge: Cambridge University Press, 2019), pp. 405–27.

'The Comic Voices of Dylan Thomas', in Kieron Smith and Rhian Barfoot (eds), *New Theoretical Perspectives on Dylan Thomas* (Cardiff: University of Wales Press, 2020), pp. 77–95.

'Two Rivers from a Common Spring', Gwen Davies (ed.), *Two Rivers from a Common Spring: The Books Council of Wales at 60* (Aberystwyth: Books Council of Wales, 2021), pp. 90–113.

'Dwy Ffrwd o'r un Ffynnon', Gwen Davies (ed.), *O Hedyn i Ddalen: Dathlu'r Cyngor Llyfrau yn 60* (Aberystwyth: Cyngor Llyfrau, 2021), pp. 94–117.

'Foreword' to *Osi Rhys Osmond: Cultural Alzheimer's* (Llandysul: Gomer, H'mm Foundation, 2023), pp. i–iv.

'Foreword' to Dafydd W. Jones, *The Reconciliation of Modernism: Ceri Richards and the second generation, 1930–1945* (Cardiff: University of Wales Press, 2024), pp. xi–xiv.

'The Wittgensteinian School of English at Swansea', in Alan Sandry (ed.), *Wittgenstein in Swansea: Philosophy and Legacy* (Cardiff: University of Wales Press, 2025).

Contributions to periodicals

'Monica Lewinsky a fi', *Y Llyfr yng Nghymru / Welsh Book Studies*, 5/5 (Aberystwyth: National Library of Wales, 2003), 23–43.

with John Turner '"Whitman the great poet has meant so much to me", Lawrence's *Studies in Classic American Literature*, 1919–23', *Walt Whitman Quarterly Review*, 21/2 (Fall 2003), 41–64.

'For Wales, see Landscape: early R. S. Thomas and the English topographical tradition', in Tony Brown (ed.), *Welsh Writing in English: A Yearbook of Critical Writing*, 10 (2005), 1–31.

'Portrait of the Artist as a Young [Brynteg] Man', *Planet*, 117 (August/September 2005), 14–22.

'Roemerstadt a Hladik', *Y Traethodydd* (Ionawr 2005), 28–33.

'Vernon Watkins: Taliesin Bro Gŵyr', *Taliesin*, 129 (Gaeaf 2006), 11–36.

'"A Grand Harlequinade": the Border Writing of Nigel Heseltine', in Tony Brown (ed.), *Welsh Writing in English: A Yearbook of Critical Writing*, 11 (2007), 51–68.

'"Fidelities where beams together run": Vernon Watkins and Henry Vaughan', *Scintilla*, 11, 168–84.

'Roland Mathias', *New Welsh Review* (Winter 2007), 64–7.

'The Fantastic Side of God: R. S. Thomas and Jorge Luis Borges', *Renascence*, 60/2 (Winter 2008), 177–93.

'Writing Merthyr', *Merthyr Historian*, 19 (2008), 137–49.

'Ukryte powiazania', *Literatura na świecie: Walia*, 7–8 (2009), 86–125.

with Jane Aaron 'Walijdska ksiega przemian; *Literatura na świecie: Walia*, 7–8 (2009), 191–223.

'"Y Genedl Anghydffurfiol" a llenyddiaeth Saesneg yng Nghymru ddiwedd y bedwaredd ganrif ar bymtheg', *Ysgrifau Beirniadol*, 29, 24–50.

'Das Walisischen Schwein und der britische Löwe, zur zweisprachigkeit der walisischen Literatur', *Sprachlandschaffen: regionale literaturwisenschaaft im europeuropäischen kontext* (Klagenflurt: Hermagoras, 2010), 146–65.

'"Dubious Affinities", Leslie Norris's Welsh-English translations', *Literature and Belief*, 29 and 30/1, 257–84.

'"Till I hit upon a name": *Calamus* and the Language of Love', *Huntington Library Quarterly*, 73/4 (2010: Sesquicentennial Impressions: A Celebration of *Leaves of Grass* 1860), 641–58.

'Morgan Llwyd, *Das Buch der drei Vögel*. Ein apokalyptischer trakt aus der zeit der Bürgerkriegs', translated by Jürgen Buchmann, *Zeitschrift für Glausbensformen und Weltanschauung/Journal for the Study of Beliefs and Worldviews* (2012), 348–410.

'Seisnigrwydd *Ymadawiad Arthur*', *Y Traethodydd* (Gorffennaf 2012), 142–67.

'Commentary', in *Raymond Williams Kenkyu/Studies*, special issue: 'Long Revolutions in Wales and Japan' (March 2013), 146–7.

'Jessie Penn-Lewis, Evan Roberts a'i gofiant di-enw *War on the Saints*', *Y Traethodydd* (Gorffennaf 2013), 167–88.

'Vernon Watkins: Taliesin in Gower', *Gower*, 64 (2013), 53–61.

'A Turbulent Priest', *New Welsh Review* (Autumn 2013), 48–54.

'"Ei luniad yn oleuni": R. S. Thomas ym myd lluniau', *Cyfatebiaethau*, ed. Christine Kinsey (Glyn-y-Weddw: Oriel Plas Glyn-y-Weddw, 2014), 6–9.

'R. S. Thomas and the "Impressed Brush"', *Correspondences*, ed. Christine Kinsey (Glyn-y-Weddw: Glyn-y-Weddw Gallery, 2014), 6–9.

'The Poet of Sarn Rhiw', John Barnie (ed.), *Encounters with R. S. Thomas* (Llandysul: Gwasg Gomer, H'mm Foundation, 2014), 28–35.

'Morgan Llwyd: tad y Genedl Anghydffurfiol', *Diwinyddiaeth*, 65 (2014), 30–47.

'Gwreiddiau'r syniad o "Genedl Anghydffurfiol"', *Cylchgrawn Hanes y Methodistiaid Calfinaidd/Historical Society of the Presbyterian Church of Wales*, 38 (2014), 85–104.

'"There's words": Dylan Thomas et la langue', Pascale Sardin et Christian Gutleben (eds), *Lire et Relire Dylan Thomas, Cycnos*, 31/2 (2015), 29–56.

'Gofod personol Tony Bianchi', yn *O'r Pedwar Gwynt* (Hydref 2017), 11–13.

'Saunders Lewis: *Gwaed yr Uchelwyr*', *Gwerddon* (2017) (online)

'Chwilio am yr enaid: Emyr Humphreys a Marilynne Robinson', *O'r Pedwar Gwynt* (Gwanwyn 2019).

'Emyr Humphreys: "Ewropead hiwmanistig"', *Y Traethodydd* (Gorffennaf 2019), 132–47.

'Yr Heriwr Anhepgor, Alwyn D. Rees', *Y Traethodydd* (Ionawr, 2020), 37–51.

'Light "thick as honey among the grasses": two unpublished notebooks by R. S. Thomas', *PN Review* (January 2020).

'"Eutopia": hanes cudd yr Euro-Gymry', *O'r Pedwar Gwynt* (Gaeaf 2020), 8–9.

'Two Rivers from a Single Source', *Anglo Files (Denmark)*, 202/4 (2021), 19–23.

'*Saeva Indignatio*: R. S. Thomas, Siôn Cent a Jonathan Swift', *Y Traethodydd* (Hydref 2022), 227–45.

'R. S. Thomas, Siôn Cent, and "the buggeration of it"', *International Journal for Welsh Writing in English*, 10/1 (2023), 1–32.

'A "singing Walt of the mower": Dylan Thomas and the Whitmanian [re]turn in the post-war poetic culture of the United States', *Walt Whitman Quarterly Review*, 40/3–4 (Winter/Spring 2023), 1–31.

'"Sacrament sicr yn [eu] sain": y dychymyg ysbrydol yng ngherddi diweddar Cymru', *O'r Pedwar Gwynt* (Gwanwyn 2023), 31–2.

'"Most of the stories have to do with vanishing": cerddi y Cymro annisgwyl W. S. Merwin', *O'r Pedwar Gwynt* (Gaeaf 2023), 36–7.

Bibliography of M. Wynn Thomas 2004–2024

'Arthur Bowen Davies: y "Cymro" a weddnewidiodd ddiwylliant celf y Taleithiau', *Y Traethodydd* (Ionawr 2024), 7–26.

Reviews

Angharad Price, *Rhwng Du a Gwyn* (*Gwales*, August 2001).

Goronwy Wyn Owen, *Rhwng Calfin a Böhme: golwg ar syniadaeth Morgan Llwyd* (*Taliesin*, June 2003).

Tony Conran, *Bronwen and other Verse Plays* (*Planet*, Autumn 2004).

Jorie Graham, *Overlord* (*Acumen*, October 2005).

Caradoc Evans, *Morgan Bible and Journal* (*Planet*, August/September 2006).

'Roland Mathias' (*New Welsh Review*, Winter 2007).

Andrew Lawson, *Walt Whitman and the Class Struggle* (*Nineteenth-Century Literature*, December 2006).

Jorie Graham, *Overlord* (*Acumen*, January 2006).

Owen Thomas (gol.), *Llenyddiaeth Mewn Theori* (*Taliesin*, Gwanwyn 2007).

Tudur Hallam, *Canon ein Llên* (*Taliesin*, Gaeaf 2008).

Dewi Z. Phillips, *Ffiniau; Myfyrdod Athronyddol ar Lenyddiaeth* (*Taliesin*, Gwanwyn 2009).

Charles Bukowski, *The Pleasures of the Damned: Collected Poems, 1951–1993* (*Acumen*, May 2010).

Günter Leypoldt, *Culture and Authority in the Age of Whitman* (*Review of English Studies*, 2010).

Ned Thomas, *Bydoedd* (*Planet*, Summer 2011).

Matt Miller, *Collage of Myself: Walt Whitman and the Making of Leaves of Grass* (*Walt Whitman Quarterly Review*, 2011).

Charles Mundye (ed.), *Keidrych Rhys, the Van Pool* (*The Welsh Agenda*, Summer 2012).

Angharad Price, *T. H. Parry-Williams* (*Y Traethodydd*, Autumn 2014).

Menna Elfyn, *Murmur* (*Planet*, Spring 2013).

John Harris, *Caradoc Evans: A Devil in Eden* (*International Journal for Welsh Writing in English*, 2022).

Betsy Erkkila, *Whitman: Sex, Poetry and Politics* (*Walt Whitman Quarterly Review*, 2020).

Reviews for *The Guardian*

Written in Water: W. S. Merwin, *Selected Poems* (2 June 2007).

Age, the equaliser: Anne Stevenson, *Stone Milk* (14 October 2007).

The Outsider: Alun Lewis, *Collected Poems* (9 February 2008).

Full Fathom Five: Jorie Graham, *Sea Change* (3 May 2008).

Called back to earth: Kathleen Raine (4 October 2008).

Flesh knew itself and spoke: Sharon Olds, *One Secret Thing* (2009).

The heart of the matter: Dannie Abse, *New Selected Poems, 1949–2009* (30 May 2009).

A Hospital Odyssey: Gwyneth Lewis, *A Hospital Odyssey* (17 April 2010).

A Masque for Wales: Geoffrey Hill, *Oraclau/Oracles* (16 October 2010).

Black Cat Bone: John Burnside, *Black Cat Bone* (6 September 2011).

Index